STUDY GUIDE

for

PARKIN
Microeconomics
ELEVENTH EDITION

Mark Rush
University of Florida

PEARSON

Boston Columbus Indianapolis New York San Francisco Upper Saddle River
Amsterdam Cape Town Dubai London Madrid Milan Munich Paris Montreal Toronto
Delhi Mexico City São Paulo Sydney Hong Kong Seoul Singapore Taipei Tokyo

Executive Acquisitions Editor: Adrienne D'Ambrosio
Editorial Project Manager: Sarah Dumouchelle
Associate Production Project Manager: Alison Eusden
Senior Manufacturing Buyer: Carol Melville

10 9 8 7 6 5 4 3 2

www.pearsonhighered.com

ISBN-10:   0-13-302182-3
ISBN-13: 978-0-13-302182-0

HOW TO EARN AN A!

■ Introduction

My experience has taught me that what students want most from a study guide is help in mastering course material in order to do well on examinations. I have developed this *Study Guide* to respond specifically to that demand. Using this *Study Guide* alone, however, is not enough to guarantee that you will do well in your course. In order to help you overcome the problems and difficulties that most students encounter, I have some general advice on how to study, as well as some specific advice on how best to use this *Study Guide*.

Economics requires a different style of thinking than what you may encounter in other courses. Economists make extensive use of assumptions to break down complex problems into simple, analytically manageable parts. This analytical style, while ultimately not more demanding than the styles of thinking in other disciplines, feels unfamiliar to most students and requires practice. As a result, it is not as easy to do well in economics on the basis of your raw intelligence and high-school knowledge as it is in many other courses. Many students who come to my office are frustrated and puzzled by the fact that they are getting A's and B's in their other courses but only a C or worse in economics. They have not recognized that economics is different and requires practice. In order to avoid a frustrating visit to your instructor after your first test, I suggest you do the following.

♦ *Don't rely solely on your high-school economics.* If you took high-school economics, you have seen the material on supply and demand which your instructor will lecture on in the first few weeks. Don't be lulled into feeling that the course will be easy. Your high-school knowledge of economic concepts will be very useful, but it will not be enough to guarantee high scores on exams. Your college or university instructors will demand much more detailed knowledge of concepts and ask you to apply them in new circumstances.

♦ *Keep up with the course material on a weekly basis.* Skim the appropriate chapter in the textbook *before* your instructor lectures on it. In this initial reading, don't worry about details or arguments you can't quite follow — just try to get a general understanding of the basic concepts and issues. You may be amazed at how your instructor's ability to teach improves when you come to class prepared. As soon as your instructor has finished covering a chapter, complete the corresponding *Study Guide* chapter. Avoid cramming the day before or even the week before an exam. Because economics requires practice, cramming is an almost certain recipe for failure. Indeed, based on data I have, students who crammed by intensively studying within three days of a test had higher SAT scores than the average student but did relatively poorer on the class tests than the average student who studied more consistently throughout the term. So, *don't* fall into this trap: Consistently study!

♦ *Keep a good set of lecture notes.* Good lecture notes are vital for focusing your studying. Your instructor will lecture on a subset of topics from the textbook. The topics your instructor covers in a lecture should usually be given priority when studying. Also give priority to studying the figures and graphs covered in the lecture.

Instructors differ in their emphasis on lecture notes and the textbook, so ask early on in the course which is *more* important in reviewing for exams — lecture notes or the textbook. If your instructor answers that both are important, then ask the following, typical economic question: which will be more beneficial — spending an extra hour re-reading your lecture notes or an extra hour re-reading the textbook? This question assumes that you have read each textbook chapter twice (once before lecture for a general understanding, and then later for a thorough understanding); that you have prepared a good set of lecture notes; and that you have worked through all of the problems in the appropriate *Study Guide* chapters. By applying this style of analysis to the problem of efficiently allocating your study time, you are already beginning to think like an economist!

♦   *Use your instructor and/or teaching assistants for help.* When you have questions or problems with course material, come to the office to ask questions. Remember, you are paying for your education and instructors are there to help you learn. I am often amazed at how few students come to see me during office hours. Don't be shy. The personal contact that comes from one-on-one tutoring is professionally gratifying for instructors as well as (hopefully) beneficial for you.

♦   *Form a study group.* A very useful way to motivate your studying and to learn economics is to discuss the course material and problems with other students. Explaining the answer to a question *out loud* is a very effective way of discovering how well you understand the question. When you answer a question only in your head, you often skip steps in the chain of reasoning without realizing it. When you are forced to explain your reasoning aloud, gaps and mistakes quickly appear, and you (with your fellow group members) can quickly correct your reasoning. The "You're the Teacher" questions in the *Study Guide* and the Review questions at the end of each textbook chapter are extremely good study group material. You might also get together *after* having worked the *Study Guide* problems, but *before* looking at the answers, and help each other solve unsolved problems.

♦   *Work old exams.* One of the most effective ways of studying is to work through exams your instructor has given in previous years. Old exams give you a feel for the style of question your instructor may ask, and give you the opportunity to get used to time pressure if you force yourself to do the exam in the allotted time. Studying from old exams is not cheating, as long as you have obtained a copy of the exam legally. Some institutions keep old exams in the library, others in the department. Students who have previously taken the course are usually a good source as well. Remember, though, that old exams are a useful study aid only if you use them to *understand* the reasoning behind each question. If you simply memorize answers in the hopes that your instructor will repeat the identical question, you are likely to fail. From year to year, instructors routinely change the questions or change the numerical values for similar questions.

♦   *Use the MyEconLab web site.* One of the most exciting features of the textbook is the opportunity it offers to use the MyEconLab web site. Michael Parkin, the author of the textbook, has been a leader in developing for the web site new, *useful* features that help students learn. You definitely should check out the web site because of all the help it offers. The textbook has complete details about the web site.

■ Using Your *Study Guide*

You should only attempt to complete a chapter in the *Study Guide* after you have read the corresponding textbook chapter and listened to your instructor lecture on the material. Each *Study Guide* chapter contains the following sections.

Key Concepts. This first section is a short summary, in point form, of all key definitions, concepts and material from the textbook chapter. Key terms from the textbook appear in bold. Each term in bold is in the glossary of the textbook. This first section is designed to focus you quickly and precisely on the core material that you *must* master. It is an excellent study aid for the night before an exam. Think of it as crib notes that will serve as a final check of the key concepts you have studied.

Helpful Hints. When you encounter difficulty in mastering concepts or techniques, you will not be alone. Many students find certain concepts difficult and often make the same kinds of mistakes. I have taught over 30,000 students the principles of economics and I have seen these common mistakes often enough to have learned how to help students avoid them. The hints point out these mistakes and offer tips to avoid them. The hints focus on the most important concepts, equations, and techniques for problem solving. They also review crucial graphs that appear on every instructor's exams. I hope that this section will be very useful, because instructors always ask exam questions designed to test these possible mistakes in your understanding.

Self-Test. This will be one of the most useful sections of the *Study Guide.* The questions are designed to give you practice and to test skills and techniques you must master to do well on exams.

There are plenty of multiple-choice type of questions and other types of questions in the Self-Test, each with a specific pedagogical purpose. Indeed, this book contains nearly 1,000 multiple choice questions in total!

Before I describe the four parts of the Self-Test section, here are some general tips that apply to all parts.

Use a pencil to write your answers in the *Study Guide* so you have neat, complete pages from which to study. Draw graphs wherever they are applicable. Some questions will ask explicitly for graphs; many others will not but will require a chain of reasoning that involves shifts of curves on a graph. *Always draw the graph.* Don't try to work through the reasoning in your head — you are much more likely to make mistakes that way. Whenever you draw a graph, even in the margins of the *Study Guide,* label the axes. You may think that you can keep the labels in your head, but you will be confronting many different graphs with many different variables on the axes. Avoid confusion and label. As an added incentive, remember that on exams where graphs are required, instructors will deduct points for unlabelled axes.

Do the Self-Test questions as if they were real exam questions, which means do them *without looking at the answers.* This is the single most important tip I can give you about effectively using the *Study Guide* to improve your exam performance. Struggling for the answers to questions that you find difficult is one of the most effective ways to learn. The adage "no pain, no gain" applies well to studying. You will learn the most from right answers you had to struggle for and from your wrong answers and mistakes. Only after you have attempted all the questions should you look at the answers. When you finally do check the answers, be sure to understand where you went wrong and why the right answer is correct.

There are many questions in each chapter, and it will take you somewhere between two and six hours to answer all of them. If you get tired (or bored), don't burn yourself out by trying to work through all of the questions in one sitting. Consider breaking up your Self-Test over two (or more) study sessions.

The four parts of the Self-Test section are:

True/False and Explain. These questions test basic knowledge of concepts and your ability to apply the concepts. Some of the questions challenge your understanding, to see if you can identify mistakes in statements using basic concepts. These questions will identify gaps in your knowledge and are useful to answer out loud in a study group.

When answering, identify each statement as *true,* or *false.* Explain your answer in *your words* in one sentence in the space underneath each question.

Multiple-Choice. These more difficult questions test your analytical abilities by asking you to apply concepts to new situations, manipulate information and solve numerical and graphical problems.

This is a most frequently used type of exam question, and the Self-Test contains many of them.

Read each question and all four choices carefully before you answer. Many of the choices will be plausible and will differ only slightly. You must choose the one *best* answer. A useful strategy in working these questions is first to eliminate any obviously wrong choices and then to focus on the remaining alternatives. Don't get frustrated or think that you are dim if you can't immediately see the correct answer. These questions are designed to make you work to find the correct choice.

Short Answer. Each chapter contains several Short Answer questions. Some are straightforward questions about basic concepts. They can generally be answered in a few sentences or, at most, in one paragraph. Others are problems. The best way to learn to do economics is to do problems. Problems are also the second-most popular type of exam question — practice them as much as possible!

You're the Teacher. Each chapter contains from one to three questions that either cover very broad issues or errors that are all too common among students. These questions may be the most valuable you will encounter for use in your study group. Take turns by pretending that you are the teacher and answer the questions for the rest of your group. Who knows, you may like this process so much that you actually do become a professor at a university teaching economics!

Answers. The Self-Test is followed by answers to all questions. Unlike other study guides on the market, I have included complete answers because I believe that reading complete answers will help you master the material ... and that's what this *Study Guide* is all about! But do *not* look at an answer until you have attempted a question. When you do finally look, use the answers to understand where you went wrong and why the right answer is correct.

As you work through the material, you'll find that the true/false and multiple choice questions, as well as their answers, are identified by a heading from the textbook. If you find that you are missing a lot of questions from one particular section, it is time to head back to the textbook and bone up on this material! In other words, *use* the textbook and this *Study Guide* to pull the A you want to earn!

Chapter Quiz. The last page in each chapter contains another 10 multiple choice questions covering the material in the chapter. These are questions that I and other instructors have included on our exams. Because these questions have been written by several instructors, they differ in style from the others in the chapter and so are a very good tool to be sure that you grasp the material. You can use the questions immediately after you finish each chapter, or else you can hoard them to help you prepare when exam time rolls around. In either case, the answers are given at the back of the book.

Part Overview Problem. Every few chapters, at the end of each of the parts of the textbook, you will find a special problem (and answer). In this section is a self-test that contains four multiple choice questions drawn from each chapter in the section. The questions are in order, with the first four from the first chapter in the section, the second four from the second chapter, and so forth. If you miss several questions from one chapter, you'll know to spend more time on that chapter when preparing for your exam. These multiple choice questions are written in a different style than those in the chapter because instructors have different ways of writing questions. By encountering different styles, you will be better prepared for *your* test.

Final Exams. At the end of the *Study Guide* are two multiple choice final exams and answers. These are final exams that I have used in my class at the University of Florida. You should use them to help you study for the final exam in your class.

If you effectively combine the use of the textbook, the *Study Guide,* the web site *MyEconLab,* and all other course resources, you will be well prepared for exams. You will also have developed analytical skills and powers of reasoning that will benefit you throughout your life and in whatever career you choose.

■ Your Future and Economics

After your class is concluded, you may well wonder about economics as a major. The last essay in this *Study Guide,* written by Robert Whaples, helps examine your future by discussing whether economics is the major for you. I invite you to read this chapter and consider the information in it. Economics is a major with a bright future so I think you'll be interested in this important chapter.

■ Final Comments

I have tried to make the *Study Guide* as helpful and useful as possible. Undoubtedly I have made some mistakes; mistakes that you may see. If you find any, I, and succeeding generations of students, would be grateful if you could point them out to me. At the end of my class at the University of Florida, when I ask my students for their advice, I point out to them that this advice won't help them at all because they have just completed the class. But, comments they make will influence how future students are taught. Thus, just as they owe a debt of gratitude for the comments and suggestions that I received from students before them, so too will students after them owe them an (unpaid and unpayable) debt. You are in the same situation. If you have questions, suggestions, or simply comments, let me know. My address is on the next page, or you can e-mail me at MARK.RUSH@CBA.UFL.EDU. Your input probably won't benefit you directly, but it will benefit following generations. And, if you give me permission, I will note your name and school in following editions so that any younger siblings (or, years down the road, maybe even your children!) will see your name and offer up thanks.

To date, students who have uncovered errors and to whom we all owe a debt of gratitude include:

- Jeanie Callen at the University of Minnesota-Twin Cities
- Brian Mulligan at the University of Florida
- Patrick Lusby at the University of Florida
- Jonathan Baskind at the University of Florida
- Breina Polk at Cook College at Rutgers University
- Ethan Schulman at the University of Iowa
- Adrian Garza at the University of Iowa
- Curtis Hazel at the University of North Florida
- Zhang Zili at American University
- Valerie Stewart at the University of Georgia
- Rob Bleeker at the Ohio State University
- Katherine Hamilton at the University of Florida
- Dennis Spinks at the Ohio State University
- Debbie McGuffie at the University of Florida
- Daniel Glassman at the University of Florida
- Thomas Cowan at the University of Florida
- Christopher Bland at the University of Florida
- Richard Caitung at the University of Florida
- Kristin L. Thistle at the University of Florida

- Michael Benkoczy at the University of Florida
- J.B. Johns at the Johns Hopkins University
- Joshua R. Levenson at the University of Miami
- Ryan Ellis at the University of Wisconsin, Madison
- Daniel Law at Butte Community College
- Katherine Kowsh at the University of Florida
- Will Broadway at the University of Florida
- Yalcyn Bican of Turkey
- Hillary Huffmire at Brigham Young University
- Michael Lagoe at the University of Florida
- Brittany Baugher at the University of Florida
- Jasmine Garcia at the University of Florida
- Elizabeth Ennis at the University of Florida
- Timothy Kirchner at the University of Florida
- Tina Jones at Indiana Wesleyan University
- Mikaila Gazzillo at the University of Florida
- Chau Tran at the University of Florida
- Nicholas Arjoon at the University of Florida
- Jennifer Cheng at the University of Florida

I owe Avi J. Cohen, of York University, and Harvey B. King, of University of Regina. Their superb study guide for the Canadian edition of Michael Parkin's book was a basis for this study guide. Much of what is good about this book is a direct reflection of their work.

Robert Whaples of Wake Forest University wrote the section of the *Study Guide* dealing with majoring in economics. He also checked an earlier edition of the manuscript for errors and provided questions that I use in this edition. Robert is a superb economist and this book is by far the better for this fact! Another brilliant teacher, Carol Dole of Jacksonville University, also supplied questions that I use with this edition. I think it fair to say that the clever questions are the work of Carol and Robert.

I also thank Michael Parkin and Robin Bade. Michael has written such a superior book that it was easy to be enthusiastic about writing the *Study Guide* to accompany it. Moreover, both Michael and Robin have played a hands on role in creating this *Study Guide* and have made suggestions that vastly improved the *Study Guide*.

I want to thank my family: Susan, Tommy, Bobby, and Katie, who, respectively: allowed me to work all hours on this book; helped me master the intricacies of FTPing computer files; let me postpone riding bicycles with him until after the book was concluded; and would run into my typing room to tell how she had advanced in her latest Zelda game. Thanks a lot! Finally, I want to thank Lucky, Pearl, and Sphynx who sat at my feet and next to the computer in a box (and occasionally meowed) while I typed.

Mark Rush
Economics Department
University of Florida
Gainesville, Florida 32611
January, 2013.

Table of Contents

Chapter 1

WHAT IS ECONOMICS?

Key Concepts

Definition of Economics

The fundamental and universal economic problem is **scarcity**: the inability to get everything we want. Because the available productive resources are never enough to satisfy everyone's wants, choices are necessary. Choices are influenced by **incentives**, which can be a reward that encourages an action or a penalty that discourages an action. Prices act as incentives.

Economics is the social science that studies the choices that individuals, businesses, governments, and entire societies make as they cope with scarcity and the incentives that influence and reconcile those choices. Economics is divided into two broad fields:

♦ **Microeconomics** is the study of choices that individuals and businesses make, the way these choices interact in markets, and the influence of governments.

♦ **Macroeconomics** is the study of the performance of the national economy and the global economy.

Two Big Economic Questions

Economics explores two big questions:

♦ How do choices end up determining *what*, *how*, and *for whom* goods and services get produced?

♦ Do the choices that people make in the pursuit of their own *self-interest* unintentionally promote the broader *social interest*?

Goods and services are the objects that people value and produce to satisfy human wants. Goods and services are produced using productive resources called **factors of production**. There are four categories:

♦ **Land:** the "gifts of nature" such as land, minerals, and water, used to produce goods and services.

♦ **Labor:** the work time and work effort people devote to producing goods and services. The quality of labor depends on **human capital**, which is the knowledge and skill that people obtain from education, on-the-job training, and work experience.

♦ **Capital:** the tools, instruments, machines, buildings, and other constructions that businesses use to produce goods and services. The productive resource "capital" differs from *financial capital*, which includes money, stocks, and bonds.

♦ **Entrepreneurship:** the human resource that organizes land, labor, and capital.

For whom the goods and services are produced depends on people's incomes. To earn an income, people sell the services of the factors of production they own. Land earns **rent;** labor earns **wages;** capital earns **interest;** and entrepreneurship earns **profit.**

People make choices that are in their **self interest,** choices that they think are the best available for them. An outcome is in the **social interest if** it is best for society as a whole. Resource use is **efficient** if it is *not* possible to make someone better off without making someone else worse off. The social interest requires efficiency and fairness but fairness is hard to define. Economists work to understand when choices made in self interest advance the social interest. For instance, does globalization best serve the social interest? Did the high-tech information-age economy result from choices made in the social interest? Are the private choices made about climate change in the social interest? Do banks' self-interested choices to loan and people's self-interested choices to borrow serve the social interest or do they lead to macroeconomic instability?

The Economic Way of Thinking

A choice involves a **tradeoff.** A tradeoff is an exchange—giving up one thing to get something else. Economists assume that people make **rational choices,** which means that they compare the costs and benefits and then make the choice that achieves the greatest benefit over cost for the person making the choice.

♦ The **benefit** of something is the pleasure that it brings and is determined by the person's **preferences**—what a person likes and by how much. Benefit is measured by the most the person is *willing* to give up to get the thing.

♦ The **opportunity cost** of something is the highest-valued alternative that must be given up to get it. Opportunity cost is not all the alternatives foregone, it is *only* the highest-valued alternative foregone. All tradeoffs involve an opportunity cost.

♦ The benefit that arises from an increase in an activity is called **marginal benefit.** The opportunity cost of an increase in an activity is called **marginal cost.**

Most choices involve deciding how much of an activity to do. Choices that compare the marginal benefit of a small change to the marginal cost of the small change are said to be made at the **margin**. If the marginal benefit of an action exceeds its marginal cost, the action is undertaken; if the marginal benefit of an action is less than its marginal cost, the action is not undertaken.

Changes in marginal cost and/or marginal benefit affect the decisions made, so choices respond to incentives. Institutions affect people's incentives and so they affect whether a self-interested choice promotes the social interest.

■ Economics as Social Science and Policy Tool

Economists distinguish between:

♦ *Positive statements* — statements about what is. A positive statement can be tested to see if it is true or false.

♦ *Normative statements* — statements about what ought to be. These are matters of opinion and are not testable.

Economists use economic models to unscramble cause and effect. An **economic model** is a description of some aspect of the economic world that includes only those features of the world that are needed for the purpose at hand. A model is tested to determine how well its predictions correspond with the facts.

Testing models is difficult because the real world outcomes used to test models reflect the simultaneous changes of many factors. To overcome this difficulty, economists use *natural experiments*, *statistical investigations*, and *economic experiment*s.

Helpful Hints

1. **CHOICES AND INCENTIVES :** The basic assumption about human behavior made by economists is that people act to make themselves as well off as possible. As a result, people respond to changed incentives by changing their decisions. The key idea is that an individual compares the additional (or "marginal") benefit from taking an action to the additional (or "marginal") cost of the action. If the marginal benefit from the action exceeds the marginal cost, taking the action makes the person better off, so the person takes the action. Conversely, if the marginal benefit falls short of the marginal cost, the action is not taken. Only the *additional* benefit—the *marginal* benefit—and *additional* cost—the *marginal* cost—are relevant because they are the benefits and costs that the person will enjoy and incur if the action is undertaken. Keeping straight the distinction between additional benefits and costs versus total benefits and costs is a vital part of economics, particularly of microeconomics.

2. **MODELS AND SIMPLIFICATION :** In attempting to understand how and why something works (for example, an airplane or an economy), we can use description or we can use theory. A description is a list of facts about something. But it does not tell us which facts are essential for understanding how an airplane works (the shape of the wings) and which facts are less important (the color of the paint). Scientists use theory to abstract from the complex descriptive facts of the real world and focus only on those elements essential for understanding. These essential elements are fashioned into models — highly simplified representations of the real world.

Models are like maps, which are useful precisely because they abstract from real world detail. A GPS map that reproduced all the details of the real world (street lights, traffic signs, billboards, overhead electric wires) would be useless because it would be too complicated to use. A useful map offers a simplified view, which is carefully selected according to the purpose of the map. A useful theory is similar: It gives guidance and insight into how the immensely complicated real world functions and reacts to changes.

Questions

■ True/False and Explain

Definition of Economics

1. Scarcity is a problem only for the poor.

2. Macroeconomics is the branch of economics that studies the factors that change national employment and income.

Two Big Economic Questions

3. Answering the question "What goods and services are produced?" automatically answers the question "How are goods and services produced?"

4. An example of the "how" part of the first big question is: "How does the nation decide who gets the goods and services that are produced?"

5. As a factor of production, capital earns profit.

6. When making choices, people consider the social interest of their decisions.

7. Choices made in self interest might also advance the social interest.

The Economic Way of Thinking

8. Tradeoffs mean that you give up one thing to get something else.

9. A person's benefit from a new portable computer is measured by the most that the person is willing to give up to get the portable computer.

10. If Sam buys a slice of pizza for $3 rather than a burrito for $3, the burrito is the opportunity cost of buying the slice of pizza.

11. When a person compares the marginal cost and marginal benefit of a small change in an activity, the person is making a choice at the margin.

Economics As Social Science and Policy Tool

12. A positive statement is about what is; a normative statement is about what will be.

13. Natural experiments can be used to test an economic model.

■ Multiple Choice

Definition of Economics

1. The fact that wants cannot be fully satisfied with available resources reflects the definition of
   a. incentives.
   b. scarcity.
   c. the output-inflation tradeoff.
   d. for whom to produce.

2. Studying the effects choices have on the national economy is part of
   a. scarcity.
   b. microeconomics.
   c. macroeconomics.
   d. global science.

Two Big Economic Questions

3. Which of the following is NOT part of the first big economic question?
   a. What goods and services are produced?
   b. How are goods and services produced?
   c. For whom are goods and services produced?
   d. Why are goods and services produced?

4. The question, "Should desktop computers or laptop computers be produced?" is an example of which part of the first big economic question?
   a. The "what" part.
   b. The "how" part.
   c. The "where" part.
   d. The "for whom" part.

5. People have different amounts of income. This observation is most directly related to which part of the first big economic question?
   a. The "what" part.
   b. The "how" part.
   c. The "why" part.
   d. The "for whom" part.

6. The factor of production that earns the most income is _____.
   a. land
   b. labor
   c. capital
   d. entrepreneurship

7. If a drug executive sets the price of a new drug at $1,000 a dose because that is the price that is best for the executive, the executive is definitely making a
   a. self-interested choice.
   b. choice in the social interest.
   c. globalization choice.
   d. factors of production choice.

8. Choices made in the pursuit of self interest _____ the social interest.
   a. always further
   b. sometimes further
   c. never further
   d. are no comparable to choices made in the

The Economic Way of Thinking

9. A rational choice
   a. must reflect the person's self interest.
   b. compares costs and benefits and selects the action that gives the greatest benefit over cost.
   c. comes close to eliminating scarcity.
   d. cannot reflect a tradeoff because the choice is rational.

10. The benefit of a good is measured by _____ and its cost is measured by _____.
    a. the dollar value of the good; the dollar cost of the good
    b. the tradeoff necessary to purchase the good; the incentives necessary to motivate the person to buy the good
    c. what a person is willing to give; what a person must give up
    d. None of the above answers are correct because benefit is impossible to measure.

11. From 9 to 10 A.M., Fred can sleep in, go to his economics lecture, or play tennis. Suppose that Fred decides to go to the lecture but thinks that, if he hadn't, he would otherwise have slept in. The opportunity cost of attending the lecture is
    a. sleeping in *and* playing tennis.
    b. playing tennis.
    c. sleeping in.
    d. one hour of time.

12. When the government chooses to use resources to build a dam, these resources are no longer available to build a highway. This fact best illustrates the concept of
    a. a market.
    b. macroeconomics.
    c. opportunity cost.
    d. marginal benefit.

13. To make a choice on the margin, an individual
    a. ignores any opportunity cost if the marginal benefit from the action is high enough.
    b. will choose to use his or her scarce resources only if there is a very large total benefit from so doing.
    c. compares the marginal cost of the choice to the marginal benefit.
    d. makes the choice with the smallest opportunity cost.

Economics As Social Science and Policy Tool

14. A positive statement is
    a. about what ought to be.
    b. about what is.
    c. always true.
    d. one used in an economic experiment.

15. Which of the following is a positive statement?
    a. The government must lower the price of a pizza so that more students can afford to buy it.
    b. The best level of taxation is zero percent because then people get to keep everything they earn.
    c. My economics class should last for two terms because it is my favorite class.
    d. An increase in college tuition will lead fewer students to apply to college.

16. Economic models
    a. include only normative statements.
    b. are tested using only statistical investigations.
    c. must include all known facts about a situation.
    d. include only details considered essential.

■ Short Answer Problems

1. "In the future, as our technology advances even further, eventually we will whip scarcity. In the high-tech future, scarcity will be gone." Do you agree or disagree with this claim? Explain your answer and what scarcity is. Why does the existence of scarcity require choices?

2. What are the factors of production? Focusing on the factors of production, describe the relationship between the question "How are goods and services produced?" and the question "For whom are goods and services produced?".

3. What is making a choice based on self interest? Making a choice based on social interest? Why is it important to determine if choices based on self interest are the same as choices based on social interest?

4. Why does your decision to buy a taco from Taco Bell reflect a tradeoff? Be sure to discuss the role played by opportunity cost in your answer.

5. "Education is a basic right. Just as kindergarten through 12th grade education is free, so, too, should a college education be free and guaranteed to every American." This statement can be analyzed by using the economic concepts discussed in this chapter to answer the following questions.

   a. What would be the opportunity cost of providing a free college education for everyone?

   b. Is providing this education free from the perspective of society as a whole?

6. What role do incentives play in making a rational choice?

7. Indicate whether each of the following statements is positive or normative. If it is normative, rewrite it so that it becomes positive. If it is positive, rewrite it so that it becomes normative.

   a. Policymakers ought to lower the inflation rate even if it lowers output.

   b. An imposition of a tax on tobacco products will decrease their consumption.

   c. Health care costs should be lower so that poorer people can afford quality health care.

■ You're the Teacher

1. Your friend asks, "Does everything have an opportunity cost?" Your friend has hit upon a very good question; provide an equally good answer!

2. "Economic theories are useless because the models on which they are based are totally unrealistic. They leave out so many descriptive details about the real world, they can't possibly be useful for understanding how the economy works." So says your skeptical friend. You'd like to keep your friend in your economics class so that you two can study together. Defend the fact that economic theories are much simpler than reality and help your friend realize that time spent studying economic theories is time well spent!

Answers

True/False Answers

Definition of Economics

1. **F** Scarcity exists because people's wants exceed their ability to meet those wants, and this fact of life is true for *any* person, rich or poor.

2. **T** Macroeconomics studies the entire economy; microeconomics studies separate parts of the economy.

Two Big Economic Questions

3. **F** Almost always, goods and services can be produced many different ways, so the "how" question must be answered separately from the "what" question.

4. **F** The "how" part of the first big question asks, "How are goods and services produced?"

5. **F** Capital earns interest; entrepreneurship earns profit.

6. **F** People make self-interested choices, that is, they make the choices they are best for them.

7. **T** A role of economics is to discover when choices made in the self interest advance the social interest and when they conflict with the social interest.

The Economic Way of Thinking

8. **T** The question gives the definition of a tradeoff.

9. **T** Benefit is measured by how much the person is *willing* to give up to get something; cost is measured by how much the person *must* give up to get something.

10. **T** The opportunity cost is the burrito that was foregone in order to buy the pizza.

11. **T** The definition of making a choice at the margin means that choice revolves around a small change.

Economics As Social Science and Policy Tool

12. **F** Although a positive statement is, indeed, about what is, a normative statement tells what policies should be followed.

13. **T** Natural experiments, along with statistical investigations and economic experiments, are used to test economic models.

Multiple Choice Answers

Definition of Economics

1. **b** Scarcity refers to the observation that wants are unlimited but that the resources available to satisfy these wants are limited.

2. **c** Macroeconomics studies the national economy as well as the global economy.

Two Big Economic Questions

3. **d** "Why" is not part of the first big economic question.

4. **a** The "what" part asks "What goods and services are produced?"

5. **d** People with high incomes will get more goods and services than those with low incomes.

6. **b** Labor earns wages, which together with fringe benefits are about 70 percent of total income.

7. **a** Because the choice is best for the executive, it is a self-interested choice.

8. **b** Part of the job of economists is to determine when choices made in self interest further social interest and when they come into conflict.

The Economic Way of Thinking

9. **b** Rational choices are made at the margin by comparing the marginal benefit of an action to its marginal cost.

10. **c** When comparing benefit to cost, the person compares what he or she is *willing* to give up to *what* he or she must give up.

11. **c** The opportunity cost of an action is the (single) highest-valued alternative foregone by taking the action.

12. **c** Because the resources are used to build a dam, the opportunity of using them to build a highway is given up.

13. **c** Comparing marginal cost and marginal benefit is an important technique, especially in microeconomics.

Economics As Social Science and Policy Tool

14. **b** Positive statements describe how the world operates.

15. **d** This statement is the only one that tries to describe how the world actually works; all the others are normative statements that describe a policy that should be pursued.

16. **d** By including only essential details, economic models are vastly simpler than reality.

■ Answers to Short Answer Problems

1. This claim is incorrect. Scarcity will always exist. Scarcity occurs because people's wants are basically unlimited, but the resources available to satisfy these wants are finite. As a result, not all of everyone's wants can be satisfied. For instance, think about the number of people who want to spend all winter skiing on uncrowded slopes. Regardless of the level of technology, there simply are not enough ski slopes available to allow everyone who wants to spend all winter skiing in near isolation to do so. Uncrowded ski slopes are scarce and will remain so.

   Because not all the goods and services wanted can be produced, choices must be made about which wants will be satisfied and which wants will be disappointed.

2. The four factors of production are land, labor, capital, and entrepreneurship. These are the resources used to produce goods and services, so the question asking how goods and services are produced asks which factors will be used. People earn their incomes by offering factors of production for use. Land earns rent, labor earns wages, capital earns interest, and entrepreneurship earns profit. The answer to the question asking for whom the goods and services are produced depends on people's incomes. So, for example, if more land is used to produce goods and services, then landowners' incomes will be higher so they will be able to acquire more of the goods and services that have been produced.

3. A choice based on self interest is a choice that is best for the person making the choice. A choice based on social interest is a choice that is best for society. It is important to determine if choices based on self interest are the same as choices based on social interest because most choices are based on self interest. If the choices are the same, then people pursuing their own self interest advance the social interest.

4. The decision to buy a taco reflects a tradeoff because you have given up your funds in exchange for the taco. The opportunity cost of buying the taco is the highest-valued alternative given up. For instance, suppose that if you had not decided to buy the taco, you would then have used the funds to buy a burger from Burger King. In this case, the opportunity cost of buying the taco is the forgone burger because that is the highest-valued alternative given up.

5. a. Even though a college education may be offered without charge ("free"), opportunity costs still exist. The opportunity cost of providing such education is the highest valued alternative use of the resources used to construct the necessary universities and the highest valued alternative use of the resources (including human resources) used in the operation of the schools.

   b. Providing a "free" college education is hardly free from the perspective of society. The resources used in this endeavor would no longer be available for other activities. For instance, the resources used to construct a new college cannot be used to construct a hospital to provide better health care. Additionally, the time and effort spent by the faculty, staff, and students operating and attending colleges has a substantial opportunity cost, namely, that these individuals cannot participate fully in other sectors of the economy. Providing a "free" college education to everyone is not free to society!

6. Incentives are rewards or penalties. Increases in the marginal benefit or decreases in the marginal cost are rewards; decreases in the marginal benefit or increases in the marginal cost are penalties. Because rational choices compare the marginal benefit of an action to the marginal cost of the action, an incentive that changes the marginal benefit or the marginal cost might change the outcome of a rational decision. For instance, an incentive that increases the marginal benefit of an action makes it more likely that the decision maker will choose to undertake the action.

7. a. This statement is normative. A positive statement is: "If policymakers lowered the inflation rate by 1 percentage point, then output would fall by 1 percent."

   b. This statement is positive. A normative statement is: "We should impose a tax on tobacco products in order to decrease their consumption."

   c. This statement is normative. A positive statement is: "If health care costs were lower, more poor people would receive health care."

■ You're the Teacher

1. "Virtually everything has an opportunity cost. People sometimes say that viewing a beautiful sunset or using sand from the middle of the Sahara Desert have no opportunity costs. But that isn't strictly true. Viewing the sunset has an opportunity cost in terms of the time spent watching it. The time could have been utilized in some other activity and, whatever the next highest-valued opportunity might have been, that is the opportunity cost of watching the sunset. Similarly, making use of sand from the Sahara also must have some opportunity cost, be it the time spent in gathering the sand or the resources spent in gathering it. So from the widest of perspectives, the answer is: Yes, everything does have an opportunity cost."

2. "Economic theories are like maps, which are useful precisely because they abstract from real world detail. A useful map offers a simplified view, which is carefully selected according to the purpose of the map. No map maker would claim that the world is as simple (or as flat) as the map, and economists do not claim that the real economy is as simple as their theories. What economists do claim is that their theories isolate the effects of real forces operating in the economy, yield predictions that can be tested against real-world data, and result in predictions that often are correct."

"I've got a book here that my parents gave to me by Milton Friedman, a Nobel Prize winner in Economics. Here's what he says on this topic: 'A theory or its 'assumptions' cannot possibly be thoroughly 'realistic' in the immediate descriptive sense.... A completely 'realistic' theory of the wheat market would have to include not only the conditions directly underlying the supply and demand for wheat but also the kind of coins or credit instruments used to make exchanges; the personal characteristics of wheat-traders such as the color of each trader's hair and eyes, ... the number of members of his family, their characteristics, ... the kind of soil on which the wheat was grown, ... the weather prevailing during the growing season; ... and so on indefinitely. Any attempt to move very far in achieving this kind of 'realism' is certain to render a theory utterly useless.' "

"I think Friedman makes a lot of sense in what he says. It seems to me that theories have to be simple in order to be powerful and so I don't see anything wrong with the fact that economic theories leave out a bunch of trivial details."

From Milton Friedman, "The Methodology of Positive Economics," in *Essays in Positive Economics.* (Chicago: University of Chicago Press, 1953), 32.

Chapter Quiz

1. The most fundamental economic problem is
   a. reducing unemployment.
   b. health and health care.
   c. scarcity.
   d. decreasing the inflation rate.

2. Studying how an individual firm decides to set its price is primarily a concern of
   a. normative economics.
   b. macroeconomics.
   c. microeconomics.
   d. all economists.

3. Which of the following is a macroeconomic topic?
   a. Why has the price of a personal computer fallen over time?
   b. How does a rise in the price of cheese affect the pizza market?
   c. What factors determine the nation's inflation rate?
   d. How does a consumer decide how many tacos to consume?

4. When the economy produces fireworks for sale at the Fourth of July, it most directly is answering the _____ question.
   a. what goods and services are produced
   b. opportunity cost
   c. for whom are goods and services produced
   d. how are goods and services produced

5. When doctors have an average income that exceeds $250,000, the economy most directly is answering the _____ part of the first big question.
   a. what goods and services are produced
   b. opportunity cost
   c. how are goods and services produced
   d. for whom are goods and services produced

6. Which of the following is microeconomic issue?
   a. How does a pharmaceutical company determine the price of a drug?
   b. What effect does a government deficit have on the unemployment rate?
   c. Is inflation harmful?
   d. Why is the unemployment rate falling?

7. Decisions made in a person's self-interest
   a. are unaffected by either marginal benefit or marginal cost.
   b. will reflect tradeoffs but are not made at the margin.
   c. might also advance the social interest.
   d. None of the above answers is correct.

8. Opportunity cost is
   a. zero for services, because services do not last for very long, and positive for goods, because goods are long lasting.
   b. paid by society not by an individual.
   c. the highest-valued alternative given up by making a choice.
   d. all the alternatives given up by making a choice.

9. In economics, positive statements
   a. are only about facts that economists are certain (are "positive") are true.
   b. tell what policy the government ought to follow.
   c. depend on value judgments.
   d. in principle, can be tested to determine if they are true or false.

10. Which of the following is a normative statement?
    a. The price of gasoline fell last month.
    b. Portable computers are more expensive than desktop computers.
    c. On the average, economics majors have higher starting salaries than management majors.
    d. The government should provide universal health care.

The answers for this Chapter Quiz are on page 345

Appendix

GRAPHS IN ECONOMICS

Key Concepts

■ Graphing Data

Graphs represent quantity as a distance on a line. On a graph, the horizontal scale line is the *x-axis*, the vertical scale line is the *y-axis*, and the intersection of the two scale lines is the *origin*. A line from a point in a graph to the vertical axis is called the *x* coordinate because its length is the same as the value marked off along the *x*-axis; a line from the point in the graph to the horizontal axis is called the *y*-coordinate because its length is the same as the value marked off along the *y*-axis.

♦ **Scatter diagrams** plot the value of one variable against the value of another variable for a number of different values of each variable. Scatter diagrams show the relationship between two variables by illustrating the "scatter" of their points. Such a relationship indicates how the variables are *correlated*, that is, occur together. But scatter diagrams cannot determine whether one variable *causes* the other.

Graphs can have breaks in the axes, over which the variable measured along that axis jumps in value. Graphs can also mislead by stretching or compressing the scale of a variable measured along either axis.

■ Graphs Used in Economic Models

The four important relationships between variables are:

♦ **Positive relationship** or **direct relationship** — the variables move together in the same direction, as illustrated in Figure A1.1. A positive relationship is upward-sloping.

♦ **Negative relationship** or **inverse relationship** — the variables move in opposite directions, as shown in Figure A1.2. A negative relationship is downward-sloping.

FIGURE **A1.1**
A Positive Relationship

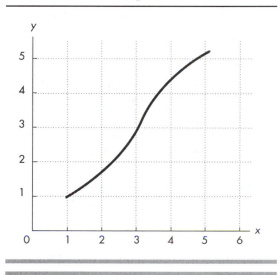

FIGURE **A1.2**
A Negative Relationship

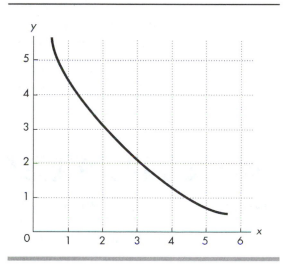

◆ Maximum or minimum — the relationship reaches a maximum or a minimum point, then changes direction. Figure A1.3 shows a minimum.

◆ Unrelated — the variables are not related so that, when one variable changes, the other is unaffected. The graph is either a vertical or horizontal straight line, as illustrated in Figure A1.4.

A relationship illustrated by a straight line is called a **linear relationship.**

■ The Slope of a Relationship

The **slope** of a relationship is the change in the value of the variable measured on the *y*-axis divided by the change in the value of the variable measured on the *x*-axis. The formula for slope is $\Delta y/\Delta x$, with Δ meaning "change in."

A straight line (or linear relationship) has a constant slope. A curved line has a varying slope, which can be calculated two ways:

◆ *Slope at a point* —draw the straight line tangent to the curve at that point and then calculate the slope of the line.

◆ *Slope across an arc* —draw a straight line between the two points on the curve and then calculate the slope of the line.

■ Graphing Relationships Among More Than Two Variables

Relationships between more than two variables can be graphed by holding constant the values of all the variables except two (the ***ceteris paribus*** assumption, that is, "if all other relevant things remain the same") and then graphing the relationship between the two with, *ceteris paribus*, only the variables being studied changing. When one of the variables not illustrated in the figure changes, the entire relationship between the two that have been graphed shifts.

Helpful Hints

1. **IMPORTANCE OF GRAPHS AND GRAPHICAL ANALYSIS :** Economists almost always use graphs to present relationships between variables. This fact should not "scare" you or give you pause.

FIGURE **A1.3**
A Minimum

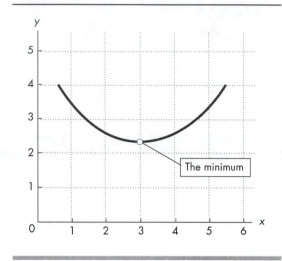

FIGURE **A1.4**
No Relationship

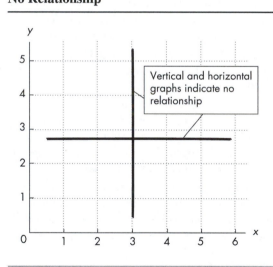

Economists do so because graphs *simplify* the analysis. All the key concepts you need to master are presented in this appendix. If your experience with graphical analysis is limited, this appendix is crucial to your ability to readily understand economic analysis. However, if you are experienced in constructing and using graphs, this appendix may be "old hat." Even so, you should skim the appendix and work through the questions in this *Study Guide.*

2. **CALCULATING THE SLOPE :** Often the slopes of various relationships are important. Usually what is key is the sign of the slope — whether the slope is positive or negative — rather than the actual value of the slope. An easy way to remember the formula for slope is to think of it as the "rise over the run," a saying used by carpenters and others. As illustrated in Figure A1.5, the *rise* is the change in the variable measured on the vertical axis, or in terms of symbols, Δy. The *run* is the change in the variable measured on the horizontal axis, or Δx. This "rise over the run" formula also makes it easy to remember whether the slope is positive or negative. If the rise is actually a drop, as shown in Figure A1.5, then the slope is negative because when the variable measured on the horizontal axis increases, the variable measured on the vertical axis decreases. However, if the rise actually is an increase, then the slope is positive. In this case, an increase in the variable measured on the *x*-axis is associated with an increase in the variable measured on the *y*-axis.

FIGURE **A1.5**
Rise Over The Run

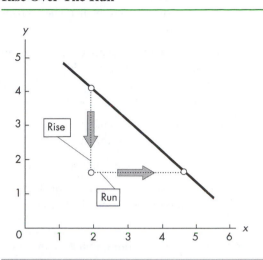

Questions

■ True/False and Explain

Graphing Data

1. The origin is the point where a graph starts.

2. The *x*-axis is the horizontal scale line.

3. In Figure A1.6 the relationship between the number of Facebook pages and the price of a Facebook ads is positive.

4. Figure A1.6 shows that a higher price for Facebook ads caused more Facebook pages to be created.

5. Figure A1.6 shows that a larger number of Facebook pages caused the price of Facebook ads to rise.

6. A graph showing a positive relationship between stock prices and the nation's production means that an increase in stock prices causes an increase in production.

Graphs Used in Economic Models

7. If the graph of the relationship between two variables slopes upward to the right, the relationship between the variables is positive.

FIGURE **A1.6**
True/False Questions 3, 4, 5

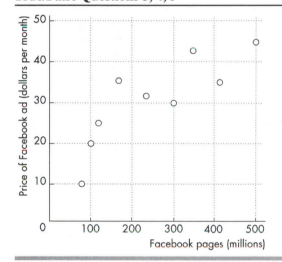

8. If the relationship between *y* (measured on the vertical axis) and *x* (measured on the horizontal axis) is one in which *y* reaches a maximum, the slope of the relationship must be negative before and positive after the maximum.

9. To the left of a minimum point, the slope is negative; to the right, the slope is positive.

10. Graphing things that are unrelated on one diagram is <u>NOT</u> possible.

The Slope of a Relationship

11. It is possible for the graph of a positive relationship to have a slope that becomes smaller when moving rightward along the graph.

12. The slope of a straight line is calculated by dividing the change in the value of the variable measured on the horizontal axis by the change in the value of the variable measured on the vertical axis.

13. For a straight line, if a large change in y is associated with a small change in x, the line is steep.

14. The slope of a curved line is <u>NOT</u> constant.

15. The slope of a curved line at a point equals the slope of a line tangent to the curved line at the point.

Graphing Relationships Among More Than Two Variables

16. *Ceteris paribus* means "everything else changes."

17. The amount of corn a farmer grows depends on its price and the amount of rainfall. The curve showing the relationship between the price of a bushel of corn and the quantity grown is the same curve regardless of the amount of rainfall.

■ **Multiple Choice**

Graphing Data

1. The two perpendicular scale lines are called the
   a. origin.
   b. graph.
   c. axes.
   d. coordinates.

2. When the inflation rate increases, the interest rate also generally increases. This fact indicates that
   a. there might be false causality between inflation and the interest rate.
   b. higher inflation rates must cause higher interest rates.
   c. a scatter diagram of the inflation rate and the interest rate will have the dots generally higher the farther they are to the right.
   d. there is no correlation between the two variables.

3. Over the past decade, the total production in the United States has ranged from $10 trillion to $15 trillion. During the same time, interest rates on U.S. government securities have ranged from 7 percent to 1 percent. If you wanted to plot the relationship between total production in the United States and government interest rates, you would probably need to
   a. plot the interest rate on the vertical axis.
   b. assume that changes in one of the variables causes changes in the other, though you do *not* need to determine which variable causes the changes in the other.
   c. use a break in the axis that measures total U.S. production so that the graph is not misleading.
   d. None of the above answers are correct because it is impossible to plot a scatter diagram between interest rates and total U.S. production since the numbers are so different.

4. Scatter diagrams _____ show causation and they _____ show correlation.
   a. can; can
   b. can; cannot
   c. cannot; can
   d. cannot; cannot.

5. Suppose that the points showing the relationship between expenditure and income are tightly clustered around a line. In this case we can be confident that
   a. a change in income causes a change in expenditure.
   b. income and expenditure must be similar in magnitude.
   c. either a change in income causes a change in expenditure or a change in expenditure causes a change in income.
   d. there is a high correlation between income and expenditure.

Graphs Used in Economic Models

6. If variables x and y move up and down together, they are
   a. positively related.
   b. negative related.
   c. unrelated.
   d. trend related.

Multiple Choice Questions 7 and 8

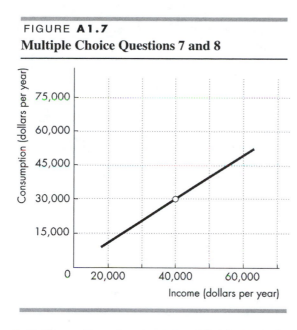

Multiple Choice Question 10

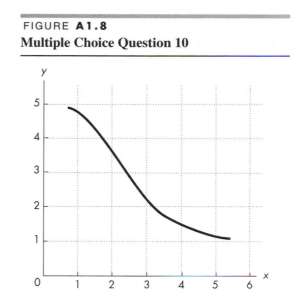

7. In Figure A1.7 when income equals $40,000, what does consumption equal?

    a. $0
    b. $15,000
    c. $30,000
    d. $40,000

8. The relationship between income and consumption illustrated in Figure A1.7 is

    a. positive and linear.
    b. positive and nonlinear.
    c. negative and linear.
    d. negative and nonlinear

9. The term "direct relationship" means the same as

    a. correlation.
    b. trend.
    c. positive relationship.
    d. negative relationship.

10. Figure A1.8 shows

    a. a positive relationship.
    b. a variable relationship.
    c. a negative relationship.
    d. no consistent relationship between the variables.

11. The relationship between two variables, x and y, is a vertical line. Thus x and y are

    a. positively correlated.
    b. negatively correlated.
    c. not related.
    d. falsely related.

The Slope of a Relationship

12. The slope of a negative relationship is

    a. negative.
    b. undefined.
    c. positive to the right of the maximum point and negative to the left.
    d. constant as long as the relationship is nonlinear.

13. A linear relationship

    a. always has a maximum.
    b. always has a constant slope.
    c. always slopes up to the right.
    d. never has a constant slope.

FIGURE **A1.9**
Multiple Choice Questions 14 and 15

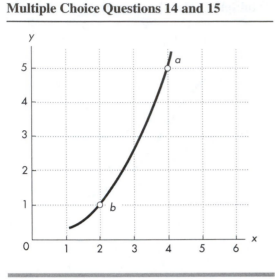

FIGURE **A1.10**
Multiple Choice Questions 16 and 17

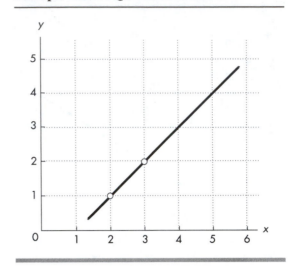

14. The relationship between *x* and *y* in Figure A1.9 is
    a. positive with an increasing slope.
    b. positive with a decreasing slope.
    c. negative with an increasing slope.
    d. negative with a decreasing slope.

15. In Figure A1.9 the slope across the arc between points *a* and *b* equals
    a. 5.
    b. 4.
    c. 2.
    d. 1.

16. In Figure A1.10, between *x* = 2 and *x* = 3, what is the slope of the line?
    a. 1
    b. −1
    c. 2
    d. 3

17. In Figure A1.10 how does the slope of the line between *x* = 4 and *x* = 5 compare with the slope between *x* = 2 and *x* = 3?
    a. The slope is greater between *x* = 4 and *x* = 5.
    b. The slope is greater between *x* = 2 and *x* = 3.
    c. The slope is the same.
    d. The slope is not comparable.

Graphing Relationships Among More Than Two Variables

FIGURE **A1.11**
Multiple Choice Questions 18, 19, 20

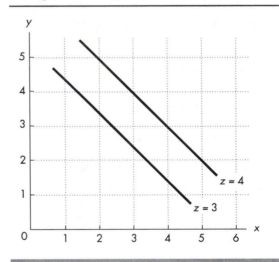

18. In Figure A1.11 *x* is
    a. positively related to *y* and negatively related to *z*.
    b. positively related to both *y* and *z*.
    c. negatively related to *y* and positively related to *z*.
    d. negatively related to both *y* and *z*.

19. In Figure A1.11, *ceteris paribus*, an increase in *x* is associated with

   a. an increase in *y*.
   b. a decrease in *y*.
   c. a decrease in *z*.
   d. None of the above answers is correct.

20. In Figure A1.11 an increase in *z* leads to a

   a. movement up along one of the lines showing the relationship between *x* and *y*.
   b. movement down along one of the lines showing the relationship between *x* and *y*.
   c. rightward shift of the line showing the relationship between *x* and *y*.
   d. leftward shift of the line showing the relationship between *x* and *y*.

■ **Short Answer Problems**

1. a. The data in Table A1.1 show the U.S. unemployment rate and the growth rate of total production between 1994 and 2011. Put the unemployment rate on the horizontal axis and draw a scatter diagram of these data.
   b. What is the relationship between these two variables?

TABLE **A1.2**

Short Answer Problem 2

x	y
1	2
2	4
3	6
4	8
5	7
6	6

2. a. Use the data in Table A1.2 to graph the relationship between *x* and *y*.
   b. Over what range of values for *x* is this relationship positive? Over what range is it negative?
   c. Calculate the slope between *x* = 1 and *x* = 2.
   d. Calculate the slope between *x* = 5 and *x* = 6.
   e. What relationships do your answers to parts c and d have to your answer for part b?

3. a. In Figure A1.12, use the tangent line in the figure to calculate the slope at point *b*.
   b. Compute the slope across the arc between points *b* and *a*.

TABLE **A1.1**

Short Answer Problem 1

Growth rate of total production (percent)	Unemployment rate (percent)
4.1	6.1
2.5	5.6
3.7	5.4
4.5	5.6
4.4	5.0
4.8	4.2
4.1	4.0
1.1	4.7
1.8	5.8
2.5	6.0
3.5	5.5
3.1	5.1
2.7	4.6
1.9	4.6
−0.5	5.8
−3.5	9.3
3.0	9.6
1.7	9.0

FIGURE **A1.12**

Short Answer Problem 3

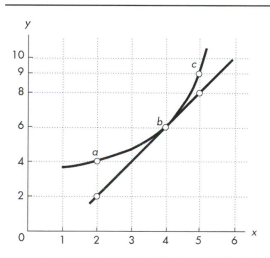

c. Calculate the slope across the arc between points *c* and *b*.

4. Can a curve have a positive but decreasing slope? If so, draw an example.

5. a. Bobby says that he buys fewer DVDs when the price of a DVD is higher. Bobby also says that he will buy more DVDs after he graduates and his income is higher. Is the relationship between the number of DVDs Bobby buys and the price positive or negative? Is the relationship between Bobby's income and the number of DVDs positive or negative?

TABLE **A1.3**

Short Answer Problem 5

Price (dollars per DVD)	Quantity of DVDs purchased, low income	Quantity of DVDs purchased, high income
$11	5	6
12	4	5
13	3	4
14	1	3
15	0	2

b. Table A1.3 shows the number of DVDs Bobby buys in a month at different prices when his income is low and when his income is high. On a diagram with price on the vertical axis and the quantity purchased on the horizontal axis, plot the relationship between the number of DVDs purchased and the price when Bobby's income is low.

c. On the same diagram, draw the relationship between the number of DVDs purchased and the price when Bobby's income is high.

d. Does an increase in Bobby's income cause the relationship between the price of a DVD and the number purchased to shift rightward or leftward?

■ **You're the Teacher**

1. "Hey, I thought this was an *economics* class, not a *math* class. Where's the economics? All I've seen so far is math!" Reassure your friend by explaining why the concentration in this chapter is on mathematics rather than economics.

2. "I don't understand why we need to learn all about graphs. Instead of this, why can't we just use numbers? If there is any sort of relationship we need to see, we can see it easier using numbers instead of all these complicated graphs!" Explain why graphs are useful when studying economics.

3. "There must be a relationship between the direction a curve is sloping, what its slope is, and whether the curve shows a positive or negative relationship between two variables. But I can't see the tie. Is there one? And what is it?" Help this student by answering the questions posed.

Answers

■ True/False Answers

Graphing Data

1. **F** The origin is where the horizontal and vertical axes start, *not* where the graph starts.

2. **T** And the *y*-axis is the vertical scale line.

3. **T** The scatter diagram shows a positive relationship; when one variable increased, so did the other.

4. **F** Scatter diagrams cannot show causation.

5. **F** Scatter diagrams show only correlation *not* causation regardless of which variable is said to be causing changes in the other.

6. **F** The graph shows a correlation between stock prices and production, but that does not necessarily mean that an increase in stock prices causes the increase in production.

Graphs Used in Economic Models

7. **T** If the graph slopes upward to the right, then an increase in the variable measured along the horizontal axis is associated with an increase in the variable measured on the vertical axis.

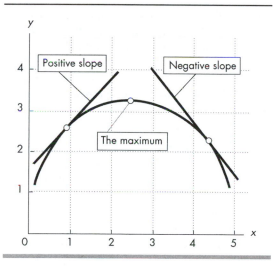

FIGURE **A1.13**
True/False Question 8

8. **F** As Figure A1.13 illustrates, before the maximum, the relationship is positive; after the maximum is reached, the relationship is negative.

9. **T** To verify this answer, flip Figure A1.13 upside down. To the left of the minimum the line is falling, so its slope is negative; to the right the line is rising, so its slope is positive.

10. **F** If two unrelated variables are graphed on the same diagram, the "relationship" between the two is either a vertical or a horizontal straight line.

The Slope of a Relationship

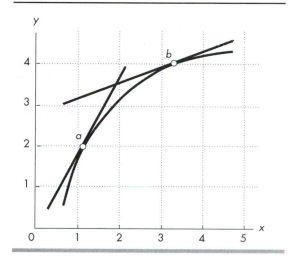

FIGURE **A1.14**
True/False Question 11

11. **T** Figure A1.14 shows a positive relationship whose slope decreases when moving rightward along it from point *a* to point *b*.

12. **F** Just the reverse is true: Divide the change in the variable on the *vertical* axis by the change in the variable on the *horizontal* axis.

13. **T** The definition of slope is $\Delta y / \Delta x$. So if a large change in *y* (the numerator) is associated with a small change in *x* (the denominator), the magnitude of the slope is relatively large. The large magnitude for the slope indicates that the line is relatively steep.

14. **T** Only the slope of a straight line is constant.

15. **T** This question tells precisely how to calculate the slope at a point on a curved line.

Graphing Relationships Among More Than Two Variables

16. **F** *Ceteris paribus* means that only the variables

being studied change; all other variables do not change.

17. **F** For different amounts of rainfall, there are different curves showing the relationship between the price of a bushel of corn and the quantity that is grown.

■ Multiple Choice Answers

Graphing Data

1. **c** The vertical scale line is the y-axis, the horizontal scale is the x-axis.

2. **c** The dots will tend to cluster along a line that slopes upward moving to the right along it.

3. **c** The break would be necessary because total U.S. production is so large.

4. **c** Scatter diagrams can only show correlation. They cannot show whether changes in one variable cause changes in another because both variables might be responding to changes in some other factor.

5. **d** The fact the points are tightly clustered together means the two variables are highly correlated.

Graphs Used in Economic Models

6. **a** In this case, an increase (or decrease) in x is associated with an increase (or decrease) in y, so the variables are positively related.

7. **c** Figure A1.7 shows that when income is $40,000 a year, then consumption is $30,000 a year.

8. **a** The relationship is positive (higher income is related to higher consumption) and is linear.

9. **c** The term "positive relationship" means the same as "direct relationship."

10. **c** As x increases, y decreases; thus the relationship between x and y is negative.

11. **c** Figure A1.15 demonstrates that the change in y from 2 to 3 has no effect on x — it remains equal to 3.

The Slope of a Relationship

12. **a** A negative relationship has a negative slope; a positive relationship has a positive slope.

13. **b** A straight line — that is, a linear relationship — has a constant slope whereas nonlinear relationships have slopes that vary. Thus the slope of a straight line is the same anywhere on the line.

FIGURE **A1.15**
Multiple Choice Question 11

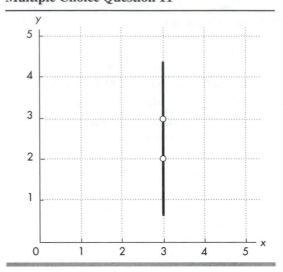

14. **a** The slope is positive and, because the line is becoming steeper, the slope is increasing.

15. **c** The slope between the two points equals the change in the vertical distance (the "rise") divided by the change in the horizontal distance (the "run"), that is, $(5 − 1)/(4 − 2) = 2$.

16. **a** The slope equals the change in the variable measured along the vertical axis divided by the change in the variable measured along the horizontal axis, or $(2 − 1)/(3 − 2) = 1$.

17. **c** The figure shows a straight line. The slope of a straight line is constant, so the slope between $x = 4$ and $x = 5$ is the same as the slope between $x = 2$ and $x = 3$.

Graphing Relationships Among More Than Two Variables

18. **c** The curves showing the relationship between x and y demonstrate that x and y are negatively related. For any value of y, an increase in z is associated with a higher value for x, so x and z are positively related.

19. **b** Moving along one of the lines showing the relationship between x and y (say, the line with $z = 3$) shows that as x increases, y decreases.

20. **c** The higher value of z shifts the entire relationship between x and y rightward.

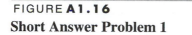

■ Answers to Short Answer Problems

FIGURE **A1.16**

FIGURE **A1.16**
Short Answer Problem 1

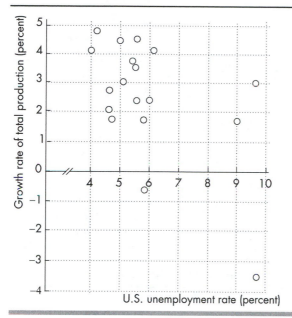

1. a. Figure A1.16 shows scatter diagram between the unemployment rate and the growth rate of total production.
    b. Though weak, the relationship is negative,.

FIGURE **A1.17**
Short Answer Problem 2

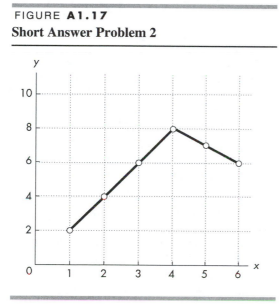

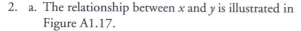

2. a. The relationship between *x* and *y* is illustrated in Figure A1.17.

b. The relationship between *x* and *y* changes when *x* is 4. The relationship is positive between *x* = 1 and *x* = 4. Between *x* = 4 and *x* = 6, the relationship is negative.

c. The slope equals Δ*y*/Δ*x* or, in this case between *x* = 1 and *x* = 2, the slope is (2 − 4)/(1 − 2) = 2.

d. Between *x* = 5 and *x* = 6, the slope is equal to (7 − 6)/(5 − 6) = −1.

e. Over the range of values where the relationship between *x* and *y* is positive — from *x* = 1 to *x* = 4 — the slope is positive. Over the range where the relationship between *x* and *y* is negative — from *x* = 4 to *x* = 6 — the slope is negative. Thus positive relationships have positive slopes, and negative relationships have negative slopes.

3. a. The slope is (8 − 2)/(5 − 2) = 2.
    b. The slope is (6 − 4)/(4 − 2) = 1.
    c. The slope is (9 − 6)/(5 − 4) = 3.

FIGURE **A1.18**
Short Answer Problem 4

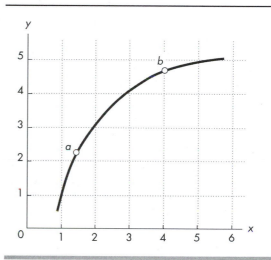

4. Yes, a curve can have a positive, decreasing slope. Figure A1.18, above, illustrates such a relationship. In it, at relatively low values of *x* the slope is quite steep, indicating a high value for the slope. But as *x* increases, the curve becomes flatter, which means that the slope decreases. (To verify these statements, draw the tangent lines at points *a* and *b* and then compare their slopes.) This figure points out that there is a major difference between the value of a curve at some point, that is, what *y* equals, and what the curve's slope is at that point!

5. a. Because Bobby buys more DVDs when their price is lower, the relationship between the number of DVDs Bobby buys and the price is negative. Similarly, the relationship between Bobby's income and the number of DVDs he buys is positive.

    b. Figure A1.19 illustrates the relationship between the price of a DVD and the number Bobby buys when his income is low.

    c. Also illustrated in Figure A1.19 is the relationship between the number of DVDs Bobby buys and their price when Bobby's income is high.

    d. An increase in Bobby's income shifts the relationship between the price of a DVD and the number Bobby buys rightward.

■ You're the Teacher

1. "This *is* an economics class. But understanding some simple graphing ideas makes economics a lot easier to learn. Learning about graphing for its own sake is not important in this class; what is important is learning about graphing to help with the economics that we'll take up in the next chapter. So look at this chapter as a resource. Whether you already knew everything in it before you looked at it or even if everything in it was brand new, anytime you get confused by something dealing with a technical point on a graph, you can look back at this chapter for help. So, chill out; we'll get to the economics in the next chapter!"

2. "Graphs make understanding economics and the relationships between economic variables easier in three ways. First, graphs are extremely useful in showing the relationship between two economic variables. Imagine trying to determine the relationship between the interest rate and inflation rate if all we had was a bunch of numbers showing the interest rate and inflation rate each year for the past 30 years. We'd have 60 numbers; good luck in trying to eyeball a relationship from them! Second, graphs can help us more easily understand what an economic theory is trying to explain because they allow us to see quickly how two variables are related. By showing us the general relationship, we can be assured that any conclusions we reach don't depend on the numbers that we decided to use. Finally, graphs sometimes show us a result we might not have otherwise noticed. If all we had were numbers,

FIGURE **A1.19**

Short Answer Problem 5

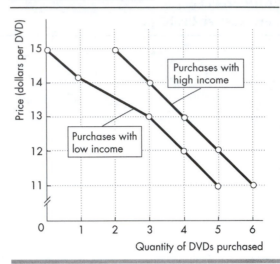

FIGURE **A1.20**

You're the Teacher Question 3

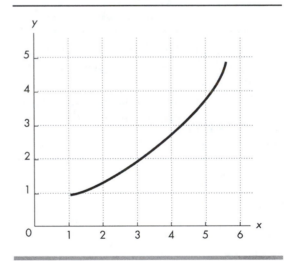

we could easily become lost trying to keep track of them. Graphs make our work easier, and for this reason we need to know how to use them!"

3. "The connection between the direction a line slopes, its slope, and whether the relationship is positive or negative is easy — once you see it! Take a look at Figure A1.20. In this figure, the line slopes upward to the right. The slope of this line is positive an increase in *x* is associated with an increase in *y*. Because increases in *x* are related to increases in *y*, the graph shows a positive relationship between *x* and *y*."

FIGURE **A1.21**
You're the Teacher Question 3

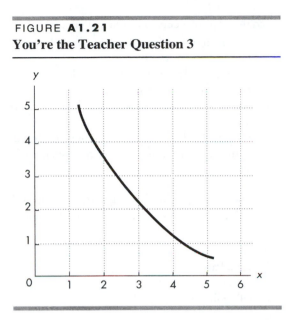

"Now look at Figure A1.21. Here the line slopes downward to the right. The slope of this line is negative: An increase in *x* is related to a decrease in *y*. Because *x* and *y* are inversely related, the relationship shown in Figure A1.21 is negative."

"So, look: Positive relationships have positive slopes and negative relationships have negative slopes!"

"We can summarize these results for you so that you'll always be able to remember them by putting them all together:

Direction of line		Sign of slope		Type of relationship
Upward to the right	⇔	Positive	⇔	Positive
Downward to the right	⇔	Negative	⇔	Negative

This summary should help you keep everything straight. Things should be easier now."

Appendix Quiz

1. The vertical scale line of a graph is called the
   a. origin.
   b. scalar.
   c. *y*-axis.
   d. *x*-axis.

2. When the variable measured on the *y*-axis rises by 8, the variable measured on the *x*-axis increases by 2. The slope of this relationship is
   a. 0.25.
   b. 8.0.
   c. 4.0.
   d. 2.0.

3. The number of pizzas purchased in a month depends on the price of a pizza and on consumer's income. If the relationship between the price and the number purchased is plotted on a graph and consumers' income then changes,
   a. the plotted relationship shifts.
   b. there is no change in the plotted relationship.
   c. there is a movement along the plotted relationship.
   d. None of the above.

4. A scatter diagram between two variables has a negative slope. So an increase in the variable measured on the vertical axis is associated with _____ the variable measured on the horizontal axis.
   a. an increase in
   b. no change in
   c. a decrease in
   d. no *consistent* change in

5. If a relationship has a positive slope, then
   a. an increase in one variable causes an increase in the other.
   b. it must be a vertical line.
   c. it slopes upward moving to the right.
   d. it becomes steeper moving to the right.

6. To the slope of a curved line across an arc
   a. is equal to the average of the slope of the curve line at both ends of the arc.
   b. cannot be calculated because the slope of a curved line is not defined.
   c. is equal to the slope of a straight line across the arc.
   d. is defined as being equal to the slope of the curve at the midway point between the two ends of the arc.

7. As a point on a graph moves upward and leftward, the value of its *x*-coordinate _____ and the value of its *y*-coordinate _____.
   a. rises; rises
   b. rises; falls
   c. falls; rises
   d. falls; falls

8. The slope of a line equals the
   a. change in *y* plus the change in *x*.
   b. change in *y* minus the change in *x*.
   c. change in *y* times the change in *x*.
   d. change in *y* divided by the change in *x*.

9. As a curve approaches a minimum, its slope will
   a. be positive before the minimum and negative after the minimum.
   b. be negative before the minimum and positive after the minimum.
   c. remain constant on either side of the minimum.
   d. change, but in no consistent way from one curve to the next.

10. If the change in *y* equals 10 and the change in *x* equals −5,
    a. the slope of the curve is positive.
    b. the slope of the curve is negative.
    c. the curve must be a straight line.
    d. the slope cannot be calculated without more information.

The answers for this Appendix Quiz are on page 345

Chapter 2 THE ECONOMIC PROBLEM

■ Production Possibilities and Opportunity Cost

The quantities of goods and services that can be produced are limited by the available amount of resources and by technology. The **production possibilities frontier** (*PPF*) is the boundary between those combinations of goods and services that can be produced and those that cannot.

FIGURE **2.1**
A *PPF* with Increasing Opportunity Costs

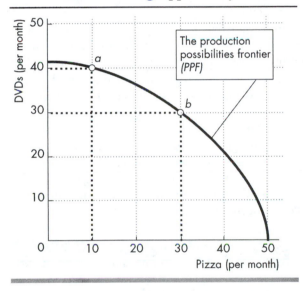

A *PPF* is illustrated in Figure 2.1. All production possibilities frontiers have two important characteristics in common:

♦ Production points inside and on the *PPF* are attainable. Points beyond the *PPF* are unattainable.

♦ Production points on the *PPF* achieve **production efficiency** because there the goods and services are produced at the lowest possible cost. Production points inside the *PPF* are *inefficient*, with misallocated or unused resources.

Moving between points *on* the *PPF* involves a *tradeoff* because something must be given up to get more of something else. The **opportunity cost** of an action is the highest-valued alternative foregone. In Figure 2.1, the opportunity cost of obtaining 20 more pizzas by moving from point *a* to point *b* is the 10 DVDs that are foregone. Opportunity cost is a ratio. It equals the decrease in the production of one good divided by the increase in the production of the other. For the movement from *a* to *b* the opportunity cost is 10 DVDs divided by 20 pizzas or 1/2 of a DVD per pizza.

When resources are not equally productive in producing different goods and services, the *PPF* has increasing opportunity costs and bows outward, as illustrated in Figure 2.1. As more pizza is produced, the opportunity cost of a pizza increases.

■ Using Resources Efficiently

Allocative efficiency is reached when goods and services are produced at the lowest possible cost and in the quantities that provide the greatest possible benefit.

♦ The **marginal cost** of a good is the opportunity cost of producing *one* more unit of it. Because of increasing opportunity cost, when moving along the production possibilities frontier the marginal cost of an additional unit of a good increases as more is produced. So the marginal cost curve, illustrated in Figure 2.2 on the next page, slopes upward.

♦ **Preferences** are a person's likes and dislikes and the intensity of these feelings. Preferences can be described using the concept of marginal benefit. The **marginal benefit** from a good or service is the benefit received from consuming one more unit of it. The marginal benefit of a good is measured by the most that people are *willing* to pay for another unit of it. The marginal benefit from additional units of a good decreases as more is consumed. The **marginal benefit curve**, which shows the relationship

FIGURE **2.2**

Efficient Use of Resources: *MB* and *MC*

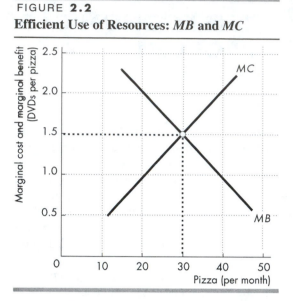

between the marginal benefit of a good and the quantity consumed, slopes downward as shown in Figure 2.2.

Allocative efficiency occurs when the marginal benefit from another unit of a good equals its marginal cost. In Figure 2.2, producing 30 pizzas is the efficient allocation of resources between pizzas and DVDs. *All* points on the *PPF* are production efficient; only the *one* point on the *PPF* where *MB* = *MC* is allocative efficient.

■ Economic Growth

Economic growth occurs when production possibilities expand. **Technological change,** the development of new goods and better ways of producing goods and services, and **capital accumulation,** the growth in capital resources including human capital, are two key factors that affect economic growth.

- ◆ Economic growth shifts the *PPF* outward. The faster it shifts, the more rapid is economic growth.
- ◆ The opportunity cost of economic growth is the lost production of goods and services that can be consumed today.
- ◆ Nations that devote more resources to capital accumulation grow more rapidly.

■ Gains from Trade

A person has a **comparative advantage** in an activity if he or she can perform the activity at a lower opportunity cost than anyone else.

- ◆ Comparative advantage differs from absolute advantage. **Absolute advantage** occurs when a person is more productive (can produce more goods in a given amount of time) than another person.

Specialization according to comparative advantage and trading for other goods creates *gains from trade* because such specialization and exchange allows consumption along the trade line at points outside the *PPF*. Production still occurs on the *PPF* but consumption can be at a point beyond the *PPF*.

■ Economic Coordination

Firms and markets have evolved to help achieve decentralized economic coordination between the billions of individuals.

- ◆ A **firm** is an economic unit that hires factors of production and organizes those factors to produce and sell goods and services.
- ◆ A **market** is any arrangement that allows buyers and sellers to get information and to do business with each other.

Markets work only when property rights exist. **Property rights** are social arrangements that govern the ownership, use, and disposal of anything people value.

Money, any commodity or token that is generally acceptable as a means of payment, is used in markets.

Goods markets are where goods and services are bought and sold; factor markets are where factors of production are bought and sold. Resources flow from household to firms through factor markets; goods and services flow from firms to household through goods markets. Markets coordinate decisions in the circular flow through price adjustments.

Helpful Hints

1. **ASSUMPTIONS OF THE *PPF*:** The *PPF* provides an example of the role played by simplifying assumptions in economic analysis. No society in the world produces only two items but by assuming that there are such "two-good" nations, we gain invaluable insights into the real world. For instance, we see that once a nation is producing on its production possibilities frontier, no matter how many goods it produces, to increase the production of one good necessarily has an opportunity cost—some other good or goods that must be foregone.

In addition, we also see that countries that devote a larger proportion of their resources to capital accumulation will have more rapid growth.

2. **INEFFICIENT PRODUCTION POINTS :** Points within the *PPF* are attainable but are inefficient. Production occurs here whenever some inefficiency or misallocation emerges within the economy, such as excessive unemployment of any resource or an inefficient use of resources. Points beyond the *PPF* are unattainable. They are *not* classified as either efficient or inefficient because they are not production combinations the society can reach.

FIGURE **2.3**

A *PPF* Between Corn and Cloth

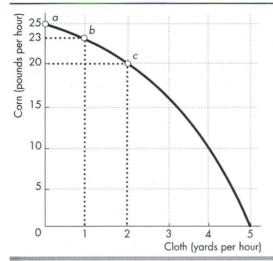

3. **CALCULATING OPPORTUNITY COST :** A helpful formula for opportunity cost results from the fact that opportunity cost is a ratio. Opportunity cost equals the quantity of goods you must give up divided by the quantity of goods you will get.

Consider the *PPF* is in Figure 2.3. If we move along the *PPF* from *a* to *b*, what is the opportunity cost of an additional yard of cloth? The nation must give up 2 pounds of corn (25 – 23) to get 1 yard of cloth (1 – 0). So the opportunity cost of the first yard of cloth is 2 pounds of corn divided by 1 yard of cloth or 2 pounds of corn per yard of cloth. Next, if we move from *b* to *c*, the opportunity cost of the second yard of cloth is calculated the same way and is 3 pounds of corn per yard of cloth.

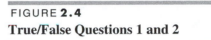

Questions

■ **True/False and Explain**

Production Possibilities and Opportunity Cost

FIGURE **2.4**

True/False Questions 1 and 2

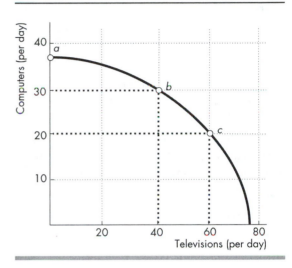

1. In Figure 2.4 production point *a* is <u>NOT</u> attainable.

2. In Figure 2.4 the opportunity cost of moving from point *b* to point *c* is 1/2 computer per television.

3. From a point on the *PPF*, rearranging production and producing more of *all* goods is possible.

4. From a point within the *PPF*, rearranging production and producing more of *all* goods is possible.

5. Production efficiency requires producing at a point on the *PPF*.

6. Along a bowed-out *PPF*, as more of a good is produced, the opportunity cost of producing the good diminishes.

Using Resources Efficiently

7. The marginal cost of the 20th ton of cement equals the cost of producing all 20 tons of cement.

8. As people consume more of a good, its marginal benefit decreases.

9. Allocative efficiency is achieved by producing the amount of a good such that the marginal benefit of

the last unit produced exceeds its marginal cost by as much as possible.

Economic Growth

10. Economic growth is illustrated by outward shifts in the *PPF*.

11. Increasing a nation's economic growth rate has an opportunity cost.

Gains from Trade

12. Daphne definitely has a comparative advantage in producing sweaters if she can produce more than can Lisa.

13. If two individuals have different opportunity costs of producing goods, both can gain from specialization and trade.

14. If the United States has an absolute advantage in growing corn and making computers, it must have a comparative advantage in growing corn.

15. Learning-by-doing can lead to dynamic comparative advantage.

Economic Coordination

16. Buyers and sellers must meet face-to-face in a market.

17. Price adjustments coordinate decisions in goods markets, but not in factor markets.

■ Multiple Choice

Production Possibilities and Opportunity Cost

1. Production points on the *PPF* itself are
   a. efficient but not attainable.
   b. efficient and attainable
   c. inefficient but not attainable.
   d. inefficient and attainable.

2. If the United States can increase its production of automobiles without decreasing its production of any other good, the United States must have been producing at a point
   a. within its *PPF*.
   b. on its *PPF*.
   c. beyond its *PPF*.
   d. None of the above are correct because increasing the production of one good without decreasing the production of another good is impossible.

FIGURE **2.5**
Multiple Choice Questions 3 and 4

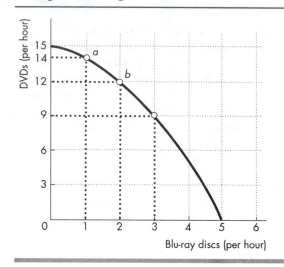

3. In Figure 2.5, at point *a* what is the opportunity cost of producing one more Blu-ray disc?
   a. 14 DVDs
   b. 3 DVDs
   c. 2 DVDs
   d. There is no opportunity cost.

4. In Figure 2.5, at point *b* what is the opportunity cost of producing one more Blu-ray disc?
   a. 12 DVDs
   b. 3 DVDs
   c. 2 DVDs
   d. There is no opportunity cost.

5. When producing at a production efficiency, than
   a. scarcity is no longer a problem.
   b. producing more of one good requires producing less of some other good.
   c. the most highly valued goods and services are being produced.
   d. producing another unit of the good has no opportunity cost.

6. The existence of the tradeoff along the *PPF* means that the *PPF* is
   a. bowed outward.
   b. linear.
   c. negatively sloped.
   d. positively sloped.

7. The bowed-outward shape of a *PPF*
   a. is due to capital accumulation.
   b. reflects the unequal application of technology in production.
   c. illustrates the fact that no opportunity cost is incurred for increasing the production of the good measured on the horizontal axis but it is incurred to increase production of the good measured along the vertical axis.
   d. is due to the existence of increasing opportunity cost.

A nation produces only two goods — yak butter and rutabagas. Three alternative combinations of production that are on its *PPF* are given in Table 2.1. Use this information to answer the next three questions.

TABLE **2.1**

Production Possibilities

Possibility	Pounds of yak butter	Number of rutabagas
a	600	0
b	400	100
c	0	200

8. In moving from combination *a* to *b*, the opportunity cost of producing more rutabagas is
   a. 6 pounds of yak butter per rutabaga.
   b. 4 pounds of yak butter per rutabaga.
   c. 2 pounds of yak butter per rutabaga.
   d. 0 pounds of yak butter per rutabaga.

9. In moving from combination *b* to *a*, the opportunity cost of producing more pounds of yak butter is
   a. 0.10 rutabaga per pound of yak butter.
   b. 0.50 rutabaga per pound of yak butter.
   c. 1.00 rutabaga per pound of yak butter.
   d. 2.00 rutabagas per pound of yak butter.

10. Producing 400 pounds of yak butter and 50 rutabagas is
    a. not possible for this nation.
    b. possible and is an efficient production point.
    c. possible, but is an inefficient production point.
    d. an abhorrent thought.

Using Resources Efficiently

11. Moving along a bowed-out *PPF* between milk and cotton, as more milk is produced the marginal cost of an additional gallon of milk
    a. rises.
    b. does not change.
    c. falls.
    d. probably changes, but in an ambiguous direction.

12. The most anyone is willing to pay for another purse is $30. Currently the price of a purse is $40, and the cost of producing another purse is $50. The marginal benefit of a purse is
    a. $50.
    b. $40.
    c. $30.
    d. An amount not given in the answers above.

13. If the marginal benefit from another computer exceeds the marginal cost of the computer, then to use resources efficiently,
    a. more resources should be used to produce computers.
    b. fewer resources should be used to produce computers.
    c. if the marginal benefit exceeds the marginal cost by as much as possible, the efficient amount of resources are being used to produce computers.
    d. none of the above is correct because marginal benefit and marginal cost have nothing to do with using resources efficiently.

Economic Growth

14. Economic growth
    a. creates unemployment.
    b. has no opportunity cost.
    c. shifts the *PPF* outward.
    d. makes it more difficult for a nation to produce on its *PPF*.

15. The *PPF* shifts if
    a. the unemployment rate falls.
    b. people decide they want more of one good and less of another.
    c. the prices of the goods and services produced rise.
    d. the resources available to the nation change.

16. An increase in the nation's capital stock will
    a. shift the *PPF* outward.
    b. lead to a movement along the *PPF* upward and leftward.
    c. lead to a movement along the *PPF* downward and rightward.
    d. move the nation from producing within the *PPF* to producing at a point closer to the *PPF*.

17. An opportunity costs of economic growth is
    a. capital accumulation.
    b. technological change.
    c. reduced current consumption.
    d. the gain in future consumption.

18. In general, the more resources that are devoted to technological research, the
    a. greater is current consumption.
    b. higher is the unemployment rate.
    c. faster the *PPF* shifts outward.
    d. more the *PPF* will bow outward.

Gains from Trade

19. In order to achieve the maximum gains from trade, people should specialize according to
    a. property rights.
    b. *PPF*.
    c. absolute advantage.
    d. comparative advantage.

In one day Brandon can either plow 40 acres of land or plant 20 acres. In one day Christopher can either plow 28 acres of land or plant 7 acres. Use this information to answer the next four questions.

20. Which of the following statements about absolute advantage is correct?
    a. Brandon has an absolute advantage in both plowing and planting.
    b. Brandon has an absolute advantage only in plowing.
    c. Brandon has an absolute advantage only in planting.
    d. Christopher has an absolute advantage both in plowing and planting.

21. Brandon has
    a. a comparative advantage both in plowing and planting.
    b. a comparative advantage only in plowing.
    c. a comparative advantage only in planting.
    d. a comparative advantage in neither in plowing and planting.

22. Christopher has
    a. an absolute advantage only in planting.
    b. an absolute advantage only in plowing.
    c. a comparative advantage only in planting.
    d. a comparative advantage only in plowing.

23. Brandon and Christopher can
    a. both gain from exchange if Brandon specializes in planting and Christopher in plowing.
    b. both gain from exchange if Brandon specializes in plowing and Christopher in planting.
    c. exchange, but only Brandon will gain from the exchange.
    d. exchange, but only Christopher will gain from the exchange.

24. A nation can *produce* at a point outside its *PPF*
    a. when it trades with other nations.
    b. when it is producing products as efficiently as possible.
    c. when there is no unemployment.
    d. at no time ever.

25. A nation can *consume* at a point outside its *PPF*
    a. when it trades with other nations.
    b. when it is producing products as efficiently as possible.
    c. when there is no unemployment.
    d. at no time ever.

Economic Coordination

26. Which of the following does <u>NOT</u> help achieve economic coordination?
    a. Firms
    b. Markets
    c. The production possibilities frontier
    d. None of the above because all these answers given help organize trade.

27. In markets, people's decisions are coordinated by
    a. specialization according to absolute advantage.
    b. changes in property rights.
    c. learning-by-doing.
    d. adjustments in prices.

■ Short Answer Problems

1. What does the negative slope of the *PPF* mean? Why is a *PPF* bowed out?

2. In Figure 2.6 indicate which points are production efficient and which are inefficient. Also show which points are attainable and which are not attainable.

FIGURE **2.6**
Short Answer Problem 2

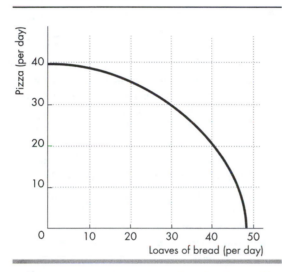

3. Sydna is stranded on a desert island and can either fish or harvest dates. Six points on her production possibilities frontier are given in Table 2.2.
   a. In Figure 2.7 plot these possibilities, label the points, and draw the *PPF*.
   b. If Sydna moves from possibility *c* to possibility *d*, what is the opportunity cost per fish?
   c. If Sydna moves from possibility *d* to possibility *e*, what is the opportunity cost per fish?
   d. In general, what happens to the opportunity cost of a fish as more fish are caught?
   e. In general, what happens to the opportunity cost of dates as more dates are harvested?
   f. Based on the original *PPF* you plotted, is a combination of 40 dates and 1 fish attainable? Is this combination an efficient one? Explain.

TABLE **2.2**
Sydna's Production Possibilities

Possibility	Dates gathered (per day)	Fish caught (per day)
a	54	0
b	50	1
c	42	2
d	32	3
e	20	4
f	0	5

FIGURE **2.7**
Short Answer Problem 3

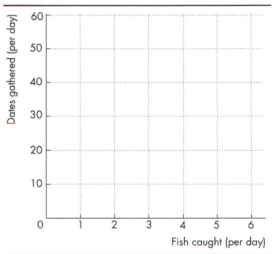

4. If the following events occurred (each is a separate event, unaccompanied by any other event), what would happen to the *PPF* in Problem 3?
   a. A new fishing pond is discovered.
   b. The output of dates is increased.
   c. Sydna finds a ladder that enables her to gather slightly more dates.
   d. A second person, with the same set of fishing and date-gathering skills as Sydna, is stranded on the island.

TABLE **2.3**

Marginal Benefit and Marginal Cost of Pizza

Slice of pizza	Marginal benefit of slice	Marginal cost of slice	Marginal benefit minus marginal cost
I	6.0	I.5	____
2	5.0	2.0	____
3	4.0	2.5	____
4	3.0	3.0	____
5	2.0	3.5	____
6	1.0	4.0	____

5. A nation produces only pizza and tacos. Table 2.3 shows the marginal benefit and marginal cost schedules for slices of pizza in terms of tacos per slice of pizza.

   a. Complete Table 2.3.

   b. For the first slice of pizza, after paying the marginal cost, how much marginal benefit — if any — is left?

   c. For the second slice, after paying the marginal cost, how much marginal benefit — if any — is left? How does your answer to this question compare to your answer to part (b)?

   d. Should the first slice of pizza be produced? Should the second one be produced? Explain you answers, especially your answer about the second slice.

   e. In a diagram, draw the marginal cost curve and the marginal benefit curve. Indicate the quantity of pizza slices that uses resources efficiently.

6. Bearing in mind the point that resources are limited, explain why is it important for a nation to use its resources efficiently.

7. Suppose that both the United States and France produce computers and wine. Table 2.4 shows what each country can produce in an hour.

   a. On graph paper, draw the *PPF* for the United States for one hour.

   b. On graph paper, draw the *PPF* for France for one hour.

   c. Complete Table 2.5.

   d. In what good(s) does the United States have a comparative advantage? France?

   e. Initially the United States uses half its resources to produce wine and half to produce computers.

TABLE **2.4**

Production in France and the United States

	Computers produced in an hour	Bottles of wine produced in an hour
United States	10,000	20,000
France	12,000	8,000

TABLE **2.5**

Short Answer Problem 7 (c)

	Opportunity cost of one computer	Opportunity cost of one bottle of wine
United States	____	____
France	____	____

How much wine and how many computers are produced in an hour in the United States? France also devotes half her resources to computers and half to wine. How many computers and bottles of wine does France produce in an hour? What is the total amount of wine produced by France and the United States in an hour? The total number of computers?

   f. Suppose that the United States specializes in wine and France in computers. What is the total amount of wine produced by France and the United States now? The total number of computers?

   g. What do your answers to parts (e) and (f) show?

8. How do property rights affect people's incentives to create new music?

■ **You're the Teacher**

1. "The idea of the production possibilities frontier is stupid. I mean, after all, who ever heard of a nation that produces only two goods. Come on, every nation produces millions, probably billions of goods. Why do I have to bother to learn about the production possibilities frontier when it is so unrealistic?" One reason for this student to learn about the production possibilities frontier is that it will probably be on the exams. But there are other reasons, too. Explain some of them to help motivate this student.

Answers

■ True/False Answers

Production Possibilities and Opportunity Cost

1. **F** *Any* point on the production possibilities frontier is attainable, even points where the *PPF* intersects the axes.

2. **T** The opportunity cost equals the number of computers foregone, 10, divided by the number of televisions gained, 20.

3. **F** Points on the frontier are production efficient, so increasing the production of one good necessarily requires producing fewer of some other good.

FIGURE **2.8**
True/False Question 4

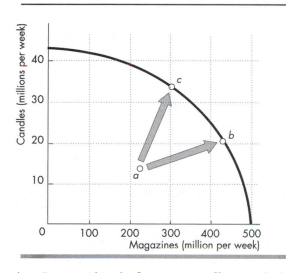

4. **T** Points within the frontier are inefficient, which means its possible to rearrange production and boost the production of all goods and services. This condition is illustrated in Figure 2.8, where from (the inefficient) point *a*, it is possible to move to points such as *b* or *c* where more of both books and magazines are produced.

5. **T** Production efficiency implies that the production of one good can be increased *only if* the production of another good is decreased, which is true only on the *PPF* itself.

6. **F** As more of a good is produced, the opportunity cost of additional units increases.

Using Resources Efficiently

7. **F** The marginal cost is the cost of the 20th ton itself, not the cost of producing all 20 tons.

8. **T** As people have more of a product, they are willing to pay less for additional units, which means that the marginal benefit of the product will decrease.

9. **F** For resources to be allocated efficiently, it is necessary for the marginal benefit of the last unit produced to equal the marginal cost of the unit.

Economic Growth

10. **T** As the *PPF* shifts outward, the nation is able to produce more of all goods.

11. **T** The opportunity cost is the loss of current consumption.

Gains from Trade

12. **F** Based on the information in the problem, Daphne definitely has an absolute advantage, but without more information we cannot tell whether she has a comparative advantage.

13. **T** A key observation is that *both* individuals gain.

14. **F** Comparative advantage requires *comparing* the opportunity cost of producing corn in the United States with the opportunity cost of producing it elsewhere.

15. **T** Learning-by-doing means that the cost of producing a good falls as more is produced, so the nation (or person) ultimately acquires a comparative advantage in making the good.

Economic Coordination

16. **F** Buyers and sellers communicate with each other in markets, but in most markets they do not meet face-to-face.

17. **F** Price adjustments coordinate decisions in markets.

■ Multiple Choice Answers

Production Possibilities and Opportunity Cost

1. **b** *Only* points on the frontier are both attainable and efficient.

2. **a** Only from points within the frontier can the production of a good increase without decreasing the production of another good.

3. **c** By producing 1 more Blu-ray disc, DVD production falls by 2 (from 14 to 12), so the opportunity cost of the Blu-ray disc is the ratio of 2 DVDs to the 1 Blu-ray, that is, 2 DVDs per Blu-ray disc.

4. **b** As more Blu-ray discs are produced, the opportunity cost of an additional Blu-ray disc gets larger.

5. **b** All production points *on* the *PPF* are production efficient.

6. **c** When production is on the *PPF*, the tradeoff is that if more of one good is produced, then some other good must be foregone. This result means that the *PPF* has a negative slope.

7. **d** Increasing opportunity cost means that, as more of a good is produced, its opportunity cost increases. As a result, the *PPF* bows outward.

8. **c** Moving from *a* to *b* gains 100 rutabagas and loses 200 pounds of yak butter, so the opportunity cost is (200 pounds of yak butter)/(100 rutabagas), or 2 pounds of yak butter per rutabaga.

9. **b** 100 rutabagas are foregone, so the opportunity cost is (100 rutabagas)/(200 pounds of yak butter), or 0.50 rutabagas per pound of yak butter. Note how the opportunity cost of a rutabaga is the inverse of the opportunity cost of a pound of yak butter, as calculated in the answer to the previous question.

10. **c** When 400 pounds of yak butter are produced, a maximum of 100 rutabagas can be produced; if only 50 rutabagas are produced, the combination is inefficient.

Using Resources Efficiently

11. **a** Along a bowed-out *PPF*, as more of a good is produced, its marginal cost — the opportunity cost of producing another unit — rises.

12. **c** The marginal benefit from a good is the maximum that a person is willing to pay for the good.

13. **a** The benefit from the computer exceeds the cost of producing the computer, so society will gain if resources are allocated so that the computer is produced.

Economic Growth

14. **c** Economic growth makes attainable previously unattainable production levels.

15. **d** An increase in resources shifts the *PPF* outward; a decrease shifts it leftward. (A decrease in the unemployment rate moves the nation from a point in the interior of the *PPF* to a point closer to the frontier.)

16. **a** Increases in a nation's resources create economic growth and shift the nation's *PPF* outward.

17. **c** If a nation devotes more resources to capital accumulation or technological development, which are the main sources of growth, fewer resources can be used to produce goods for current consumption.

18. **c** The more resources used for technological research, the more rapid is economic growth.

Gains from Trade

19. **d** Specializing according to comparative advantage reduces the opportunity cost of producing goods and services.

20. **a** Brandon can produce more of both goods than Christopher, so Brandon has an absolute advantage in both goods.

21. **c** Brandon's opportunity cost of planting an acre of land is plowing 2 acres, whereas Christopher's opportunity cost of planting an acre is plowing 4 acres.

22. **d** Christopher's opportunity cost of plowing an acre is planting 1/4 an acre, while Brandon's opportunity cost is planting 1/2 an acre.

23. **a** By specializing according to their comparative advantages, both can gain from exchange.

24. **d** The *PPF* shows the maximum amounts that can be produced.

25. **a** When a nation specializes according to its comparative advantage and trades with another specialist nation, both can consume at levels beyond their *PPFs*.

Economic Coordination

26. **c** The production possibilities frontier shows the limits to production and does not help achieve economic coordination.

27. **d** Changes in prices create incentives for people to change their actions.

■ Answers to Short Answer Problems

1. The negative slope of the *PPF* indicates that increasing the production of one good means that the production of some other good decreases.

   A *PPF* is bowed out because the existence of non-identical resources creates an increasing opportunity cost as the production of a good is increased. Because resources are not identical, some are better suited for producing one good than another. So when resources are switched from producing items for which they are well suited to producing goods for which they are ill suited, the opportunity cost of increasing the output of these goods rises.

FIGURE 2.9
Short Answer Problem 2

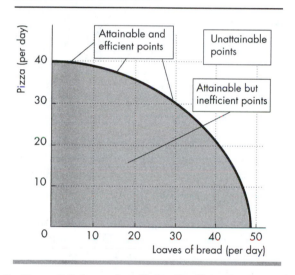

2. Figure 2.9 shows the efficient/inefficient points and attainable/not attainable points. The attainable but inefficient points are shaded; the attainable and efficient points lie on the *PPF* itself; and the unattainable points are located beyond the *PPF*.

3. a. Figure 2.10 shows the *PPF*.

    b. Moving from *c* to *d* increases the number of fish caught by 1 and decreases the number of dates gathered from 42 to 32. Catching 1 fish costs 10 dates, so the opportunity cost of the fish is 10 dates. The opportunity cost of this fish is:

    $$\frac{42 \text{ dates} - 32 \text{ dates}}{3 \text{ fish} - 2 \text{ fish}} = 10 \text{ dates per fish.}$$

    c. Moving from *d* to *e* indicates that the opportunity cost of the fish is 12 dates: The number of

FIGURE 2.10
Short Answer Problem 3

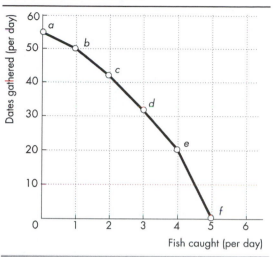

dates gathered falls from 32 to 20 while the number of fish caught increases by 1.

d. As more fish are caught, the opportunity cost of an additional fish rises. In particular, the first fish has an opportunity cost of only 4 dates; the second, 8 dates; the third, 10 dates; the fourth, 12 dates; and the fifth, 20 dates.

e. As more dates are gathered, the opportunity cost of a date rises. Moving from *f* to *e* shows that the first 20 dates cost only 1 fish so that the opportunity cost of a date here is 1/20 of a fish. Going from *e* to *d*, however, makes the opportunity cost of a date 1/12 of a fish. This pattern continues so that as more dates are gathered, their opportunity cost increases. Finally, moving from *b* to *a* has the largest opportunity cost for a date, 1/4 of a fish.

As parts (d) and (e) demonstrate, there is increasing opportunity cost moving along the *PPF*. That is, as more fish are caught, their opportunity cost — in terms of foregone dates — increases and as more dates are gathered, their opportunity cost — in terms of foregone fish — also increases. It is these increasing opportunity costs that account for the bowed-outward shape of the *PPF*.

f. This combination is within the *PPF* and is attainable. It is inefficient because Sydna could produce more of either or both goods. Sydna is not organizing her activities efficiently.

FIGURE **2.11**
Short Answer Problem 4 (a)

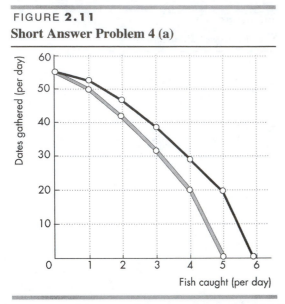

4. a. A new fishing pond increases the number of fish Sydna can catch, but it does not affect the maximum number of dates she can gather. Her *PPF* shifts generally as shown in Figure 2.11.

   b. Increasing her output of dates does not affect the *PPF*. Sydna might increase her gathering of dates either by moving from a point within the *PPF* to a point on (or closer to) the frontier or by moving along the frontier. Neither of these actions shifts the *PPF*.

FIGURE **2.12**
Short Answer Problem 4 (c)

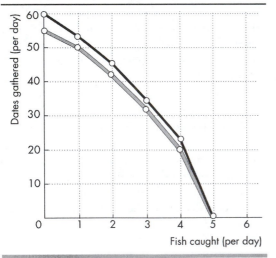
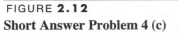

   c. The ladder increases the number of dates that Sydna can gather, but has no effect on the fish

that she can catch. As a result, the maximum number of dates increases, but the maximum number of fish does not change. The *PPF* shifts in the same general pattern as shown in Figure 2.12.

FIGURE **2.13**
Short Answer Problem 4 (d)

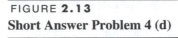
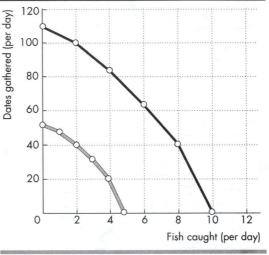

   d. Having a second worker on the island boosts both the number of dates that can be gathered *and* the number of fish that can be caught. If the second person has the same set of skills as Sydna, the *PPF* shifts out in a "parallel" manner, as illustrated in Figure 2.13. Be sure to note that the scales on the axes in Figure 2.13 are different from those on the axes in Figures 2.10–2.12.

TABLE **2.6**
Marginal Benefit and Marginal Cost of Pizza

Slice of pizza	Marginal benefit of slice	Marginal cost of slice	Marginal benefit minus marginal cost
1	6.0	1.5	4.5
2	5.0	2.0	3.0
3	4.0	2.5	1.5
4	3.0	3.0	0.0
5	2.0	3.5	−1.5
6	1.0	4.0	−3.0

5. a. Table 2.6 shows the answers.
   b. For the first slice of pizza, after paying the marginal cost, there is 4.5 of marginal benefit left.

c. For the second slice of pizza, after paying the marginal cost, there is 3.0 of marginal benefit left over. There is less left over for the second slice than the first slice because the marginal benefit of the second slice is less than that of the first slice and the marginal cost the second slice is more than that of the first one.

d. The first slice should be produced because the marginal benefit from the first slice exceeds its marginal cost. The second slice also should be produced for the same reason. As long as the marginal benefit from a slice of pizza exceeds its marginal cost, society benefits if the slice is produced. The "net benefit" from the first slice is more than that of the second slice, but as long as there is a positive net benefit, society benefits.

FIGURE 2.14
Short Answer Problem 5 (e)

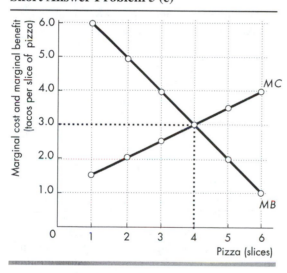

e. Figure 2.14 shows the marginal cost and marginal benefit curves. Four slices of pizza are the allocatively efficient quantity, that is, the quantity that uses resources efficiently, because the marginal benefit from the fourth slice equals its marginal cost. The marginal benefit for any greater quantity of pizza slices is less than the marginal cost of the slice, so producing these units would result in a net loss for society.

6. A nation should use its resources efficiently because it has only a limited quantity of them. If resources are used inefficiently, there is waste and fewer of people's wants can be satisfied. By using its resources efficiency and thereby producing at the

point of allocative efficiency, society ensures that as many of the most important wants, measured by the marginal benefit from the goods that satisfy those wants, are satisfied.

FIGURE 2.15
Short Answer Problem 7 (a)

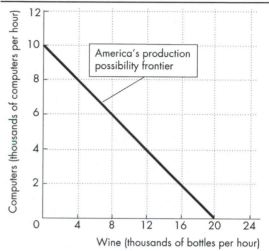

7. a. Figure 2.15 shows the *PPF* for the United States. The maximum amount of wine that can be produced is 20,000 bottles and the maximum number of computers that can be produced is 10,000.

FIGURE 2.16
Short Answer Problem 7 (b)

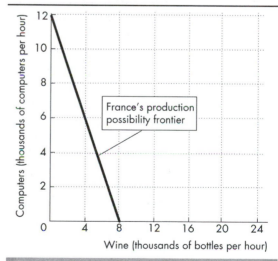

b. Figure 2.16 shows the French *PPF*.

TABLE 2.7
Short Answer Problem 7 (c)

	Opportunity cost of one computer	Opportunity cost of one bottle of wine
United States	2 bottles of wine	½ computer
France	2/3 bottles of wine	1½ computer

c. Table 2.7 shows the opportunity costs for the goods. To illustrate how this table was obtained, we can use the opportunity cost of a computer in the United States as an example. To produce one computer in the United States requires that resources work for 1/10,000 of an hour at manufacturing computers. So to produce an additional computer, resources must be switched from the wine industry to the computer industry for 1/10,000 of an hour. During this time, if left in the wine industry, the resources could otherwise have produced (1/10,000) × (20,000 bottles of wine) or 2 bottles of wine. Hence to produce one additional computer in the United States, 2 bottles of wine are foregone. Two bottles of wine, then, are the opportunity cost of the computer. The rest of the opportunity costs are calculated similarly.

d. The United States has a comparative advantage in wine because the opportunity cost of a bottle of wine in the United States — 1/2 computer — is less than the opportunity cost of a bottle of wine in France —1½ computer. France has a comparative advantage in the production of computers, because its opportunity cost —2/3 of a bottle of wine — is less than that in the United States — 2 bottles of wine.

e. In the United States, 5,000 computers and 10,000 bottles of wine are produced in an hour. In France, 6,000 computers and 4,000 bottles of wine are produced in an hour. Overall, 11,000 computers and 14,000 bottles of wine are produced in an hour.

f. With the United States specializing in wine, 20,000 bottles of wine are produced in an hour. Because France specializes in computers, 12,000 computers are produced in an hour.

g. With specialization, world computer production rises by 1,000 computers per hour and world production of wine rises by 6,000 bottles per hour. The fact that world production of wine and computers *both* increase demonstrates that specialization, according to comparative advantage, can boost world output of all goods.

8. Property rights play a key role in shaping the incentive to create new music or, more generally, to create *any* new computer program, book, pharmaceutical drug, and so forth. Creation is costly because resources, time, and effort must be devoted to this process. By securing the property right to new music, the musician stands to benefit greatly from the resources expended. But if the person cannot obtain a property right, anyone can copy the new music. In that case the musician's return will be dissipated when a lot of people copy the music and, indeed, someone else might reap the rewards. Property rights, by promising that the musician will personally benefit from the effort involved in creating the music, motivate significantly more new music than would occur in the absence of property rights.

■ **You're the Teacher**

1. "*All* economic models vastly simplify the complex reality. But that is no reason to throw them away. The lessons that can be learned from the simple two-good *PPF* carry over to the real world. For instance, the two-good *PPF* shows that there are limits to production. These limits are represented by the *PPF*, which divides attainable from unattainable production points. Now, just as you say, in the real world billions of goods are produced. But there are still limits. But no matter how many goods a nation produces, every nation faces a limit of how much it can produce, just as in the simple two-good *PPF* case."

"Plus, the simple *PPF* model demonstrates that production can be efficient or inefficient. This result is also true in the real world. "And, the two-good *PPF* shows that once production is efficient — a point on the *PPF* — increasing the output of one good has an opportunity cost because the production of the other good must be reduced. The same is true in our real world. If we are producing efficiently, if we want to produce more of one good, we have to give up other goods. So, based on the assumption that there are only two goods, the *PPF* teaches us stuff that we can apply everywhere, not just on the next test."

Chapter Quiz

1. Consider a linear *PPF* with a vertical intercept of 80 guns and a horizontal intercept of 120 tons of butter. The opportunity cost of increasing butter output from 30 to 31 tons is
   a. 1/2 of a gun.
   b. 2/3 of a gun.
   c. 1 gun.
   d. 1 1/2 guns.

2. A nation can produce at a point outside its *PPF*
   a. when it trades with other nations.
   b. when it produces inefficiently.
   c. when it produces efficiently.
   d. never.

3. Which of the following statements is true?
   a. All resources are made by people.
   b. Human resources are called labor.
   c. Capital is made only by labor.
   d. Human capital is a contradiction in terms.

4. A situation in which some resources are used inefficiently is represented in a *PPF* diagram by
   a. any point on either the vertical or horizontal axis.
   b. the midpoint of the *PPF*.
   c. a point outside the *PPF*.
   d. a point inside the *PPF*.

5. Robert has decided to write the essay that is due in his economics class rather than watch a movie. The movie he will miss is Robert's _____ of writing the essay.
   a. opportunity cost
   b. explicit cost
   c. implicit cost
   d. discretionary cost

6. The goods given up to pay for the cost of textbooks _____ and the earnings foregone because of attending college _____ part of the opportunity cost of attending college.
   a. are; are
   b. are; are not
   c. are not; are
   d. are not; are not

7. The highest-valued alternative foregone from an action is called the action's
   a. "loss."
   b. "money cost."
   c. "direct cost."
   d. "opportunity cost."

8. The marginal benefit of a good is the
   a. benefit that the good gives to someone other than the buyer.
   b. maximum someone is willing to pay for that unit of the good.
   c. benefit of the good that exceeds the marginal cost of the product.
   d. benefit of the good divided by the total number of units purchased.

9. A marginal benefit curve has a _____ slope; a marginal cost curve has a _____ slope.
   a. positive; positive
   b. positive; negative
   c. negative; positive
   d. negative; negative

10. The production possibilities frontier shifts inward as a result of
    a. an increase in the production of consumption goods.
    b. an increase in R&D expenditure.
    c. an increase in population.
    d. destruction of part of the nation's capital stock.

The answers for this Chapter Quiz are on page 345

Mid-Term Examination

■ **Chapter 1**

1. Suppose your economics instructor decides to give 10 percent extra credit on the next test to students who either increase their score from the last test or else score 90 or above on the test. If you decide to study for an additional 3 hours, you _____ made a choice on the margin and you _____ responded to an incentive.

   a. have not; have not
   b. have not; have
   c. have; have not
   d. have; have

2. For dinner you are very hungry so you decide to buy a delivered pizza from Pizza Hut. Your choice

   a. is made in the social interest.
   b. is made in your self interest.
   c. reflects an example of the big tradeoff.
   d. has no opportunity cost because you must eat to survive.

3. Positive statements are statements about

   a. prices.
   b. quantities.
   c. what is.
   d. what ought to be.

4. The branch of economics that studies individual markets within the economy is called

   a. macroeconomics.
   b. microeconomics.
   c. individual economics.
   d. market economy.

5. Decisions made in the self interest _____ decisions made in the social interest.

   a. must conflict with
   b. must coincide with
   c. might conflict with or might coincide with
   d. are not comparable to

■ **Chapter 2**

6. Output combinations beyond the production possibility frontier
   a. result in more rapid growth.
   b. are associated with unused resources.
   c. are attainable only with the full utilization of all resources.
   d. are unattainable.

7. The *PPF* curve shifts inward as a result of
   a. a decrease in the production of consumption goods.
   b. an increase in R&D expenditure.
   c. an increase in population.
   d. the destruction of a portion of the capital stock.

8. The decentralized coordination that our economy uses depends, in part, on the following social organizations:
   a. land, labor, and capital.
   b. markets, property rights, and firms.
   c. wages, rent, interest, and profit.
   d. comparative advantage and absolute advantage.

9. To obtain all the gains available from comparative advantage, individuals or countries must do more than trade, they must also
   a. specialize.
   b. save.
   c. invest.
   d. engage in research and development.

10. To produce at the allocatively efficient point, it must be the case that the
    a. *MC* is at its minimum.
    b. *MB* exceed the *MC* by as much as possible.
    c. *MB* equal the *MC*.
    d. None of the above are correct.

Answers

■ Mid-Term Exam Answers

1. d;   2. b;   3. c;   4. b;   5. c;   6. d;   7. d;   8. b;   9. a;   10. c.

Chapter 3 DEMAND AND SUPPLY

■ Markets and Prices

A **competitive market** is a market that has many buyers and sellers, so no single buyer or seller can influence the price. The **money price** of a good is the number of dollars that must be given up it. The ratio of one price to another is the **relative price**. A good's relative price is its opportunity cost. The demand and supply of a good determine its relative price, so a prediction that the "price falls" means the relative price falls.

■ Demand

The **quantity demanded** of a good is the amount that consumers plan to buy during a given time period at a particular price. The **law of demand** states that "other things remaining the same, the higher the price of a good, the smaller is the quantity demanded; and the lower the price of a good, the greater is the quantity demanded." Higher prices reduce the quantity demanded for two reasons:

♦ *Substitution effect* — a higher relative price raises the opportunity cost of buying a good, so people buy less of it.

♦ *Income effect* — a higher relative price reduces the amount of goods people can buy. Usually this effect decreases the amount people buy of the good that rose in price.

Demand is the entire relationship between the price of a good and the quantity demanded. A **demand curve** shows the relationship between the quantity demanded of a good and its price, everything else remaining the same. Demand curves are negatively sloped, as illustrated in Figure 3.1. For each quantity, a demand curve shows the highest price someone is willing to pay for that unit. This highest price is the *marginal benefit* a consumer receives for that unit of output.

♦ A change in the price of the good or service leads to a **change in the quantity demanded** and *a move-*

FIGURE 3.1
Demand Curves

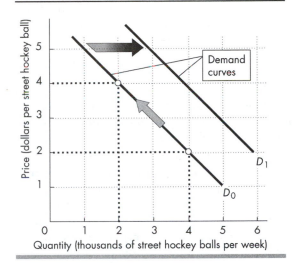

ment along the demand curve. The higher the price of a good or service, the lower the quantity demanded. In Figure 3.1, along demand curve D_0 when street hockey balls rise in price from \$2 to \$4, the quantity demanded decreases from 4,000 to 2,000 street hockey balls per week.

A **change in demand** and *a shift of the demand curve*, occur when any factor that influences buying plans changes, other than the price of the good. An increase in demand means that the demand curve shifts rightward, such as the shift from D_0 to D_1 in Figure 3.1. A decrease in demand refers to the demand curve shifting leftward. The demand curve shifts with changes in:

● *prices of related goods* — a rise in the price of a **substitute** (a good that can be used in place of another good) increases demand and shifts the demand curve rightward; a rise in the price of a **complement** (a good that is used with another good) decreases demand and shifts the demand curve leftward.

● *expected future prices* — if the price of a good is expected to rise in the future, the opportunity cost of buying it now is lower than in the future. The current demand increases and the demand curve shifts rightward.

- *income* — for a **normal good**, an increase in income increases demand and shifts the demand curve rightward; for an **inferior good** an increase in income decreases demand and shifts the demand curve leftward.

- *expected future income and credit* — when expected future income increases or when credit is easy to obtain, current demand might increase.

- *population* — an increase in population increases demand and shifts the demand curve rightward.

- *preferences* — if people like a good more, its demand increases and the demand curve shifts rightward.

■ Supply

The **quantity supplied** of a good or service is the amount that producers plan to sell during a given time period at a particular price.

The **law of supply** states that "other things remaining the same, the higher the price of a good, the greater is the quantity supplied; and the lower the price of a good, the smaller is the quantity supplied." **Supply** is the entire relationship between the quantity supplied and the price of a good. A **supply curve** shows the relationship between the price and the quantity supplied. Supply curves are positively sloped, as shown in Figure 3.2. For each quantity, the supply curve shows the minimum price a supplier must receive in order to produce that unit of output.

- A change in the price of the good leads to a **change in the quantity supplied** and a *movement along the supply curve*. In Figure 3.2, along supply curve S_0 when street hockey balls rise in price from $2 to $4, the quantity supplied increases from 2,000 to 4,000 street hockey balls per week.

When any factor that influences selling plans other than the price of the good changes, there is a **change in supply** and a *shift of the supply curve*. An increase in supply shifts the supply curve rightward, shown in Figure 3.2 as the shift from S_0 to S_1; a decrease in supply shifts the supply curve leftward. The supply curve shifts in response to changes in:

- *prices of factors of production* — a rise in the price of a factor of production used to produce the good decreases supply and the supply curve shifts leftward.

- *prices of related goods produced* — a rise in the price of a *substitute in production* decreases supply and

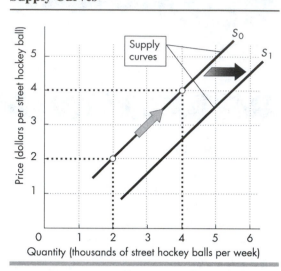

FIGURE 3.2
Supply Curves

the supply curve shifts leftward; a rise in the price of a *complement in production* increases supply and the supply curve shifts rightward.

- *expected future prices* — if the price is expected to rise in the future, the current supply decreases and the supply curve shifts leftward.

- *the number of suppliers* — an increase in the number of suppliers increases supply and the supply curve shifts rightward.

- *technology* — an advance in technology increases supply and the supply curve shifts rightward.

- *the state of nature* — good states of nature, such as a good growing season for an agricultural good or cloudless days for solar energy plants, increase supply and the supply curve shifts rightward.

■ Market Equilibrium

The **equilibrium price** is the price at which the quantity demanded equals the quantity supplied. It is determined by the intersection of the demand and supply curves. The **equilibrium quantity** is the quantity bought and sold at the equilibrium price. Figure 3.3 shows the equilibrium price, $3, and the equilibrium quantity, 3,000 street hockey balls per week. The price acts as a regulator driving the quantity supplied to equal the quantity demanded. At prices below the equilibrium price, a shortage exists and the price rises. At prices above the equilibrium price, a surplus exists and

FIGURE **3.3**
The Equilibrium Price and Quantity

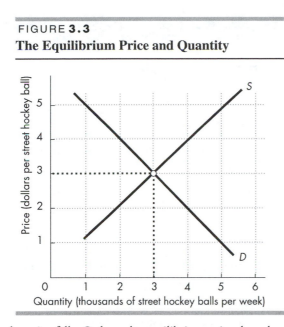

the price falls. Only at the equilibrium price does the price not change.

■ Predicting Changes in Price and Quantity

When either the demand *or* supply changes so that *one* of the demand or supply curves shifts, the effect on both the price (P) and quantity (Q) can be determined:

- An increase in demand (a rightward shift of the demand curve) raises P and increases Q.

- A decrease in demand (a leftward shift of the demand curve) lowers P and decreases Q.

- An increase in supply (a rightward shift of the supply curve) lowers P and increases Q.

- A decrease in supply (a leftward shift of the supply curve) raises P and decreases Q.

When both the demand and supply change so that both the demand and supply curves shift, the effect on the price *or* the quantity can be determined, but without information about the relative sizes of the shifts, the effect on the other is ambiguous.

- If both demand and supply increases (both curves shift rightward), the quantity increases but the price might rise, fall, or remain the same.

- If demand decreases (the demand curve shifts leftward) and supply increases (the supply curve shifts rightward), the price falls but the quantity might increase, decrease, or not change.

Helpful Hints

1. **DEVELOPING INTUITION ABOUT DEMAND :**
   When you are first learning about demand and supply, think in terms of concrete examples. Have some favorite examples in the back of your mind. For instance, when you hear "complementary goods" (goods used together), think about hot dogs and hot dog buns because few people eat hot dogs without using a hot dog bun. For "substitute goods" (things that take each other's place) think about hot dogs and hamburgers because they are obvious substitutes.

2. **DEVELOPING INTUITION ABOUT SUPPLY :** An easy and concrete way to identify with suppliers is to think of "profit": Anything that increases the profit from producing a good (except for the price of the good itself) increases the supply and shifts the supply curve rightward, whereas anything that decreases profit decreases the supply and shifts the supply curve leftward.

3. **SHIFT OF A CURVE VERSUS A MOVEMENT ALONG A CURVE :** Failing to distinguish correctly between a shift of a curve and a movement along a curve can lead to error and lost points on examinations. The difference applies equally to both demand and supply curves.

   Think about demand. The important point to remember is *that a change in the price of a good does not shift its demand curve;* the shortage leads to a movement along the demand curve. If one of the other factors affecting demand changes, the demand curve itself shifts.

   Similarly, a change in the price of the good leads to a movement along the supply curve. The supply curve shifts if some relevant factor that affects the supply, *other than the price of the good,* changes.

4. **RULES FOR USING A SUPPLY/DEMAND DIAGRAM :** The safest way to solve any demand and supply problem is always to draw a graph. A few mechanical rules can make using demand and supply graphs easy. First, when you draw the graph, be sure to label the axes. As the course progresses, you will encounter many graphs with different variables on the axes. You can become confused if you do not develop the habit of labeling the axes. Second, for simplicity and clarity, draw the demand and supply curves as straight lines.

Third, again for clarity, be sure to indicate and label the initial equilibrium price and quantity.

Now come two more difficult parts that you must practice. Suppose that you are dealing with a situation in which one influence changes. First, determine whether the influence shifts the demand or the supply curve. Aside from the effect of the expected future price, most factors generally shift only one curve and you must decide which one. Next determine whether the curve that is affected shifts rightward (increases) or shifts leftward (decreases). From here on, it's more straightforward: Take the figure you have already drawn, shift the appropriate curve, and read off the answer!

FIGURE **3.4**
The Effect of an Increase in Demand

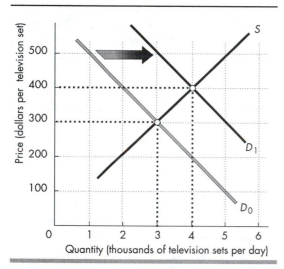

5. **CHANGES IN DEMAND DO NOT CAUSE CHANGES IN SUPPLY ; CHANGES IN SUPPLY DO NOT CAUSE CHANGES IN DEMAND :** Do not make the common error of believing that an increase in demand, that is, a rightward shift in the demand curve, causes an increase in supply, a rightward shift in the supply curve. Use Figure 3.4, which illustrates the market for television sets, as an example. An increase in demand shifts the demand curve rightward, as shown. This shift means the equilibrium price of a television rises (from $300 for a set to $400) and the equilibrium quantity increases (from 3,000 sets per day to 4,000). But the shift in the demand curve does not cause the supply curve to *shift*. Instead, there is a *movement along* the unchanging supply curve.

Questions

■ True/False and Explain

Markets and Prices

1. A good with a high relative price must have a low opportunity cost.

2. A good's relative price can fall even though its money price rises.

Demand

3. The law of demand states that, if nothing else changes, as the price of a good rises, the quantity demanded decreases.

4. A decrease in income decreases the demand for all goods and services.

5. "An increase in demand" means a movement down and rightward along a demand curve.

6. New technology for manufacturing computer chips shifts the demand curve for computer chips.

Supply

7. A supply curve shows the maximum price required in order to have the last unit of output produced.

8. If the price of chicken feed rises, the supply of chickens decreases.

9. If the price of orange juice rises, the supply curve of orange juice shifts rightward.

Market Equilibrium

10. If a market is at its equilibrium price, unless something changes, the price will not change.

11. If there is a surplus of a good, its price falls.

Predicting Changes in Price and Quantity

12. If the expected future price of a good rises, its current price rises.

13. A rise in the price of a good decreases the quantity demanded, so there can never be a situation with both the good's equilibrium price rising and its equilibrium quantity increasing.

14. If both the demand and supply curves shift rightward, the equilibrium quantity definitely increases.

15. If both the demand and supply curves shift rightward, the equilibrium price definitely rises.

■ **Multiple Choice**

Markets and Prices

1. The opportunity cost of a good is the same as its
   a. money price.
   b. relative price.
   c. price index.
   d. None of the above.

2. The money price of a pizza is $12 per pizza and the money price of a taco is $2 per taco. The relative price of a pizza is
   a. $12 per pizza.
   b. $24 per pizza.
   c. 6 tacos per pizza.
   d. 1/6 pizza.

Demand

3. The law of demand concludes that a rise in the price of a golf ball _____ the quantity demanded and _____.
   a. increases; shifts the demand curve for golf balls rightward
   b. decreases; shifts the demand curve for golf balls leftward
   c. decreases; creates a movement up along the demand curve for golf balls
   d. increases; creates a movement down along the demand curve for golf balls

4. If a rise in the price of gasoline decreases the demand for large cars,
   a. gasoline and large cars are substitutes for consumers.
   b. gasoline and large cars are complements for consumers.
   c. gasoline is an inferior good.
   d. large cars are an inferior good.

5. A normal good is one
   a. with a downward sloping demand curve.
   b. for which demand increases when the price of a substitute rises.
   c. for which demand increases when income increases.
   d. None of the above.

6. Some sales managers are talking shop. Which of the following quotations refers to a movement along the demand curve?
   a. "Since our competitors raised their prices our sales have doubled."
   b. "It has been an unusually mild winter; our sales of wool scarves are down from last year."
   c. "We decided to cut our prices, and the increase in our sales has been remarkable."
   d. None of the above.

FIGURE **3.5**
Multiple Choice Question 7

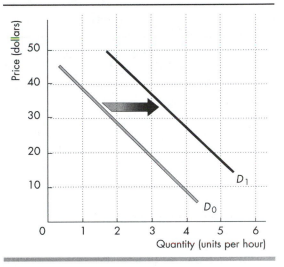

7. Which of the following could lead to the shift in the demand curve illustrated in Figure 3.5?
   a. An increase in the quantity demanded
   b. A rise in the price of a substitute good
   c. A rise in the price of a complement
   d. A fall in the price of the good

Supply

8. A fall in the price of a good leads producers to decrease the quantity of the good supplied. This statement reflects
   a. the law of supply.
   b. the law of demand.
   c. a change in supply.
   d. the nature of an inferior good.

9. Which of the following influences does <u>NOT</u> shift the supply curve?

   a. A rise in the wages paid workers
   b. Development of new technology
   c. People deciding that they want to buy more of the good
   d. A decrease in the number of suppliers

10. The price of jet fuel rises, so the

    a. demand for airplane trips increases.
    b. demand for airplane trips decreases.
    c. supply of airplane trips increases.
    d. supply of airplane trips decreases.

11. In addition to showing the quantity that will be supplied at different prices, a supply curve is also a

    a. willingness-and-ability-to-pay curve.
    b. marginal benefit curve.
    c. minimum-supply price curve.
    d. maximum-supply price curve.

12. An increase in the number of producers of gruel _____ the supply of gruel and shifts the supply curve of gruel _____.

    a. increases; rightward
    b. increases; leftward
    c. decreases; rightward
    d. decreases; leftward

13. An increase in the price of the cheese used to produce pizza shifts the supply curve of pizza _____ and shifts the demand curve for pizza _____.

    a. rightward; leftward
    b. leftward; leftward
    c. leftward; not at all
    d. not at all; leftward

14. To say that "supply increases" for any reason, means there is a

    a. rightward movement along a supply curve.
    b. leftward movement along a supply curve.
    c. rightward shift in the supply curve.
    d. leftward shift in the supply curve.

Market Equilibrium

15. If the market for Twinkies is in equilibrium, then

    a. Twinkies must be a normal good.
    b. producers would like to sell more at the current price.
    c. consumers would like to buy more at the current price.
    d. the quantity supplied equals the quantity demanded.

16. If there is a shortage of a good, the quantity demanded is _____ than the quantity supplied and the price will _____.

    a. less; rise
    b. less; fall
    c. greater; rise
    d. greater; fall

FIGURE **3.6**
Multiple Choice Question 17

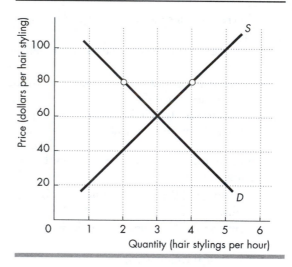

17. In Figure 3.6 at the price of $80 there is a

    a. shortage and the price will rise.
    b. shortage and the price will fall.
    c. surplus and the price will rise.
    d. surplus and the price will fall.

18. In a market, at the equilibrium price,
    a. neither buyers nor sellers can do business at a better price.
    b. buyers are willing to pay a higher price, but sellers do not ask for a higher price.
    c. buyers are paying the minimum price they are willing to pay for any amount of output and sellers are charging the maximum price they are willing to charge for any amount of production.
    d. None of the above is true.

Predicting Changes in Price and Quantity

19. Pizza and hamburgers are substitutes for consumers. A rise in the price of pizza ____ the equilibrium price of a hamburger and ____ in the equilibrium quantity of hamburgers.
    a. raises; increases
    b. raises; decreases
    c. lowers; increases
    d. lowers; decreases

20. How does an unusually cold winter affect the equilibrium price and equilibrium quantity of antifreeze?
    a. It raises the price and increases the quantity.
    b. It raises the price and decreases the quantity.
    c. It lowers the price and increases the quantity.
    d. It lowers the price and decreases the quantity.

21. You notice that the price of wheat rises and the quantity of wheat increases. This set of observations can be the result of the
    a. demand for wheat curve shifting rightward.
    b. demand for wheat curve shifting leftward.
    c. supply of wheat curve shifting rightward.
    d. supply of wheat curve shifting leftward.

22. A technological improvement lowers the cost of producing coffee. The technological improvement ____ the equilibrium price of a pound of coffee and ____ the equilibrium quantity of coffee
    a. rises; increases
    b. rises; decreases
    c. falls; increases
    d. falls; decreases

23. The number of firms producing computer memory chips decreases. As a result, the price of a memory chip ____ and the quantity of memory chips ____.
    a. rises; increases
    b. rises; decreases
    c. falls; increases
    d. falls; decreases

For the next five questions, suppose that the price of paper used in books rises and simultaneously (and independently) fewer people decide they want to read paper books.

24. The rise in the price of paper shifts the
    a. demand curve rightward.
    b. demand curve leftward.
    c. supply curve rightward.
    d. supply curve leftward.

25. The fact that fewer people want to read paper books shifts the
    a. demand curve rightward.
    b. demand curve leftward.
    c. supply curve rightward.
    d. supply curve leftward.

26. The equilibrium quantity of paper books
    a. definitely increases.
    b. definitely does not change.
    c. definitely decreases.
    d. might increase, not change, or decrease.

27. The equilibrium price of a paper book
    a. definitely rises.
    b. definitely does not change.
    c. definitely falls.
    d. might rise, not change, or fall.

28. Suppose that the effect from people deciding they want to read fewer books is larger than the effect from the increase in the price of paper. In this case, the equilibrium quantity of paper books
    a. definitely increases.
    b. definitely does not change.
    c. definitely decreases.
    d. might increase, not change, or decrease.

29. Which of the following definitely raises the equilibrium price?
    a. An increase in both demand and supply.
    b. A decrease in both demand and supply.
    c. An increase in demand combined with a decrease in supply.
    d. A decrease in demand combined with an increase in supply.

30. Is it possible for the price of a good to stay the same while the quantity increases?
    a. Yes, if both the demand and supply of the good increase by the same amount.
    b. Yes, if the demand increases by the same amount the supply decreases.
    c. Yes, if the supply increases and the demand does not change.
    d. No, it is not possible.

■ **Short Answer Problems**

1. a. This year the price of a hamburger is $2 and the price of a DVD is $12. In terms of hamburgers, what is the relative price of a DVD? In terms of hamburgers, what is the opportunity cost of buying a DVD? How are the two answers related?
   b. Next year the (money) price of a DVD doubles to $24 and the (money) price of a hamburger remains at $2. Now what is the relative price of a DVD?
   c. The following year the (money) price of a DVD stays at $24 and the (money) price of a hamburger doubles to $4. What is the relative price of a DVD?
   d. In the next year, the (money) price of a DVD doubles to $48 and the money price of a hamburger triples to $12. What is the relative price of a DVD?
   e. Can a good's relative price fall even though its money price has risen? Why or why not?

2. a. When drawing a demand curve, what six factors are assumed not to change?
   b. If any of these influences change, what happens to the demand curve?
   c. When drawing a supply curve, what six factors are assumed not to change?
   d. If any of these influences change, what happens to the supply curve?

TABLE **3.1**

Demand and Supply Schedules

Price (per comic book)	Quantity demanded (per month)	Quantity supplied (per month)
$2.50	14,000,000	8,000,000
3.00	13,000,000	10,000,000
3.50	12,000,000	12,000,000
4.00	11,000,000	13,000,000
4.50	10,000,000	14,000,000

FIGURE **3.7**

Short Answer Problem 3

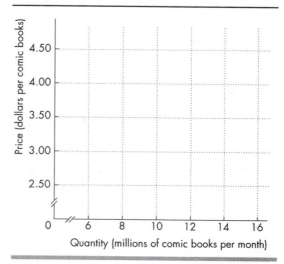

3. a. Table 3.1 presents the demand and supply schedules for comic books. Graph these demand and supply schedules in Figure 3.7. What is the equilibrium price? The equilibrium quantity?
   b. What is the marginal benefit received by the consumer of the 12,000,000th comic book? What is the minimum price for which a producer is willing to produce the 12,000,000th comic book?
   c. Suppose that the price of a movie, a substitute for comic books, rises so that at every price of a comic book consumers now want to buy 2,000,000 more comic books than before. That is, at the price of $2.50, consumers now will buy 16,000,000 comics; and so on. Plot this new demand curve in Figure 3.7. What is the new equilibrium price? The new equilibrium quantity?

4. New cars are a normal good. Suppose that the economy enters a period of strong economic expansion so that people's incomes increase substantially. Use a demand and supply diagram to determine what happens to the equilibrium price and quantity of new cars.

5. DVDs and Blu-ray discs are substitutes. Use a supply and demand diagram to determine what happens to the equilibrium price and quantity of DVDs when the price of a Blu-ray falls because of an increase in the supply of Blu-ray discs.

6. Suppose we observe that the consumption of peanut butter increases at the same time its price rises. What must have happened in the market for peanut butter? Is the observation that the price rose and the quantity increased consistent with the law of demand? Why or why not?

7. Gasoline is produced when oil is refined. Suppose that the wages paid refinery workers fall. Use a demand and supply diagram to determine the effect this action has on the equilibrium price and quantity of gasoline.

8. Companies discover a new, more efficient technology for producing ethanol. Use a demand and supply model to determine the impact that this new method has on the equilibrium price and quantity of ethanol.

9. The price of a personal computer has continued to fall in the face of increasing demand. Explain.

10. a. The market for chickens initially is in equilibrium. Suppose that eating buffalo wings (which, contrary to the name, are made from chicken wings) becomes so stylish that people eat them for breakfast, lunch, and dinner. Use a demand and supply diagram to determine how the equilibrium price and quantity of chicken change.

b. Return to the initial equilibrium, before eating buffalo wings became stylish. Now suppose that a heat wave occurred and caused tens of thousands of chickens to die or commit suicide. Keeping in mind that dead chickens cannot be marketed, use a demand and supply diagram to determine what happens to the equilibrium price and quantity of chicken.

c. Now assume that both the heat wave and fad strike at the same time. Use a demand and supply diagram to show what happens to the equilibrium price and quantity of chicken. (Hint: Can you tell for sure what happens to the price? The quantity?)

■ You're the Teacher

1. When you and a friend are studying Chapter 3, the friend says to you, "I really don't understand the difference between a 'shift in a curve' and a 'movement along' a curve. Can you help me? It's probably important to understand this, so what's the difference?" Explain the difference to your friend.

2. "This demand and supply model is nonsense. It says that if demand for some good decreases, the price of that good falls. But, come on — except for computers, how many times have you actually seen a price fall? Prices *always* rise, so don't try telling me that that they fall." The demand and supply model is sound; it is this statement that is nonsense. Show the speaker the error in that analysis.

Answers

■ True/False Answers

Markets and Prices

1. **F** A good's relative price is its opportunity cost.

2. **T** A good's relative price will fall if its money price rises less than the money prices of other goods.

Demand

3. **T** The law of demand points out the negative relationship between a good or service's price and the quantity demanded.

4. **F** Demand decreases for normal goods but increases for inferior goods.

5. **F** The term "increase in demand" refers to a rightward shift in the demand curve.

6. **F** Changes in technology are not a factor that shifts the demand curve. (Changes in technology shift the supply curve.)

Supply

7. **F** The supply curve shows the *minimum* price that suppliers must receive in order to produce the last unit supplied.

8. **T** Chicken feed is a factor used to produce chickens, so a rise in its price shifts the supply curve of chickens leftward.

9. **F** The rise in the price of orange juice creates a movement along the supply curve to a larger quantity supplied (that is, upward and rightward), but it does not shift the supply curve.

Market Equilibrium

10. **T** Once at the equilibrium price, because the opposing forces of demand and supply are in balance, the situation can persist indefinitely until something changes.

11. **T** A surplus of a good results in its price falling until it reaches the equilibrium price.

Predicting Changes in Price and Quantity

12. **T** The rise in the future price shifts the demand curve rightward and the supply curve leftward, unambiguously raising the current price.

13. **F** The inverse relationship between the price and quantity demanded holds along a fixed demand curve. But if the demand curve shifts rightward,

the equilibrium price rises and the equilibrium quantity increases.

14. **T** The equilibrium quantity definitely increases when both the demand and supply increase.

15. **F** The price rises if the shift in the demand curve is larger than that in the supply curve; but if the shifts are the same size, the price does not change and if the supply shift is larger, the price falls.

■ Multiple Choice Answers

Markets and Prices

1. **b** A good's relative price tells how much of another good must be foregone to have another unit of the good, which is the opportunity cost of the good.

2. **c** The relative price of the pizza is its money price relative to the money price of a taco, which equals ($12 per pizza)/($2 per taco) or 6 tacos per pizza.

Demand

3. **c** The law of demand points out that a higher price decreases the quantity demanded and creates a movement up along the demand curve for golf balls.

4. **b** For complementary goods, a rise in the price of one decreases the demand for the other.

5. **c** This answer is the definition of a "normal good."

6. **c** A reduction in the price of the good leads to a movement along its demand curve.

7. **b** A rise in the price of a substitute shifts the demand curve rightward.

Supply

8. **a** The law of supply points out the positive relationship between the price of a good or service and the quantity supplied.

9. **c** A change in preferences shifts the demand curve, not the supply curve.

10. **d** Jet fuel is a factor used to produce airplane trips, so a rise in the price of this resource decreases the supply of airplane trips.

11. **c** For any unit of output, the supply curve shows the minimum price for which a producer is willing to produce and sell that unit of output.

12. **a** An increase in supply is reflected by a rightward shift of the supply curve.

13. **c** A change in the price of a factor used to produce a good shifts the supply curve but does not shift the demand curve.

14. **c** An "increase in supply" means that the supply curve shifts rightward; a "decrease in supply" means the supply curve shifts leftward.

Market Equilibrium

15. **d** At equilibrium, consumers and suppliers are simultaneously satisfied insofar as the quantity consumers are willing to buy matches the quantity producers are willing to sell.

16. **c** A shortage occurs when the price is below the equilibrium price. The quantity demanded exceeds the quantity supplied and the resulting shortage means the price rises until it reaches its equilibrium.

FIGURE **3.8**
Multiple Choice Question 17

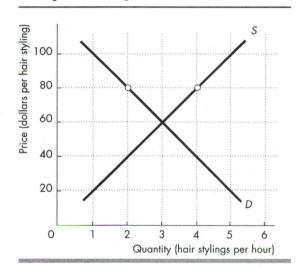

17. **d** There is surplus because, as illustrated in Figure 3.8, the quantity supplied at the price of $80 is 4. This quantity exceeds 2, the quantity demanded.

18. **a** Buyers cannot find anyone willing to sell to at a lower price and sellers cannot find anyone willing to buy at a higher price.

Predicting Changes in Price and Quantity

19. **a** The rise in the price of a pizza increases the demand for hamburgers, which results in a rise in the price of a hamburger and an increase in the quantity of hamburgers.

20. **a** The cold winter shifts the demand curve rightward, as consumers increase their demand for antifreeze; the supply curve does not shift. As a result, the equilibrium price rises and the quantity increases.

FIGURE **3.9**
Multiple Choice Question 21

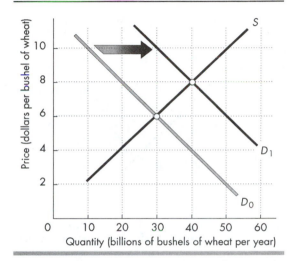

21. **a** Figure 3.9 shows that an increase in the demand for wheat, so that the demand curve shifts from D_0 to D_1, raises the price of wheat from $6 a bushel to $8 and increases its quantity from 30 billion bushels of wheat a year to 40 billion.

22. **c** The technological improvement increases the supply, that is, the supply curve shifts rightward. As a result, the quantity increases and the price falls.

23. **b** The decrease in the number of firms producing memory chips decreases the supply of memory chips, which raises the price and decreases the quantity of chips.

24. **d** Paper is used in the manufacture of paper books, so a rise in the price of paper increases the cost and shifts the supply curve of books leftward.

25. **b** When people's preferences change so that they want to read fewer paper books, the demand curve for books shifts leftward.

26. **c** Both the decrease in demand and the decrease in supply lead to a decrease in the quantity, so the equilibrium quantity unambiguously decreases.

27. **d** The equilibrium price of a paper work rises if the decrease in supply is larger than the decrease in demand, falls if the decrease in demand is larger than the decrease in supply, and does not change if the decrease in demand equals the decrease in supply.

FIGURE **3.10**

Multiple Choice Question 28

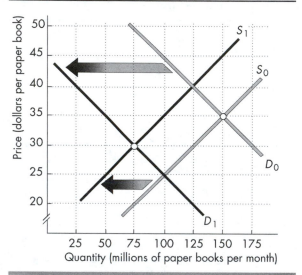

28. **a** If the shift in the demand curve exceeds the shift in the supply curve, the equilibrium price decreases. This result is illustrated in Figure 3.10, where the equilibrium price decreases from $35 to $30.

29. **c** Separately, the increase in demand and decrease in supply both raise the equilibrium price, so the two of them occurring together definitely raise the price.

30. **a** If both the demand and supply increase by the same amount, the equilibrium price will not change and the equilibrium quantity will increase.

■ **Answers to Short Answer Problems**

1. a. The money price of a DVD is $12 per DVD; the money price of a hamburger is $2 per hamburger. The relative price of a DVD is the ratio of the money prices, $12 per DVD /$2 per hamburger, or 6 hamburgers per DVD. For the opportunity cost, buying 1 DVD means using the funds that otherwise could purchase 6 ham-

burgers. Hence the opportunity cost of buying 1 DVD is 6 hamburgers. The relative price and the opportunity cost are identical.

b. The relative price of a DVD is $24 per DVD/$2 per hamburger or 12 hamburgers per DVD.

c. The relative price of a DVD is $24 per DVD/$4 per hamburger, or 6 hamburgers per DVD.

d. The relative price of a DVD is $48 per DVD/$12 per hamburger, or 4 hamburgers per DVD.

e. Yes, a good's relative price can fall even though its money price rises. Part (d) gives an example of how that can occur: If a good's money price rises by a smaller percentage than the money price of other goods, then the good's relative price falls. Keep this result in mind when you use the demand and supply model because when the model predicts that the equilibrium price will fall, it means that the *relative* price, and not necessarily the money price, falls.

2. a. The six factors that do not change along a demand curve are: prices of related goods; expected future prices; income; expected future income and credit; population; and, preferences.

b. If any of these influences change, the demand curve shifts.

c. The six factors that are held constant when you draw a supply curve are prices of factors of production; prices of related goods produced; expected future prices; the number of suppliers; technology; and, the state of nature.

d. If any of these influences change, the supply curve shifts. It is very important to remember what influences shift a supply curve and what shift a demand curve.

3. a. Figure 3.11 (on the next page) shows the graph of the demand and supply schedules as S and D_0. The equilibrium price is $3.50 a comic book, and the equilibrium quantity is 12,000,000 comic books.

b. The person who buys the 12,000,000th comic book pays $3.50 for the comic book, and so $3.50 is the benefit this person receives from this comic book. The firm that produces the 12,000,000th comic book receives $3.50 for the book, and the supply curve shows that $3.50 is the minimum price for which this firm is willing to produce and sell the comic book.

FIGURE **3.11**

Short Answer Problem 3

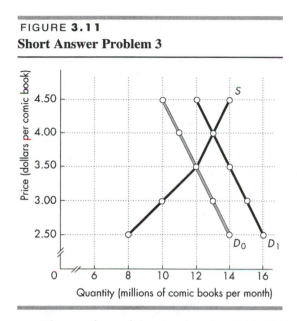

Quantity (millions of comic books per month)

c. The new demand curve is plotted in Figure 3.11 as D_1. The new equilibrium price is $4, and the new equilibrium quantity is 13 million.

FIGURE **3.12**

Short Answer Problem 4

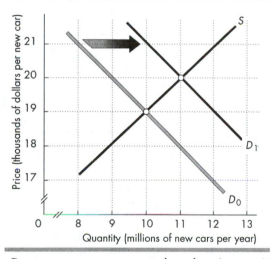

Quantity (millions of new cars per year)

4. Because new cars are a normal good, an increase in income increases the demand for them. Hence the demand curve shifts rightward, as shown in Figure 3.12. As a result, the equilibrium price rises (from $19,000 to $20,000 in the figure) and the equilibrium quantity also increases (from 10 million a year to 11 million in the figure).

FIGURE **3.13**

Short Answer Problem 5

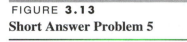

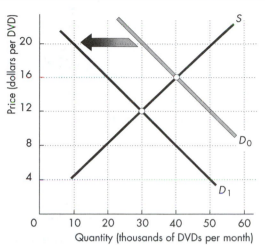

Quantity (thousands of DVDs per month)

5. The fall in the price of a Blu-ray disc, a substitute for DVDs, decreases the demand for DVDs. This change means the demand curve for DVDs shifts leftward, as shown in Figure 3.13. As a result, the price of a DVD falls, (from $16 per DVD to $12 per DVD in the figure) and the quantity decreases (from 40,000 per month to 30,000 in the figure). Note that it is the shift in the demand curve that changed the price and that the shift in the demand curve did *not* shift the supply curve.

6. In order for both the equilibrium price and quantity of peanut butter to increase, the demand for peanut butter must have increased. The increase in demand leads to a rise in the price and an increase in the quantity of peanut butter.

   The observation that both the price rose and the quantity increased is not at all inconsistent with the law of demand. The law of demand states that "other things remaining the same, the higher the price of a good, the smaller is the quantity demanded." A key part of this law is the "other things remaining the same" clause. When the demand curve for peanut butter shifts rightward, something else that increased the demand for peanut butter changed. Hence "other things" have not remained the same and by changing have resulted in a higher price and an increased quantity of peanut butter.

FIGURE **3.14**
Short Answer Problem 7

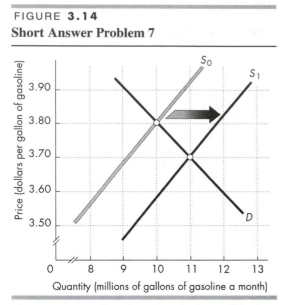

7. Lower wages reduce the price of a factor (labor) used to produce gasoline. As a result, the supply of gasoline increases. This change is illustrated in Figure 3.14, where the supply curve shifts rightward from S_0 to S_1. The increase in supply lowers the price of gasoline (from $3.80 a gallon to $3.70 in the figure) and increases the quantity (from 10 million gallons a month to 11 million).

FIGURE **3.15**
Short Answer Problem 8

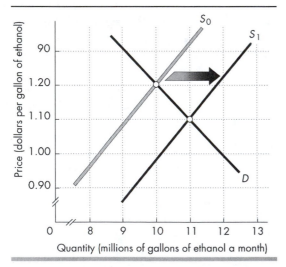

8. New technology increases the supply, so the supply curve shifts rightward. Then, as Figure 3.15 shows, the price falls (from $1.20 per gallon to $1.10 per gallon in the figure) and the equilibrium quantity

increases from (10 million gallons of ethanol per month to 11 million gallons of ethanol per month). This answer and the figure are virtually the same as those in problem 7. Even though a fall in wages and the development of new technology appear dissimilar, the demand and supply model reveals that both have the same effect on the price and quantity of the good. This model can easily accommodate these quite different changes. For this reason the demand and supply model is a very important economic tool.

FIGURE **3.16**
Short Answer Problem 9

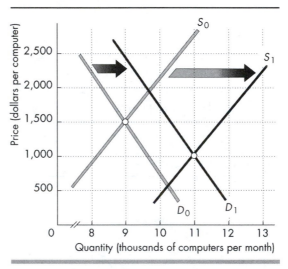

9. Personal computers have fallen in price although the demand for them has increased because the supply has increased even more rapidly. Figure 3.16 illustrates this situation. From one year to the next the demand curve shifted from D_0 to D_1. But over the year the supply curve shifted from S_0 to S_1. Because the supply has increased more than the demand, the price of a personal computer fell (in the figure, from $1,500 for a personal computer to $1,000). The quantity increased (from 9,000 personal computers a month to 11,000 in the figure).

10. a. With the change in people's preferences — they want more chicken wings and hence more chickens — the demand for chickens increases. The increase in the demand for chickens means that the demand curve for chickens shifts rightward. Figure 3.17 (on the next page) shows this change. As it demonstrates, the equilibrium

FIGURE **3.17**
Short Answer Problem 10 (a)

FIGURE **3.17**
Short Answer Problem 10 (a)

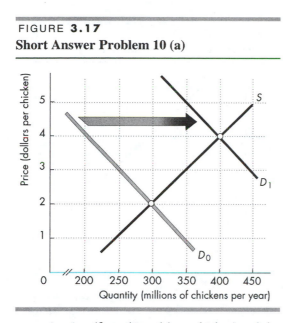

price rises (from \$2 to \$4 per chicken) and the equilibrium quantity of chickens increase (from 300 million to 400 million). Note that the change in people's preferences does not affect the supply of chicken, so the supply curve does *not* shift.

FIGURE **3.18**
Short Answer Problem 10 (b)

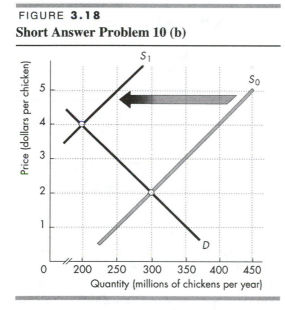

b. The heat wave decreases the number of chickens that can be supplied. This change shifts the supply curve for chickens leftward, as Figure 3.18 shows. As a result, the heat wave raises the price

FIGURE **3.19**
Short Answer Problem 10 (c)

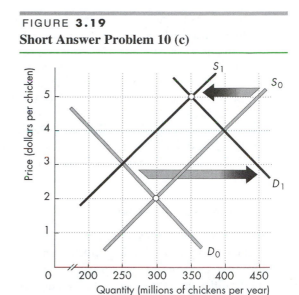

FIGURE **3.20**
Short Answer Problem 10 (c)

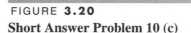
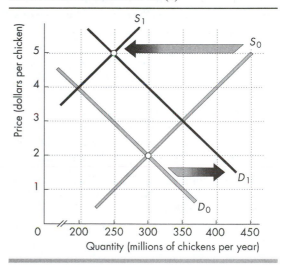

of a chicken (from \$2 to \$4) and decreases the quantity (from 300 million to 200 million).

c. If the demand increases *and* the supply decreases, the equilibrium price of a chicken rises. But the effect on the quantity is ambiguous. Figures 3.19 and 3.20 reveal the nature of this ambiguity. In Figure 3.19, the demand shift is larger than the supply shift, and the equilibrium quantity increases to 350 million chickens. But in Figure 3.20, the magnitude of the shifts is reversed, and the supply shift exceeds the demand shift. Because the supply shift is larger, the equilibrium quantity decreases to 250 million chickens. So unless you know which shift is larger, you cannot determine whether the quantity increases (when the demand shift is larger); decreases (when the supply shift is larger); or stays the same (when both shifts are the same size). However, regardless of the relative sizes, Figures 3.19 and 3.20 show that the price will unambiguously rise, coincidentally to $5 in both figures.

■ You're the Teacher Answers

1. "The distinction between a 'shift in a curve' and a 'movement along a curve' is really crucial. Let's think about the demand curve; once you understand the difference for the demand curve, understanding it for the supply curve is easier. Take movies, OK? A lot of things affect how many movies we see in a month: the ticket price, our income, and so on. Start with the price. Obviously, if the price of a movie ticket rises, we'll buy fewer. The slope of a demand curve shows this effect. For the demand curve in Figure 3.21, when the price rises from $10 to $11 for a movie, the movement is from point a on the demand curve to point b. Our quantity demanded decreases from 5 movies a month to 4. So the rise in the price of the good has lead to a movement along the demand curve. The negative slope of the demand curve shows the negative effect that higher prices have on the quantity demanded."

"Now, let's suppose that our incomes fall and that as a result we're going to go to fewer movies. The demand curve's slope can't show us this effect because the slope indicates the relationship between the price and the quantity demanded. Instead, the whole demand curve is going to shift. That is, at any price we'll buy fewer tickets. Look at Figure 3.22 for instance. If the price stays at $11 a movie, the quantity we demand decreases from 4 movies a month to 2."

"But the same is true if the price is $10: If the price stays at $10 the quantity we demand decreases from 5 movies a month to only 3. Now, I don't mean to say that the price has to stay at $11 or at $10. All I'm saying is that at any possible price, the number of movies we'll see has decreased and I'm just using $11 and $10 as examples. So we're going to decrease the quantity demanded at $11 and at $10, *and* at

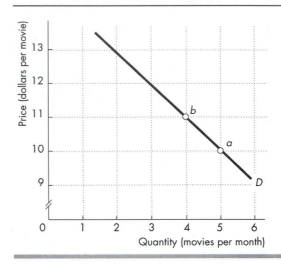

FIGURE **3.21**
You're the Teacher Question 1

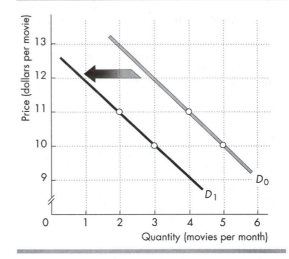

FIGURE **3.22**
You're the Teacher Question 1

every other possible price. That means that we can draw a new demand curve (D_1) to show how much we demand at every price after our incomes fall. So, the drop in income has shifted the demand curve from D_0 to D_1. And, that's all there is to the difference between a 'movement along the demand curve' and a 'shift in the demand curve.'"

2. "You're missing a key point about the demand and supply model. This model predicts what happens to *relative* prices, not *money* prices. You're certainly right when you say that we don't often see a money

DEMAND AND SUPPLY   6 I

price fall. We live in inflationary times and most money prices usually rise. But when the demand and supply model says that the price falls, it means that the *relative* price falls. A good's relative price can fall even though its money price rises. For instance, if the money price of some good rises by 2 percent when the money prices of all other goods are rising by 4 percent, the first good's relative price has fallen. That is, its money price relative to every other money price is lower. If you think about it, relative prices change all the time, and at least half the time relative prices fall. Drops in relative prices aren't rare; they're common. So, don't be too hasty to throw away the demand and supply model. Not only are we going to see it on tests in this class, but it also works well to help us understand what happens to a good's (relative) price and quantity whenever there's a change in a relevant factor."

Chapter Quiz

1. When demand increases, the
   a. price falls and the quantity decreases.
   b. price falls and the quantity increases.
   c. price rises and the quantity decreases.
   d. price rises and the quantity increases.

2. Wants differ from demands insofar as
   a. wants are limited by income but demands are unlimited.
   b. wants require a plan to acquire a good, while demands require no such plan.
   c. wants imply a decision about which demands to satisfy, while demands require no such specific plans.
   d. wants are unlimited and involve no specific plan to acquire the good, while demands reflect a decision about which wants to satisfy and a plan to buy the good.

3. A complement is a good
   a. that can be used in place of another good.
   b. that is used with another good.
   c. of lower quality than another.
   d. of higher quality than another.

4. Suppose that people buy less of good 1 when the price of good 2 falls. These goods are
   a. complements.
   b. substitutes.
   c. normal.
   d. inferior.

5. A change in the price of a good _____ its supply curve and _____ a movement along its supply curve.
   a. shifts; results in
   b. shifts; does not result in
   c. does not shift; results in
   d. does not shift; does not result in

6. Which of the following shifts the supply curve of plywood leftward?
   a. A situation in which the quantity demanded of plywood exceeds the quantity supplied.
   b. An increase in the price of machinery used to produce plywood.
   c. A technological improvement in the production of plywood.
   d. A decrease in the wages of workers employed to produce plywood.

7. A surplus results in the
   a. demand curve shifting rightward.
   b. supply curve shifting rightward.
   c. price falling.
   d. price rising.

8. If new cars are a normal good and people's incomes rise, then the new equilibrium quantity is _____ the initial equilibrium quantity.
   a. greater than
   b. equal to
   c. less than
   d. perhaps greater than, less than, or equal to depending on how suppliers react to the change in demand.

9. In the market for oil, the development of a new deep sea drilling technology _____ the demand curve for oil and _____ the supply curve of oil.
   a. shifts rightward; shifts rightward
   b. does not shift; shifts rightward
   c. shifts leftward; shifts leftward
   d. does not shift; shifts leftward

10. Taken by itself, an increase in supply results in
    a. the price rising.
    b. the price falling.
    c. the demand curve shifting rightward.
    d. the demand curve shifting leftward.

The answers for this Chapter Quiz are on page 345

Key Concepts

■ Price Elasticity of Demand

◆ The **price elasticity of demand** is a units-free measure of responsiveness of the quantity demanded of a good to a change in its price when all other influences on buyers' plans remain the same.

The price elasticity of demand equals the magnitude of:

$$\frac{\text{(percentage change in quantity demanded)}}{\text{(percentage change in price)}} = \frac{\Delta Q / Q_{ave}}{\Delta P / P_{ave}}$$

where "*ave*" stands for average. The percentage change in the quantity between two points on a demand curve is equal to $\Delta Q / Q_{ave} \times 100$.

◆ When the elasticity equals 0, the good has **perfectly inelastic demand** and the demand curve is vertical.

◆ When the elasticity is less than 1 and greater than 0, the good has **inelastic demand**.

◆ When the elasticity equals 1, the good has **unit elastic demand**.

◆ When the elasticity is greater than 1 and less than infinity, the good has **elastic demand**.

◆ When the elasticity equals infinity, the good has **perfectly elastic demand** and the demand curve is horizontal.

The price elasticity of demand depends on three factors:

◆ *Closeness of ssubstitutes* — the more close substitutes there are for the good, the larger is its price elasticity. Necessities generally have few substitutes and so have a small elasticity; luxuries generally have many substitutes and so have a large elasticity.

◆ *Proportion of income spent on the good* — the greater the proportion of income spent on a good, the larger is its price elasticity of demand.

◆ *Time elapsed since the price change* — the longer the time that has passed since the price changed, the larger is the price elasticity of demand.

Elasticity is *not* equal to the slope of the demand curve. Along a downward sloping linear demand curve the slope ($\Delta P / \Delta Q$) is constant but the elasticity falls in magnitude moving downward along the curve. At the midpoint of a downward sloping linear demand curve the elasticity equals 1.0; above the midpoint the elasticity is greater than 1.0; and' below the midpoint the elasticity is less than 1.0.

Total revenue equals the price of the good multiplied by the quantity sold, $P \times Q$. The **total revenue test** estimates the price elasticity of demand by noting how a change in price affects the total revenue.

◆ The total revenue test is:

When demand is	A price cut results in
Inelastic (elasticity < 1)	a decrease in total revenue
Unit elastic (elasticity = 1)	no change in total revenue
Elastic (elasticity > 1)	an increase in total revenue

The expenditure on a good follows the same rules: If the good has an elastic demand, a price cut increases expenditure; if it has a unit elastic demand, a price cut does not change expenditure; and, if it has an inelastic demand, a price cut decreases expenditure.

■ More Elasticities of Demand

The **income elasticity of demand** measures the responsiveness of the demand for a good to a change in income, other things remaining the same. The income elasticity of demand is defined as:

$$\frac{\text{(percentage change in the quantity demanded)}}{\text{(percentage change in income)}}$$

When	Demand is
income elasticity > 1	normal good; income elastic
0 < income elasticity < 1	normal good; income inelastic
income elasticity < 0	inferior good

The **cross elasticity of demand** measures the responsiveness of demand for a good to a change in the price of a substitute or complement, other things remaining the same.

The cross elasticity of demand equals:

$$\frac{\text{(percentage change in the quantity demanded)}}{\text{(percentage change in the price of a related good)}}.$$

The sign of the cross elasticity of demand depends on whether the goods are substitutes or complements.

When	Then
the goods are substitutes	cross-elasticity > 0
the goods are complements	cross-elasticity < 0

■ Elasticity of Supply

The **elasticity of supply** measures the responsiveness of the quantity supplied to a change in its price when all other influences on selling plans remain the same.

The elasticity of supply equals:

$$\frac{\text{(percentage change in the quantity supplied)}}{\text{(percentage change in the price)}}$$

The size of the price elasticity of supply depends on:

♦ the ease with which additional resources can be substituted into the production process. The easier the substitution, the larger the elasticity of supply.

♦ the time frame for the supply decision. The *momentary supply* shows the immediate response to a price change. The *short-run supply* shows how the quantity supplied responds to a change in price after some of the possible adjustments have been made. The *long-run supply* shows the response of the quantity supplied to a price change after all possible adjustments have been made.

Helpful Hints

1. **INTUITION BEHIND THE CONCEPT OF ELASTICITY :** Though there are many elasticity formulas in this chapter, *all* of the elasticity formulas measure how strongly a relationship responds to some change. The price elasticity of demand, for instance, indicates how strongly a change in a good's price affects the quantity demanded of the good, while the income elasticity of demand measures how strongly a change in income affects the demand for a good.

2. **WHY ELASTICITIES USE PERCENTAGES :** Percentages are a natural way to determine the importance of a change in price, income, or quantity. For example, which seems larger: a $1 hike in the price of a Big Mac served at the local McDonald's or a $1 increase in the price of the least expensive BMW sold at the nearest BMW dealer? A Big Mac might be about $3, so the $1 rise in the price of the Big Mac is larger because it represents a 33 percent boost. With a BMW selling for around $30,000, a $1 rise in its price is minuscule, a 0.0033 percent rise. Many consumers would respond to a $1 change in the price of a Big Mac; few would to a $1 change in the price of a BMW. Thus a good measure of the size of a price change is the percentage change.

3. **HOW TO RECALL THE ELASTICITY FORMULA :** Whether the percentage change in the quantity demanded or the percentage change in the price goes in the numerator for the price elasticity of demand is easy to forget. If you think of a kewpie doll, the sort of doll that is given away at carnivals for a display of an otherwise fairly useless talent, you should be able to keep the formula straight. The word kewpie is pronounced *q-p*, thereby telling us that "*q*" goes first (in the numerator) and that "*p*" goes second (in the denominator).

4. **PRICE ELASTICITY AND TOTAL REVENUE :** Total revenue equals price multiplied by quantity. To see why the price elasticity of demand tells how a price change affects total revenue, think about a price hike. A price rise has two separate effects on total revenue. First, a higher price directly raises total revenue. Second, consumers respond to the higher price by decreasing the quantity they demand. The decrease in the quantity reduces total revenue. Which effect is larger? That depends on the price elasticity of demand. If demand is elastic, the percentage decrease in the quantity demanded exceeds the percentage rise in price so the effect from the decreased quantity exceeds the impact from the higher price. Total revenue falls. But if demand is inelastic, the higher price dominates the decreased quantity and total revenue rises. Finally, if demand is unit elastic, the percentage decrease in the quantity demanded equals the percentage rise in price so the two effects offset each other, with no change in total revenue.

5. **WHY ONLY THE PRICE ELASTICITY OF DEMAND USES THE MAGNITUDE OF THE PERCENTAGE CHANGES :** The price elasticity of demand uses the *magnitude* of the percentage change in quantity demanded divided by the percentage change in price. However, neither the income elasticity nor the cross elasticity use the magnitude. Why the difference? Because the sign of the last two elasticities is important. The price elasticity of demand would *always* be negative so using its magnitude simply eliminates a potentially confusing negative sign. The income elasticity, however, can be either negative or positive. A negative income elasticity indicates that the good is an inferior good and a positive income elasticity signifies that the good is a normal good. The sign of the cross elasticity also is important. A negative cross elasticity shows that the two goods are complements and a positive cross elasticity means that the two goods are substitutes. Because the signs of the income elasticity and cross elasticity tell us something, we retain the signs rather than discard them.

Questions

■ True/False and Explain

Price Elasticity of Demand

1. The price elasticity of demand is the same as the slope of the demand curve.

2. The price elasticity of demand ranges from 0 to ∞.

3. The more demanders respond to a price change, the larger the price elasticity of demand.

4. If the price elasticity of demand is positive, the demand is elastic.

5. Exxon brand gasoline is likely to have an elastic demand.

6. People spend more on rent than on soap, so the price elasticity of demand for housing is likely to be larger than the price elasticity of demand for soap.

7. The price elasticity of demand for food is largest in poor nations.

8. As time passes after a price change, the price elasticity of demand becomes smaller.

9. Moving along a linear demand curve to lower prices and increased quantities, the price elasticity of demand does not change.

10. Your local Domino's Pizza outlet estimates that the price elasticity of demand for its pizzas is 4.00, so if it raises the price it charges for its pizza, its total revenue will increase.

More Elasticities of Demand

11. A good has an elastic demand if its income elasticity of demand exceeds 1.0.

12. An inferior good has an income elasticity that is negative; a normal good has an income elasticity that is positive.

13. The cross elasticity of demand between hot dogs and hot dog buns is negative.

Elasticity of Supply

14. The elasticity of supply equals the change in the quantity supplied divided by the change in price.

15. If a good has a vertical supply curve, its elasticity of supply equals 0.

■ Multiple Choice

Price Elasticity of Demand

1. A 10 percent hike in the price of a textbook decreases the quantity demanded by 2 percent. The price elasticity of demand for textbooks is
   a. 0.2.
   b. 2.0.
   c. 5.0.
   d. 10.0.

TABLE **4.1**

Multiple Choice Question 2

Price per volleyball (dollars)	Quantity demanded (volleyballs per year)
19	55
21	45

2. Two points on the demand curve for volleyballs are shown in Table 4.1. What is the price elasticity of demand between these two points?
   a. 2.5.
   b. 2.0.
   c. 0.5.
   d. 0.4.

3. The quantity of new cars increases by 5 percent. If the price elasticity of demand for new cars is 1.25, the price of a new car will
   a. fall by 4 percent.
   b. fall by 5 percent.
   c. fall by 6.25 percent.
   d. fall by 1.25 percent.

4. Business people often speak about price elasticity without actually using the term. Which statement describes a good with an elastic demand?
   a. "A price cut won't help me. It won't increase my sales, and I'll just get less money for each unit."
   b. "I don't think a price cut will help my bottom line any. Sure, I'll sell a bit more, but I'll more than lose because the price will be lower."
   c. "My customers are real shoppers. After I cut my prices just a few cents below those my competitors charge, customers have been flocking to my store and sales are booming."
   d. "The economic expansion has done wonders for my sales. With more people back at work, my sales are taking off!"

5. For a perfectly vertical demand curve, the price elasticity of demand
   a. equals 0.
   b. is greater than 0 but less than 1.0.
   c. equals 1.0.
   d. is negative.

6. If the demand for a good is perfectly elastic, then its demand curve
   a. is vertical.
   b. is horizontal.
   c. has a 45° slope.
   d. is a rectangular hyperbola.

7. The demand for a good is more price inelastic if
   a. its price is higher.
   b. the percentage of income spent on it is larger.
   c. it is a luxury good.
   d. it has no close substitutes.

8. Which of the following is likely to have the largest price elasticity of demand?
   a. An automobile
   b. A new automobile
   c. A new Ford automobile
   d. A new Ford Mustang

9. Moving up along a linear demand curve past the midpoint, the demand becomes
   a. inelastic.
   b. unit elastic.
   c. elastic.
   d. first elastic and then inelastic.

10. If the price elasticity of demand equals 1.0, then as the price falls the
    a. quantity demanded decreases.
    b. total revenue falls.
    c. quantity demanded does not change.
    d. total revenue does not change.

11. A rise in the price of a good increases the total revenue from the good if the
    a. income elasticity of demand exceeds 1.
    b. good is an inferior good.
    c. good has an inelastic demand.
    d. good has an elastic demand.

12. By reviewing its sales records, Dell's economists discover that when it lowers the price of its personal computers, the total revenue Dell obtains from the sale of its personal computers rises. Hence Dell's economists know that the
    a. supply of Dell personal computers is elastic.
    b. demand for Dell personal computers is elastic.
    c. supply of Dell personal computers is inelastic.
    d. demand for Dell personal computers is inelastic.

13. If a 4 percent rise in the price of peanut butter causes total revenue from sales of peanut butter to fall by 8 percent, then the demand for peanut butter is
    a. elastic.
    b. inelastic.
    c. unit elastic.
    d. There is not enough information given to determine whether the demand for peanut butter is elastic, unit elastic, or inelastic.

14. When the price of a hot dog rises 10 percent, your expenditure on hot dogs increases. Hence, it is certain that
    a. hot dogs are a normal good for you.
    b. hot dogs are an inferior good for you.
    c. your demand for hot dogs is elastic.
    d. your demand for hot dogs is inelastic.

More Elasticities of Demand

15. Suppose that the *income* elasticity of demand for apartments is –0.2. This value indicates that
    a. the demand for apartments is price inelastic.
    b. the demand for apartments is unit elastic.
    c. a rise in the rent for apartments lowers the total revenue from renting apartments.
    d. apartments are an inferior good.

16. Beans are an inferior good; chicken is a normal good. When people's incomes rise, the demand for beans _____ and the demand for chicken _____.
    a. increases; increases
    b. increases; decreases
    c. decreases; increases
    d. decreases; decreases

17. A 10 percent hike in income increases the demand for coffee by 3 percent. Then the income elasticity of demand for coffee is
    a. –0.3.
    b. 3.3.
    c. 0.3.
    d. 10.0

18. *All* normal goods have
    a. income elasticities of demand greater than 1.0.
    b. price elasticities of demand greater than 1.0.
    c. negative price elasticities of demand.
    d. positive income elasticities of demand.

19. For which of the following pairs of goods is the cross elasticity of demand positive?
    a. Tennis balls and tennis rackets
    b. Videotapes and laundry detergent
    c. Airline trips and textbooks
    d. Beef and chicken

20. A 10 percent increase in the price of a Pepsi increases the demand for a Coca Cola by 50 percent. Thus the cross elasticity of demand between Pepsi and Coca Cola is
    a. 50.0.
    b. 10.0.
    c. 5.0.
    d. 0.2.

21. A fall in the price of a paperback book from $6 to $4 causes a decrease in the quantity of magazines demanded from 1,100 to 900. What is the cross elasticity of demand between paperback books and magazines?
    a. 0.5
    b. –0.5
    c. 2.0
    d. Without information about what was the change in income, it is not possible to calculate the cross elasticity of demand.

Elasticity of Supply

22. Suppose that the price elasticity of supply for oil is 0.1. Then, if the price of oil rises by 20 percent, the quantity of oil supplied will increase
    a. by 200 percent.
    b. by 20 percent.
    c. by 2 percent.
    d. by 0.2 percent.

23. When the price of a CD is $13 per CD, 39,000,000 CDs per year are supplied. When the price is $15 per CD, 41,000,000 CDs per year are supplied. What is the elasticity of supply for CDs?
    a. 2.86
    b. 0.35
    c. 0.14
    d. 0.05

24. If the long-run supply of rice is perfectly elastic, then
    a. as people's incomes rise, the quantity of rice supplied decreases.
    b. as the price of *corn* falls, the quantity of *rice* demanded decreases.
    c. in the long run, a large rise in the price of rice causes no change in the quantity of rice supplied.
    d. in the long run, an increase in the demand for rice leaves the price of rice unchanged.

25. The elasticity of supply does <u>NOT</u> depend on
    a. resource substitution possibilities.
    b. the fraction of income spent on the good.
    c. the time elapsed since the price change.
    d. None of the above because all of the factors listed affect the elasticity of supply.

■ Short Answer Problems

1. Assume that the price elasticity of demand for oil is 0.2 in the short run and 0.8 in the long run. To raise the price of oil by 10 percent in the short run, what must be the decrease in the quantity of oil? In the long run, to have a 10 percent rise in the price of oil, what must be the decrease?

FIGURE **4.1**

Short Answer Problem 2

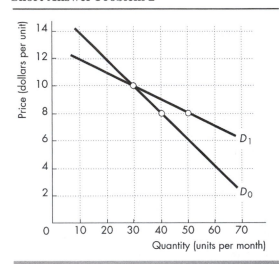

2. In Figure 4.1 which demand is more elastic between prices $10 and $8?

3. Why is the price elasticity of demand for food larger in poor nations than in rich nations?

4. Explain what perfectly elastic demand means. Sketch an example of a demand curve for a good with perfectly elastic demand. When will perfectly elastic demand occur? Be sure to use the notion of substitutes in your answer.

5. The supply curve for blank DVDs is illustrated in Figure 4.2. Perhaps because of a rise in wages, the supply of blank DVDs decreases so that for every possible quantity, the new supply curve lies above the old supply curve by $5.

   a. Suppose the demand for blank DVDs is perfectly elastic and is such that the initial equilibrium price is $2 for a DVD. After the decrease in supply, by how much does the price of a DVD rise? Draw a figure to illustrate your answer.

   b. Suppose the demand for DVDs is perfectly inelastic and is such that the initial equilibrium

FIGURE **4.2**

Short Answer Problem 5

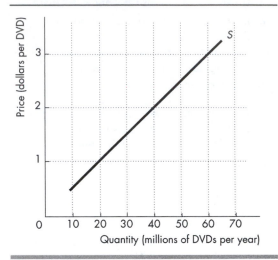

   price of a DVD is $2. In this case, by how much does the price of a DVD rise? Draw a figure to illustrate this situation.

   c. Based on your answers to parts (a) and (b), when will an increase in cost raise the price of a good or service the most: When demand is elastic or when it is inelastic? When will it decrease the quantity the most? When demand is elastic or inelastic? Is there any situation under which the price does not change?

TABLE **4.2**

The Demand for Burritos

Price (dollars per burrito)	Quantity demanded (burritos per week)	Total revenue per week (dollars)
$8	30	_____
7	40	_____
6	50	_____
5	60	_____
4	70	_____
3	80	_____
2	90	_____
I	100	_____

6. Table 4.2 gives eight points on a demand curve for burritos.

   a. Graph this demand curve.

   b. Calculate the price elasticity of demand between

$1 and $2; $2 and $3; $3 and $4; $4 and $5; $5 and $6; $6 and $7; and $7 and $8.

c. In Table 4.2, complete the last column.

d. Based on your answer to part (b), how does the price elasticity of demand change for a movement downward along this demand curve? How does this change relate to your answers in part (c) for total revenue at the different prices?

TABLE **4.3**

The Demand For Pizza

Price (dollars per slice of pizza)	Quantity demanded (slices of pizza per week)	Total revenue per week (dollars)
$8	12.5	_____
7	14.3	_____
6	16.7	_____
5	20.0	_____
4	25.0	_____
3	33.3	_____
2	50.0	_____
1	100.0	_____

---

7. Table 4.3 gives eight points on a demand curve for slices of pizza.

a. Graph the demand curve.

b. Calculate the price elasticity of demand between $1 and $2; $2 and $3; $3 and $4; $4 and $5; $5 and $6; $6 and $7; and $7 and $8.

c. Complete the last column in Table 4.3.

d. Based on your answers to parts (b) and (c), how does the total revenue per week relate to the price elasticity of demand at the different prices?

8. You are the manager of a local restaurant. You notice that when you lower the price of your meals, your total revenue rises. What conclusion can you draw about the demand for your restaurant's meals?

9. Why does the elasticity of supply of automobiles generally increase as more time passes after a price change?

10. The demand for a peanut butter permanently increases. Suppose that the long-run supply is more elastic than the short-run supply. When will the price of peanut butter rise the most? Immediately after the demand change or in the long run? When will the quantity increase the most? Draw a graph to illustrate your answers.

■ **You're the Teacher**

1. "How can I use the price elasticity of demand formula to calculate the price elasticity of demand? Also how can I determine how much a decrease in quantity boosts the price or how much a price change affects the quantity demanded?" Your classmate is having trouble with some algebra. Once more, help out your friend by demonstrating how to use the formula for price elasticity to answer the questions.

2. "The whole idea of 'elasticity' is unnecessarily complicated! Take the price elasticity of demand; it tries to measure how strongly demanders respond to a price change. But the slope of the demand curve shows us that. The flatter the demand curve, the more consumers react to a price change. Clearly, economists should just use the slope of the demand curve as their measure of 'elasticity'. I don't know why they bother to use percentages except to make this idea hard!" Economists enjoy simple things as much as anyone, so they surely do not use percentages to make elasticity difficult to understand. Thus the speaker is making an error; correct the error in the analysis.

Answers

■ True/False Answers

Price Elasticity of Demand

1. **F** The slope of the demand curve equals $\Delta P/\Delta Q$, whereas the price elasticity of demand equals $(\Delta Q/Q_{ave})/(\Delta P/P_{ave})$.

2. **T** The smallest value for the price elasticity of demand, 0, means demand is perfectly inelastic; the largest, ∞, indicates perfectly elastic demand.

3. **T** The stronger the response to a price change, the larger is the elasticity.

4. **F** Demand is elastic when the price elasticity of demand exceeds 1.0.

5. **T** Other brands of gasoline, such as Shell or BP, are close substitutes for Exxon, so the demand for Exxon gasoline is likely to be elastic.

6. **T** Generally, the larger the total budget share spent on a good, the larger is the price elasticity of demand.

7. **T** The price elasticity of demand for food in poor nations is larger than that in rich nations because in poor nations, food takes a larger portion of consumer's incomes.

8. **F** As more time passes, more changes in demand can occur, so demand becomes *more* elastic.

9. **F** Moving downward along a linear demand curve, the price elasticity of demand falls.

10. **F** The demand for Domino's Pizza is elastic. Raising the price decreases the quantity by so much that total revenue declines.

More Elasticities of Demand

11. **F** To be elastic, the *price* elasticity of demand must exceed 1.0.

12. **T** An increase in income decreases the demand for inferior goods and increases it for normal goods.

13. **T** Hot dogs and hot dog buns are complements, so the cross elasticity of demand is negative.

Elasticity of Supply

14. **F** The price elasticity of supply equals the *percentage* change in the quantity supplied divided by the *percentage* change in price.

15. **T** When the elasticity of supply equals zero, the supply is perfectly inelastic.

■ Multiple Choice Answers

Price Elasticity of Demand

1. **a** The price elasticity of demand is equal to (2 percent)/(10 percent) = 0.2.

2. **b** The price elasticity of demand between two points equals $[(\Delta Q/Q_{ave}) \times 100] / [(\Delta P/P_{ave}) \times 100]$. In this case the elasticity of demand is 2.

3. **a** Rearranging the formula for the price elasticity of demand gives (percentage change in price) = (percentage change in quantity demanded)/(elasticity of demand). So, the percentage change in price equals (5 percent)/(1.25) = 4 percent.

4. **c** When a small cut in price increases the quantity demanded substantially, the demand is elastic.

5. **a** When a good has a perfectly inelastic demand, the price elasticity of demand equals zero and the demand curve is vertical.

6. **b** When demand is perfectly elastic, a very small rise in the price decreases the quantity demanded to 0, which is the situation with a horizontal demand curve.

7. **d** If there are no close substitutes, demanders continue to buy the good even if its price is boosted substantially, which means that the demand is inelastic.

8. **d** There are many more substitutes for a new Ford Mustang than for the other goods. The more narrowly defined a good, the larger is its price elasticity of demand.

9. **c** Above the midpoint of a linear demand curve, the price elasticity of demand is elastic.

10. **d** If demand is unit price elastic, a change in the price of the good creates an offsetting change in the quantity demanded so that total revenue does not change.

11. **c** If the demand is inelastic, the percentage rise in price exceeds the percentage decrease in the quantity demanded, so total revenue from sales of the good increases.

12. **b** When the demand is elastic, the percentage increase in the quantity demanded exceeds the percentage fall in the price, so total revenue rises.

13. **a** When demand is elastic, a rise in the price of the good decreases the quantity demanded by proportionally more, so that total revenue falls when the price is boosted.

14. **d** When an increase in the price of a good increases your expenditure on the good, your demand for the good is inelastic.

More Elasticities of Demand

15. **d** If the income elasticity is negative, the good is an inferior good.

16. **c** For an inferior good an increase in income decreases demand; for a normal good an increase in income increases demand.

17. **c** The income elasticity of demand in this case equals (3 percent)/(10 percent) or 0.3.

18. **d** An increase in income increases the demand for a normal good.

19. **d** The cross elasticity of demand is positive for substitutes. Beef and chicken are substitutes, so their cross elasticity of demand is positive.

20. **c** The cross elasticity of demand equals the percentage change in the quantity of Coca Cola divided by the percentage change in the price of a Pepsi. Hence the cross elasticity of demand equals (50 percent)/(10 percent) = 5.0.

21. **a** The cross elasticity of demand is calculated as $[(\Delta Q/Q_{ave}) \times 100] / [(\Delta P/P_{ave}) \times 100]$, in which the quantity refers to magazines and the price to paperback books. Using the formula gives $[(-200/1{,}000) \times 100] / [(-\$2/\$5) \times 100] = 0.5$.

Elasticity of Supply

22. **c** Rearranging the formula for the price elasticity of supply gives (percentage change in quantity supplied) = (price elasticity of supply) × (percentage change in price) = (0.1) × (20 percent) = 2 percent.

23. **b** The elasticity of supply is $[(\Delta Q/Q_{ave}) \times 100] / [(\Delta P/P_{ave}) \times 100]$, or $[(2{,}000{,}000/40{,}000{,}000) \times 100] / [(\$2/\$14) \times 100] = 0.35$.

24. **d** When the supply is perfectly elastic, an increase in demand has no effect on the equilibrium price. This result is illustrated in Figure 4.3, in which the increase in demand from D_0 to D_1 leaves the price constant at $50 a ton.

25. **b** The proportion of income spent on the good affects the price elasticity of demand, *not* the price elasticity of supply.

FIGURE **4.3**

Multiple Choice Question 24

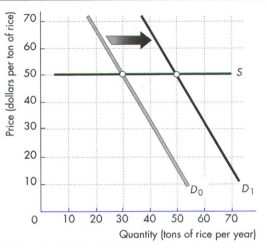

■ Answers to Short Answer Problems

1. Rearranging the formula for the price elasticity of demand gives (price elasticity of demand) × (percentage change in price) = (percentage change in quantity). The price rise is 10 percent, so the amount by which the quantity must be restricted in the short run is (0.2) × (10 percent) = 2 percent.

   In the long run, the price elasticity of demand is 0.8, so the decrease in the quantity is (0.8) × (10 percent) = 8 percent. To raise the price by 10 percent, the long-run decrease in the quantity must be four times the short-run decrease.

2. The demand represented by D_1 is more elastic than the demand given by D_0. To see why, recall the formula for the price elasticity of demand

   $$\frac{\text{(percentage change in quantity demanded)}}{\text{(percentage change in price)}}$$

   Along both demand curves, the percentage change in the price from $10 to $8 is the same. But Figure 4.4 (on the next page) shows that the percentage change in the quantity demanded is greater along D_1 where the quantity demanded increases from 30 to 50, a 50 percent increase, then along D_0 where the quantity demanded increases to 40, only a 29 percent increase. Because the percentage increase in the quantity demanded is greater along D_1, the price elasticity of demand over this price range is larger for demand D_1.

FIGURE **4.4**

Short Answer Problem 2

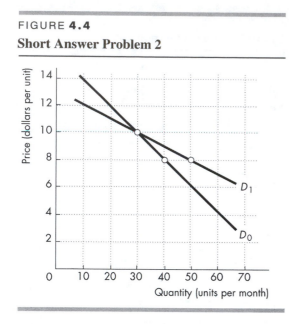

3. The larger the fraction of their income that consumers spend on a good, the greater the price elasticity of demand. People in poor nations spend a larger proportion of their income on food than do people in wealthy nations, so the price elasticity of demand for food is larger in poor nations.

FIGURE **4.5**

Short Answer Problem 4

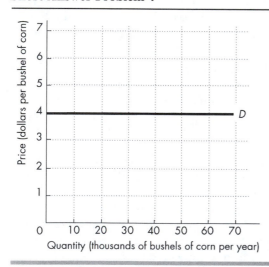

4. A perfectly elastic demand is illustrated in Figure 4.5. Demand is perfectly elastic when demanders can find perfect substitutes for a good. For example,

consider corn grown by one farmer. Other farmers' corn is a perfect substitute for the first farmer's corn. If there are perfect substitutes for the good, even the smallest rise in the price of the good leads the quantity demanded to decrease to 0. The horizontal demand curve in Figure 4.5 indicates that any rise in the price above $4 a bushel will decrease the quantity demanded to 0.

FIGURE **4.6**

Short Answer Problem 5 (a)

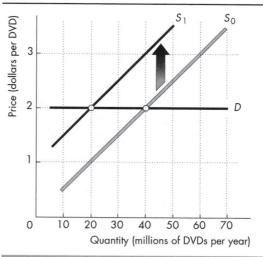
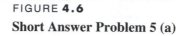

5. a. In Figure 4.6 the rise in costs shifts the supply curve from S_0 to S_1. The arrow indicates $1, the amount by which the new supply curve lies above the old supply curve. The price stays at $2 per DVD; in other words, the price does not rise. The quantity, however decreases from 40 million DVDs to 20 million DVDs per year.

   b. In Figure 4.7 (on the next page), the supply curve again shifts from S_0 to S_1 and the length of the arrow again indicates $1. In this case, when the demand is perfectly inelastic, the price rises by the full amount indicated by the arrow; that is, the price climbs from $2 to $3 per DVD, which is a rise of exactly $1. The quantity, however, remains constant at 40 million DVDs.

   c. As Figures 4.6 and 4.7 show, the rise in costs increases the price the most when demand is inelastic. When demand is perfectly inelastic, the price goes up by the full amount of the rise in costs. Then, as demand becomes more elastic, the price rises by less. At the other extreme,

FIGURE **4.7**

Short Answer Problem 5 (b)

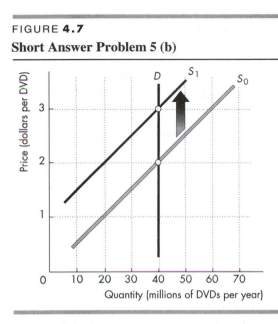

Quantity (millions of DVDs per year)

when demand is perfectly elastic, the price does not change.

The quantity decreases most when demand is perfectly elastic. As demand becomes less elastic, the change in the quantity becomes smaller.

FIGURE **4.8**

Short Answer Problem 6 (a)

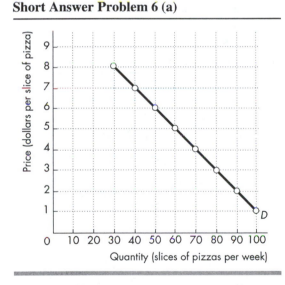

Quantity (slices of pizzas per week)

6. a. Figure 4.8 shows the demand curve.

b. Table 4.4 contains the price elasticities of demand. To see how these elasticities are calculated, take the elasticity between $1 and $2 as an example. The elasticity of demand is defined as

TABLE **4.4**

Short Answer Problem 6 (b)

Prices	Elasticity
$7 to $8	2.14
6 to 7	1.44
5 to 6	1.00
4 to 5	0.69
3 to 4	0.47
2 to 3	0.29
1 to 2	0.16

TABLE **4.5**

Short Answer Problem 6 (c)

Price	Total Revenue
$8	$240
7	280
6	300
5	300
4	280
3	240
2	180
1	100

$[(\Delta Q/Q_{ave}) \times 100] / [(\Delta P/P_{ave}) \times 100]$, which is $[(10/95) \times 100] / [($1/$1.50) \times 100] = 0.16$.

c. The total revenues are given in Table 4.5. Total revenue equals $(P \times Q)$, so at a price of $6, ($6 \times 50) = 300.

d. Moving along the *linear* demand curve from $8 to $1 results in the elasticity falling, from 2.14 when the price is between $8 and $7, to 0.16 when the price is between $2 and $1. When demand is elastic, at prices above the midpoint, a fall in price (with its corresponding increase in sales) raises total revenue. When demand is unit elastic, at the midpoint of $5.50, total revenue is at its maximum and a fall in price (with the increase in sales) does not change the total revenue. Finally, at prices less than the midpoint, the range over which the demand is inelastic, even though a fall in price raises the quantity sold, it does so by a smaller percentage so that the price cut lowers total revenue.

FIGURE **4.9**

Short Answer Problem 7 (a)

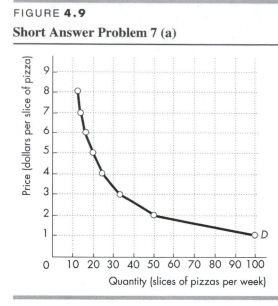

7. a. Figure 4.9 illustrates the demand curve.
    b. Table 4.6 contains the price elasticities of de-
       mand. For example, at a price between $4 and
       $5, the price elasticity of demand equals
       $[(\Delta Q/Q_{ave}) \times 100] / [(\Delta P/P_{ave}) \times 100] =$
       $[(5/22.5) \times 100] / [(\$1/\$4.50) \times 100] = 1.00.$
    c. The total revenues are in Table 4.7. Total reve-
       nue equals $(P \times Q)$. To calculate the total reve-
       nue at a price of, say, $2, multiply the price by
       the quantity, or $(\$2 \times 50) = \$100$.
    d. The price elasticity of demand along this de-
       mand curve always equals 1.00. In other words,
       this demand is always unit elastic. With unit
       elasticity, changes in price do not change total
       revenue, which is precisely what Table 4.7 illus-
       trates.

TABLE **4.6**

Short Answer Problem 7 (b)

Prices	Elasticity
$7 to $8	1.00
6 to 7	1.00
5 to 6	1.00
4 to 5	1.00
3 to 4	1.00
2 to 3	1.00
1 to 2	1.00

TABLE **4.7**

Short Answer Problem 7 (c)

Price	Total Revenue
$8	$100
7	100
6	100
5	100
4	100
3	100
2	100
1	100

8. The demand for the meals is elastic. Why? When
   the demand is elastic, a fall in price raises total revenue, which is precisely what you have observed.
9. The elasticity of supply increases as time passes after
   a price change because making changes in the production process becomes easier. For instance, to
   meet a permanent increase in the demand for automobiles, initially automakers might only be able
   to add an additional shift of workers at existing factories. But with the passage of time, the companies
   can make larger changes, such as building more factories. As more capacity is added, more cars will be
   manufactured, increasing the elasticity of supply.

FIGURE **4.10**

Short Answer Problem 10

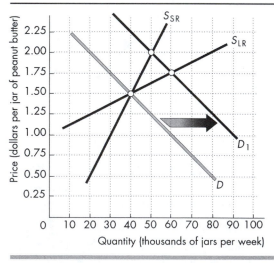

10. The price of peanut butter rises the most immedi-
    ately after the increase in demand and the quantity

increases the most in the long run. These results are illustrated in Figure 4.10. Here the short-run supply curve is labeled S_{SR} and the long-run supply curve is labeled S_{LR}. Demand increases from D to D_1. Immediately after the increase, the price rises from $1.50 per jar to $2.00 per jar and the quantity increases from 40,000 jars per week to 50,000 jars per week. In the long run, supply becomes more elastic and so the long run supply curve, S_{LR}, becomes relevant. Hence the price rises ultimately only to $1.75 per jar while the quantity increases all the way to 60,000 jars per week.

■ **You're the Teacher Answers**

1. "This is not so hard if you think about it the right way! The formula is price elasticity of demand =

$$\frac{\text{(percentage change in quantity demanded)}}{\text{(percentage change in price)}}$$

This formula contains three numbers: price elasticity of demand, (percentage change in quantity demanded), and (percentage change in price). Now, just so you can really see these as symbols and numbers, let me call the (percentage change in price) %ΔP and the (percentage change in quantity demanded) %ΔQ. I think that by using these symbols, it makes the formulas even clearer."

"Now, the whole deal is that if you have any two of the numbers, you can solve for the third. For instance, if you have the %ΔQ and %ΔP, you can determine the price elasticity of demand. Similarly, if you know the price elasticity of demand and %ΔQ, you can quickly rearrange the basic elasticity formula to solve for %ΔP, as %ΔP = (%ΔQ) ÷ (Price elasticity of demand). Finally, if you have the price

elasticity of demand and %ΔP, you can calculate (%ΔQ) by rearranging the basic formula to get %ΔQ = (Price elasticity of demand) × (%ΔP). Just plug the numbers into these formulas and that's all there is to it!"

TABLE **4.8**
You're the Teacher Question 2

Price	Quantity	Price	Quantity
$1.00	11	100¢	11
2.00	10	200	10

2. "You're basically right: All elasticity does is measure how strongly a relationship responds to some sort of change. But you're missing an important point about the slope. The slope of, say, the demand curve depends on the units involved and changes when the units used change. For example, two points on a demand curve are presented in different units in Table 4.8. In one case the prices are in dollars and in the other case the prices are in cents. The magnitude of the slope of the demand curve (ΔP/ΔQ) in the first part of the table is 1.00 and in the second part is 100.0. If the measure of elasticity changed every time we changed units, we would have a problem. For instance, we couldn't easily compare, say, the price elasticity of demand for food in Japan, where prices are stated in yen, with that in the United States, where they are stated in dollars. Using percentages, however, avoids this problem. In each of the two columns, the price elasticity of demand is the same: 0.14. That's why percentages are used in the elasticity formulas, not because economists want to make us study more in order to understand elasticity!"

Chapter Quiz

1. On a demand and supply diagram, the total revenue from sales of a good is shown as
   a. a vertical distance.
   b. a horizontal distance.
   c. the area of a triangle.
   d. the area of a rectangle.

2. The fewer substitutes available for a good, the
   a. larger is the income elasticity of demand.
   b. smaller is the income elasticity of demand.
   c. larger is the price elasticity of demand.
   d. smaller is the price elasticity of demand.

3. If the price elasticity of demand exceeds 1.0 but is less than infinity, demand is
   a. inelastic.
   b. unit elastic.
   c. elastic.
   d. perfectly elastic.

4. If the price elasticity of demand is _____, the demand curve is _____
   a. infinity; horizontal
   b. infinity; vertical
   c. one; horizontal
   d. one; vertical

5. A fall in the price of lemons from $10.50 per bushel to $9.50 increases the quantity demanded from 19,200 bushels to 20,800. The price elasticity of demand in this range of the demand is
   a. 0.80.
   b. 1.20.
   c. 1.25.
   d. 8.00.

6. If an increase in the price of corn increases the total expenditure on corn, then it is definitely the case that the
   a. supply of corn is elastic.
   b. supply of corn is inelastic.
   c. demand for corn is elastic.
   d. demand for corn is inelastic.

7. If the demand for a good is price inelastic, but *not* perfectly price inelastic, then a 10 percent decrease in its price causes the quantity demanded to increase by
   a. more than 10 percent.
   b. 10 percent.
   c. less than 10 percent.
   d. 0 percent.

8. If two different goods are complements, their
   a. cross elasticity of demand is negative.
   b. cross elasticity of demand is positive.
   c. income elasticity of demand is negative.
   d. income elasticity of demand is positive.

9. The price elasticity of supply measures
   a. how often the price of the good changes.
   b. the slope of the supply curve.
   c. how sensitive the quantity supplied is to changes in supply.
   d. how sensitive the quantity supplied is to changes in the price.

10. The supply of a good such as fresh fish is usually least elastic in the
    a. momentary period.
    b. short run.
    c. long run.
    d. competitive period.

The answers for this Chapter Quiz are on page 345

5 EFFICIENCY AND EQUITY

Resource Allocation Methods

Resources are scarce so they *must* be allocated to producing different goods. Some methods of resource allocation include:

♦ Market price — people who are willing and able to pay the price get the resource.

♦ Command — a **command system** allocates resources by the order of (command) someone in authority.

♦ Majority rule — the majority vote decides how resources are allocated, for example, what will be the tax rates on income.

♦ Contest — winners receive the resource. Sports are an example, but more generally contests occur when many people are competing to win one big prize, such as being named CEO of a company.

♦ First-come, first-served — people first in line get the resource, be it a table at a restaurant or a space on a highway.

♦ Lottery — the randomly selected winners receive the resource.

♦ Personal characteristics — people with the "right" characteristics get the resource.

♦ Force — the stronger person or group gets the resource. Force includes wars but it also includes the ability of the state to protect voluntary exchange.

Benefit, Cost, and Surplus

Resources are allocated efficiently and in the social interest when they are used in the ways that are most highly valued by people. This outcome occurs when the marginal benefit, the benefit a person receives from consuming one more unit of a good or service, equals the marginal cost, the opportunity cost of producing one more unit of a good or service.

The *value* of one more unit of a good is its marginal benefit. Marginal benefit is measured as the maximum that someone is willing to pay for another unit of the good. The demand curve shows the maximum some-

one is willing to pay for each unit of a good, so the demand curve for a good is its marginal benefit curve.

The relationship between the price and the quantity demanded by one person is the individual demand. The *market demand curve* is the horizontal summation of all the individual demand curves.

The value of a good can be different than the good's price. **Consumer surplus** is the excess of the benefit received from a good over the amount paid for it. Consumer surplus equals the marginal benefit of a good minus its price, summed over the quantity bought.

♦ Because the demand curve shows the marginal benefit, consumer surplus is the area under the demand curve (the benefit) and above the market price. Figure 5.1 shows the consumer surplus for the good. It is the darkened triangle under the market demand curve and above the market price.

FIGURE **5.1**

Consumer Surplus

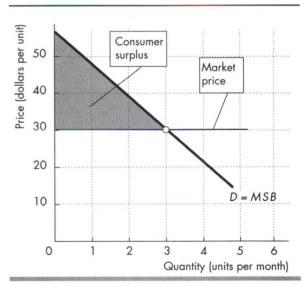

The cost of producing a good is what the producer pays to produce it; the price of a good is what the producer receives when it is sold. The marginal cost of a good is equal to the minimum price a producer must receive to produce the unit of the good because this amount just covers all the costs of producing it. A supply curve shows the minimum price a producer must receive to produce another unit of a good, so the supply curve of a good is its marginal cost curve.

The relationship between the price and the quantity supplied by one producer is the individual supply. The *market supply curve* is the horizontal summation of all the individual supply curves.

If a firm sells a good for more than it costs to produce it, the firm receives a producer surplus. **Producer surplus** is the excess of the amount received from the sale of a good over the cost of producing it.

♦ Because the supply curve is the marginal cost curve, producer surplus equals the area below the market price of the good and above the market supply curve. Figure 5.2 shows a producer surplus.

FIGURE **5.2**
Producer Surplus

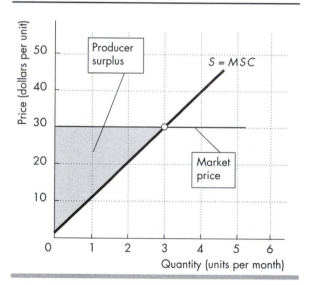
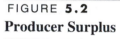

■ Is the Competitive Market Efficient?

♦ If the entire benefit from a good is enjoyed by the buyers, then the marginal benefit to the society, *MSB*, equals the marginal benefit to the consumers and the demand curve is the *MSB* curve.

♦ If the entire cost of producing a good is paid by the producers, then the marginal cost to the society, *MSC*, equals the marginal cost to the producers and the supply curve is the *MSC* curve.

The allocatively efficient amount of a good is produced when the marginal social benefit equals its marginal social cost.

♦ If the marginal social benefit exceeds the marginal social cost, then the benefit of another unit exceeds the cost to produce it, so it is in the social interest to produce the unit.

♦ If the marginal social cost exceeds the marginal social benefit, the benefit of the last unit being produced is less than the cost of producing it, so it is in the social interest that the unit not be produced.

FIGURE **5.3**
Efficiency of Perfect Competition

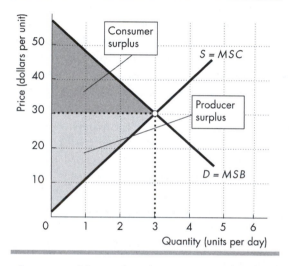

♦ In a competitive market, the quantity produced is the equilibrium quantity. In Figure 5.3, the equilibrium quantity is 30 units, determined by the *D* and *S* curves.

♦ The efficient quantity sets the marginal social benefit equal to the marginal social cost, *MSB* = *MSC*. In Figure 5.3, the efficient quantity is 30 units, determined by the *MSB* and *MSC* curves. A competitive market is efficient because the quantity produced is the same as the efficient quantity.

♦ When the market is using resources efficiently, the **total surplus**—the sum of consumer surplus plus producer surplus—is as large as possible, as illustrated in Figure 5.3.

♦ Adam Smith's idea of the invisible hand concludes that competitive markets send resources to their highest-valued use, that is, competitive markets are efficient.

FIGURE **5.4**
Deadweight Loss

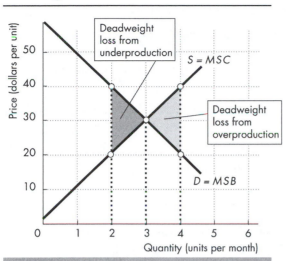

Contrary to the invisible hand idea, markets are not always efficient. **Market failure** occurs when a market delivers an inefficient outcome. When a market under-produces or overproduces a good, a deadweight loss is created. **Deadweight loss** is decrease in the total sur-plus that results from an inefficient level of production.

♦ The deadweight loss is inflicted on the entire society; it is not something that the producer gains at the expense of the consumer or vice versa.

♦ Figure 5.4 illustrates the deadweight loss triangles from overproduction (producing 4 units rather than 3) and underproduction (producing 2 units rather than 3).

The major obstacles that can lead to market failure and inefficiency are:

♦ *Price and quantity regulations* — price regulations that set the highest legal price or the lowest legal price sometimes block price adjustments and pre-vent the market from reaching its (efficient) equilib-rium. Quantity regulations also can prevent the market from reaching its unregulated equilibrium.

♦ *Taxes and subsidies* — taxes increase the price paid by buyers and lower the price received by sellers; subsidies decrease the price paid by buyers and raise the price received by sellers. Taxes lead to under-production; subsidies lead to overproduction.

♦ *Externalities*— an externality is a cost or benefit that affects someone other than the seller or buyer of the good. In these cases the participants do not consider

all the costs or benefits *to others* of their actions. Ex-ternal costs lead to overproduction; external benefits lead to underproduction.

♦ *Public goods and common resources* — a public good is a good or service that is consumed simultaneously by everyone regardless of whether they paid for it. Public goods create a free rider problem, in which people are unwilling to pay for the good. A com-mon resource is a resource that no one owns but everyone can use, such as fish in the ocean. Com-mon resources are over-used.

♦ *Monopoly* — a monopoly is a single firm that con-trols the entire market. A monopoly underproduces because it decreases its production in order to raise the price and increase its profit.

♦ *High transactions costs* — the opportunity cost of bringing buyers and sellers together in a market are **transactions costs**. Transactions costs can make some markets too costly to operate.

Competitive markets can be efficient. When a market is inefficient, one of the alternative non-market methods described in the first section might do a better job of allocating resources.

■ Is the Competitive Market Fair?

While there is general agreement about what consti-tutes efficiency, there is not the same general agreement about fairness. The two approaches to fairness are "It's not fair if the result isn't fair" and "It's not fair if the rules aren't fair."

♦ **Utilitarianism** — aims for "the greatest happiness for the greatest number of people." Utilitarianism looks at the results of the process so redistribution of income can lead to fairness. Redistribution to achieve equality in incomes (the "fair" outcome) leads to the **big tradeoff**, the tradeoff between effi-ciency and fairness. Redistribution weakens the in-centive to work so that a more equal income distribution leads to inefficiency.

♦ **Symmetry Principle** — the requirement that sim-ilar people should be treated similarly. The sym-metry principle looks at the rules of the process and judges fairness on the basis of rules. If a mar-ket is efficient (there are no price and quantity reg-ulations, taxes or subsidies, externalities, public goods and common resources, monopolies, and transac-tions costs are not too high), then a competitive market is fair according to the symmetry principle.

Helpful Hints

1. **MARGINAL BENEFIT AND MARGINAL COST :** In casual conversation we talk about "how much a good cost us" or "how much a firm benefited by selling us the good." But be careful not to confuse conversation with the precise language of economic science. In particular, the marginal benefit from a good is received by the consumer and the marginal cost is paid by the producer. It is that the consumer of the good who benefits from the good. You, when you drive your car, benefit from your car. It is the producer of the good who pays for the production. The firm that manufactured your car paid the steel mill for the steel used to produce it.

FIGURE **5.5**

Efficiency and *MSB = MSC*

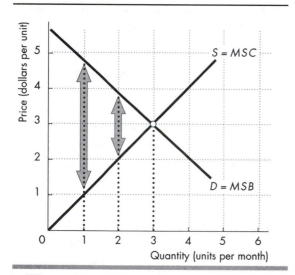

2. **WHY *MSB = MSC* IS EFFICIENT :** Why does producing where *MSB = MSC* lead to efficiency? If *MSB > MSC*, society's total surplus increases if the unit is produced. For instance, in Figure 5.5 the first unit has a large difference between *MSB* and *MSC*, shown by the long arrow. The second unit also has *MSB* greater than *MSC* but by less than the first unit. However, producing this unit still adds to society's *total* net surplus; it just adds less than the first unit. As long as *MSB* exceeds *MSC* total surplus increases if the unit is produced. By producing at the point where *MSB = MSC, all* the units that have a total surplus to society are produced and *none* of the units that impose a loss on society, units for which *MSB < MSC*, are produced.

Questions

■ True/False and Explain

Resource Allocation Methods

1. When market prices are used to allocate resources, only the people who are able and willing to pay get the resources.

2. A boss telling a worker what to do is an example of a command system of allocating resources.

3. In the U.S. economy, resources are never allocated according to random chance.

4. Force is used as an allocation method force only for illegal activities, such as theft or robbery.

Benefit, Cost, and Surplus

5. Allocative efficiency occurs when resources are used to produce the goods and services that people value most highly.

6. The price of a good or service always equals its value.

7. The market demand curve for tacos shows the maximum price a consumer is willing to pay for the ten millionth taco.

8. As more of a good or service is consumed, its marginal benefit decreases.

9. Consumer surplus equals the area above the market demand curve and below the market price.

10. Cost and price are the same thing.

11. The marginal cost of the one millionth pizza is another name for the total cost of producing all one million pizzas.

12. The market supply curve and the marginal social benefit curve are the same.

13. Producer surplus equals the price of a good minus the cost of producing it summed over the quantity sold.

Is the Competitive Market Efficient?

14. If the marginal social benefit from a good exceeds its marginal social cost, resources are used more efficiently if less of the good is produced.

15. Allocative efficiency requires that the marginal social benefit of a good equal its marginal social cost.

16. A competitive market is always efficient.

17. When producing the efficient quantity of a good, the sum of consumer surplus plus producer surplus is as large as possible.

18. Deadweight loss is comprised of a loss of consumer surplus and/or producer surplus.

Is the Competitive Market Fair?

19. Utilitarianism says that a competitive market producing the efficient quantity is always fair.

20. The idea of making the poorest as well off as possible uses the "results" to judge fairness.

21. The symmetry principle states that people should have identical incomes, that is, "symmetric" incomes.

■ Multiple Choice

Resource Allocation Methods

1. Allocating resources by the order of someone in authority is a _____ allocation method.
   a. first-come, first-served
   b. market price
   c. majority rule
   d. command

2. Often people trying to withdraw money from their bank must wait in line, which reflects a _____ allocation method.
   a. first-come, first-served
   b. market price
   c. contest
   d. command

3. If a person will rent an apartment only to married couples over 30 years old, that person is allocating resources using a _____ allocation method.
   a. first-come, first-served
   b. market price
   c. personal characteristics
   d. command

Benefit, Cost, and Surplus

4. Allocative efficiency occurs when
   a. the *MSB* of the good is zero.
   b. the *MSB* from a good exceeds its *MSC* by as much as possible.
   c. resources are used in the ways that people value most highly.
   d. the *MSC* of a good is set equal to zero.

5. Which of the following statements is <u>TRUE</u>?
   a. The value of one more unit of a good is not the same as the good's marginal benefit.
   b. A good's marginal benefit is the maximum price someone is willing to pay for another unit.
   c. The maximum price someone is willing to pay for one more unit of a good equals its consumer surplus.
   d. None of the above are correct because all the statements are false.

6. The marginal social benefit curve for a good is the same as the good's
   a. marginal social cost curve.
   b. market supply curve.
   c. market demand curve.
   d. consumer surplus curve.

7. Susan is willing to pay $5.00 for the second slice of pizza she eats. The price she actually pays is $4.00. Susan's consumer surplus for *this slice* of pizza is
   a. $5.00.
   b. $4.00.
   c. $2.00.
   d. $1.00.

8. Because of decreasing marginal benefit, the consumer surplus from the first unit of a good is _____ the consumer surplus from the second unit.
   a. greater than
   b. equal to
   c. less than
   d. not comparable to

9. The cost of producing one more unit of a good is that good's
   a. price.
   b. marginal benefit.
   c. marginal cost.
   d. producer surplus.

10. The market supply curve shows the
    a. minimum price suppliers must receive in order to produce another unit of the good.
    b. maximum price suppliers must receive in order to produce another unit of the good.
    c. amount of producer surplus suppliers receive.
    d. profit that suppliers receive from producing another unit of the good.

11. The producer surplus from computers is equal to the
   a. maximum amount a consumer is willing to pay for the computer minus the price that actually must be paid summed over the quantity sold.
   b. actual price of the computer minus the maximum amount a consumer is willing to pay for it.
   c. cost of producing the computer minus the its price summed over the quantity sold.
   d. computer's price minus the cost of producing it summed over the quantity sold..

Is the Competitive Market Efficient?

Figure 5.6 illustrates the perfectly competitive market for shirts. There are no externalities, taxes, subsidies, price or quantity regulations, or high transactions costs. Use Figure 5.6 for the next two questions.

FIGURE **5.6**

Multiple Choice Questions 12 and 13

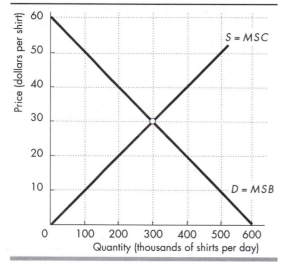

12. The equilibrium quantity of shirts equals ____ per day.
   a. 0 shirts
   b. 300,000 shirts
   c. 600,000 shirts
   d. None of the above.

13. The efficient quantity of shirts equals ____ per day.
   a. 0 shirts
   b. 300,000 shirts
   c. 600,000 shirts
   d. None of the above.

Use Figure 5.7, and the areas illustrated in it, for the next four questions.

FIGURE **5.7**

Multiple Choice Questions 14, 15, 16, 17

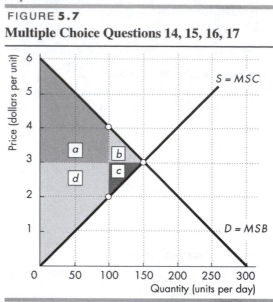

14. When production is 150 units with a price of $3, consumer surplus in the market illustrated in Figure 5.7 equals
   a. area *a*.
   b. area *b*.
   c. area *a* + *b*.
   d. area *a* + *d*.

15. When production is 150 units with a price of $3, producer surplus in this market equals
   a. area *a* + *b*.
   b. area *c*.
   c. area *c* + *d*.
   d. area *a* + *c*.

16. If the quantity is restricted to 100 units, then the deadweight loss equals
   a. area *c*.
   b. area *c* + *d*.
   c. area *a* + *b*.
   d. area *b* + *c*.

17. The total surplus when 150 units are produced ____ the total surplus when 100 units are produced?
   a. is larger than
   b. the same as
   c. is less than
   d. cannot be compared to

FIGURE **5.8**

Multiple Choice Question 18

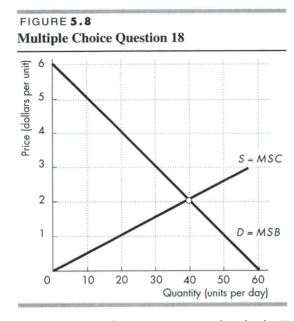

18. In Figure 5.8, when 20 units are produced, what is the dollar value of the deadweight loss?

  a. $0
  b. $20
  c. $30
  d. $80

19. A deadweight loss

  a. is possible only if the good is underproduced but is not possible if the good is overproduced.
  b. subtracts only from producer surplus.
  c. is a loss to consumers and a gain to producers.
  d. is a loss inflicted on the entire society.

20. Which of the following is <u>NOT</u> a potential source of inefficiency?

  a. External costs
  b. Decreasing marginal benefit
  c. Monopoly
  d. A tax

21. Suppose consumers decide they value a good more highly than before. Then the efficient quantity to produce of that good _____.

  a. increases.
  b. does not change.
  c. decreases.
  d. perhaps changes, but without more information the direction of the change cannot be told.

22. If a market results market failure, then

  a. it is impossible to achieve efficiency.
  b. the market must be supplied by a monopoly.
  c. there can be no consumer surplus in the market.
  d. some other allocation scheme might be more efficient.

Is the Competitive Market Fair?

23. Susan thinks the only fair outcome is one in which she receives three slices of pizza a week. Susan is using a _____ concept of fairness.

  a. "it's not fair if the result isn't fair"
  b. "it's not fair if the rules aren't fair"
  c. "big tradeoff"
  d. "symmetry principle"

24. The assertion that if resources are allocated efficiently, they also are allocated fairly is made by

  a. all utilitarians.
  b. John Rawls, who proposed making the poorest as well off as possible.
  c. Robert Nozick, who believes that equality of opportunity is fair.
  d. all economists who understand the big tradeoff.

■ **Short Answer Problems**

1. Why must resources be allocated?

2. a. Table 5.1 presents the marginal benefit and marginal cost schedules for video games. There are no externalities, so the marginal benefit to the consumer is the same as the marginal social benefit and the marginal cost paid by the producer is the same as the marginal social cost. Based on Table 5.1, complete Table 5.2 (on the next page).

TABLE **5.1**

Marginal Benefit and Marginal Cost of Video Games

Quantity (millions of video games)	Marginal benefit (dollars per game)	Marginal cost (dollars per game)
1	50	10
2	40	20
3	30	30
4	20	40
5	10	50

TABLE **5.2**

Short Answer Problem 2 (a)

Quantity (millions of video games)	Marginal social benefit minus marginal social cost
1	____
2	____
3	____
4	____
5	____

FIGURE **5.9**

Short Answer Problems 2 and 3

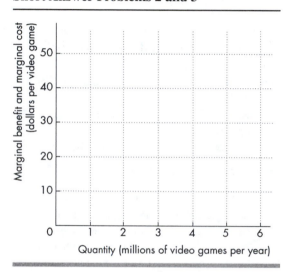

Quantity (millions of video games per year)

b. In Figure 5.9 draw the marginal social benefit and marginal social cost curves from Table 5.1.

c. What is the efficient number of video games to produce?

3. a. Using the data in Table 5.1, in Figure 5.9 now draw the demand curve for video games and the supply curve for video games.

b. There are no price or quantity regulations, no taxes, and no subsidies in this market. The market is competitive so it is not a monopoly. What quantity of video games will be produced?

c. Compare your answer to part (c) of problem 2 with your answer to part (c) of problem 1.

4. What is the relationship between the marginal benefit of a good, its value, and the maximum amount that a consumer is willing to pay for the good?

FIGURE **5.10**

The Demand For Jeans

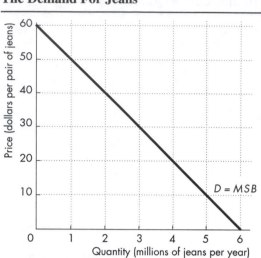

Quantity (millions of jeans per year)

5. a. Figure 5.10 shows the market demand curve for jeans. In the figure, indicate consumer surplus if the market price is $40 for a pair of jeans. What dollar amount does the consumer surplus equal?

b. In Figure 5.10, indicate the consumer surplus if the market price is $30 for a pair of jeans. What does the consumer surplus now equal?

c. When is the consumer surplus larger?

FIGURE **5.11**

The Supply Of Jeans

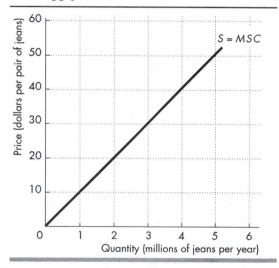

Quantity (millions of jeans per year)

6. a. Figure 5.11 shows the market supply curve for jeans. In the figure, indicate the producer surplus if the market price is $40 for a pair of jeans.

What is the dollar amount of the producer surplus?

b. In Figure 5.11, indicate the producer surplus if the market price is $30 for a pair of jeans. What does the producer surplus now equal?

c. When is the producer surplus larger?

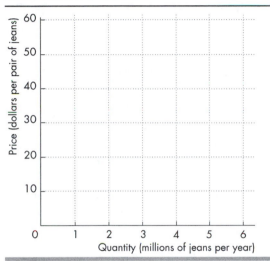

FIGURE **5.12**

Short Answer Problem 7

7. a. Using the demand curve from Figure 5.10 and the supply curve from Figure 5.11, in Figure 5.12 determine the equilibrium price and quantity of jeans.

b. In Figure 5.12 illustrate the consumer surplus and the producer surplus. What are the dollar amounts of consumer surplus and producer surplus? What amount does the sum of consumer surplus and producer surplus equal?

c. Suppose that output is restricted to 2 million pairs of jeans. In a figure similar to Figure 5.12, show the deadweight loss. What does the deadweight loss equal? What now is the sum of consumer surplus and producer surplus?

d. Suppose that output is equal to 4 million pairs of jeans. In another figure similar to Figure 5.12, show the deadweight loss. What does the deadweight loss equal? What now is the sum of consumer surplus and producer surplus?

e. When is the total surplus the largest: When 2 million jeans are produced? When 4 million jeans are produced? Or when the efficient quantity of jeans is produced?

8. What is a deadweight loss?

9. a. Igor has a job as Minister of Agriculture. He is interested in the market for mushrooms because he has a fondness for mushrooms. Igor realizes that this market is competitive. He also knows that there are no external benefits or external costs and that there are no government policies, such as taxes or subsidies, affecting the market. Mushrooms are not a common resource. The equilibrium quantity of mushrooms is 10 million pounds a year. Igor wants to know what would be the quantity produced if resources are being used efficiently. Based on the information given, what is the efficient quantity of mushrooms?

b. Igor can't believe that the efficient quantity is as low as you answered. (He *really* likes mushrooms!) Igor asks: What would be the loss if 11 million pounds of mushrooms are grown? In a diagram, show Igor the loss.

c. Igor now claims that the efficient quantity isn't fair because it is too small. What concept of fairness is Igor using?

d. Given Igor's view in the previous question, is Igor likely to agree that "it isn't fair if the rules aren't fair?" Why or why not?

■ **You're the Teacher**

1. "You know, there's one point about this chapter that bugs me. I can't understand how it's possible to have too much of a good. After all, in Chapter 2 we talked a lot about scarcity and about how there aren't enough resources available to produce enough stuff so that everyone's wants are met. Now here's this chapter that says we can produce too much of a good. What is going on?" Explain to your friend why it is possible to "overproduce" a good and, if you feel ambitious, further explain how the fact that resources *are* scarce implies that such overproduction harms society.

Answers

■ True/False Answers

Resource Allocation Methods

1. **T** Market prices allocate goods to consumers who both want the good and are able to pay for it.

2. **T** The boss is "commanding" the worker to use his or her time doing a specific task.

3. **F** Lotteries are one of the resource allocation methods occasionally used in the U.S. economy.

4. **F** The government also uses force to insure that property rights are protected.

Benefit, Cost, and Surplus

5. **T** Allocative efficiency occurs when marginal benefit equals marginal cost.

6. **F** The value of a good equals the maximum that someone is willing to pay for it, which often exceeds the price.

7. **T** Because the demand curve shows the maximum someone is willing to pay for each unit, the demand curve is the same as the marginal benefit curve.

8. **T** The download slope of the demand (and marginal benefit) curve shows that as more of a good is consumed, its marginal benefit decreases.

9. **F** Consumer surplus equals the area *under* the market demand curve and *above* the price.

10. **F** Cost is what a producer pays to produce a good; price is what a producer receives when the good is sold.

11. **F** The marginal cost of the one millionth pizza is the cost of producing only the one millionth pizza.

12. **F** The market supply curve is the same as the marginal cost curve.

13. **T** The statement defines producer surplus.

Is the Competitive Market Efficient?

14. **F** If the marginal benefit exceeds the marginal cost, resources are used more efficiently if production of the good is increased.

15. **T** The equality between marginal social benefit and marginal social cost signals that resources are being used efficiently.

16. **F** Government imposed taxes, subsidies, and price or quantity regulations can lead a competitive market to produce inefficiently. In addition, if there are externalities, the good is a public good or common resource, the good is sold by a monopoly, or there are high transactions costs, then the market will not necessarily be efficient.

17. **T** The fact that the sum of consumer surplus and producer surplus is as large as possible indicates that the gains from trade are as large as possible.

18. **T** A deadweight loss is a total loss to society; no one benefits from a deadweight loss.

Is the Competitive Market Fair?

19. **F** Utilitarianism argues that income should be taken from the rich and given to the poor. It does *not* claim that efficiency is fair.

20. **T** Making the poorest as well off as possible changes the economic game's results after the game is over.

21. **F** The symmetry principle is the assertion that people in similar circumstances should be treated similarly.

■ Multiple Choice Answers

Resource Allocation Methods

1. **d** Command is used because the person in charge is issuing orders ("commands") telling how resources will be allocated.

2. **a** The earlier someone arrives, the closer to the start of the line and the sooner the person is served.

3. **c** The person is using the personal characteristics of the potential tenants to determine to whom the apartment will be rented.

Benefit, Cost, and Surplus

4. **c** Efficiency occurs when the goods people value most highly are the goods being produced.

5. **b** The marginal benefit of the good equals the maximum price consumers are willing to pay for another unit of the good. The value of the good also equals its marginal benefit.

6. **c** Because the marginal benefit is the maximum amount someone is willing to pay for another unit of the good, the demand curve, which shows this maximum price, is the same as the marginal benefit curve.

7. **d** Susan's consumer surplus equals the benefit from the slice, which is maximum she is willing to pay for the slice, $5, minus what she actually pays, $4.

8. **a** With decreasing marginal benefit, the marginal benefit a consumer receives from the first unit of the good exceeds the marginal benefit the consumer receives from the second unit of the good.

9. **c** The question gives the definition of marginal cost.

10. **a** For any unit of output, the market supply curve shows the minimum price for which that unit will be produced and sold. Because the minimum price is the marginal social cost of the unit, the market supply curve is the same as the marginal cost curve.

11. **d** Producer surplus accrues to suppliers, and answer d is the definition of producer surplus.

Is the Competitive Market Efficient?

12. **b** The quantity produced is determined by the intersection of supply and demand curves.

13. **b** The efficient quantity is determined by the intersection of the marginal social benefit and marginal social cost curves. In comparison with the last answer, when demand equals the marginal benefit and supply equals the marginal cost, the equilibrium quantity is the efficient quantity.

14. **c** Consumer surplus equals the area under the demand curve and above the price.

15. **c** Producer surplus is the area above the supply curve and below the price.

16. **d** The deadweight loss is the sum of the lost consumer surplus (area *b*) plus the lost producer surplus (area *c*).

17. **a** When 150 units are produced, the total surplus is the area *a + b + c + d*; when 100 units are produced, the total surplus is only the area *a + d*.

18. **c** The deadweight loss is the area of the darkened triangle in Figure 5.13. The area of a triangle equals (½) × (base) × (height). The base equals 40 units minus 20 units, or 20. The height equals $4 per unit minus $1 per unit, or $3. So the deadweight loss is (½) × (20) × ($3) = $30.

19. **d** *No one* benefits from a deadweight loss.

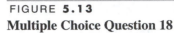

FIGURE **5.13**
Multiple Choice Question 18

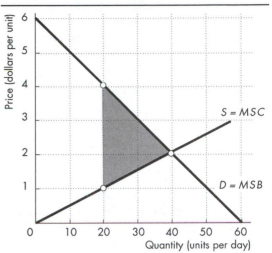

20. **b** Decreasing marginal benefit simply implies that the value of the initial units consumed exceeds the value of last units consumed.

21. **a** When a good is valued more highly, the marginal benefit increases and so efficiency requires that more of the good be produced.

22. **d** If a market allocation of resources results in market failure, then perhaps one of the other resource allocation methods might lead to allocative efficiency.

Is the Competitive Market Fair?

23. **a** Susan is judging fairness by looking at the outcome — she must have three slices of pizza a week — so she is using a "it's not fair if the result isn't fair" approach.

24. **c** Robert Nozick asserts that the government must establish and protect private property and that all exchanges must be voluntary, in which case the resulting outcome is efficient and fair.

■ Answers to Short Answer Problems

1. Resources must be allocated because they are scarce. Because of the scarcity of resources, not everyone's wants can be met. The resource allocation method used will determine whose wants are fulfilled and whose wants are left unfulfilled.

TABLE **5.3**

Short Answer Problem 2 (a)

Quantity (millions of video games)	Marginal social benefit minus marginal social cost
1	40
2	20
3	0
4	−20
5	−40

2.   a. See the completed Table 5.3. For each quantity, the answer in the table is obtained by subtracting the marginal benefit from the marginal cost.

FIGURE **5.14**

Short Answer Problem 2

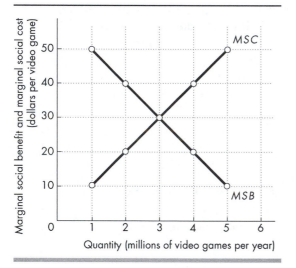

b. Figure 5.14 shows the marginal social benefit and marginal social cost schedules.

c. Both the table and the figure demonstrate that the efficient number of video games is 3 million because this quantity sets the marginal social benefit from an additional game equal to the game's marginal social cost.

3.   a. Figure 5.15 shows the demand and supply curves for video games. The key point in drawing Figure 5.15 is the fact that the demand curve, *D*, is the same as the marginal social benefit curve, *MSB*, and the supply curve, *S*, is the same as the marginal social cost curve, *MSC*. These equivalencies are noted in the figure.

FIGURE **5.15**

Short Answer Problem 3

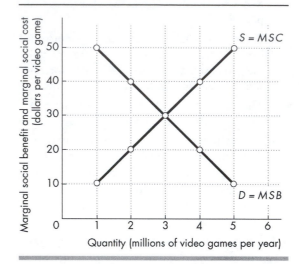

b. The quantity produced is 3 million video games, determined by where the supply and demand curves cross.

c. The two answers are identical, 3 million video games. In other words, the efficient quantity of video games is the same as the quantity actually produced.

4. All three concepts are the same. In other words, the marginal benefit of a good is defined as the good's value. And the value of a good is the maximum price that someone is willing to pay for it. Hence all three terms are interchangeable.

5.   a. Figure 5.16 (on the next page) shows the consumer surplus as the area of the shaded triangle. The amount of consumer surplus is equal to the area of the triangle. Use the formula for the area of a triangle, (½) × (base) × (height). The base equals 2 million pairs of jeans, the quantity demanded. The height is $20 per jean. Thus consumer surplus is (½) × (2 million jeans) × ($20 per jean) or $20 million.

b. Figure 5.17 (on the next page) shows the consumer surplus when the price of jeans is $30 a pair. The consumer surplus in this case is $45 million, from (½) × (3 million jeans) × ($30 per jean). As the price falls, the consumer surplus rises.

FIGURE **5.16**
Short Answer Problem 5 (a)

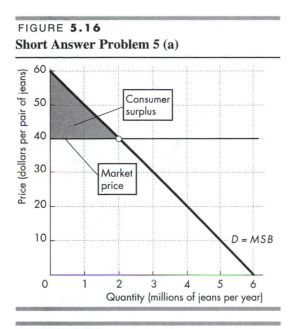

FIGURE **5.18**
Short Answer Problem 6 (a)

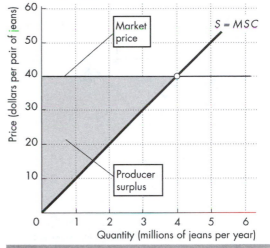
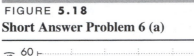

FIGURE **5.17**
Short Answer Problem 5 (b)

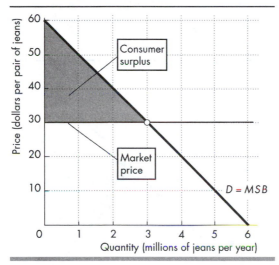

FIGURE **5.19**
Short Answer Problem 6 (b)

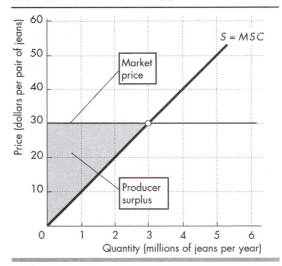

   c. Consumer surplus is larger when the price is lower. This result reflects the conclusion that consumers are better off when the prices of the goods they buy are lower.

6. a. Figure 5.18 shows the producer surplus as the area of the grey triangle. The amount of the producer surplus can be determined by using the formula for the area of a triangle, specifically (½) × (base) × (height). The base equals 4 million pairs of jeans, the quantity supplied. The height equals $40 per jean. Producer surplus is (½) × (4 million jeans) × ($40 per jean) or $80 million.

  b. Figure 5.19 shows the producer surplus when the price of a pair of jeans is $30. Producer surplus equals (½) × (base) × (height), which is equal to (½) × (3 million jeans) × ($30 per jean), or $45 million.

  c. Producer surplus is larger when the price is higher. This result illustrates the fact that producers are better off when the price of the good they sell is higher.

FIGURE **5.20**

Short Answer Problem 7 (a) and (b)

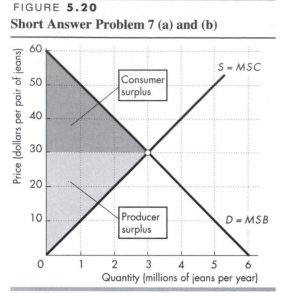

FIGURE **5.21**

Short Answer Problem 7 (c)

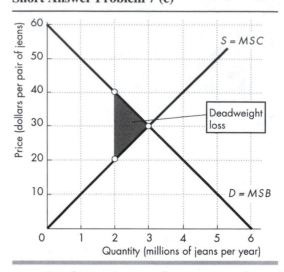

7. a. Figure 5.20 demonstrates that the quantity is 3 million jeans and the price is $30 a pair.

    b. Consumer surplus and producer surplus are illustrated in Figure 5.20. The price of a pair of jeans is $30. From Problem 5 (b), the consumer surplus is $45 million. From Problem 6 (b), producer surplus is $45 million. (The result that the consumer surplus equals the producer surplus is a coincidence; in general there is no particular relationship between the amount of consumer surplus and the amount of producer surplus.) The sum of consumer surplus plus producer surplus is $90 million.

    c. Figure 5.21 illustrates the case when production of jeans is limited to 2 million pairs. The deadweight loss is the dark triangle in the figure. Use (½)(base)(height), the formula for the area of a triangle, to calculate it. The base is 1 million pairs of jeans. The height is $20 per jean, the difference between what consumers are willing to pay for another pair of jeans, $40, and the amount suppliers need to receive to produce an additional pair, $20. The deadweight loss equals (½) × (1 million jeans) × ($20 per jean) or $10 million. The sum of consumer surplus and producer surplus is most easily calculated by subtracting the deadweight loss from the sum when the market produces the efficient quantity. From part (b) of this problem, the sum when the market is efficient is $90 million. So when the market underproduces by producing only 2 million

pairs of jeans, the sum of consumer surplus and producer surplus equals $90 million minus $10 million or $80 million.

FIGURE **5.22**

Short Answer Problem 7 (d)

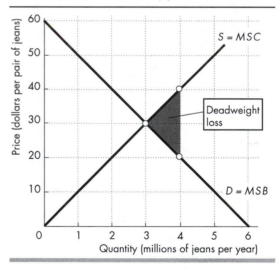

    d. Figure 5.22 shows the situation when 4 million pairs of jeans are produced. The deadweight loss is again illustrated by the dark triangle. The amount of deadweight loss equals the area of the triangle, or (½) × (base) × (height). The base is 1 million pairs of jeans, the amount of overproduction. The height is $20, the difference between the marginal social cost of another pair of jeans and the marginal social benefit from another pair. The deadweight loss is equal to (½) × (1 million jeans) × ($20 per jean) = $10 million. The result that the deadweight loss in part (d) from overproducing 1 million pairs of jeans equals the deadweight loss from underproducing 1 million pairs of jeans, in part (c), is a coincidence. In general these amounts are not equal. The sum of consumer surplus and producer surplus equals the sum when the efficient quantity is produced, $90 million, minus the deadweight loss, $10 million. So with this overproduction, the sum of consumer surplus and producer surplus is $80 million.

e. The total surplus equals the sum of consumer surplus and producer surplus. It is largest when the efficient quantity of jeans is produced, when 3 million pairs of jeans are produced.

8. A deadweight loss is the loss to society when resources are used inefficiently. When resources are used efficiently, the sum of the consumer surplus plus the producer surplus is as large as possible. Any sort of inefficiency decreases the total sum, and the decrease is the deadweight loss. It is important to note that a deadweight loss is a loss to *society* as a whole. In other words, no one benefits from a deadweight loss.

9. a. Based on the data in the question, the efficient quantity of mushrooms to produce is 10 million pounds a year. Why? The mushroom market meets all the criteria to be efficient: It is a competitive market, there are no externalities, and there are no government policies (such as price controls or taxes) that lead the amount produced to differ from the equilibrium quantity. So the amount produced, the equilibrium quantity, is the efficient amount.

b. Figure 5.23 shows the deadweight loss from producing 11 million pounds of mushrooms. The deadweight loss exists because past 10 million pounds of mushrooms, the value people place on an additional pound of mushrooms — their marginal benefit — is less than the cost to produce an additional pound — the marginal cost. Hence all the pounds past 10 million subtract from the gains from trade, and the amount subtracted is equal to the deadweight loss.

c. Igor thinks that too few mushrooms are produced. Hence, Igor is using the result (not enough mushrooms) to judge fairness. Thus Igor

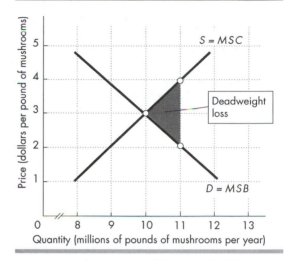

FIGURE 5.23
Short Answer Problem 9 (b)

is using the concept of "it's not fair if the result isn't fair."

d. Igor is unlikely to agree that "it isn't fair if the rules aren't fair" because when the rules are "fair", that is, when there is no government interference in the market, Igor does not like the outcome. Basically, Igor wants to bend the rules so that more mushrooms are grown, perhaps by giving growers a subsidy to encourage more production.

■ **You're the Teacher**

1. "Yeah, I know what you mean that there seems to be a contradiction between the idea that 'resources are limited and therefore not everyone can have everything they want' and a lesson in this chapter that 'it is possible to produce too much of a good'. But, once you think about it a bit, the two ideas actually fit together okay."

"Think about sodas. We both drink a lot of them, but you know we'd both like to drink more. The fact that we'd like more shows us that sodas are 'scarce,' that is, some of our wants for more sodas won't be satisfied. But now suppose that 100 times more sodas were produced. We'd have soda coming out of our ears! We'd have plenty to drink, but we'd have to brush our teeth in it and use it in the shower. I like soda as much as anybody, but taking a bath in soda sounds gross! In this situation obviously too much soda is being produced. We'd be a lot better off if production was cut back."

"In fact, in some sense it's precisely because resources are limited that we can overproduce a good. Look, if society produced 100 times the amount of soda we produce now, the fact that our resources are limited means that we'd have to give up a bunch of other things: We'd have no cars because all the metal was being used to make soda cans; we'd have no books or magazines because all the paper was being used to make six-pack holders; we'd lose a *lot* of stuff because the resources were devoted to making soda. If we had unlimited resources, we would not lose anything and so in this case, we really couldn't overproduce a good. But, because our resources are limited, we want to use them the best we can, which means we want to produce the efficient amount of each good!"

Chapter Quiz

1. If the marginal social cost of the sixth slice of pizza is greater than the marginal social benefit, then the output level is
   a. efficient and more pizza should be produced.
   b. efficient and less pizza should be produced.
   c. inefficient and more pizza should be produced.
   d. inefficient and less pizza should be produced.

2. When the city of Fresno holds a referendum to determine if taxes will be raised to pay for road repairs, the city is using a _____ allocation method.
   a. majority rule
   b. market price
   c. contest
   d. personal characteristics

3. If the only people who benefit from a pizza are those who buy the pizza, the demand curve for pizza
   a. lies above the marginal social benefit curve for pizza.
   b. lies below the marginal social benefit curve for pizza.
   c. is the same as the marginal social benefit curve for pizza.
   d. has one point in common with the marginal social benefit curve for pizza.

4. The value of a good minus the price paid for it is the
   a. producer surplus from the good.
   b. consumer surplus from the good.
   c. total surplus from the good.
   d. exchange surplus from the good.

5. Which of the following can be a source of inefficiency?
   a. Competition
   b. Taxes
   c. Markets
   d. None of the above are sources of economic inefficiency.

6. Competitive markets will generally
   a. produce too much of a public good.
   b. produce too little of a public good.
   c. produce the efficient amount of a public good.
   d. produce too much, too little, or the efficient amount of a public good depending on whether the market demand curve accurately reflects the marginal social benefit.

7. Which of the following statements about a deadweight loss is correct?
   a. The deadweight loss is largest in a perfectly competitive market producing a good with no external costs or benefits.
   b. A deadweight loss is a loss to consumers and a gain to producers.
   c. A deadweight loss is a loss to producers and a gain to consumers.
   d. None of the above are correct.

8. If the marginal social cost of the last unit of a good produced is less than the marginal social benefit,
   a. the amount produced is efficient.
   b. less than the efficient amount is being produced.
   c. more than the efficient amount is being produced.
   d. as time passes, consumers will increase their benefit from the good.

9. Deadweight loss can be the result of
   a. overproduction but not underproduction.
   b. underproduction but not overproduction.
   c. both overproduction and underproduction.
   d. neither overproduction nor underproduction.

10. The "Big Tradeoff" points out that
    a. the symmetry principle is not fair.
    b. taking income from rich people and giving it to poor people can create inefficiency.
    c. making the poorest as well off as possible is not compatible with fairness.
    d. utilitarianism is fair.

The answers for this Chapter Quiz are on page 345

■ A Housing Market with a Rent Ceiling

The government might regulate a market. A **price ceiling** or a **price cap** is a government regulation that makes it illegal to charge a price higher than a specified level. A price ceiling imposed *above* the equilibrium price has no effect. A price ceiling set *below* the equilibrium price has major effects.

A price ceiling imposed in a housing market is a **rent ceiling**. A rent ceiling prohibits charging rent that exceeds the ceiling amount. Rent ceilings below the equilibrium rent creates a housing shortage.

♦ In Figure 6.1, in the absence of a rent ceiling the equilibrium rent is $750 per month and quantity of apartments is 3,000. With a rent ceiling of $500 per month, the quantity of apartments demanded increases to 4,000 and the quantity of apartments supplied decreases to 2,000. The grey arrow shows the shortage of 2,000 apartments.

A shortage leads to:

♦ increased **search activity** — time spent looking for someone with whom to do business.

♦ **black markets** — an illegal market in which the equilibrium price exceeds the imposed price ceiling.

Rent ceilings create inefficiency and a deadweight loss. Figure 6.1 illustrates the deadweight loss created by a rent ceiling. The producer surplus shrinks to the triangular area shown in Figure 6.1. Tenants are willing to expend resources equal to the rectangular area in Figure 6.1 searching for an apartment. If they spend this amount of resources, the total consumer surplus shrinks to the triangular area indicated in Figure 6.1.

Because rent ceilings block voluntary exchange, they are unfair according to the *fair rules* view of fairness. Rent ceilings do not necessarily allocate more apartments to

FIGURE 6.1
The Deadweight Loss from a Rent Ceiling

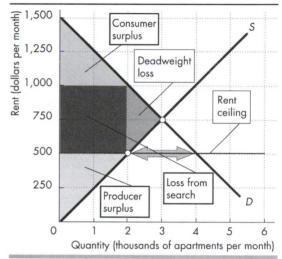

the poorest. Instead they allocate apartments to those who are lucky or to those who are first in line. They also can lead to increased discrimination. Because they do not allocate apartments to the poor, rent ceilings violate the *fair results* view of fairness.

■ A Labor Market with a Minimum Wage

A **price floor** is a government imposed regulation that makes it illegal to charge a price lower than the specified level. A price flow set *below* the equilibrium price has no effect. A price flow set *above* the equilibrium price changes the market outcome.

A price floor in a labor market is a **minimum wage**. A minimum wage makes hiring workers for less than the specified wage rate illegal. A minimum wage set above the equilibrium wage rate creates unemployment.

♦ In Figure 6.2 (on the next page), in the absence of a minimum wage the equilibrium wage rate is $9.00 per hour and quantity of hours is 3 million per year.

FIGURE 6.2
The Deadweight Loss from a Minimum Wage

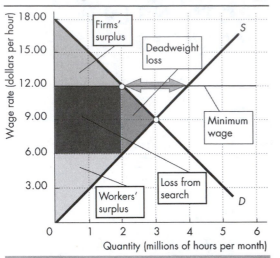

With a minimum wage of $12 per hour, the quantity of labor supplied increases to 4 million hours and the quantity of labor demanded decreases to 2 million hours. The grey arrow shows the unemployment of 2 million hours of labor.

Unemployment leads to increased job search.

A minimum wage set above the equilibrium wage rate results in inefficiency and a deadweight loss. Figure 6.2 illustrates the deadweight loss created by the minimum wage. Firms' surplus shrinks to the triangular area shown in Figure 6.2. Workers are willing to expend resources equal to the rectangular area in Figure 6.2 searching for employment. If they spend this amount of resources, workers' surplus shrinks to the triangular area illustrated in Figure 6.2.

♦ Most economists believe that minimum wage laws contribute to high unemployment among low-skilled young workers.

Based on a "fair results" approach to fairness, the minimum wage is unfair because the unemployed wind up worse off with the minimum wage and those who keep their jobs are not necessarily the poorest. The minimum wage is unfair under a "fair rules" approach to fairness because it blocks voluntary exchange.

■ Taxes

Tax incidence is the division of the burden of a tax between buyers the sellers. If the price paid by the buyers rises by the full amount of the tax, then the full amount of the burden falls on the buyers; if the price rises by less than the amount of the tax, the burden falls on both the buyers and the sellers; and if the price does not rise, then the full amount of the burden falls on the sellers.

♦ A tax on sellers decreases the supply of the taxed good, so the supply curve shifts leftward. The vertical distance between the supply curve with the tax and without it equals the amount of the tax. The price paid by buyers rises and the price received by sellers, net of the tax, falls.

♦ A tax on buyers decreases the demand for the taxed good, so the demand curve shifts leftward. The vertical distance between the demand curve with the tax and without it equals the amount of the tax. The price paid by buyers, including the tax, rises and the price received by sellers falls.

The price paid by buyers and the price received by sellers is the same regardless of whether the tax is imposed on buyers or sellers.

The division of the tax depends on the elasticities of demand and supply. The more inelastic the demand, the larger the fraction of the tax demanders pay.

♦ Perfectly inelastic demand — buyers pay all the tax.

♦ Perfectly elastic demand — sellers pay all the tax.

The more inelastic the supply, the larger the fraction of the tax sellers pay.

♦ Perfectly inelastic supply — sellers pay all the tax.

♦ Perfectly elastic supply — buyers pay all the tax.

Usually goods with inelastic demands are taxed. Compared to a good with an elastic demand, taxing a good with an inelastic demand results in more tax revenue and a smaller deadweight loss demand because with an inelastic demand the tax does not reduce the quantity purchased by much.

In general, imposing a tax on a product creates a deadweight loss. (If the demand or supply is perfectly inelastic, imposing the tax creates no deadweight loss.)

Two (conflicting) principles of fairness for taxes have been suggested:

♦ Benefits principle — people should pay taxes equal to the benefits they receive from the services provided by the government. The benefits principle justifies gas taxes used to maintain roads.

♦ Ability-to-pay principle — people should pay taxes according to how easily they can bear the burden of the tax.

■ Production Quotas and Subsidies

Price floors are sometimes used to boost farmers' incomes. Production quotas and subsidies are also used.

♦ A **production quota** is an upper limit to the quantity of a good that may be produced in a given time period.

A production quota decreases the quantity and raises the price paid by buyers and received by sellers. It creates a deadweight loss and inefficiency. Because the price exceeds the marginal cost, producers have an incentive to produce more than their assigned quota.

♦ A **subsidy** is a payment made by the government to a producer. A subsidy is like a negative tax: It increases the supply so that the vertical distance between the initial supply curve and the supply curve with the subsidy is equal to the subsidy.

A subsidy increases the quantity produced, lowers the price paid by buyers, and raises the price, including the subsidy, received by producers. It creates a deadweight loss because the good is overproduced.

■ Markets for Illegal Goods

The purchase and sale of some goods is illegal. Penalties can be levied on sellers and/or buyers. Compared to the situation if the good was legal, if sellers are penalized:

♦ The cost of selling the good rises because of the penalty, so the supply curve shifts leftward.

♦ These penalties boost the price and decrease the quantity.

Compared to the situation if the good was legal, if buyers are penalized:

♦ The benefits from the good fall because of the penalty, so the demand curve shifts leftward.

♦ These penalties lead to a fall in the price and a decrease in the quantity.

If buyers and sellers are each penalized:

♦ Both the demand and supply curves shift leftward.

♦ The quantity definitely decreases. The price rises if the decrease in supply is larger and falls if the decrease in demand is larger.

A policy of decriminalizing and then taxing the good, such as an illegal drug, might be able to achieve the same consumption levels as prohibition. But the required tax rate might be high, leading to substantial tax evasion. And legalization might send the wrong signal to potential consumers.

Helpful Hints

1. **THE HARM FROM RENT CEILINGS :** Whenever some influence disturbs an equilibrium in an unregulated (free) market, the differing desires of buyers and sellers are brought back into balance by price movements. If prices are controlled by government regulation, however, the price mechanism no longer can serve this purpose. In the case of price ceilings, increased search activity will emerge. By creating increased search, price ceilings waste society's scarce resources. For instance, with rent controls, would-be apartment dwellers, fruitlessly driving around the city searching for an apartment, accomplish nothing from a social perspective. The time and energy that these people dissipate in futile search activity creates nothing socially useful.

   In addition, price ceilings deliver the wrong signals to suppliers. In a free market, a shortage of apartments means rents are driven higher. Higher rents give apartment owners the incentive to increase the number of apartments they rent, which helps overcome the initial shortage. With rent controls, rents do not rise. Hence apartment owners have no incentive to increase the number of apartments they rent.

2. **INTUITIVE EXPLANATION OF WHO PAYS A TAX:** Consider the intuition of how the demand elasticity affects the division of the tax. Suppliers always want to pass all of the tax along to buyers in the form of a higher price. But if the demand for the product is very elastic, consumers can find good substitutes for the product being taxed. If sellers tried to stick demanders with a large part of the tax, buyers would substitute other products, and suppliers would find themselves unable to sell anything. In this case suppliers absorb a large portion of the tax. However, if the demand for the good is inelastic, consumers cannot readily find anything to take the product's place. In this situation, consumers pay a large part of the tax.

   Similar reasoning applies to the elasticity of supply. If supply is very elastic, suppliers can find other products to make and buyers wind up paying most of the tax. However, if the supply is inelastic, producers cannot easily switch to producing another product. Buyers do not have to pay much of the tax in this case because suppliers can't find anything else to produce.

Questions

■ True/False and Explain

A Housing Market with a Rent Ceiling

1. To change the market outcome, a rent ceiling must be set at an amount less than the equilibrium rent.

2. With a rent ceiling set below the equilibrium rent, there is no way to allocate apartments among potential renters.

3. Suppose that a price control is holding the price of gasoline below its equilibrium level. When the control is abolished and the price rises, the amount of gasoline purchased by consumers will decrease.

4. A rent ceiling below the equilibrium rent increases economic efficiency and decreases the deadweight loss because more people can afford apartments.

A Labor Market with a Minimum Wage

5. In a labor market, a minimum wage is an example of a price floor.

6. If the minimum wage is above the equilibrium wage, raising the minimum wage decreases the number of workers employed.

7. Most economists believe that raising the minimum wage has no effect on unemployment.

Taxes

8. When a tax is imposed on sellers of a good, the supply curve with the tax lies below the supply curve without the tax.

9. Imposing a tax on buyers rather than on sellers means that buyers must pay a larger part of the tax.

10. Buyers always pay a larger amount of a tax than do sellers.

11. The more elastic the demand for a good or service, the larger the amount of a sales tax paid by the buyers.

Production Quotas and Subsidies

12. If demand for a farm product is inelastic, a crop failure decreases farmers' total revenue.

13. Subsidies increase the equilibrium quantity.

Markets for Illegal Goods

14. Imposing penalties on sellers of an illegal product raises the price of the illegal product.

15. Imposing penalties on *both* buyers and sellers of an illegal good always raises the price of the illegal good.

■ Multiple Choice

A Housing Market with a Rent Ceiling

1. A price ceiling set below the equilibrium price _____ a shortage and _____ a deadweight loss.
    a. creates; creates
    b. creates; does not create
    c. does not create; creates
    d. does not create; does not create

For the next five questions, use Table 6.1, which shows the supply and demand schedules for apples.

TABLE 6.1
Multiple Choice Questions 2, 3, 4, 5, 6

Price (dollars per pound)	Quantity demanded (tons per year)	Quantity supplied (tons per year)
$1.10	24	30
1.00	28	28
0.90	32	26
0.80	36	24
0.70	40	22

2. What is the equilibrium price of an apple?
    a. $1.10 per pound
    b. $1.00 per pound
    c. $0.80 per pound
    d. $0.60 per pound

3. What is the equilibrium quantity of apples?
    a. 24 tons
    b. 28 tons
    c. 32 tons
    d. 36 tons

4. The government imposes a price ceiling of 80¢ per pound. At this price, how many apples are supplied?
    a. 24 tons
    b. 28 tons
    c. 32 tons
    d. 36 tons

5. At the ceiling price of 80¢ per pound, how many apples are consumed?

   a. 24 tons
   b. 28 tons
   c. 32 tons
   d. 36 tons

6. At the ceiling price of 80¢ per pound of apples, what is the shortage of apples?

   a. 0 tons
   b. 12 tons
   c. 24 tons
   d. 36 tons

FIGURE **6.3**

Multiple Choice Questions 7, 8 and 9

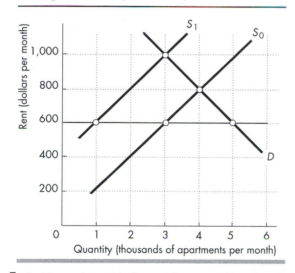

7. In Figure 6.3, with the supply curve of housing S_0 and with a rent ceiling of $600 a month, there is

   a. a surplus of $200 a month.
   b. a shortage of 5,000 apartments a month.
   c. a shortage of 2,000 apartments a month.
   d. neither a shortage nor surplus of apartments.

8. In Figure 6.3 a disaster strikes so that the housing supply curve shifts from S_0 to S_1. If the rent ceiling remains at $600, there is a

   a. surplus of $400 a month.
   b. shortage of 5,000 apartments a month.
   c. shortage of 4,000 apartments a month.
   d. shortage of 1,000 apartments a month.

9. In Figure 6.3 a disaster strikes so that the housing supply curve shifts from S_0 to S_1. If the rent ceiling remains at $600, the deadweight loss is

   a. larger before the disaster.
   b. larger after the disaster.
   c. the same before and after the disaster.
   d. not comparable before and after the disaster.

10. If the government sets a price ceiling on pizza that is below the equilibrium price of a pizza, then

    a. there will be a shortage of pizza.
    b. there will be a surplus of pizza.
    c. existing firms will expand their production to meet the increased quantity demanded.
    d. new firms will enter the market to meet the increase in the quantity demanded.

11. Which of the following is an example of a black market?

    a. A market where legal transactions take place at prices lower than a government imposed price ceiling.
    b. A market where illegal transactions take place at prices higher than a government imposed price ceiling.
    c. A legal market where buyers and sellers search for each other.
    d. An illegal market in which the lights are not turned on.

12. A price ceiling below the equilibrium price _____ search and _____ a deadweight loss.

    a. creates; creates
    b. creates; does not create
    c. does not create; creates
    d. does not create; does not create

A Labor Market with a Minimum Wage

13. The deadweight loss from the minimum wage is larger when the minimum wage is set _____ the equilibrium wage rate.

    a. above
    b. equal to
    c. below
    d. The deadweight loss is the same no matter if the minimum wage is set above, below, or equal to the equilibrium wage.

FIGURE **6.4**
Multiple Choice Questions 14, 15, and 16

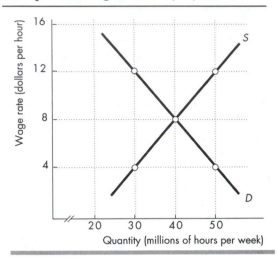

FIGURE **6.5**
Multiple Choice Questions 18, 19, 20, and 21

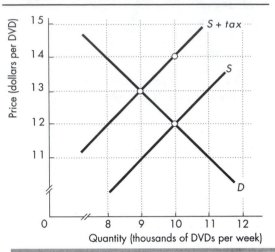

14. In Figure 6.4 if the minimum wage was set at $4 per hour, what would be the level of unemployment?

    a. 50 million hours.
    b. 40 million hours.
    c. 20 million hours.
    d. 0.

15. In Figure 6.4 if the minimum wage was set at $12 per hour, what would be the level of unemployment?

    a. 50 million hours
    b. 40 million hours
    c. 20 million hours
    d. 0 hours

16. In Figure 6.4 if the minimum wage was set at $4 per hour, what does the deadweight loss equal?

    a. $60 million
    b. $30 million
    c. $20 million
    d. $0

17. According to the fair results approach to fairness, a minimum wage _____ fair and according to the fair rules approach to fairness, a minimum wage _____ fair.

    a. is; is
    b. is; is not
    c. is not; is
    d. is not; is not

Taxes

18. In Figure 6.5 what is the amount of the tax on DVDs?

    a. $14 per DVD
    b. $13 per DVD
    c. $2 per DVD
    d. $1 per DVD

19. In Figure 6.5, the tax law imposes the tax on

    a. only the buyers.
    b. only the sellers.
    c. both the sellers and the buyers.
    d. neither the sellers nor the buyers.

20. In Figure 6.5, how much of the tax is paid by buyers?

    a. $14 per DVD
    b. $13 per DVD
    c. $2 per DVD
    d. $1 per DVD

21. In Figure 6.5, how much of the tax is paid by the sellers?

    a. $14 per DVD
    b. $13 per DVD
    c. $2 per DVD
    d. $1 per DVD

22. The division of a tax falls heaviest on buyers when
    a. demand is perfectly elastic.
    b. demand is inelastic but not perfectly inelastic.
    c. demand is perfectly inelastic.
    d. supply is perfectly inelastic.

23. Suppose that the government wants to discourage the use of cigarettes. If it imposes a tax on cigarettes, the equilibrium quantity decreases the most when the elasticity of demand equals
    a. 2.00.
    b. 1.00.
    c. 0.50.
    d. 0.

24. The more elastic the supply, the
    a. more likely the government is to tax the product.
    b. more likely the government is to impose a price ceiling.
    c. smaller the amount of any tax imposed on the product paid by the suppliers.
    d. more elastic is the demand.

Production Quotas and Subsidies

25. A production quota set on sugar below the equilibrium quantity of sugar _____ paid by buyers and _____ the price received by sellers.
    a. raises; raises
    b. raises; lowers
    c. lowers; raises
    d. lowers; lowers

26. A subsidy paid to corn farmers _____ the supply of corn and _____ a deadweight loss.
    a. increases; creates
    b. increases; does not create
    c. decreases; creates
    d. decreases; does not create

27. A production quota set on wheat below the equilibrium quantity of gives wheat farmers the incentive to cheat on the quota. A subsidy paid to peanut farmers raises the price paid by buyers.
    a. Both sentences are correct.
    b. The first sentence is correct and the second is incorrect.
    c. The first sentence is incorrect and the second is correct.
    d. Both sentences are incorrect.

Markets for Illegal Goods

28. By imposing sanctions on buyers of an illegal good, the government shifts the good's
    a. demand curve rightward.
    b. demand curve leftward.
    c. supply curve leftward.
    d. supply curve rightward.

29. If sanctions are imposed on sellers but not users of an illegal good, the equilibrium price of the good _____ and the equilibrium quantity _____.
    a. falls; decreases
    b. rises; increases
    c. rises; decreases
    d. falls; increases

30. If the government wants to discourage consumption of a good, it can
    a. impose penalties on buyers of the good.
    b. impose penalties on sellers of the good.
    c. tax the product.
    d. do all of the above because all the policies serve to decrease consumption of the good.

■ Short Answer Problems

1. For a price ceiling to have an effect in the market, it needs to be set below the equilibrium price. Why?

TABLE **6.2**

Short Answer Questions 2, 3

Price (dollars per gallon)	Quantity demanded (millions of gallons per year)	Quantity supplied (millions of gallons per year)
4.40	8	24
4.30	10	22
4.20	12	20
4.10	14	18
4.00	16	16
3.90	18	14

2. Table 6.2 presents the supply and demand schedules for gasoline.
    a. With no government intervention in the market, what is the equilibrium price of gasoline? The equilibrium quantity?
    b. If there is a deadweight loss, what does it equal?

c. Suppose that the government imposes a price ceiling of $3.90 a gallon. Now what is the quantity demanded? The quantity supplied?

d. With the price ceiling of $3.90 a gallon, how much gasoline do consumers buy? What is the amount of the shortage?

e. If there is a deadweight loss, what does it equal?

3. Suppose that the supply schedule of gasoline in Table 6.2 suddenly decreases, perhaps because of events in the Middle East. In particular, suppose that at every possible price of gasoline, the quantity supplied is now 8 million gallons less per year.

a. If the government did not impose any price controls, what is the new equilibrium price of gasoline? The new equilibrium quantity? How is the gasoline allocated among potential consumers?

b. Suppose that the government imposed a price ceiling of $3.90. Now what is the quantity demanded? The quantity supplied?

c. With a price ceiling of $3.90 in place, how much gasoline do consumers buy? What is the amount of the shortage? How is gasoline allocated among potential consumers?

d. When are demanders able to consume more gasoline? When the price is controlled at $3.90 a gallon, or when the price is left free to reach its equilibrium? Explain.

4. Suppose that policymakers decide that the price of a pizza is too high and that not enough people can afford to buy pizza. As a result, they impose a price ceiling on pizza that is below the current equilibrium price. When are consumers able to buy more pizza: before the price ceiling or after? Use a demand and supply diagram to support your answer.

TABLE 6.3

Short Answer Problem 5

Price (dollars per slice)	Quantity demanded (millions of slices per year)	Quantity supplied (millions of slices per year)
4.20	30	42
4.10	34	40
4.00	38	38
3.90	42	36
3.80	46	34
3.70	50	32

5. Table 6.3 presents the demand and supply sched-

FIGURE 6.6

Short Answer Problem 5

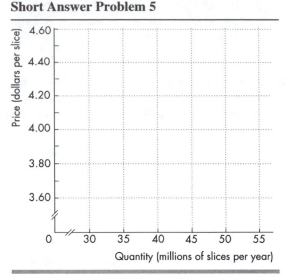

ules for slices of pizza.

a. Plot the demand and supply curves in Figure 6.6.

b. What is the equilibrium price of a slice of pizza? The equilibrium quantity?

c. Suppose the government imposes a price ceiling of $3.90 per slice of pizza. On your diagram, show the quantities demanded and supplied and identify any shortage or surplus. Illustrate the deadweight loss.

FIGURE 6.7

Short Answer Problem 6

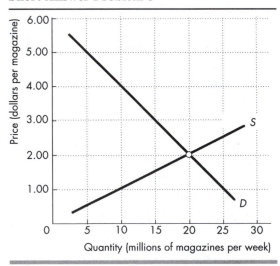

6. Figure 6.7 shows the market for magazines. Suppose the government imposes a $3.00 per magazine

tax on suppliers. In Figure 6.7, illustrate the impact of this tax.

  a. How much of the tax is paid by buyers?

  b. How much of the tax is paid by sellers?

  c. What does the deadweight loss equal?

FIGURE **6.8**
Short Answer Problem 7

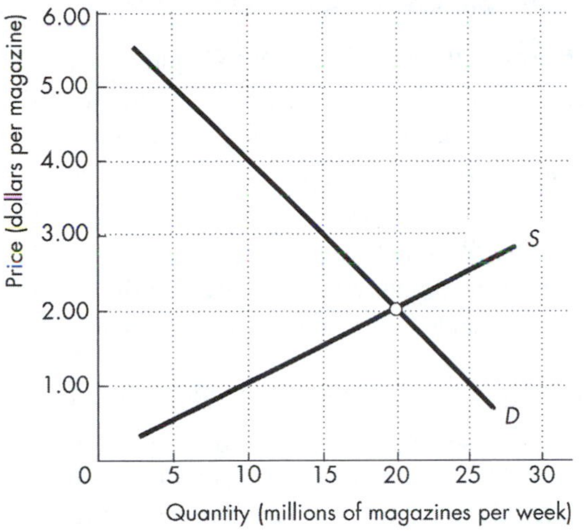

7. Figure 6.8 shows the market for magazines. Suppose the government imposes a $3.00 per magazine tax on buyers. In Figure 6.8, illustrate the impact of this tax.

  a. How much of the tax is paid by buyers?

  b. How much of the tax is paid by sellers?

  c. Comparing your answers to questions 6 and 7, do buyers pay more or less of the tax when the tax is imposed on them?

8. After graduating, you land a plush job advising the president on economic matters. One day the president asks you for your suggestions about products to tax.

  a. The president asks you to produce a list of items to be taxed that will yield substantial tax revenue to the government and for which consumers pay a large amount of the tax. Without trying to name specific products, what is the general characteristic of the demand for the products that you will suggest for taxation? Why?

  b. After you discuss this first list with the president, the president realizes that this year is an election year. As a result, the president changes your assignment a bit. Now the president asks you for a list of products that will still yield a lot of revenue for the government, but whose tax will fall more heavily on producers. Again without trying to name specific products, what is the general characteristic of the supply of the products that would comprise your second list? Why?

9. How does a subsidy compare to a tax?

10. You are in charge of combating illegal drug use in the United States. You must decide between imprisoning users or imprisoning sellers of drugs.

  a. If you decide to imprison users, what effect do you expect this policy to have on the price and quantity of illegal drugs?

  b. If you decide to imprison sellers, what effect do you think this policy will have on the price and quantity of illegal drugs?

  c. Without knowing which policy is being followed, can changes in the price of illegal drugs alone determine the success of a policy designed to reduce the consumption of illegal drugs?

■ You're the Teacher

1. "I don't get this stuff about how suppliers and demanders split the sales tax. Every time *I* go to the store, I pay *all* the sales tax. I have never seen a store that offered to split the tax with me. So, how can our text say that suppliers usually have to pay part of a tax? I'm lost; can you help me out?" Your classmate is befuddled. Point your friend in the right direction.

A n s w e r s

■ True/False Answers

A Housing Market with a Rent Ceiling

1. **T** If a rent ceiling is set above the equilibrium rent, it does not make the equilibrium rent illegal and therefore has no impact.

2. **F** Lines and payments on the black market help allocate apartments among potential renters.

3. **F** With the price control, there was a shortage of gasoline; when the price rises, suppliers produce more gasoline and demanders are able to buy more.

4. **F** A rent ceiling below the equilibrium rent creates inefficiency and a deadweight loss.

A Labor Market with a Minimum Wage

5. **T** A price floor sets the lowest legal price and that is precisely what a minimum wage does: It sets the lowest legal wage rate.

6. **T** By raising the wage that must be paid, firms respond by decreasing the quantity of workers they demand, that is, decreasing the number of workers they will hire.

7. **F** Most economists believe that a rise in the minimum wage increases unemployment.

Taxes

8. **F** The supply curve with the tax *above* the initial supply curve without the tax. The vertical distance between the two curves is the amount of the tax.

9. **F** The amount of the tax paid by buyers is the same *regardless* of whether the tax is imposed on the buyers or on the sellers.

10. **F** The amount paid by buyers depends on the relative elasticities of demand and supply.

11. **F** The more elastic the demand, the larger the amount of the tax paid by sellers.

Production Quotas and Subsidies

12. **F** The crop failure raises the price of the crop and, because the demand for it is inelastic, boosts farmers' total revenue.

13. **T** The increase in quantity means that the price on the world market falls.

Markets for Illegal Goods

14. **T** The penalties increase the cost of supplying the good, which decreases the supply and raises the price.

15. **F** The price rises if the penalties are more severe on sellers and falls if they are more severe on buyers.

■ Multiple Choice Answers

A Housing Market with a Rent Ceiling

1. **a** If the price ceiling makes the equilibrium price illegal, it creates a shortage and a deadweight loss.

2. **b** The quantity of apples demanded equals the quantity of apples supplied when the price is $1.00 per pound.

3. **b** At the equilibrium price, the quantity of apples demanded equals the quantity of apples supplied, 28 tons.

4. **a** At a price of 80¢ a pound, the supply schedule shows that producers supply 24 tons per year.

5. **a** Although consumers demand 36 tons of apples, only 24 tons are produced, so only 24 tons can be consumed.

6. **b** The shortage equals the quantity of apples demanded, 36 tons, minus the quantity of apples supplied, 24 tons.

7. **c** The shortage equals the quantity demanded at the ceiling price (5,000) minus the quantity supplied at that price (3,000).

8. **c** The shortage increases because the quantity demanded remains at 5,000 apartments while the quantity supplied falls to 1,000 apartments.

9. **b** The deadweight loss is larger after the disaster because the difference between the quantity supplied at the ceiling price and the equilibrium quantity is larger.

10. **a** The price ceiling has made the equilibrium price illegal, so a shortage results.

11. **b** Black markets are illegal markets wherein people conduct transactions at prices forbidden by the government.

12. **a** The price ceiling makes the equilibrium price illegal, so a shortage and a deadweight loss occur.

A Labor Market with a Minimum Wage

13. **a** If a minimum wage is set above the equilibrium

price, it creates a surplus of labor and a deadweight loss. If it is set equal to or below the equilibrium wage, it does not create a surplus of labor or a deadweight loss.

14. **d** A minimum wage of $4 falls below the equilibrium wage, so no unemployment is created.

15. **c** If the minimum wage is raised to $12, the quantity of labor supplied, 50 million hours, exceeds the quantity demanded, 30 million hours, by 20 million hours.

16. **d** Because the minimum wage is *below* the equilibrium wage rate, the labor market remains at is equilibrium so there is no deadweight loss.

17. **d** The minimum wage is unfair by both measures of fairness.

Taxes

18. **c** The supply curve with the tax lies above the supply without the tax by a distance equal to the amount of the tax. The vertical distance in Figure 6.5 is $2, so this amount is the tax.

19. **b** Because only the supply curve shifted, the tax law has imposed the tax on only the sellers.

20. **d** The total price, including the tax, paid by buyers climbs from $12 to $13, so buyers pay $1 of the tax.

21. **d** The price the sellers keep per DVD falls from $12 to $11, so sellers pay $1 of the tax.

22. **c** When demand is perfectly inelastic, the price of the product rises by the entire amount of the tax so buyers pay the entire tax.

23. **a** The greater the elasticity of demand, the more the tax decreases the equilibrium quantity consumed.

24. **c** The more elastic the supply, the greater the amount of a tax paid by buyers and the smaller the amount paid be sellers..

Production Quotas and Subsidies

25. **a** The production quota decreases the supply, which raises the price.

26. **a** The subsidy increases the supply and creates a deadweight loss from overproduction.

27. **b** Farmers have the incentive to cheat on a production quota because their marginal cost of producing a bushel of wheat is less is less than the price they would receive from selling it.

Markets for Illegal Goods

28. **b** The sanctions decrease the benefits buyers receive from the good, thereby decreasing demand for the product.

29. **c** The sanctions shift the supply curve leftward, thereby raising the price and decreasing the quantity.

30. **d** All of the policies decrease the quantity so all could be used to discourage consumption of a good.

■ Answers to Short Answer Problems

1. For a price ceiling to have an effect it must make the equilibrium price illegal. If the price ceiling does not make the equilibrium price illegal, the market price remains equal to the equilibrium price and nothing changes. However, if the price ceiling is set below the equilibrium price, then the equilibrium price becomes illegal. In this situation the market is affected: At the ceiling price there is a shortage but the price cannot (legally) rise to eliminate the shortage. The shortage persists and a deadweight loss is created.

2. a. The equilibrium price of gasoline is $4.00 a gallon because that price equates the quantity supplied to the quantity demanded. The equilibrium quantity is 16 million gallons a year.

   b. There is no deadweight loss in this unregulated market.

   c. If the government imposes a price ceiling of $3.90 a gallon, the demand schedule shows that consumers demand 18 million gallons of gasoline a year. At the ceiling price, the supply schedule indicates that producers supply 14 million gallons of gasoline a year.

   d. With the price ceiling, only 14 million gallons of gasoline are available. Thus even though consumers would be willing to purchase 18 million gallons, all they can actually buy is 14 million gallons. The shortage equals the amount consumers are willing to buy (18 million gallons) minus the amount actually available (14 million gallons), or 4 million gallons.

   e. The easiest way to calculate the deadweight loss uses Figure 6.9 (on the next page), which shows the deadweight loss triangle. The height of the

FIGURE **6.9**
Short Answer Problem 2 (e)

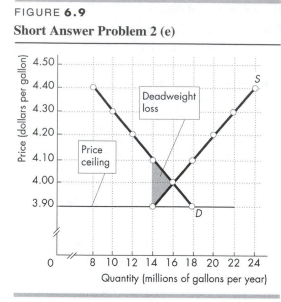

triangle is $0.20 per gallon (= $4.10 – $3.90) and the base of the triangle is 2 million gallons (= 16 million gallons – 14 million gallons). Using the formula for the area of a triangle, the deadweight loss therefore equals ½ × $0.20 per gallon × 2 million gallons, or $200,000.

TABLE **6.4**
Short Answer Question 3

Price (dollars per gallon)	Quantity demanded (millions of gallons per year)	New quantity supplied (millions of gallons per year)
$4.40	8	16
4.30	10	14
4.20	12	12
4.10	14	10
4.00	16	8
3.90	18	6

3. a. Table 6.4 makes answering this question easier. It shows the new supply schedule after the decrease in supply. The demand schedule is unchanged. The new equilibrium price is $4.20 a gallon, and the new equilibrium quantity is 12 million gallons a year. The gasoline is allocated among consumers by price. Faced with the higher price, consumers will decrease the quantity they demand. Essentially, those consumers willing and able to pay the higher price buy gas-

oline and consumers either unwilling or unable to pay the higher price do not.

b. If the government imposes a price ceiling of $3.90 a gallon, the demand schedule shows that the quantity demanded is 18 million gallons. The quantity supplied at the ceiling price is 6 million gallons.

c. With the price ceiling, consumers are able to purchase only the amount of gasoline actually made available. That is, consumers can buy only 6 million gallons of gasoline, and there is a shortage of 12 million gallons (18 million gallons – 6 million gallons). Because the price cannot allocate gasoline among consumers, other mechanisms come into play. Long lines will form at gasoline stations, so people willing and able to wait in the lines will buy gasoline. Black markets, where bribes and other side payments are made to suppliers by consumers, will spring up. Thus consumers willing and able to participate in black markets will buy gasoline.

d. When the price is left free to reach its equilibrium, consumers can consume 12 million gallons of gasoline. With the price ceiling, consumers can consume 6 million gallons of gasoline. Hence, as a group, consumers are able to consume more gasoline when the market is left unregulated.

FIGURE **6.10**
Short Answer Problem 4

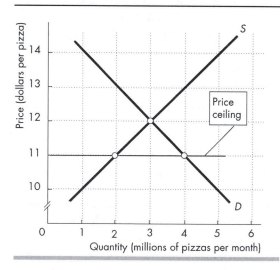

4. Figure 6.10 illustrates the pizza market before and after the price ceiling has been imposed. Before a

price ceiling of, say, $11 is imposed, the equilibrium price is $12 a pizza and the quantity produced and consumed is 3 million per month. With the price ceiling of $11 a pizza, suppliers are willing to produce only 2 million pizzas a month. Consumers would like to buy more pizza, 4 million a month, but they cannot buy what is not produced. Thus only 2 million pizzas rather than 3 million pizzas are consumed after the price ceiling. So even though the price ceiling might have been imposed to give more consumers the ability to afford to buy pizza, in aggregate more pizza is consumed without the price ceiling than with it.

FIGURE **6.11**
Short Answer Problem 5

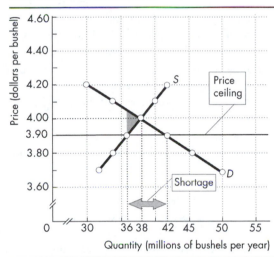

5. a. Figure 6.11 presents the demand and supply curves.

    b. The equilibrium price of slice of pizza is $4.00 a slice, where the demand and supply curves intersect. The equilibrium quantity is 38 million slices per year.

    c. Figure 6.11 shows that, with a price ceiling of $3.90, the quantity demanded is 42 million slices and the quantity supplied is 36 million slices. There is a shortage is 6 million slices of pizza. The deadweight loss is the area of the gray triangle.

6. a. The tax imposed on sellers decreases the supply. The distance between the supply curve with the tax and the initial supply curve is the amount of the tax. This situation is illustrated in Figure 6.12 where the double headed arrow equals the amount of the tax, $3.00. The price paid by the

FIGURE **6.12**
Short Answer Problem 6

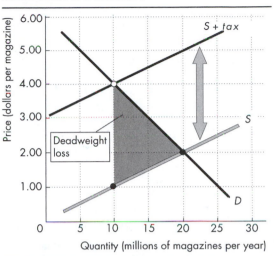

buyers rises from $2.00 per magazine to $4.00 per magazine, so the buyers pay $2.00 of the tax.

    b. As Figure 6.12 shows, before the tax the sellers received $2.00 per magazine. After the tax is imposed, the sellers receive $4.00 per magazine but $3.00 must be sent to the government as the tax. So after the tax the price (net of the tax) that sellers keep is $4.00 − $3.00 or $1.00. The price received and kept by the sellers falls from $2.00 per magazine to $1.00 per magazine, so the sellers pay $1.00 of the tax.

    c. Figure 6.12 shows the triangular deadweight loss. The deadweight loss equals the area of the triangle, ½ ×(20 million − 10 million) × ($4 − $1), which is $15 million.

7. a. The tax imposed on buyers decreases the demand. The distance between the demand curve with the tax and the initial demand curve is the amount of the tax. This situation is illustrated in Figure 6.13 (on the next page) where the double headed arrow equals the amount of the tax, $3.00. Before the tax, the price paid by the buyers was $2.00 per magazine. After the tax, the price, including the tax rises to $4.00 per magazine. So the buyers pay $2.00 of the tax.

    b. As Figure 6.13 shows, before the tax the sellers received $2.00 per magazine. After the tax is imposed, the sellers receive $1.00 per magazine. So the sellers pay $1.00 of the tax.

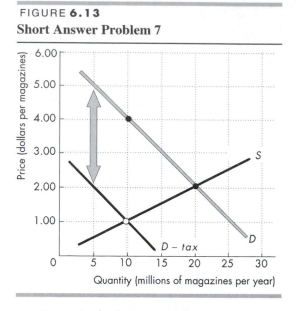

FIGURE **6.13**
Short Answer Problem 7

c. Buyers (and sellers) pay the same amount of the tax regardless of whether the tax law imposes the tax on buyers or on sellers.

8. a. You want to find products for which the demand is relatively inelastic. Taxing products with inelastic demands has two effects. First, the decrease in the equilibrium quantity is less than it would be if a good with an elastic demand were taxed; and, second, the amount of the tax paid by consumers is higher for goods with inelastic demands. Because the president wants the taxes to fall most heavily on consumers, the second effect directly achieves the president's second goal. In addition, the president also wants to generate substantial tax revenues. Because the equilibrium quantity is not decreased much, more of this product will be bought and sold. With more transactions, the government will collect more tax. So the first effect means that the government will collect significant tax revenues — the president's first goal.

   b. You recommend that the government tax products with relatively inelastic supplies. First a relatively inelastic supply means that a tax does not reduce the equilibrium quantity by much. As a result, the government collects more tax revenues than if it taxed products with elastic supplies. Second, the amount of the tax paid by suppliers increases as the supply becomes less

elastic. So by taxing products with inelastic supplies, the producers pay a larger part of the tax.

9. A subsidy is like a "reverse tax." In particular, when a firm is taxed, it *sends* money to the government when it sells the product, which decreases the supply thereby raising the price and decreasing the quantity. When a firm is subsidized, it *receives* money from the government when it sells the product, which increases the supply thereby lowering the price and increasing the quantity. Both a tax and a subsidy can create a deadweight loss. A tax creates a deadweight loss because it leads to less than the efficient quantity being produced; a subsidy creates a deadweight loss because it leads to more than the efficient quantity being produced.

10. a. Imposing sanctions on consumers (users) decreases the demand and shifts the demand curve for illegal drugs leftward. The price falls and the quantity of illegal drugs consumed decreases.

    b. If sellers are penalized, the supply decreases and the supply curve shifts leftward. In this case, the price of illegal drugs rises and the quantity consumed decreases.

    c. The answers to parts (a) and (b) illustrate that the price of illegal drugs cannot be used to judge the success of a policy against drugs. For instance, if the price rises when sanctions are imposed against sellers, the policy is effective. But if the price rises when sanctions are imposed against users, the policy is failing because even with the sanctions demand is increasing enough so that consumption is rising. So to use price changes as a signal of the success or failure of a policy also requires knowledge of what type of policy is being pursued.

■ You're the Teacher

1. "You're getting a bit confused. It's easiest to explain this concept with a concrete example: I'm hungry so let's think about pizza. Suppose that the government did not tax pizza and that the equilibrium price is $11 per pizza. Okay, now suppose that the government slaps a $2 per pizza tax on pizza. What our textbook has shown me is that this tax raises the price, say, to $11.50 per pizza. In other words, the price — *including* the tax — is $11.50 per pizza. That also means that the price without the tax falls to $9.50 per pizza. So when we call the people at

the pizza shop on the phone, they tell us that the price is $9.50 plus $2 tax, or $11.50. It looks like we're getting stuck with the entire $2 tax. But we're not. Actually, after the tax is imposed, we pay only $0.50 more because the price we pay rises only from $11.00 to $11.50. The pizza makers wind up pay- ing $1.50 of this tax: Before the tax they got to keep $11.00 per pizza, but after the tax they get to keep only $9.50 per pizza. The moral here is that appear- ances can be deceiving. Another moral is that you need to study your economics more!"

Chapter Quiz

1. Buyers pay more of a tax if the tax is imposed on
   a. only the sellers.
   b. the sellers and the buyers equally.
   c. None of the above answers is correct because the buyers pay the same proportion of the tax regardless of upon whom the tax is levied.
   d. None of the above answers is correct because buyers *always* pay 100 percent of any tax.

2. Effective rent controls
   a. increase search activity.
   b. increase the long-run housing supply.
   c. have no effect on the quantity of apartments rented.
   d. increase the vacancy rate of apartments.

3. When search costs are taken into account, a price ceiling set below the equilibrium price _____ consumer surplus and _____ producer surplus.
   a. decreases; decreases
   b. increases; decreases
   c. decreases; increases
   d. increases; increases

4. A price floor set below the equilibrium price
   a. decreases only the quantity demanded.
   b. decreases only the quantity supplied.
   c. decreases both the quantity supplied and the quantity demanded.
   d. has no effect.

5. The minimum wage boosts firms' incentive to
   a. hire more workers.
   b. increase output.
   c. use labor-saving technology.
   d. hire teens.

6. The equilibrium price of a gallon of gasoline is $4 per gallon. Of the following prices, the deadweight is the largest of a price ceiling is set at _____ per gallon of gasoline.
   a. $2
   b. $3
   c. $4
   d. $5

7. A production quota set less than the equilibrium quantity _____ the price received by sellers and _____ a deadweight loss.
   a. lowers; creates
   b. raises; does not create
   c. does not change; creates
   d. raises; creates

8. The supply and demand for a good are neither perfectly elastic nor perfectly inelastic. Hence imposing a tax on the good burdens
   a. only buyers.
   b. only sellers.
   c. both buyers and sellers.
   d. neither buyers nor sellers.

9. If the government declares that selling certain drugs is illegal, then the
   a. demand curve shifts rightward.
   b. demand curve shifts leftward.
   c. supply curve shifts rightward.
   d. supply curve shifts leftward.

10. A minimum wage _____ based on the fair rules approach to fairness and _____ based on the fair results approach to fairness.
    a. is not; is not
    b. is; is not
    c. is not; is
    d. is; is

The answers for this Chapter Quiz are on page 345

Chapter 7 GLOBAL MARKETS IN ACTION

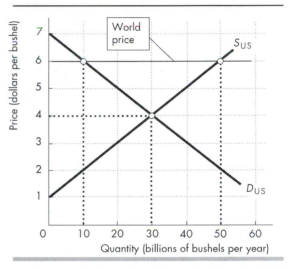

How Global Markets Work

The goods and services we buy from producers in other nations are our **imports**; the goods and services we sell to people in other nations are our **exports**. In 2011 U.S. exports were $2.1 trillion, about 14 percent of total U.S. production, and U.S. imports were $2.7 trillion, about 18 percent of total U.S. expenditure. Both goods and services are traded.

Comparative advantage is the factor that drives international trade. National comparative advantage occurs when a nation can perform an activity or produce a good or service at lower opportunity cost than any other nation. Nations reap gains from trade by specializing in the production of the good or service in which they have a comparative advantage and trading with other nations.

♦ Figure 7.1 shows the wheat market, a market in which the United States has a comparative advantage. The no-trade price in the United States, $4 per bushel, is less than the world price, $6 per bushel. At the world price, the quantity of wheat demanded by U.S. residents is 10 billion bushels per year, the quantity of wheat produced in the United States is 50 billion bushels per year, and the difference, 40 billion bushels per year, is exported.

♦ Figure 7.2 shows the market for blouses, a market in which foreign countries have a comparative advantage. The no-trade price in the United States, $60 per blouse, is greater than the world price, $30 per blouse. At the world price, the quantity of blouses demanded by U.S. residents is 25 million per year, the quantity of blouses produced in the United States is 5 million per year, and the difference, 20 million blouses per year, is imported.

FIGURE 7.1

A Market with U.S. Exports

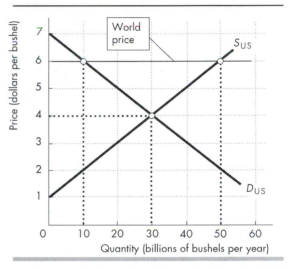

FIGURE 7.2

A Market with U.S. Imports

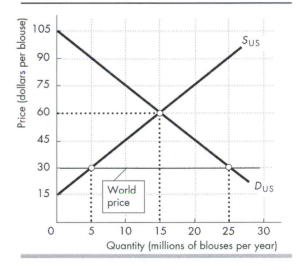

■ Winners, Losers, and the Net Gain from Trade

The gains and losses from trade are measured as the changes in consumer surplus, producer surplus, and total surplus.

♦ Figure 7.3 shows the wheat market, a market in which the United States has a comparative advantage. With no international trade the price in the United States is $4 per bushel and 30 billion bushels are produced and consumed. Consumer surplus is equal to area *A* + area *B* and producer surplus is equal to area *C*. With international trade the price is $6 per bushel, the world price. 10 billion bushels are consumed in the United States, 50 billion bushels are produced in the United States, and the difference, 40 billion bushels, is exported. Consumer surplus shrinks to area *A* and producer surplus expands to area *B* + area *C* + area *D*. Consumers lose from this trade and producers gain. On net, total surplus in the United States increases by area *D*.

♦ Figure 7.4 shows the market for blouses, a market in which other countries have a comparative advantage. With no international trade the price in the United States is $60 per blouse and 15 million blouses per year are produced and consumed. Consumer surplus is equal to area *A* and producer surplus is equal to area *B* + area *C*. With international trade the price is $30 per blouse, the world price. 25 million blouses per year are consumed in the United States, 5 million blouses per year are produced in the United States, and the difference, 20 million blouses per year, is imported. Consumer surplus expands to area *A* + area *B* + area *D* and producer surplus shrinks to area *C*. Consumers gain from this trade and producers lose. On net, total surplus in the United States increases by area *D*.

For both imports and exports, the United States has a net gain because the total surplus increases. However for both imports and exports one group—consumers for exports and producers for imports—loses.

■ International Trade Restrictions

Governments restrict trade to protect domestic industries. The four main methods used to restrict trade are:

♦ **Tariffs** — a tax imposed by the importing country when an imported good crosses its boundary.

♦ **Import quotas** — a restriction that limits the max-

FIGURE **7.3**

Surpluses in a Market with U.S. Exports

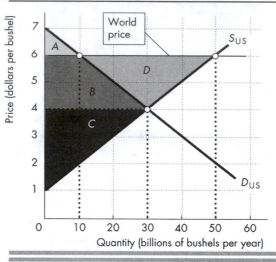
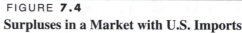

FIGURE **7.4**

Surpluses in a Market with U.S. Imports

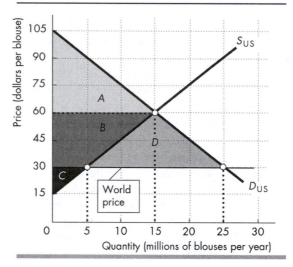

imum quantity of a good that may be imported in a given period.

♦ Other import barriers — other barriers include health, safety, and regulation barriers and voluntary export restraints. A voluntary export restraint is the same as a quota that is given to foreign exporters of the good.

♦ Export subsidies — payments given by the government to firms that produce exported goods and services.

Today, U.S. tariffs are low compared to their historical

levels. The **General Agreement on Tariffs and Trade** (GATT) is an international agreement designed to reduce tariffs. Figure 7.5 illustrates the effects of a tariff.

♦ Because the supply from the rest of world is perfectly elastic, a tariff of $15 per blouse raises the price in the United States the full amount of the tariff, in the figure from $30 per blouse to $45 per blouse. In the United States the quantity of blouses demanded decreases to 20 million per year and the quantity produced increases to 10 million per year so imports decrease to 10 million blouses per year.

♦ Consumer surplus shrinks from area *A* + area *B* + area *C* + area *D* + area *E* before the tariff to only area *A* after the tariff. Producer surplus expands from area *F* before the tariff to area *B* + area *F* after the tariff. The government gains tariff revenue equal to area *D*. Area *C* and area *E* are deadweight losses.

♦ Producers and the government gain from a tariff. Consumers lose from a tariff. On net society loses from a tariff because deadweight losses are created.

An import quota decreases the amount of the good that can be imported. Figure 7.6 shows the effect of a quota.

♦ An import quota of 10 million blouses means that at prices above the world price 10 million blouses are added to the U.S. supply. The supply curve to the United States becomes *S*$_{US}$ + *quota*. The price of blouses rises to $45 per blouse. At this price the quantity of blouses demanded decreases to 20 million and the quantity produced increases to 10 million. Imports decrease to 10 million blouses.

♦ Consumer surplus shrinks from area *A* + area *B* + area *C* + area *D* + area *E* before the quota to only area *A* after the quota. Producer surplus expands from area *F* before the quota to area *B* + area *F* after the tariff. Importers gain a profit equal to area *D*. Area *C* and area *E* are deadweight losses.

♦ Producers and importers gain from an import quota. Consumers lose from an import quota. On net society loses from an import quota because deadweight losses are created.

Tariffs, import quotas, other import barriers and export subsidies reduce the gains from trade and create deadweight losses and inefficiency.

■ The Case Against Protection

Arguments in favor of protection are flawed. The seven

FIGURE **7.5**
Effects of a Tariff

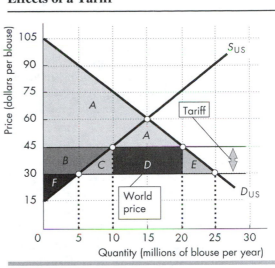

FIGURE **7.6**
Effects of a Quota

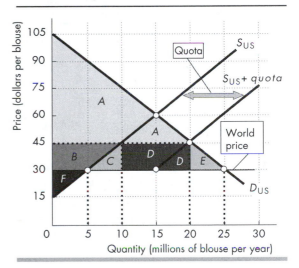

arguments and their errors are:

♦ *Helps an infant-industry grow* — the nation should protect a new industry that will grow into a mature industry that can compete in the world market by reaping learning-by-doing gains in productivity. Error: *If* firms will reap learning-by-doing benefits, then this argument fails because these firms can finance their own start-ups.

♦ *Counteracts* **Dumping** — the nation should protect an industry from foreign competitors who sell their exports at a lower price than the cost of production.

Error: Determining when a firm sells below cost is very difficult; and it is rational for a firm to charge a low price in a market in which the demand is sensitive to the price and a high price in a market in which the demand is insensitive to the price.

♦ *Saves domestic jobs* — imports cost U.S. jobs.
Error: Free trade costs jobs in importing industries, but it creates them in exporting industries; tariffs that protect jobs in import-competing industries do so at an exceedingly high cost.

♦ *Compete with cheap foreign labor* — tariffs are necessary to compete with cheap foreign labor.
Error: U.S. labor is more productive than cheap foreign labor; U.S. firms can compete successfully in industries in which they have a comparative advantage because of their productivity relative to other nations.

♦ *Penalize lax environmental standards* — protection is needed to compete against nations with weak environmental standards.
Error: Not all poor nations have weak standards; poor nations' concerns about the environment will increase when they grow richer through trade; currently poor nations might have a comparative advantage in pollution-intensive goods.

♦ *Rich nations exploit developing countries* — protection prevents developed nations from forcing people in poor nations to work for slave wages.
Error: By allowing poor nations to trade with rich ones, wages in poor nations rise because of the increased demand for labor.

♦ *Reduce offshore outsourcing* — (**offshore outsourcing** occurs when U.S. firms buy goods, components, or services from firms in other countries) offshore outsourcing sends good jobs to other countries. Offshore outsourcing inflicts losses on some parts of society, such as U.S. workers who lose jobs, but also brings gains to other sector4s, such as education which is exported. Overall, the economy gains.

Trade is restricted for two reasons:

♦ Tariff revenue — The government collects revenue from tariffs. This revenue source is important in developing nations.

♦ Rent seeking — **Rent seeking** is lobbying for special treatment by the government to create economic profit or to divert consumer surplus or producer surplus away from others. The people harmed by international trade lobby politicians to limit free trade.

Helpful Hints

1. **DOES PROTECTION SAVE JOBS ?** This argument is popular but incorrect. Imposing a tariff on imports costs jobs in export industries. We lose jobs because foreigners, unable to sell as much to us, are thus unable to buy as much from us. Hence our export industries shrink, or fail to grow as much as otherwise.

   Moreover, saving the jobs in the import-competing industry comes at a very high cost. For example, protection in the textile industry annually costs American residents $221,000 per job; in the automobile industry, $105,000 per job; in dairy products, $220,000 per job; and in steel, $750,000 per job. These costs greatly exceed the wages in these jobs. Just as it would be foolish to spend $221,000 to obtain $45,000, so, too, is it foolish for the nation to protect jobs when the cost of the protection exceeds the wages paid for the jobs!

2. **WHY DOES PROTECTION PERSIST ?** Gains from free trade can be considerable, so why do countries impose trade restrictions? The key is that, although free trade creates overall benefits to the economy as a whole, there are both winners and losers. The winners gain more in total than the losers lose, but the latter tend to be concentrated in a few industries. In other words, the gains from free trade are spread amongst many people — so the gain per person is small — while the costs are concentrated amongst only a few people— so the costs per person are large.

   Because of this concentration, free trade is resisted. Even though trade restrictions benefit only a small minority while the overwhelming majority are harmed, implementation of trade barriers is not surprising. The cost of a particular trade restriction to each of the majority individually is quite small, but the benefit to each of the few individually is large. So the minority has a strong incentive to have a restriction imposed, whereas the majority has little incentive to expend time and energy in resisting a trade barrier. The net result is that governments frequently wind up restricting free trade, even though the restrictions cost their nations more than they benefit it.

Questions

True/False and Explain

How Global Markets Work

1. Nations can trade goods but not services.

2. In 2011, the value of American imports exceeded the value of American exports.

3. If the U.S. price of a good before international trade is lower than the world price, the U.S. will export this good when it trades internationally.

4. Compared to the situation before international trade, the price of a good rises in the United States when the United States exports the good.

5. Compared to the situation before international trade, U.S. consumption of a good increases when the United States imports the good.

Winners, Losers, and the Net Gain from Trade

6. U.S. producer surplus decreases when the United States imports a good.

7. Because U.S. total surplus rises when the United States imports a good, no one in the United States loses from importing the good.

8. The U.S. consumer surplus from wheat increases when the United States exports wheat.

9. Domestic producers gain and domestic consumers lose from exports.

10. Only the nation that exports the good gains from international trade.

International Trade Restrictions

11. When governments impose tariffs, they increase their citizens' consumer surplus.

12. When France imposes a tariff on wheat, production of wheat in France increases.

13. Tariffs in the United States are at an all-time high.

14. An import quota has no effect on consumer surplus because quotas do not change the price of the good.

15. If Chile imposes an import quota on U.S. wheat, on net Chile gains.

16. An import quota and a voluntary export restraint both raise revenue for the government.

The Case Against Protection

17. The only argument for protection without any error is the infant-industry argument.

18. U.S. workers can compete with lower paid foreign workers in industries in which the U.S. has a comparative advantage.

19. International trade lowers wages in poor nations.

20. Governments gain more revenue from import quotas than from tariffs.

Multiple Choice

How Global Markets Work

1. Which of the following statements about U.S. international trade in 2011 is correct?
   a. The value of U.S. exports exceeded the value of U.S. imports.
   b. The value of U.S. exports was about 33 percent of the value of total U.S. production.
   c. The United States imported only goods.
   d. The United States was the world's largest trader.

2. The United States has a comparative advantage in producing cotton if the U.S. price of cotton before international trade is _____ the world price.
   a. less than
   b. equal to
   c. greater than
   d. not comparable to

3. Compared to the situation before international trade, after the United States exports a good production in the United States _____ and consumption in the United States _____.
   a. increases; increases
   b. increases; decreases
   c. decreases; increases
   d. decreases; decreases

4. Compared to the situation before international trade, after the United States imports a good production in the United States _____ and consumption in the United States _____.
   a. increases; increases
   b. increases; decreases
   c. decreases; increases
   d. decreases; decreases

Winners, Losers, and the Net Gain from Trade

Figure 7.7 illustrates the market for cardboard, which is imported into the United States. Use Figure 7.7 for the next three questions.

FIGURE 7.7
Multiple Choice Questions 5, 6, and 7

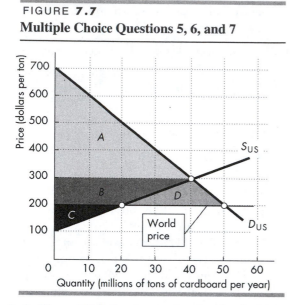

5. In Figure 7.7, before international trade, the U.S. price of cardboard was ____ per ton and the quantity consumed in the United States was ____ million tons per year.
   a. $200; 50
   b. $300; 40
   c. $100; 20
   d. $200; 20

6. In Figure 7.7, consumer surplus before international trade is ____ and consumer surplus after international trade is ____.
   a. Area A; Area A + Area B + Area C
   b. Area A + Area B; Area A + Area B
   c. Area A; Area A + Area B + Area C + Area D
   d. Area A; Area A + Area B + Area D

7. In Figure 7.7, producer surplus before international trade is ____ and producer surplus after international trade is ____.
   a. Area C; Area A + Area B + Area C + Area D
   b. Area C; Area C
   c. Area B + Area C; Area C
   d. Area A + Area B + Area D; Area C

8. U.S. producer surplus ____ when the United States imports a good and U.S. producer surplus ____ when the United States exports a good.
   a. increases; increases
   b. increases; decreases
   c. decreases; increases
   d. decreases; decreases

9. When the United States exports a good, U.S. consumer surplus ____ and U.S. total surplus ____.
   a. increases; increases
   b. increases; decreases
   c. decreases; increases
   d. decreases; decreases

10. When the United States exports a good, the amount of the ____ in U.S. consumer surplus is ____ the amount of the ____ in U.S. producer surplus.
    a. increase; smaller than; increase
    b. increase; larger than; decrease
    c. decrease; smaller than; increase
    d. decrease; equal to; increase

International Trade Restrictions

11. A tariff is
    a. a government imposed limit on the amount of a good that can be exported from a nation.
    b. a government imposed barrier that sets a fixed limit on the amount of a good that can be imported into a nation.
    c. a tax on a good imported into a nation.
    d. an agreement between governments to limit exports from a nation.

12. When the United States imposes a tariff on a good, the amount of the ____ in U.S. consumer surplus is ____ the amount of the ____ in U.S. producer surplus
    a. increase; smaller than; increase
    b. increase; larger than; decrease
    c. decrease; larger than; increase
    d. decrease; equal to; increase

13. Who benefits from a tariff on a good?
    a. Domestic consumers of the good
    b. Domestic producers of the good
    c. Foreign governments
    d. Foreign producers of the good

14. When the United States imposes an import quota on a good, the amount of the _____ in U.S. consumer surplus is _____ the amount of the _____ in U.S. producer surplus

    a. increase; smaller than; increase
    b. increase; larger than; decrease
    c. decrease; larger than; increase
    d. decrease; equal to; increase

15. Who benefits from an import quota on a good?

    a. Domestic consumers of the good
    b. Domestic producers of the good
    c. Foreign governments
    d. Domestic government

16. Tariffs _____ consumer surplus and import quotas _____ consumer surplus.

    a. increase; increase
    b. increase; decrease
    c. decrease; increase
    d. decrease; decrease

17. Tariffs _____ the domestic price of the good and import quotas _____ the domestic price of the good.

    a. raise; raise
    b. raise; lower
    c. lower; raise
    d. lower; lower

18. Tariffs _____ a deadweight loss and import quotas _____ a deadweight loss.

    a. create; create
    b. create; do not create
    c. do not create; create
    d. do not create; do not create

19. When does the government gain the most revenue?

    a. When it imposes a tariff.
    b. When it imposes an import quota.
    c. When it negotiates a voluntary export restraint.
    d. When it offers an export subsidy.

The Case Against Protection

20. Selling a product in a foreign nation at a price less than its cost of production is called

    a. infant industry exploitation.
    b. absolute advantage.
    c. dumping.
    d. net exporting.

21. The (false) idea that an industry should be protected because of learning-by-doing until it is large enough to compete successfully in world markets is the _____ argument for protection.

    a. cheap foreign labor
    b. infant industry
    c. dumping
    d. comparative advantage

22. When a rich nation buys a product made in a poor nation, in the poor nation the demand for labor _____ and the wage rate _____.

    a. increases; rises
    b. increases; falls
    c. decreases; rises
    d. decreases; falls

23. Which of the following is a valid reason for protecting an industry?

    a. The industry is unable to compete with low-wage foreign competitors.
    b. Protection penalizes lax environmental standards.
    c. Protection keeps richer nations from exploiting the workers of poorer countries.
    d. None of the above reasons is a valid reason for protection.

24. Which of the following statements about the gains from international trade is correct?

    a. Everyone gains from international trade.
    b. Some people gain from international trade and some lose, though overall the gains exceed the losses.
    c. Some people gain and some people lose from international trade; overall the losses exceed the gains.
    d. Everyone loses from international trade.

■ **Short Answer Problems**

1. Table 7.1 (on the next page) gives the domestic supply and demand schedules for watches for the nation of Norolex.

    a. Draw the supply and demand schedules in Figure 7.8 (on the next page).
    b. What is the equilibrium price?
    c. How many watches are produced in Norolex? How many are purchased by consumers in Norolex?

TABLE **7.1**

Market for Watches in Norolex

Price (dollars per watch)	Quantity demanded (millions of watches)	Quantity supplied (millions of watches)
$20	65	15
25	60	20
30	55	25
35	50	30
40	45	35
45	40	40
50	35	45

FIGURE **7.9**

Short Answer Problem 2

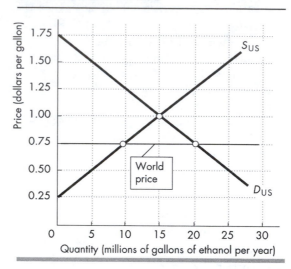

FIGURE **7.8**

Short Answer Problem 1

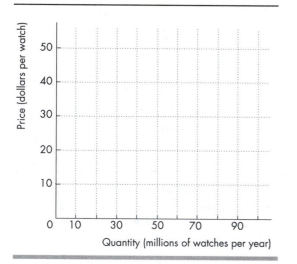

d. If the world price of a watch is $35 per watch, how many watches are produced in Norolex and how many are consumed? Does Norolex import or export watches? How many?

e. At what world prices would Norolex export watches? At what world prices would Norolex import watches?

2. Figure 7.9 shows the U.S. market for ethanol.

a. If ethanol is not traded internationally, what is the U.S. price and quantity of ethanol? In dollars, what is the amount of consumer surplus, producer surplus, and total surplus?

b. Now suppose the United States allows international trade in ethanol. In Figure 7.9 show the U.S. consumer surplus and U.S. producer surplus

when ethanol is imported at the world price. In dollars, what is the amount of consumer surplus, producer surplus, and total surplus?

c. How do the changes in the surpluses relate to the gainers and losers from international trade?

3. How does a tariff on an imported good affect the domestic price of the good? The quantity imported and the quantity produced domestically?

4. Return to the watch industry in Norolex, with the demand and supply schedules in Table 7.1. The world price of a watch is $35. The watch industry in Norolex is unhappy with the situation after trade has occurred and so it lobbies the government to impose a $5 per watch tariff.

a. With the tariff, what is the price of a watch in Norolex? How many watches are consumed in Norolex, produced in Norolex, and imported into Norolex? What is the government's revenue from this tariff?

b. In Figure 7.10 (on the next page) draw the demand and supply curves in Norolex. Show the world price of $35 a watch. Indicate the effect of the tariff and show the deadweight loss from the tariff.

c. What is the action of the watch industry lobby group called?

5. How does an import quota on an imported good affect the domestic price of the good, the quantity produced domestically, and the quantity imported?

FIGURE **7.10**
Short Answer Problem 4

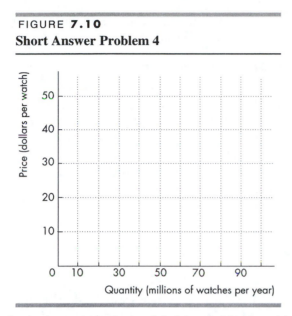

FIGURE **7.11**
Short Answer Problem 7

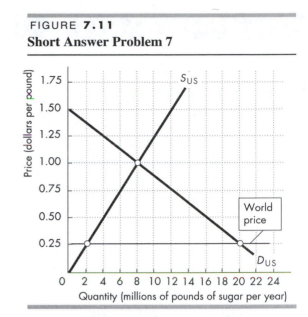

6. Again return to the watch industry in Norolex with the supply and demand schedules given in Table 71. Suppose the watch industry lobby group in Norolex convinces the government to impose an import quota of 10 million watches. With the import quota, what is the price of a watch in Norolex? How many watches are consumed in Norolex, produced in Norolex, and imported into Norolex? What is the government's revenue from this import quota?

7. Figure 7.11 shows the market for sugar.

   a. With international trade in sugar and no protection, what is the price of sugar in the United States, how much sugar is consumed in the United States and how much is produced? What is the U.S. consumer surplus from sugar, the U.S. producer surplus from sugar, and the total surplus?

   b. Show the effect of an import quota of 6 million tons of sugar per year in Figure 7.11. What is the price of sugar in the United States, how much sugar is consumed in the United States and how much is produced? What is the U.S. consumer surplus from sugar and the U.S. producer surplus from sugar? Who gains and who loses from the import quota? What is the deadweight loss?

   c. How does the deadweight loss with the import quota compare to the deadweight loss without the import quota? Are import quotas good or bad for the economy?

■ **You're the Teacher**

1. "I understand the stuff about comparative advantage. But I can't see how the United States can compete with nations like Mexico, where the wages are so low. We have to protect our high wages by keeping Mexican products out of our markets." Your friend thinks he understands comparative advantage, but he does not. Help him understand comparative advantage. Explain how American firms can compete with Mexican companies.

2. After you explain the error in question 1, your friend makes another mistake: "OK, now I see how U.S. firms can compete. But, still, international trade can't be good. After all, if this trade helps Mexico, we must lose. So I still think that international trade should be banned." Explain to your friend how international trade benefits both America and Mexico.

Answers

■ True/False Answers

How Global Markets Work

1. **F** Services, such as travel abroad, transportation, and insurance, can be traded internationally.

2. **T** In 2011, as throughout the past three decades, the value of U.S. imports exceeded the value of U.S. exports.

3. **T** The lower U.S. price means that the United States has a comparative advantage in the production of the good.

4. **T** The U.S. price rises to equal the world price.

5. **T** The rise in consumption is the benefit the United States receives from imports.

Winners, Losers, and the Net Gain from Trade

6. **T** When the United States imports a good, the U.S. price falls and the quantity produced in the United States decreases, both of which decrease U.S. producer surplus.

7. **F** While U.S. total surplus rises, U.S. producer surplus falls and U.S. producers are harmed by imports.

8. **F** U.S. consumer surplus falls because the U.S. price of wheat rises when the United States exports wheat.

9. **T** When the United States exports a good, the U.S. price rises, which benefits U.S. producers and harms U.S. consumers.

10. **F** The total surplus rises in *both* the nation that exports the good and the nation that imports the good.

International Trade Restrictions

11. **F** By raising the price of imported goods, tariffs harm consumers.

12. **T** By raising the French price of wheat, French producers respond by increasing the quantity of wheat they produce.

13. **F** Tariffs in the United States are near an all-time low.

14. **F** A quota raises the domestic price of the good, thereby decreasing the consumer surplus.

15. **F** A quota creates a deadweight loss in Chile, indicating that Chile loses from the quota.

16. **F** The government gains no revenue from either a quota or a voluntary export restraint.

The Case Against Protection

17. **F** All arguments for protection are flawed.

18. **T** In industries with a comparative advantage, higher productivity more than offsets higher wages, so American firms can successfully compete.

19. **F** International trade *raises* wages in poor nations.

20. **F** Governments gain no revenue from import quotas whereas they gain some revenue from tariffs.

■ Multiple Choice Answers

How Global Markets Work

1. **d** The United States is by far the world's largest trader, accounting for 10 percent of world exports and 13 percent of world imports.

2. **a** If the U.S. price of cotton before international trade is lower than the world price, the United States has a comparative advantage in producing cotton and will export cotton.

3. **b** If the United States exports a good, its U.S. price rises, which increases its U.S. production and decreases its U.S. consumption.

4. **c** If the United States imports a good, its U.S. price falls, which decreases its U.S. production and increases its U.S. consumption.

Winners, Losers, and the Net Gain from Trade

5. **b** The equilibrium is determined by the intersection of the supply and demand curves.

6. **d** Imports benefit consumers because their consumer surplus increases.

7. **c** Imports harm producers because their producer surplus decreases.

8. **c** Imports harm producers and exports benefit producers.

9. **c** Exports harm consumers, because their consumer surplus decreases, but exports benefit the overall economy because total surplus increases.

10. **c** Consumers lose from exports while producers gain. The gain to producers exceeds the loss to consumers so, on net, society gains.

International Trade Restrictions

11. **c** Answer (c) is the definition of a tariff.

12. **c** Consumers lose from a tariff while producers gain. The loss to consumers exceeds the gain to producers so that, on net, society loses.

13. **b** Domestic producers gain because the price of the product rises.

14. **c** Analogous to the situation with a tariff, consumers lose from a quota and producers gain. The loss to consumers again exceeds the gain to producers so that, on net, society loses.

15. **b** An import quota increases domestic producers' producer surplus.

16. **d** Tariffs and import quotas both harm consumers by decreasing consumer surplus.

17. **a** Tariffs and import quotas both raise the domestic price of the good.

18. **a** All trade barriers create deadweight losses.

19. **a** Unlike tariffs, the government gets no revenue from import quotas and voluntary export restraints.

The Case Against Protection

20. **c** Although often alleged, dumping is difficult to prove because it is difficult to determine whether a firm is selling below its cost.

21. **b** The description in the problem is the definition of the infant industry argument for protection.

22. **a** By increasing the demand for the goods produced in the poor nation, the demand for labor increases, thereby raising the wage rate in that nation.

23. **d** All of the reasons offered for protection are faulty.

24. **b** Because the overall gains exceed the overall loses, in principle the losers from international trade can be compensated so that, on balance, everyone gains from the trade.

■ Answers to Short Answer Problems

1. a. Figure 7.12 shows the demand and supply curves.
   b. Either from Figure 7.12 or from the demand and supply schedules, the equilibrium price with no international trade is $45 because at this price the quantity demanded equals the quantity supplied.

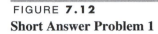

FIGURE **7.12**

Short Answer Problem 1

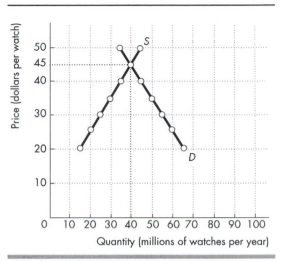

c. With no trade, 40 million watches per year are produced domestically, and so 40 million watches per year are purchased by consumers in Norolex.

d. If the world price of a watch is $35, then 30 million watches are produced in Norolex and 50 million are consumed. Norolex imports 20 million watches.

e. Norolex exports watches if the world price exceeds $45, the no-trade equilibrium price in Norolex. For prices higher than $45, Norolex has a comparative advantage in producing watches. Norolex imports watches for world prices lower than $45. If the world price of a watch is less than $45, Norolex does not have a comparative advantage in producing watches.

2. a. With no international trade, the price of a gallon of ethanol in the United States is $1.00 and 15 million gallons are produced. The consumer surplus is identified in Figure 7.13 (on the next page) as area *A*. The area of this triangle is equal to ½ × base × height or ½ × ($1.75 − $1.00) × 15 million, or $5,625,000. The producer surplus in Figure 7.13 is equal to the area of the triangle comprised of area *B* + area *C*. The producer surplus is equal to ½ × ($1.00 − $0.25) × 15 million, or (again) $5,625,000. The total surplus is equal to the sum of the consumer surplus and producer surplus, or $11,250,000.

FIGURE **7.13**
Short Answer Problem 2

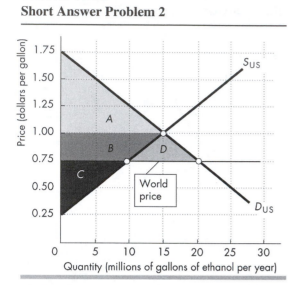

FIGURE **7.14**
Short Answer Problem 4

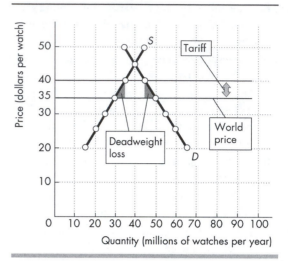

b. With international trade, the price in the United States falls to the world price, $0.75 per gallon. 20 million gallons of ethanol are consumed in the United States and 10 million gallons are produced. Consumer surplus becomes equal to area A + area B + area D, which is equal to $5,625,000 + $3,125,000 + $1,250,000, or $10,000,000. Producer surplus becomes equal to area C, which is $2,500,000. Total surplus equals the sum of consumer surplus and producer surplus, $12,500,000.

c. Consumers gain from imports, which is demonstrated by the point that the consumer surplus increases with imports. Producers lose with imports, which is demonstrated by the point that producer surplus decreases with imports. Society overall benefits from imports, which is demonstrated by the point that total surplus increases with imports.

3. A tariff on an imported good raises its price to domestic consumers because the foreign export supply decreases. As the domestic price of the good climbs, the quantity of the good demanded domestically decreases. The rise in the domestic price leads to an increase in the quantity of the good produced domestically. The quantity imported decreases.

4. a. The tariff increases the price of a watch in Norolex to $40. In Norolex at this price, 45 million watches are consumed, 35 million watches are produced, and 10 million watches are imported. The government gains tariff revenue of 10 million

watches × $5, or $50 million.

b. Figure 7.14 shows the situation in Norolex. The amount of the tariff is equal to the length of the arrow. The deadweight loss is equal to the area of the two grey triangles.

c. The producers are rent seeking.

5. The effect of an import quota on the domestic price of the good, the quantity imported, and the quantity produced domestically are exactly the same as the effects of a tariff: The import quota raises the price to domestic consumers, so the quantity of the good demanded domestically decreases and the quantity of the good produced domestically increases. For both reasons the quantity imported decreases.

6. The 10 million watch quota increases the price of a watch in Norolex to $40. In Norolex at this price, 45 million watches are consumed and 35 million watches are produced, so the quantity imported is equal to the quota amount, 10 million watches. The government gains *no* revenue from the import quota.

7. a. The price of a pound of sugar in the United States is $0.25 a pound. At this price 20 million pounds of sugar are consumed in the United States and 2 million pounds are produced. In Figure 7.15 (on the next page) U.S. consumer surplus is area A + area B + area C + area D + area E, which is $12,500,000. U.S. producer surplus is equal to area F, $250,000. Total surplus is equal to consumer surplus plus producer surplus, or $12,750,000.

FIGURE **7.15**
Short Answer Problem 7

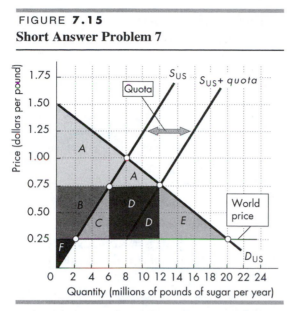

b. Figure 7.15 shows the situation with the import quota. The amount of the quota is equal to the length of the arrow. The quota changes the supply curve from S_{US} to S_{US} + *quota*. The price of a pound of sugar rises to $0.75. At this price, in the United States 12 million pounds of sugar are consumed and 6 million pounds of sugar are produced. With the quota consumer surplus is equal to area *A*, which is $4,500,000 and producer surplus is equal to area *B* + area *F*, which is $2,250,000. With the quota, consumer surplus decreases from $12,500,000 to $4,500,000 and producer surplus increases from $225,000 to $2,225,000. Consumers lose from the import quota and producers gain. The deadweight loss is equal to area *C* + area *E*, which is $3,000,000.

c. The deadweight loss without the quota is zero; with the quota it is $3,000,000. The deadweight loss is *much* larger with the import quota, which shows that import quotas harm the economy.

■ **You're the Teacher**

1. "Look, you don't have the main idea here. Let's use some numbers because they should help you catch on. Suppose that American wages are 10 times higher than Mexican wages. Now, it's also a fact that American workers are more productive than Mexican workers. Let's take two industries. In the first, call it industry A, suppose that American workers are 2 times as productive as Mexican workers; in the second, say, industry B, American workers are 20 times as productive. In industry A, American firms won't be able to compete with Mexican firms. Sure, our workers are twice as productive, but they are paid ten times as much. Therefore American firms will lose out in this industry. But in industry B, American companies will drive Mexican firms out of business. Even though our workers are paid 10 times as much as Mexican workers are paid, they produce 20 times as much as Mexican workers produce. The per unit cost of the good is less in the United States, so American firms are going to be able to compete and compete successfully."

"The United States won't be able to compete successfully with Mexico in producing every type of good or service but the reason is that the United States does not (and cannot) have a comparative advantage in all goods and services. But in the industry with the comparative advantage — industry B in my example — the United States is going to be able to compete and to win the competition."

2. "You're missing another key point. The chapter explains how trade allows all nations to increase their total surplus. Remember the diagrams showing this result? Obviously, this fact has to make nations engaged in international trade better off."

"But there's also another way to tackle this point. I read somewhere that 'trade is not a zero-sum game.' Here's what that means: If you and I voluntarily agree to a trade, like I'll trade my economics notes for your chemistry notes, the trade has to make us both better off. After all, if the trade didn't make me better off, I wouldn't agree to it and if it didn't make you better off, you wouldn't agree to it."

"Well, it's the same idea with trading between nations. Suppose that we import a DVD player from Mexico and the Mexicans use the money we sent them to buy 5 bushels of wheat from Kansas. Essentially, we've traded the 5 bushels of wheat for the DVD player. If this trade didn't make us better off, we wouldn't do it. So, too, for the Mexicans involved: If they didn't want the wheat more than the DVD player, they won't agree to the transaction. And, as the chapter explained, if we specialize in wheat and Mexico in DVD players, we both will be better off, with both gaining more total surplus."

"You know, I think this is really cool. Trade between us makes both of us better off and trade between nations makes both nations better off!"

Chapter Quiz

1. It is _____ to import a service and it is _____ to export a service.
   a. possible; possible
   b. possible; not possible
   c. not possible; possible
   d. not possible; not possible

2. If the U.S. price of an airplane before international trade is _____ the world price, the United States will _____ airplanes.
   a. the same as; both import and export
   b. lower than; import
   c. higher than; export
   d. lower than; export

3. A tariff _____ consumer surplus and an import quota _____ consumer surplus.
   a. increases; increases
   b. increases; decreases
   c. decreases; decreases
   d. decreases; increases

4. If the United States exports wheat, U.S. producer surplus _____ and U.S. total surplus _____,
   a. decreases; decreases
   b. increases; increases
   c. increases; does not change
   d. does not change; increases

5. If Mexico imposes a tariff on imported sugar, _____ gains from the tariff.
   a. Mexican sugar producers and the Mexican government
   b. Mexican sugar consumers and the Mexican government
   c. Mexican sugar consumers and Mexican sugar producers
   d. only Mexican sugar producers

6. A tariff restricts _____ and benefits _____.
   a. exports; producers
   b. exports; consumers
   c. imports; producers
   d. imports; consumers

7. If Germany imposes an import quota on imports of copper, the price of copper in Germany _____ and the quantity of copper consumed in Germany _____.
   a. rises; decreases
   b. falls; increases
   c. rises; increases
   d. falls; decreases

8. When an import quota is imposed, the difference between the domestic price and the world price is collected by
   a. the domestic government.
   b. the foreign government.
   c. domestic consumers.
   d. domestic importers of the good.

9. It is possible for expensive U.S. labor to compete successfully against less expensive foreign labor because U.S. labor
   a. pays taxes in the United States.
   b. can travel abroad to produce the goods in other nations.
   c. frequently belongs to powerful labor unions that protect their interest.
   d. is more productive.

10. If a poor nation exports a good to a rich nation, in the poor nation wages in the export sector _____ and employment _____.
    a. rise; increases
    b. rise; decreases
    c. fall; decreases
    d. fall; increases

The answers for this Chapter Quiz are on page 345

2 HOW MARKETS WORK

Mid-Term Examination

■ **Chapter 3**

1. The law of demand states that, other things remaining the same, the higher the price of a good, the
   a. smaller is the demand for the good.
   b. larger is the demand for the good.
   c. smaller is the quantity of the good demanded.
   d. larger is the quantity of the good demanded.

2. Which of the following shifts the supply curve?
   a. An increase in income but only if the good is a normal good.
   b. An increase in income regardless of whether the good is normal or inferior.
   c. A rise in the price of the good.
   d. An increase in the cost of producing the product.

3. A surplus
   a. shifts the demand curve leftward.
   b. shifts the supply curve rightward.
   c. leads to the price falling.
   d. leads to the price rising.

4. When supply increases, the equilibrium quantity _____ and the equilibrium price _____.
   a. increases; rises
   b. decreases; falls
   c. increases; falls
   d. decreases; rises

5. Butter made from milk and the price of milk rises. The equilibrium price of butter _____ and the equilibrium quantity of butter _____.
   a. rises; increases
   b. rises; decreases
   c. falls; increases
   d. falls; decreases

■ Chapter 4

6. If a rightward shift of the supply curve leads to a 5 percent decrease in price and a 10 percent increase in the quantity demanded, then the price elasticity of demand is
   a. 0.50.
   b. 2.0.
   c. 5.0.
   d. 10.0.

7. If the price elasticity of demand exceeds 1, then demand is
   a. elastic.
   b. unit elastic.
   c. inelastic.
   d. positively related to the price of the product.

8. The elasticity of demand for Pizza Hut pizza is probably _____ and is _____ in magnitude than the elasticity of demand for pizza in general.
   a. inelastic; smaller
   b. inelastic; larger
   c. elastic; larger
   d. elastic; smaller

9. A fall in the price of rutabagas from $10.50 to $9.50 a bushel raises the quantity demanded from 19,200 bushels to 20,800 bushels. The price elasticity of demand over this range of the demand curve is
   a. 0.80.
   b. 1.20.
   c. 1.25.
   d. 8.00.

10. The price elasticity of demand for wheat is 0.4 and the price of wheat rises 10 percent. The quantity of wheat demanded decreases _____ percent.
    a. 40.0
    b. 4.0
    c. 2.5
    d. None of the above are correct.

■ Chapter 5

11. Resource use is efficient when
    a. marginal social benefit exceeds marginal social cost by as much as possible.
    b. it is not possible to rearrange production.
    c. the goods and services produced are those valued most highly.
    d. whenever supply equals demand.

12. As more of a good is consumed, the marginal social benefit _____; as more of a good is produced; the marginal social cost _____.
    a. increases; increases
    b. increases; decreases
    c. decreases; increases
    d. decreases; decreases

13. If the marginal social benefit exceeds the marginal social cost of producing a unit of output, then
    a. resource use is efficient.
    b. resource use is inefficient and less should be produced.
    c. resource use is inefficient and more should be produced.
    d. It is impossible to determine if resource use is efficient without information about the demand and supply.

14. In a perfectly competitive market with no external costs or benefits, the marginal social benefit curve is the same as the demand curve. In the same situation, the marginal social cost curve is the same as the supply curve.
    a. Both sentences are true.
    b. The first sentence is true and the second sentence is false.
    c. The first sentence is false and the second sentence is true.
    d. Both sentences are false.

15. A deadweight loss can be the loss of _____ and can result _____.
    a. only consumer surplus; only from producing less than the efficient quantity
    b. only consumer surplus; only from producing more than the efficient quantity
    c. consumer surplus and producer surplus; only from producing less than the efficient quantity
    d. consumer surplus and producer surplus; either from producing less than the efficient quantity or producing more than the efficient quantity

■ **Chapter 6**

16. A good has an upward sloping supply curve and a perfectly elastic demand. Imposing a sales tax on sellers of this good shifts the supply curve
    a. leftward and the buyers pay the entire amount of the tax.
    b. rightward and the buyers pay the entire amount of the tax.
    c. rightward and the sellers pay the entire amount of the tax.
    d. leftward and the sellers pay the entire amount of the tax.

17. If buying a drug is made illegal, the demand curve shifts
    a. leftward and the price falls.
    b. leftward and the price rises.
    c. rightward and the price falls.
    d. rightward and the price rises.

18. Once the cost of search is taken into effect, workers _____ from a minimum wage and _____ firms from a minimum wage.

    a. lose; lose
    b. gain; gain
    c. lose; gain
    d. gain; lose

19. A price ceiling set below the equilibrium price _____ a deadweight loss and a price floor set above the equilibrium price _____ a deadweight loss.

    a. does not create; does not create
    b. creates; creates
    c. does not create; creates
    d. creates; does not create

20. Consumers pay a larger part of a tax when

    a. the government imposed the tax on them rather than on producers.
    b. there are a large number of suppliers.
    c. the demand for the good is elastic.
    d. the demand for the good is inelastic.

■ **Chapter 7**

21. If a tariff is imposed on tomatoes imported in the United States, U.S. tomato consumers _____ and U.S. tomato producers _____.

    a. gain; gain
    b. gain; lose
    c. lose; gain
    d. lose; lose

22. If the government imposes a tariff on imported automobiles, the price of an imported automobile ___ and if the government imposes an import quota on imported automobiles, the price of an imported automobile _____.

    a. rises; does not change
    b. rises; rises
    c. does not change; rises
    d. rises; falls

23. Which of the following creates a deadweight loss?

    a. importing a good or service but not exporting a good or service.
    b. exporting a good or service but not importing a good or service.
    c. both importing and exporting a good or service
    d. imposing a tariff on an imported good.

24. Consumers _____ from exports and producers _____ from exports.

    a. gain; gain
    b. lose; lose
    c. gain; lose
    d. lose; gain

25. Imposing an import quota on a good increases the domestic _____ and decreases the domestic _____.
    a. producer surplus; total surplus
    b. consumer surplus; producer surplus
    c. total surplus; consumer surplus
    d. consumer surplus; total surplus

Answers

■ Mid-Term Exam Answers

1. c;   2. d;   3. c;   4. c;   5. b;   6. b;   7. a;   8. c;   9. a;   10. b;
11. c;   12. c;   13. c;   14. a;   15. d;   16. d;   17. a;   18. a;   19. b;   20. d;
21. c;   22. b;   23. d;   24. d;   25. a.

Chapter 8 UTILITY AND DEMAND

■ Consumption Choices

Consumption choices are determined by the interaction of the household's consumption possibilities and its preferences.

The household's consumption possibilities, that is, its purchases are limited by its income and by the prices of the goods and services. A **budget line**, illustrated in Figure 8.1, marks the boundary between those combinations of goods and services that a household can afford to buy and those that it cannot afford. Consumption points on or within the budget line are affordable; those beyond it are unaffordable.

From the affordable combinations of goods and services, the consumer's choice about which combination to consume depends on his or her **preferences**. Preferences are a description of the consumer's likes and dislikes. To describe the consumer's preferences, we define **utility** as the benefit or satisfaction from consumption of goods or services.

- **Total utility** is the *total* benefit that a person gets from the consumption of *all* the goods and services he or she consumes.

- **Marginal utility** (*MU*) is the *change* in total utility from a one-unit *increase* in the quantity of a good consumed. *MU* is positive, but because of **diminishing marginal utility**, falls as the consumption of the good increases.

■ Utility-Maximizing Choice

Consumers' goal is to obtain the most total utility; they maximize their total utility.

A **consumer equilibrium** occurs when all the consumer's available income is allocated in the way that maximizes his or her total utility.

FIGURE 8.1
A Budget Line

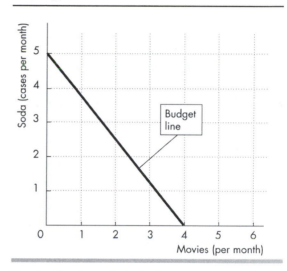

Total utility is maximized when:

- all the consumer's income is spent; and

- the **marginal utility per dollar**, which is the marginal utility from a good that results from spending one more dollar on it, is equal for all goods. The marginal utility per dollar equals the marginal utility of the good divided by its price.

In terms of a formula, for the choice between two goods, movies and sodas, the second requirement for maximizing utility is that movie and soda consumption is such that:

$$\frac{MU_m}{P_m} = \frac{MU_s}{P_s}$$

with MU_m the marginal utility from an additional movie, P_m the price of a movie, and MU_s and P_s the analogous variables for soda. If the two marginal utilities per dollar are not equal, the consumer can increase his or her total utility by rearranging his or her spending. For instance, if the marginal utility per dollar from a movie exceeds the marginal utility per dollar from a soda, the consumer can increase his or her utility by switching a dollar from sodas to movies.

Equating the marginal utilities per dollar is an example of *marginal analysis*. Marginal analysis says that if the marginal gain from an action exceeds its marginal loss, take the action but if the marginal gain from an action is less than its marginal loss, do not take the action. The units of utility are arbitrary. Rearranging the formula for utility maximization, $\dfrac{MU_m}{P_m} = \dfrac{MU_s}{P_s}$, as

$MU_S = \dfrac{P_S}{P_m} \times MU_m$ shows that we can determine

how much larger one marginal utility, MU_S in the rearranged formula, is than the other marginal utility.

■ Predictions of Marginal Utility Theory

Marginal utility theory predicts the law of demand:

♦ A fall in the price of a movie raises the marginal utility per dollar from movies. Consumers increase the quantity of movies viewed as they substitute movies for sodas. The lower price increases the quantity demanded so there is a movement down along the demand curve to the increased quantity of movies. Similarly, a rise in the price of a movie decreases the quantity demanded and creates an upward movement along a negatively sloped demand curve.

♦ A change in the price of a movie affects the demand curve for soda. Soda is a substitute for movies, so when movies fall in price, the demand curve for soda shifts leftward. Similarly when movies rise in price the demand curve for soda shifts rightward.

♦ Movies and soda are normal goods, so an increase in income increases the consumption of both products and thereby increases the demand for both products. Both demand curves shift rightward.

Marginal utility theory resolves the paradox of value, that is, why is water, which is essential for life, less expensive than diamonds, which are baubles. The distinction between total utility and marginal utility solves the paradox of value. Water is more useful (it has higher total utility) than diamonds, but water has a lower price because it has a lower *marginal* utility since the quantity of water consumed is large. Diamonds are less useful than water (they have lower total utility), but diamonds have a higher price because they have higher *marginal* utility since most people have only a few diamonds.

■ New Ways of Explaining Consumer Choices

Behavior economics studies the ways in which limits to the human brain's ability to compute and implement rational decisions influences economic behavior. Generally people are assumed to have three limitations that prevent purely rational choice:

♦ *Bounded rationality* – the human brain can't always compute the rational choice.

♦ *Bounded willpower* – people make choices that they know they will later regret.

♦ *Bounded self-interest* – people sometimes make choices that help others even if it harms themselves.

Neuroeconomics studies the activity of the human brain when a person makes an economic decision. Neuroeconomics has seen that some economic decisions activate the region of the brain (the prefrontal cortex) in which people store memories, analyze data, and calculate the consequences of actions. These decisions might be classified as rational. But other economic decisions activate the region of the brain (the hippocampus) in which people store memories of anxiety and fear. These decisions might be classified as non-rational.

Most economists believe that the apparent anomalies behavioral economists focus upon need to be studied more carefully to be sure they are not the result of utility-maximizing behavior. Most economists also believe that economics should explain the decisions people make and not study how they make the decisions.

Helpful Hints

1. **THE MEANING OF CONSUMER EQUILIBRIUM :** This chapter introduces another equilibrium: the consumer equilibrium. What does consumer equilibrium mean? Recall that the general definition of equilibrium is a situation "where opposing forces balance." When that occurs, there is no incentive for any change. In the supply and demand model, equilibrium is attained at the price at which the quantity supplied equals the quantity demanded. At that price neither demanders nor suppliers have an incentive to change their behavior. Consumer equilibrium is similar. When the equilibrium conditions are satisfied, the consumer has the most total utility that can be attained. The consumer has

no incentive to change the combination of goods consumed.

2. **THE MARGINAL UTILITY PER DOLLAR FORMULA:** One condition for consumer equilibrium is that the marginal utility per dollar from a good must equal the marginal utility per dollar from the other goods. In terms of a formula, for two goods, X and Y, the requirement is that the consumer allocate his or her income so that

$$\frac{MU_X}{P_X} = \frac{MU_Y}{P_Y}.$$

Why is this condition necessary for consumer equilibrium? Recall that the term MU_X/P_X is the marginal utility per dollar from good X, so it is the utility gained if spending on X is increased a dollar or the utility lost if spending on X is decreased by a dollar. MU_Y/P_Y tells us similar information

about Y. Anytime there is an inequality between the marginal utility per dollar from the different goods, the consumer can increase his or her total utility by buying less of the product with the low MU/P and by buying more of the good with the high MU/P. Only when the marginal utilities per dollar are equal does the consumer not gain by re-arranging the consumption bundle. As a result, only when this equality holds (and the consumer spends all his or her income) is the consumer in equilibrium obtaining the maximum total utility.

Questions

■ True/False and Explain

Consumption Choices

1. A budget line shows the different combinations of goods and services a consumer can afford to buy.

2. Marginal utility measures the *additional* utility from consuming an *additional* unit of a good.

3. As more of a good is consumed, diminishing marginal utility means that the total utility from the good diminishes.

Utility-Maximizing Choice

4. Economists assume that households choose their consumption to maximize their marginal utility per dollar from each good.

5. The marginal utility per dollar from a soda is MU_s/P_s where MU_s is the marginal utility from a soda and P_s is the price of a soda.

6. If the marginal utilities from consuming all goods are equal and the consumer is spending all of his or her income, the consumer is in equilibrium.

7. A person is maximizing utility if the marginal utility per dollar is equal for all goods and the household is spending all its income.

8. If the marginal utility per dollar from a pizza exceeds the marginal utility per dollar from a taco, total utility rises by increasing consumption of pizza by a dollar and decreasing consumption of tacos by a dollar.

Predictions of Marginal Utility Theory

9. Marginal utility theory predicts that when the price of a good rises, a consumer buys more because the marginal utility from the good is larger.

10. Marginal utility theory makes predictions that disagree with the law of demand.

11. Marginal utility theory predicts that when Shaniq's income rises, her demand for normal goods increases.

12. Marginal utility theory shows that goods with high prices (such as diamonds) have high total utilities.

New Ways of Explaining Consumer Choices

13. Behavioral economists assert that bounded rationality sometimes makes it impossible to determine the rational choice.

14. Neuroeconomics have discovered that humans never make rational choices.

■ Multiple Choice

Consumption Choices

1. A budget line is graphed with the _____ on the vertical axis and the _____ on the horizontal axis.
    a. prices of one good; quantities of another good
    b. prices of one good; prices of another good
    c. quantities of one good; quantities of another good
    d. production points of one good; consumption points of the same good

2. Marginal utility theory assumes that consumers' objectives are to

   a. maximize their total utility.
   b. maximize their marginal utility.
   c. maximize their income.
   d. none of the above.

3. As more of a good is consumed, its marginal utility _____ and its total utility _____.

   a. rises; rises
   b. rises; falls
   c. falls; rises
   d. falls; falls

4. Jeannie's marginal utility from her 3rd book in a month is 50. Her marginal utility from her 4th book

   a. is greater than 50.
   b. equals 50.
   c. is less than 50.
   d. might be more than, less than, or equal to 50 but more information is needed.

5. When Alex eats 1 slice of pizza, his total utility is 80; when Alex eats 2 slices of pizza, his total utility is 120. Alex's marginal utility from the second pizza is

   a. 200.
   b. 80.
   c. 60.
   d. 40.

Utility-Maximizing Choices

6. Andrew finds that the marginal utility from a BMW exceeds that from a slice of pizza. Andrew is spending all of his income. Andrew

   a. is not maximizing his utility.
   b. is maximizing his utility.
   c. must increase his income in order to maximize his utility.
   d. might be maximizing his utility, but we cannot tell without more information.

7. When Kelly maximizes her utility, she spends all of her income and makes sure that the

   a. marginal utility from each good she buys is as high as possible.
   b. marginal utility from each good she buys is equal.
   c. amount of each good she buys is the same.
   d. marginal utility from a good divided by its price is equal for each good she buys.

8. June bowls and listens to MP3s. Her marginal utility from bowling a game is 100 and her marginal utility from an MP3 is 20. The price of bowling a game is $5 and the price of an MP3 is $1. She spends all her income. June

   a. is maximizing her utility.
   b. must increase her consumption of bowling to maximize her utility.
   c. must increase her consumption of MP3s to maximize her utility.
   d. must increase her consumption of both bowling and MP3s to maximize her utility.

Use the following table for the next four questions.

TABLE 8.1
Multiple Choice Questions 9, 10, 11, 12

| | Marginal utility | |
Quantity	Pencils	Paper pads
1	12	16
2	10	12
3	8	8
4	6	4
5	4	2

9. Amy spends her entire income of $10 on pencils and yellow paper pads. Pencils cost $2 and paper pads cost $4. The marginal utility of each good is given in Table 8.1. If Amy is maximizing her utility, how many yellow paper pads does she buy?

   a. 0
   b. 1
   c. 2
   d. 3

10. Amy's total utility at her consumer equilibrium is

    a. 82
    b. 48
    c. 46
    d. 40

11. Amy's income rises to $16. She continues to buy only pencils and yellow paper pads and she continues to maximize her utility. How many yellow paper pads does she buy after her income increases?

    a. 0
    b. 1
    c. 2
    d. 3

12. After Amy's income rises to $16, what is her total utility?
    a. 82
    b. 64
    c. 40
    d. 36

13. Bobby buys only soda and pizza and is buying the amounts that maximize his utility. The marginal utility from a soda is 10, and the price of the soda is $1. The marginal utility from a slice of pizza is 30. The price of a slice of pizza must be
    a. $30.
    b. $3.
    c. $1.
    d. some amount that cannot be calculated without more information.

14. Meg buys only soda and pizza and is buying the amounts that maximize her utility. The marginal utility from a soda is 30 and the price of the soda is $1. The marginal utility from a slice of pizza is 90. The price of a slice of pizza must be
    a. $30.
    b. $3.
    c. $2.
    d. some amount that cannot be calculated without more information.

15. If Shaniq is maximizing her utility, when two goods have the same price she will
    a. buy only one.
    b. buy equal quantities of both.
    c. get the same marginal utility from each.
    d. get the same total utility from each.

Predictions of Marginal Utility Theory

16. Michael consumes only steak and lobster. Suppose that the price of a steak rises but Michael's income does not change. After he is back at a consumer equilibrium, compared to the situation when steak was cheaper, the marginal utility from the last steak will
    a. have increased.
    b. have not changed.
    c. have decreased.
    d. not be comparable with the marginal utility from before the price hike.

17. Michael consumes only steak and lobster. Both are normal goods. Michael's income increases but the prices of neither steak nor lobster change. After he is back at equilibrium, compared to the situation when Michael's income was less, the marginal utility from the last steak will
    a. have increased.
    b. have not changed.
    c. have decreased.
    d. not be comparable with the marginal utility from before the increase in income.

18. Marginal utility theory predicts that a rise in the price of a banana leads to
    a. the demand curve for bananas shifting rightward.
    b. the demand curve for bananas shifting leftward.
    c. a movement upward along the demand curve for bananas.
    d. a movement downward along the demand curve for bananas.

19. Which of the following statements is true?
    a. Marginal utility theory predicts that an increase in a consumer's income increases consumption of *all* goods.
    b. It is possible to derive the law of demand — that a higher price decreases the quantity demanded — using marginal utility theory.
    c. Marginal utility theory makes no prediction about a consumer's responses to hikes in the prices of the goods and services he or she consumes.
    d. Marginal utility theory predicts that all goods are normal goods and that all goods are substitutes for each other.

20. Because we cannot observe or measure utility,
    a. the predictions of marginal utility theory cannot be verified.
    b. marginal utility theory is incomplete and so its predictions might not be valid.
    c. marginal utility theory must be derived from assumptions about demand curves because demand curves can be measured.
    d. None of the above answers are correct.

21. The fact that rubies are more expensive than milk reflects the fact that for most consumers
    a. the total utility from rubies exceeds that from milk.
    b. the marginal utility from rubies equals that from milk.
    c. more milk is consumed than rubies.
    d. a quart of rubies is prettier than a quart of milk.

New Ways of Explaining Consumer Choices

22. Gene plays another hour of computer games rather than study for the hour. He knows that the next day, when he takes his test, he will regret his decision. Gene is showing
    a. the endowment effect.
    b. bounded rationality.
    c. bounded self-interest.
    d. bounded willpower.

23. Lucky buys hats for $20 but Lucky will not sell one of her hats for less than $35. Lucky is
    a. displaying the endowment effect.
    b. making her decisions using her prefrontal cortex.
    c. exhibiting bounded self-interest.
    d. showing unbounded willpower.

■ Short Answer Problems

1. Explain how the consumer equilibrium condition and the principle of diminishing marginal utility can be used to derive the law of demand.

2. Jake consumes only fish sticks and broccoli. He is initially maximizing his utility, so he spends all of his income on fish sticks and broccoli and sets

$$\frac{MU_{FS}}{P_{FS}} = \frac{MU_B}{P_B}$$

with MU_{FS} the marginal utility from fish sticks; P_{FS} the price of fish sticks; MU_B the marginal utility from broccoli; and P_B the price of broccoli. The price of fish sticks rises (from 70 cents a pound to 80 cents) as a result of the shift in the supply curve shown in Figure 8.2. Use the condition for utility maximization to explain how Jake will move to a new utility-maximizing consumer equilibrium. Also show the connection between your explanation and the change in the figure from 11,000 pounds of fish sticks being consumed to 10,000 pounds.

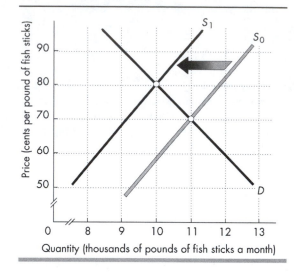

FIGURE **8.2**
Short Answer Problem 2

3. Loren is in equilibrium, spending her income of $200 buying 2 video games at a price of $40 each and 8 DVDs at a price of $15 each. Then, inflation causes the price of a DVD and a video game to double (to $80 and $30, respectively) while Loren's income also doubles (to $400). What happens to Loren's purchases of video games and DVDs: Do both increase, decrease, not change, or change in some direction that cannot be determined?

TABLE **8.2**
Short Answer Problem 4

| | Marginal utility | |
Quantity	Bats	Lizards
1	20	50
2	18	44
3	14	36
4	8	26

4. Igor maximizes his utility by spending his entire income of $16 on bats and lizards. Table 8.2 has Igor's marginal utility from each good. The price of a bat is $2, and he buys 2 bats. The marginal utility from the last lizard he buys is 36.
    a. Calculate the price of a lizard using the condition that Igor's marginal utilities per dollar are equal.
    b. What is Igor's total utility?
    c. Igor could buy 4 lizards. If he did so and also purchased the maximum number of bats possi-

ble given his income, what would be his total utility then?

d. The marginal utility from even the fourth lizard exceeds the marginal utility from the first bat; yet when maximizing his utility, Igor nonetheless buys some bats. Explain why Igor buys some bats. (Hint: Igor is not batty.)

TABLE 8.3
Liz's Utility from Popcorn

Bags of popcorn	Total utility	Marginal utility from last bag
0	0	XX
1	20	20
2	36	16
3	50	___
4	___	12
5	72	___
6	80	___

TABLE 8.4
Liz's Utility from Candy Bars

Candy bars	Total utility	Marginal utility from last bar
0	0	XX
1	14	14
2	26	12
3	___	10
4	44	___
5	51	___
6	57	___

5. Tables 8.3 and 8.4 give Liz's utility from her consumption of popcorn and candy.

   a. Complete Tables 8.3 and 8.4.

   b. Suppose that the price of a bag of popcorn is $1 and that the price of a candy bar is $0.50. Use the information in Tables 8.3 and 8.4 to complete Table 8.5. There *MU/P* means marginal utility divided by price, which is equivalent to marginal utility per dollar from popcorn and from candy.

   c. Liz's weekly allowance is $4. If she spends her entire allowance on popcorn and candy, how much popcorn and how many candy bars will Liz consume each week?

TABLE 8.5
Liz's Marginal Utilities per Dollar

Bags of popcorn	MU/P	Candy bars	MU/P
1	___	1	___
2	___	2	___
3	___	3	___
4	___	4	___
5	___	5	___
6	___	6	___

   d. In part (c), what is Liz's total utility?

   e. Suppose that Liz consumes 3 bags of popcorn and 2 candy bars. Explain why she is not maximizing her utility. Be sure to compare her total utilities for the consumption bundle in part (c) and the 3 bags of popcorn, 2 candy bars used in this question. Also use the *MU/P* terms to explain why consuming 3 bags of popcorn and 2 candy bars is not optimal.

6. Suppose that Liz's utility remains as it is in Problem 5 but the price of a candy bar doubles to $1. The price of a bag of popcorn, however, does not change — it remains equal to $1 per bag.

   a. Construct a new table (similar to Table 8.5) of the marginal utility per dollar from popcorn and candy bars.

   b. Liz's allowance continues to be $4. After the price change, how much popcorn and how many candy bars will she consume each week?

   c. Are popcorn and candy bars substitutes or complements for Liz? Why?

   d. Based on the information you have obtained, draw Liz's demand curve for candy bars.

7. Lori has $40 a week that she spends on playing tennis and buying comic books. A set of tennis costs $1 and a comic book costs $2. One week when Lori spent all her income, she found that the marginal utility from the last set of tennis was 16 and that the marginal utility from the last comic book was 20.

   a. Show that Lori's choice of tennis sets and comic books was not optimal.

   b. To increase her utility, Lori should increase her consumption of which good and decrease her consumption of which good?

8. How does marginal utility theory resolve the diamond / water paradox of value?

■ You're the Teacher

1. "This whole idea of marginal utility is stupid. I mean, after all, who goes into a store and calculates the marginal utility from something before deciding to buy it? I just look at something, look at the price, think about how much money I've got in my pocket, and then decide whether or not to buy the thing. No one I know calculates marginal utilities when they go shopping, so why do I have to learn this stuff?" What response do you make to your classmate? (*Don't* agree!)

2. "One thing I don't understand about all this material dealing with consumers and their choices is how I am supposed to think about products like apartments. Suppose that the rent in my apartment goes up. Marginal utility theory says that I will consume fewer apartments. But what does this mean? I'll still rent *one* apartment. And, if rent goes down, I sure won't go out and rent two! How does marginal utility theory account for this fact?" Your friend has come up with a good question; provide an equally good explanation to help your friend understand this point.

Answers

■ True/False Answers

Consumption Choices

1. **T** The budget line shows the limits to what a consumer can afford to purchase.

2. **T** As this definition stresses, marginal utility is the extra utility from an extra unit of a good.

3. **F** The principle of diminishing marginal utility means that the *marginal* utility—not total utility—from additional units declines.

Utility-Maximizing Choice

4. **F** Economists assume that households maximize their total utility.

5. **T** The question presents the definition of marginal utility per dollar.

6. **F** To be in equilibrium, the marginal utilities per dollar, MU/P, must be equal.

7. **T** These are the two conditions necessary for a household to maximize its utility.

8. **T** In this case, the gain in utility from consuming one dollar more of pizza exceeds the loss in utility from consuming one dollar less of tacos.

Predictions of Marginal Utility Theory

9. **F** Marginal utility theory predicts that a price rise decreases the quantity demanded.

10. **F** Marginal utility theory concludes that when the price of a good falls, consumers increase the quantity they consume, which is in accord with the law of demand.

11. **T** When Shaniq's income increases, Shaniq rearranges her consumption to maximize her utility and she increases her consumption of normal goods.

12. **F** Products with high prices must have high marginal utilities, not necessarily high total utilities.

New Ways of Explaining Consumer Choices

13. **T** The question is essentially the definition of "bounded rationality."

14. **F** Decisions made in the prefrontal cortex can be considered rational.

■ Multiple Choice Answers

Consumption Choices

1. **c** A budget line shows the *quantities* of the two goods the person can afford to consume.

2. **a** By maximizing their total utilities, people make themselves as well off as possible.

3. **c** The marginal utility diminishes and, as a result, total utility increases but by less as each additional unit of the good is consumed.

4. **c** Diminishing marginal utility means that the marginal utility from the 4th book must be less than the marginal utility from the 3rd book.

5. **d** Marginal utility equals the change in total utility from a one-unit change in consumption. Alex's marginal utility equals $(120 − 80)/1$, or 40.

Utility-Maximizing Choice

6. **d** If Andrew is maximizing his utility, we know that $MU_{\text{pizza}}/P_{\text{pizza}} = MU_{\text{BMW}}/P_{\text{BMW}}$ but without information about the price of a BMW and a pizza, we cannot determine whether this condition is satisfied.

7. **d** To maximize her utility, Kelly consumes the amounts of the different goods that equalize the marginal utility per dollar from each good.

8. **a** June's marginal utility per dollar from bowling, which 100/$5 or 20 per dollar, equals her marginal utility per dollar from MP3s, which is 20/$1 or 20 per dollar. June also spends all her income, so she is maximizing her utility.

9. **b** When Amy buys 1 yellow paper pad, she can buy 3 pencils. With this consumption bundle, $MU_{\text{pad}}/P_{\text{pad}} = 4$ and $MU_{\text{pencil}}/P_{\text{pencil}} = 4$.

10. **c** Amy receives utility of 16 from yellow paper pads and 30 (12 + 10 + 8) from pencils, for total utility of 46.

11. **c** Amy now buys 2 paper pads and 4 pencils because this combination of pads and pencils uses all her income and sets $MU_{\text{pad}}/P_{\text{pad}} = MU_{\text{pencil}}/P_{\text{pencil}} = 3$.

12. **b** Amy has utility of 28 (16 +12) from yellow paper pads and 36 (12 + 10 + 8 + 6) from pencils for total utility of 64.

13. **b** To maximize his utility, Bobby must set $MU_{\text{soda}}/P_{\text{soda}} = MU_{\text{pizza}}/P_{\text{pizza}}$. Because $MU_{\text{soda}}/P_{\text{soda}} = 10/1 = 10$, in order for $MU_{\text{pizza}}/P_{\text{pizza}}$ also to equal 10 when $MU_{\text{pizza}} = 30$, then $P_{\text{pizza}} = \$3$.

14. **b** The same reasoning outlined in the answer to

Question 12 applies and P_{pizza} = \$3. Even though Bobby's and Meg's marginal utilities are not the same, nonetheless to maximize their utility, both set $MU_{\text{soda}}/P_{\text{soda}}$ equal to $MU_{\text{pizza}}/P_{\text{pizza}}$.

15. **c** Because MU/P is equal for all goods, if two products have the same P, they must have the same MU.

Predictions of Marginal Utility Theory

16. **a** Michael consumes fewer steaks, so the marginal utility from the last steak he consumes is higher.

17. **c** Michael consumes more steak because steak is a normal good. Because he consumes more steak, the marginal utility from the last steak he consumes is lower than before.

18. **c** With a higher price for a banana, consumers decrease the quantity they consume, which raises the marginal utility of bananas.

19. **b** By making assumptions about people's behavior — that they aim to obtain the maximum total utility and that their marginal utility diminishes as they consume more of a product — it is possible to derive the law of demand.

20. **d** Marginal utility theory makes predictions about the real world that can be checked. For instance, marginal utility theory predicts the law of demand, that a higher price decreases the quantity demanded. It also predicts that the demand for a normal good increases when income increases. So even though utility cannot be measured or observed, still the predictions it makes about the real world are observable and are accurate.

21. **c** Because more milk is consumed, the MU from milk is lower than the MU from rubies.

New Ways of Explaining Consumer Choices

22. **d** Gene does not have the will power to take the action that he rationally knows will maximize his utility over the long run.

23. **a** Lucky values the hat more than its price because she owns the hat, which shows the endowment effect—people value what they own more than is rational.

■ Answers to Short Answer Problems

1. Suppose that an individual in consumer equilibrium consumes only two goods, X_0 units of good X and Y_0 units of good Y. Therefore at consumption levels X_0 and Y_0, the marginal utility per dollar from X equals the marginal utility per dollar from Y. If the price of X rises, how does the consumer respond? The marginal utility per dollar from X declines and becomes less than the marginal utility per dollar from Y. To restore equilibrium, the consumer must increase the marginal utility from X and decrease the marginal utility from Y. From the principle of diminishing marginal utility, the only way to do so is to decrease the consumption of X and increase the consumption of Y. This action, then, demonstrates the law of demand: A rise in the price of X results in a decrease in the consumption of X.

2. 2. When the price of a fish stick rises,

$$\frac{MU_{FS}}{P_{FS}} < \frac{MU_B}{P_B}.$$

Jake no longer is in equilibrium because the utility per dollar for fish sticks is less than that for broccoli. So Jake increases his total utility by spending fewer dollars on fish sticks and more on broccoli. These changes make MU_{FS} rise and MU_B fall, which will eventually result in equality between the marginal utility per dollar from fish sticks and broccoli. Jake's decreased consumption of fish sticks moves him along his demand curve for fish sticks. Indeed, consumers in general decrease the quantity of fish sticks they consume, which accounts for the movement along the market demand curve in the figure from the initial equilibrium (with 11,000 pounds of fish sticks produced and consumed) to the new equilibrium (with only 10,000 pounds of fish sticks produced and consumed).

3. After the inflation Loren still purchases 2 video games and 8 DVDs. Loren buys the combination of games and DVDs that maximizes her utility, setting $MU_{\text{games}}/P_{\text{games}} = MU_{\text{DVDs}}/P_{\text{DVDs}}$ and spending all her income. For the first requirement, before the inflation the combination of 2 games and 8 DVDs maximized Loren's utility so that it was the case that $MU_{\text{games}}/P_{\text{games}} = MU_{\text{DVDs}}/P_{\text{DVDs}}$. After the inflation, the marginal utilities do not change, but the prices double. So, MU/P for games equals $MU_{\text{games}}/(2 \times P_{\text{games}})$ and MU/P for DVDs equals $MU_{\text{DVDs}}/(2 \times P_{\text{DVDs}})$. The MU/P for video games is half what it was before,

as is the MU/P for DVDs. Because they were equal before the inflation, dividing each by 2 does not change their equality; that is, after the inflation the equality of the marginal utilities per dollar condition for utility maximization is still met. For the second condition, that all income is spent, after the inflation, buying 2 video games and 8 DVDs uses up all of Loren's income, so the second criteria is met. The combination of 2 games and 8 DVDs continues to maximize Loren's utility, so that is the combination she will purchase. One important point to note from this result is that the inflation did *not* change any of the relative prices. Changes in a relative price or changes in her real income will lead Loren to change the quantity of DVDs she buys but a pure inflation that does not change a relative price or real income has no effect.

4. a. To determine the price of a lizard use the condition for utility maximization, that the marginal utility per dollar from a lizard equals the marginal utility per dollar from a bat. In terms of a formula, we have that

$$\frac{MU_l}{P_l} = \frac{MU_b}{P_b}.$$

We know that $MU_l = 36$, $P_b = \$2$, and, if Igor buys 2 bats, that $MU_b = 18$. Substituting these values, we solve for P_l :

$$\frac{36}{P_l} = \frac{18}{\$2}$$

$$\frac{36}{9} = P_l$$

$$\$4 = P_l$$

b. Igor receives total utility of 38 from his bats (20 + 18) and total utility of 130 from his lizards (50 + 44 + 36). Igor's overall total utility from bats and lizards is 168.

c. If Igor buys 4 lizards, because each lizard costs $4, he spends all his income and so can purchase no bats. In this case, Igor's total utility is 156 (50 + 44 + 36 + 26).

d. Even though each bat returns less marginal utility than a lizard, bats are less expensive then lizards. So when Igor is selecting his utility-maximizing combination of bats and lizards, the cheapness of bats means that he will buy some. For example, compare Igor's total utility when he buys 2 bats and 3 lizards, given in part (b) as

168, with his total utility when he buys 0 bats and 4 lizards, computed in part (c) as 156. Igor's *total* utility is higher when he buys 2 bats and 3 lizards than when he concentrates solely on lizards by purchasing 4 lizards and 0 bats.

TABLE 8.7

Liz's Utility from Popcorn

Bags of popcorn	Total utility	Marginal utility from last bag
0	0	XX
1	20	20
2	36	16
3	50	14
4	62	12
5	72	10
6	80	8

TABLE 8.8

Liz's Utility from Candy Bars

Candy bars	Total utility	Marginal utility from last bar
0	0	XX
1	14	14
2	26	12
3	36	10
4	44	8
5	51	7
6	57	6

5. a. Tables 8.7 and 8.8 are completed versions of Tables 8.3 and 8.4, respectively.

TABLE 8.9

Liz's Marginal Utilities Per Dollar

Bags of popcorn	MU/P	Candy bars	MU/P
1	20	1	28
2	16	2	24
3	14	3	20
4	12	4	16
5	10	5	14
6	8	6	12

b. Table 8.9 completes Table 8.5.

c. 2 bags of popcorn and 4 candy bars. This combination uses up all of Liz's income and also equates the marginal utility per dollar from pop-corn and candy bars (both are 16).

d. Total utility is the utility from the consumption of 2 bags of popcorn (36) plus the utility from the consumption of 4 candy bars (44) or 80.

e. If Liz consumed 3 bags of popcorn and 2 candy bars, total utility would be 76, less than 80, the total utility from the consumption of 2 bags of popcorn and 4 candy bars. For the combination of 3 bags of popcorn and 2 candy bars, *MU/P* for popcorn is 14 and *MU/P* for candy bars is 24. Because *MU/P* is not the same for both goods, this combination does not maximize Liz's utility. More specifically, Liz could decrease her consumption of popcorn by a dollar, use the dollar to buy more candy bars, and thereby would raise her total utility. This marginal analysis shows that Liz can increase her total utility by consuming less popcorn and more candy whenever the *MU/P* from popcorn is less than the *MU/P* from candy bars.

TABLE **8.10**

Liz's (New) Marginal Utilities Per Dollar

Bags of popcorn	MU/P	Candy bars	MU/P
1	20	1	14
2	16	2	12
3	14	3	10
4	12	4	8
5	10	5	7
6	8	6	6

6. a. Table 8.10 shows Liz's *MU/P* from popcorn and candy after the price hike for candy. The price rise did not change Liz's *MU*s.

b. Liz will consume 3 bags of popcorn and 1 candy bar. This combination of popcorn and candy spends all of Liz's income ($4), and the marginal utility per dollar is the same for popcorn and candy bars (both are 14).

c. Popcorn and candy bars are substitutes for Liz because a rise in the price of a candy bar leads to an increase in the demand for popcorn.

d. Two points on Liz's demand curve have been identified. When the price of a candy bar is $1, 1 candy bar will be demanded, and when the price is $0.50, 4 candy bars will be demanded.

The demand curve is a line through these two points, as illustrated in Figure 8.3.

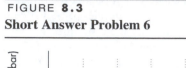

FIGURE **8.3**
Short Answer Problem 6

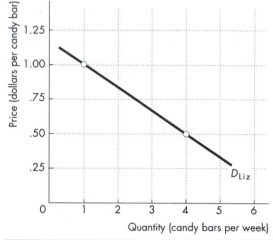

7. a. Lori is not maximizing her utility because the marginal utility per dollar from the set of tennis (16/$1 = 16) is not the same as the marginal utility per dollar from comic books (20/$2 = 10).

b. To equate the marginal utilities per dollar (and by so doing increase her total utility), Lori will increase her consumption of tennis and decrease her consumption of comic books. To show that this change raises her utility, we can use marginal analysis. By cutting back a dollar on comic books, Lori loses 10 units of utility; but then by spending the dollar on tennis, Lori gains 16 units. Therefore on net, Lori gains 6 units of utility (16 gained from tennis minus 10 lost from comic books) by changing her consumption bundle.

8. The paradox of value is resolved by recognizing the difference between the total utility from a good and its marginal utility. For instance, the total utility from consumption of water is large but because we consume a lot of water, the marginal utility from the last gallon of water is small. The total utility from the consumption of diamonds is small, but because we consume few diamonds, the marginal utility of the last diamond is large. In consumer equilibrium, because the marginal utility per dollar is the same for water and diamonds, with the low

marginal utility of water and the high marginal utility of diamonds, the price of water must be low and the price of diamonds must be high. The paradox of value is solved because it is the marginal utilities — not the total utilities — that are related to the price of diamonds and water.

■ You're the Teacher

1. "You're right that no one goes into a store and calculates marginal utility before deciding whether to buy something. But that is not the point of marginal utility theory. Marginal utility theory is *not* trying to explain how people make decisions about what to buy. Instead, it is based on the assumption that people make themselves as well off as possible —

maximize their utility — to explain how people respond to changes in prices and incomes. It's not a theory of people's thoughts. It's a theory of people's actions."

2. "What you are missing is the fact that apartments are not all identical. My apartment is larger than yours. If the price of an apartment rose — rents go up — I'd move to a smaller apartment. Or, if the price went down, I wouldn't rent two apartments, but I'd move to a still larger one. So think about it this way: If the price of an apartment goes up, we'll consume 'fewer' apartments by renting smaller apartments; and, if the price goes down, we'll consume 'more' apartments by renting larger ones."

Chapter Quiz

1. As Sam's consumption of rice decreases, his
   a. average utility from rice falls.
   b. total utility from rice falls.
   c. marginal utility from rice decreases.
   d. elasticity of utility from rise increases.

2. When Romona is in consumer equilibrium,
   a. her marginal utilities from all goods are equal.
   b. her total utilities from all goods are equal.
   c. her total utility per dollar from all goods are equal.
   d. her marginal utility per dollar from all goods are equal.

3. According to marginal utility theory, consumers
   a. maximize their total utility and minimize their marginal utility.
   b. maximize their total utility given the prices of goods and their income.
   c. maximize their income.
   d. spend the most on least expensive goods.

4. The price of a soda is $2 and the price of a movie is $10. Bobby spends all of his income on sodas and movies. If Bobby's marginal utility from a soda is 10 and his marginal utility from a movie is 20, to maximize his utility Bobby definitely _____ the number of movies he sees and _____ his consumption of sodas.
   a. increases; increases
   b. increases; decreases
   c. decreases; increases
   d. decreases; decreases

5. When economists talk of inferior goods they mean only goods for which
   a. the demand curve slopes downward.
   b. marginal utility falls as more of the good is consumed.
   c. marginal utility is always negative.
   d. demand decreases when income rises.

6. The statement that more consumption yields more utility is
   a. a prediction of marginal utility theory.
   b. an assumption of marginal utility theory.
   c. a fallacy disproven by marginal utility theory.
   d. true of goods but not of services.

7. Marginal utility theory predicts that an increase in the price of a good _____ the quantity demanded.
   a. increases
   b. has no effect on
   c. decreases
   d. perhaps increases, has no effect on, or decreases, depending on whether the good is a normal good or inferior good.

8. If less of a good is consumed, its marginal utility _____ and if more of a good is consumed, its marginal utility _____.
   a. increases; increases
   b. increases; decreases
   c. decreases; increases
   d. decreases; decreases

9. Katie is in consumer equilibrium and consumes many goods. For her, purses are a normal good. An increase in her income changes her to a new equilibrium in which her consumer surplus from purses is
   a. zero, as it was in the old equilibrium.
   b. positive and equal to what it was in the old equilibrium.
   c. smaller than in the old equilibrium.
   d. larger than in the old equilibrium.

10. Megan buys only soda and pizza and is buying the amounts that maximize her utility. The marginal utility from a soda is 10 and the price of a soda is $1. The marginal utility from a pizza is 80. Hence the price of a pizza must be
    a. $80.
    b. $10.
    c. $8.
    d. $4.

The answers for this Chapter Quiz are on page 345

9 POSSIBILITIES, PREFERENCES, AND CHOICES

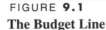

Key Concepts

■ Consumption Possibilities

The **budget line** shows the limits to a household's consumption. Figure 9.1 graphs a budget line. Consumption points beyond the budget line are unaffordable; consumption points on and within the budget line are affordable.

The *budget equation* for the budget line in Figure 9.1 is:

$$Q_{\text{soda}} = \frac{y}{P_{\text{soda}}} - \left(\frac{P_{\text{movies}}}{P_{\text{soda}}}\right) \times Q_{\text{movies}}$$

- ◆ A household's **real income** is the income expressed as a quantity of goods the household can afford to buy. In terms of soda, (y/P_{soda}) is the household's real income. An increase in income (y) shifts the budget line rightward but does not change its slope.

- ◆ A **relative price** is the price of one good divided by the price of another. The magnitude of the slope of the budget line $(P_{\text{movies}}/P_{\text{soda}})$ is the relative price of a movie in terms of a soda. Changes in the relative price rotate the budget line. A fall in the price of movies, the product on the horizontal axis, rotates the budget line outward so that it becomes flatter.

■ Preferences and Indifference Curves

An **indifference curve** is a curve showing combinations of goods among which a person is indifferent. Figure 9.2 illustrates a family of indifference curves.

- ◆ Indifference curves farther from the origin are preferred over those closer to the origin.

The **marginal rate of substitution** (*MRS*) is the rate at which a person is willing to give up the good on the vertical axis (soda) to get an additional unit of the good on the horizontal axis (movies) while remaining indifferent. The magnitude of the slope of the indifference curve equals the *MRS*.

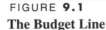

FIGURE **9.1**
The Budget Line

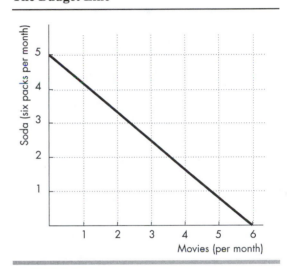

FIGURE **9.2**
Indifference Curves

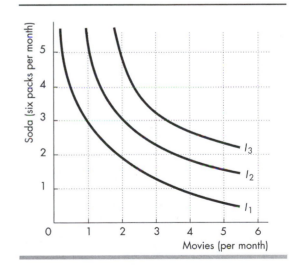

♦ The **diminishing marginal rate of substitution** is
the tendency for a person to be willing to give up
less of the good on the vertical axis to get one more
unit of the good on the horizontal axis, while remaining indifferent (that is, on the same indifference curve) as the quantity of the good on the
horizontal axis increases.

♦ Goods that are substitutes have straighter indifference curves; goods that are complements have more
bowed indifference curves.

■ Predicting Consumer Choices

The household chooses the *best affordable point* for its
consumption. This point is the combination of goods
on the budget line and on the highest possible indifference curve. Figure 9.3 illustrates the best affordable
point, where the household consumes 2 movies and 2
six-packs of soda per month. At this optimal point:

♦ the budget line and indifference curve are tangent
so that the marginal rate of substitution equals the
relative price.

The **price effect** is the change in the quantity consumed of a good resulting from a change in its price.
When the price of a movie falls, the budget line rotates
as shown in Figure 9.4 and the consumption of movies
increases from 2 per month to 2½ per month. The fall
in the price of a movie increases the quantity of movies
demanded, which shows how this analysis can be used
to derive the demand curve for movies.

The **income effect** is the change in buying plans resulting from a change in income. When income increases,
the budget line shifts outward and the consumer moves
to a new best affordable point. For normal goods, higher income increases consumption of the good and the
demand curve shifts rightward. For inferior goods,
higher income decreases consumption of the good and
the demand curve shifts leftward.

The price effect can be divided into the substitution
effect plus the income effect.

♦ The **substitution effect** is the effect of a change in
price on the quantity bought when the consumer
(hypothetically) remains indifferent (on the same
indifference curve) between the original situation
and the new one. To keep the consumer (hypothetically on the same indifference curve after the fall in
price, the consumer's income must (hypothetically)
be decreased. With this, a fall in the price results in

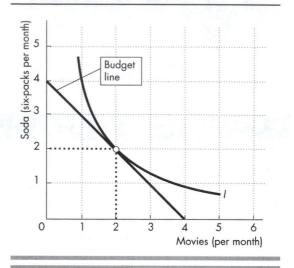

FIGURE **9.3**
The Best Affordable Point

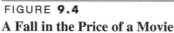

FIGURE **9.4**
A Fall in the Price of a Movie

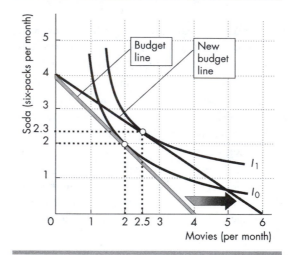

a movement downward along the indifference curve
so for all goods, the substitution effect of a fall in the
price increases consumption of the good.

♦ The income effect restores the (hypothetical) decrease in income, thereby shifting the budget line
outward. For normal goods, the substitution and
income effects from a fall in price both increase
consumption, so a lower price unambiguously increases consumption. For inferior goods, the substitution effect from a fall in the price increases
consumption but the income effects decreases consumption.

Helpful Hints

1. **A PERSPECTIVE ON THE CHAPTER :** The analysis in this chapter clarifies economists' general view that people strive to make themselves as well off as possible. However, people face constraints. These constraints, which limit the range of possible choices, depend on income and the prices of goods and are represented graphically by the budget line. Doing the best means finding the most preferred outcome consistent with those constraints. Graphically, the problem is to find the highest indifference curve attainable given the budget line. To make graphical analysis feasible, we restrict ourselves to choices between only two goods, but the same principles apply in the real world to a broader array of choices.

2. **INCOME, PRICES, AND INDIFFERENCE CURVES :** Indifference curves plot people's preferences and do not depend on their incomes or the prices of the goods. For example, an indifference curve indicates how much a person likes (or dislikes) lobster without regard to the price of a lobster or the person's income. When the price of a lobster or the individual's income changes, the budget line changes, but the indifference curves do not change. If lobster is a normal good, higher income leads to more lobster being consumed. But the reason that more lobster is consumed is that the budget line has shifted outward, making more combinations of goods affordable, and thereby enabling the person to reach a higher indifference curve.

Questions

■ True/False and Explain

Consumption Possibilities

1. The budget line has a negative slope and is linear.

2. The magnitude of the slope of the budget line is a relative price.

3. An increase in income shifts the budget line outward and makes it steeper.

Preferences and Indifference Curves

4. A person is indifferent between any combination of goods on a particular indifference curve.

5. An indifference curve measures the same things as does a demand curve.

6. Indifference curves farther from the origin are preferred to those closer to the origin.

7. The magnitude of the slope of a person's indifference curve is the marginal rate of substitution.

8. The marginal rate of substitution falls when moving upward along an indifference curve.

9. Goods that are perfect substitutes have L-shaped indifference curves.

Predicting Consumer Choices

10. The best affordable point of consumption is on the budget line and on the highest attainable indifference curve.

11. The law of demand can be derived from an indifference curve diagram by using the diagram to determine the impact changes in price have on the person's consumption bundle.

12. The substitution effect can be divided into the price effect and the income effect.

13. For an inferior good, an increase in income shifts the budget line leftward.

14. When the price of a good falls, the income effect always leads to increased consumption of the good.

15. For a normal good, both the substitution effect and income effect from a higher price lead to a decrease in the consumption of the good.

■ Multiple Choice

Consumption Possibilities

1. Which of the following statements best describes a consumer's budget line?
   a. It shows all combinations of goods among which the consumer is indifferent.
   b. It shows the limits to a consumer's set of affordable consumption choices.
   c. It shows the desired level of consumption for the consumer.
   d. It shows the consumption choices made by a consumer.

2. The magnitude of the slope of the budget line
   a. is defined as marginal rate of substitution.
   b. equals the relative price of the good measured along the horizontal axis.
   c. increases when income increases.
   d. decreases when income increases.

3. The budget line can shift or rotate
   a. only when income changes.
   b. only when prices change.
   c. when either income or prices change.
   d. None of the above because changes in income and prices do not shift or rotate the budget line.

Use Figure 9.5 for the next two questions.

FIGURE **9.5**
Multiple Choice Questions 4 and 5

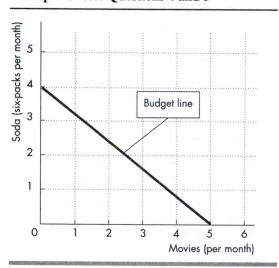

4. Suppose that this consumer's income increases and nothing else changes. As a result, the consumer's budget line
   a. rotates around the vertical intercept and becomes steeper.
   b. rotates around the vertical axis and becomes shallower.
   c. shifts rightward and becomes steeper.
   d. shifts rightward and its slope does not change.

5. Suppose that the price of a movie rises and nothing else changes. This change means the budget line
   a. rotates around the vertical intercept and becomes steeper.
   b. rotates around the vertical axis and becomes flatter.
   c. shifts rightward and becomes steeper.
   d. shifts rightward and does not change its slope.

6. Sue consumes apples and bananas. Suppose that Sue's income doubles *and* that the prices of apples and bananas also double. Sue's budget line will
   a. shift leftward but not change slope.
   b. remain unchanged.
   c. shift rightward but not change slope.
   d. shift rightward and become steeper.

Preferences and Indifference Curves

7. As a consumer moves rightward along an indifference curve, the
   a. consumer remains indifferent among the different combinations of goods.
   b. consumer generally prefers the combinations of goods farther rightward along the indifference curve.
   c. income required to buy the combinations of the goods always increases.
   d. relative price of both goods falls.

8. Indifference curves shift or rotate
   a. only when income changes.
   b. only when prices change.
   c. when either income or prices change.
   d. with none of the above because changes in income and prices do not shift indifference curves.

9. If your local newspaper reported that wearing plaid clothing was a sure way to obtain good grades, students'
   a. budget lines would shift rightward to compensate for the higher price of plaid clothing.
   b. budget lines would rotate so that more plaid clothing would be purchased.
   c. preferences would change in favor of more plaid clothing.
   d. None of the above.

10. The assumption of diminishing marginal rate of substitution means that
    a. the budget line has a negative slope.
    b. the budget line does not shift when people's preferences change.
    c. indifference curves might have a positive slope.
    d. indifference curves will be concave.

11. If two goods are perfect substitutes, their
    a. indifference curves are positively sloped straight lines.
    b. indifference curves are negatively sloped straight lines.
    c. indifference curves are L-shaped.
    d. marginal rate of substitution is infinity.

12. If the indifference curves between two goods are L-shaped, the goods are
    a. complementary goods.
    b. substitute goods.
    c. normal goods.
    d. inferior goods.

Predicting Consumer Choices

Use Figure 9.6 for the next two questions.

FIGURE **9.6**
Multiple Choice Questions 13 and 14

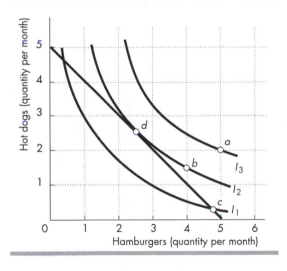

13. Which of the following statements about Figure 9.6 is correct?
    a. Point *a* is preferred to point *d*, but *a* is not affordable.
    b. The consumer is indifferent between points *d* and *c*, but *c* is more affordable.
    c. Point *b* is preferred to point *d*, but *b* is not affordable.
    d. Both points *a* and *d* cost the same, but *a* is preferred to *d*.

14. What is the best affordable point of consumption?
    a. *a*
    b. *b*
    c. *c*
    d. *d*

15. A consumer is in equilibrium when the consumption point is on
    a. the budget line.
    b. an indifference curve.
    c. the highest indifference curve that just touches the budget line.
    d. None of the above.

16. Which of the following is true when the consumer is at the best affordable point?
    a. The point is on the budget line and highest attainable indifference curve.
    b. The slope of the budget line equals the slope of the indifference curve.
    c. The MRS equals the relative price.
    d. All of the above are true at the best affordable point.

17. Which of the following statements is true?
    a. The law of diminishing marginal rate of substitution means that indifference curves are convex (bowed out).
    b. A demand curve can be derived from the indifference curve/budget line analysis.
    c. Demand curves and indifference curves measure the same things.
    d. Demand curves and indifference curves have negative slopes for the same reason.

18. In a budget line/indifference curve diagram between apples and oranges, when the price of an orange rises, the budget line _____ and the indifference curves ___.
    a. rotates outward; shift outward.
    b. rotates inward; do not shift
    c. rotates outward; shift inward
    d. rotates inward; shift inward.

19. When the price of an orange falls, the income effect
    a. increases the consumption of oranges if oranges are a normal good.
    b. increases the consumption of oranges if oranges are an inferior good.
    c. always increases the consumption of oranges.
    d. always decreases the consumption of oranges.

20. When oranges fall in price, the substitution effect
    a. increases the consumption of oranges if oranges are a normal good.
    b. increases the consumption of oranges if oranges are an inferior good.
    c. always increases the consumption of oranges.
    d. always decreases the consumption of oranges.

Use Figure 9.7 for the next three questions.

FIGURE **9.7**

Multiple Choice Questions 21, 22, 23

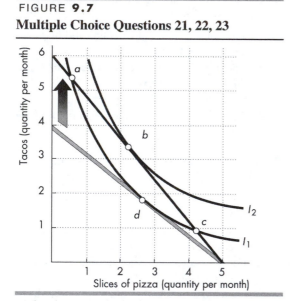

21. The change in the budget line is the result of a(n)
    a. fall in the price of a slice of pizza.
    b. fall in the price of a taco.
    c. increase in income.
    d. None of the above

22. With the change in the budget line, the consumer's real income measured in units of tacos
    a. definitely increased.
    b. definitely decreased.
    c. did not change.
    d. might have changed, but it is impossible to tell from the figure.

23. The new consumer equilibrium is at point
    a. *a.*
    b. *b.*
    c. *c.*
    d. *d.*

24. The effect from a change in price while (hypothetically) changing income to keep the consumer on the same indifference curve, is called the
    a. price effect.
    b. income effect.
    c. substitution effect.
    d. *ceterus paribus* effect.

25. When the price of a normal good falls, the income effect _____ the quantity demanded and the substitution effect _____ the quantity demanded.
    a. increases; increases
    b. increases; decreases
    c. decreases; increases
    d. decreases; decreases

26. An inferior good has
    a. a substitution effect opposite that of a normal good.
    b. an income effect opposite that of a normal good.
    c. a price effect opposite that of a normal good.
    d. no income effect.

■ **Short Answer Problems**

1. Why do indifference curves have negative slopes?

2. Jan and Dan eat bread and peanut butter and have the same income. Because they face the same prices, they have identical budget lines. Currently, Jan and Dan consume the same quantities of bread and peanut butter; they have the same best affordable consumption point. Jan views bread and peanut butter as close (though not perfect) substitutes and Dan considers bread and peanut butter to be quite (but not perfectly) complementary. On the same diagram, draw a budget line and indifference curves for Jan and Dan. (Measure the quantity of bread on the horizontal axis.)

FIGURE **9.8**
Short Answer Problem 3

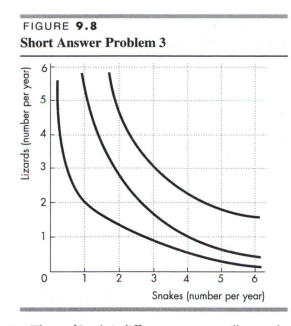

FIGURE **9.9**
Short Answer Problem 4

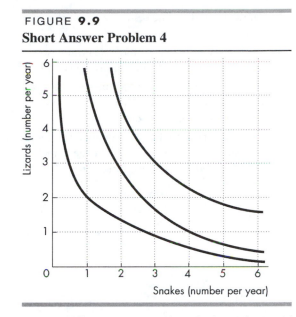

3. Three of Igor's indifference curves are illustrated Figure 9.8.

   a. Suppose that the price of a snake is $10, the price of a lizard is $20, and Igor has $60 to spend on snakes and lizards. Carefully draw his budget line in Figure 9.8. How many snakes does Igor buy? How many lizards?

   b. Suppose that the price of a snake spirals to $20 while the price of a lizard does not change. If Igor's income stays at $60, draw his new budget line in Figure 9.8. Now how many snakes does Igor buy? How many lizards? Are snakes and lizards substitutes or complements?

   c. When is Igor better off: before or after snakes go up in price? How can you tell?

4. Figure 9.9 again shows Igor's indifference curves.

   a. Snakes cost $20, lizards cost $20, and Igor's income is $60. Draw Igor's budget line in Figure 9.9. How many snakes does Igor buy? How many lizards?

   b. For his superior work in finding brains, Igor's master gives him a raise to $120. In Figure 9.9 draw Igor's new budget line. After the raise, how many snakes does Igor buy? How many lizards? For Igor, are snakes and/or lizards a normal good?

5. Ms. Muffet consumes curds and whey. The initial price of curds is $1 per unit, and the price of whey is $1.50 per unit. Ms. Muffet's income is $12.

   a. What is the relative price of curds?

   b. Derive Ms. Muffet's budget equation and draw her budget line on a graph. (Measure curds on the horizontal axis.)

   c. On your graph, draw an indifference curve so that the best affordable point corresponds to 6 units of curds and 4 units of whey.

   d. What is the marginal rate of substitution of curds for whey at this point?

   e. Show that any other point on the budget line is inferior.

6. For the initial situation described in problem 5, suppose that Ms. Muffet's income now increases.

   a. Illustrate graphically how the consumption of curds and whey are affected if both goods are normal. (Precise numerical answers are not necessary here. In your graph, just show whether consumption increases or decreases but do not worry about specific numbers.)

   b. Draw a new graph showing the effect of an increase in Ms. Muffet's income if whey is an inferior good.

7. Return to the initial circumstances in problem 5. Now, suppose that the price of curds doubles to $2 a unit while the price of whey remains at $1.50 per unit and income remains at $12.

a. Draw the budget line before and after the price change.

b. Why is the initial best affordable point (label it point *a*) no longer the best affordable point?

c. Use your graph and show the new best affordable point and label it *d*. What has happened to the consumption of curds?

d. Use your graph to illustrate the substitution and income effects from the price change. Label the point created by the substitution effect *b*.

FIGURE **9.10**

Short Answer Problem 8 (a) and 8 (b)

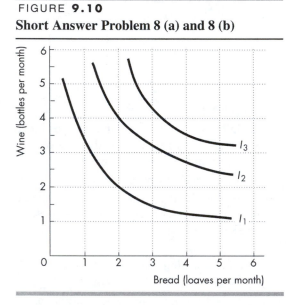

8. Figure 9.10 illustrates Carolyn's indifference map between bread and wine.

a. The price of a bottle of wine is $2, and the price of a loaf of bread is $1. Carolyn has $6 to spend on bread and wine. In Figure 9.10 draw her budget line. How many bottles of wine does Carolyn buy?

b. The price of a bottle of wine falls to $1. The price of a loaf of bread remains at $1, and Carolyn's income is constant at $6. Draw her new budget line in Figure 9.10. How many bottles of wine does Carolyn now buy?

c. Assume that Carolyn's demand curve is linear. In Figure 9.11 draw Carolyn's demand curve for wine.

FIGURE **9.11**

Short Answer Problem 8 (c)

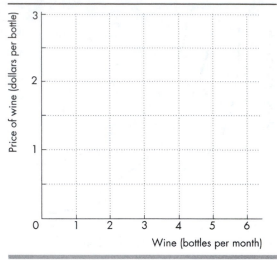

■ **You're the Teacher**

1. "I see that we can use this indifference curve/budget line approach to derive demand curves. But why bother? I mean, after all, why not just use the demand curves like we've been doing all along and not worry about this other stuff?" This question is reasonable. Tell your friend why this other stuff is worth bothering about.

2. "I finally understand this chapter: Indifference curves and demand curves are the same thing! My studying is beginning to pay off." Actually your friend is *not* studying enough. Help your friend by explaining why indifference curves and demand curves are not the same.

A n s w e r s

■ True/False Answers

Consumption Possibilities

1. **T** The budget line is straight; indifference curves are concave (bowed toward the origin).

2. **T** The magnitude of the slope of the budget line is the relative price of the good on the horizontal axis in terms of the good on the vertical axis.

3. **F** An increase in income shifts the budget line outward, but does not change its slope.

Preferences and Indifference Curves

4. **T** This definition is why a consumer is indifferent between points on a particular indifference curve.

5. **F** An indifference curve shows different combinations of two goods among which the consumer is indifferent; a demand curve shows how the quantity of one good changes when its price changes.

6. **T** Indifference curves farther from the origin have more potential consumption of *all* goods and services and so are preferred.

7. **T** The statement tells how to measure the marginal rate of substitution.

8. **F** The principle of diminishing marginal rate of substitution means that the marginal rate of substitution falls while moving *downward* along an indifference curve.

9. **F** Goods that are complements have L-shaped indifference curves.

Predicting Consumer Choices

10. **T** The best affordable point is best because it is on the highest indifference curve and is affordable because it is on the budget line.

11. **T** The question tells how a demand curve can be derived.

12. **F** The price effect can be divided into the substitution effect and the income effect.

13. **F** The budget line shifts rightward, but the equilibrium amount of the good consumed decreases.

14. **F** The income effect leads to increased consumption for normal goods and decreased consumption for inferior goods.

15. **T** For a normal good, the income effect and the substitution effect always have the same impact on consumption of the good.

■ Multiple Choice Answers

Consumption Possibilities

1. **b** The budget line illustrates the different combinations of goods an individual can afford. In this sense it is like a menu, showing what can be purchased. But in order to determine what will be purchased, information is needed on the consumer's preferences about the different combinations of goods.

2. **b** The slope indicates how many units of the good measured on the vertical axis must be given up in order to gain another unit of the good measured on the horizontal axis.

3. **c** Income and price changes shift or rotate the budget line, not indifference curves.

4. **d** Changes in the relative price rotate the budget line; changes in income shift it in a parallel fashion.

5. **a** A rise in the price of a movie does not change the vertical intercept (y/P_soda), but the magnitude of the slope $(P_\text{movies}/P_\text{soda})$ increases.

6. **b** The relative price of bananas and apples does not change because both prices doubled, so the slope of the budget line is unchanged. In addition, the intercepts do not change because the higher income matches the higher prices. So, the budget line does not change.

Preferences and Indifference Curves

7. **a** By definition, the consumer is indifferent between any consumption combination on an indifference curve.

8. **d** Only changes in the individual's preferences shift the indifference curves.

9. **c** Preferences change because now students "like" plaid clothing more than before.

10. **d** The diminishing marginal rate of substitution means that an indifference curve becomes flatter while moving rightward along it so that more of

the good measured on the horizontal axis is consumed.

11. **b** The more closely two goods substitute for each other, the more closely their indifference curves approach being straight lines.

12. **a** Perfect complements have L-shaped indifference curves.

Predicting Consumer Choices

13. **a** Point *a* is preferred because it is on a higher indifference curve, but it is not affordable because it lies beyond the budget line.

14. **d** Point *d* is the point on the highest indifference curve that is affordable.

15. **c** The consumption bundle represented by the point on the budget line where the highest indifference curve touches the budget line is the best affordable consumption bundle.

16. **d** All the statements accurately characterize consumer equilibrium.

17. **b** In other words, demand curves are the result of people selecting the best affordable consumption combination.

18. **b** The budget line changes only when either the prices or income change; the indifference curves change only when a person's preferences change.

19. **a** The income effect of a lower price motivates an increase in the consumption of normal goods only. The income effect motivates a *decrease* in the consumption of inferior goods.

20. **c** The substitution effect from a lower price *always* motivates an increase in the consumption of the relatively cheaper good.

21. **b** When the price of a taco falls, the maximum amount of tacos that can be purchased increases, but the maximum amount of pizza slices that can be purchased does not change.

22. **a** Real income increased because more tacos can be purchased.

23. **b** After the price change, point *b* is on the highest affordable indifference curve.

24. **c** This question defines the substitution effect.

25. **a** For normal goods, both the substitution and income effects from a lower price will increase the quantity demanded.

26. **b** Increases in income increase the demand for a normal good and decrease the demand for an inferior good.

■ Answers to Short Answer Problems

1. An indifference curve shows how much the consumption of one good must increase as the consumption of another good decreases in order to leave the consumer indifferent (no better or worse off).

    It has a negative slope because both goods are desirable. In order to not be made worse off, as the consumption of one good decreases, consumption of the other good must increase. This relationship implies a negative slope.

FIGURE **9.12**
Short Answer Problem 2

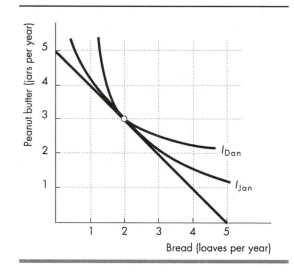

2. Figure 9.12 shows Jan and Dan's budget line and their indifference curves. Because Jan views bread and peanut butter as substitutes and Dan views them as complements, Jan's indifference curve is more linear than Dan's and Dan's is more L-shaped than Jan's.

    In general, the more the goods are viewed as substitutes, the more linear are the indifference curves. The more the goods are viewed as complements, the more L-shaped are the indifference curves.

FIGURE **9.13**
Short Answer Problem 3 (a)

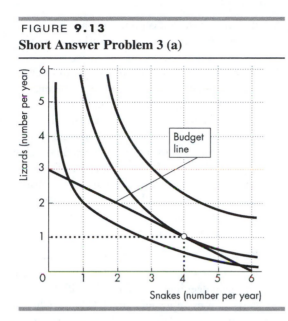

3. a. Figure 9.13 shows the budget line. The point with the highest attainable utility is indicated by the circle, where the budget line touches the highest possible indifference curve. At this point Igor buys 4 snakes and 1 lizard.

FIGURE **9.14**
Short Answer Problem 3 (b)

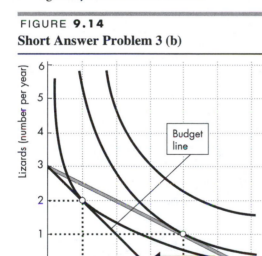

b. Figure 9.14 illustrates Igor's new budget line. After the price hike for snakes, Igor buys 1 snake and 2 lizards. Lizards and snakes are substitutes. The increase in the price of a snake increases the quantity of lizards that Igor buys.

c. Igor was better off before the price of a snake rose. A comparison of Figures 9.13 and 9.14 reveals that Igor was on a higher indifference curve before the price of a snake rose, so he preferred the situation before snakes rose in price.

FIGURE **9.15**
Short Answer Problem 4 (a)

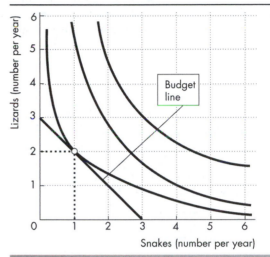

4. a. Figure 9.15 shows that Igor buys 1 snake and 2 lizards.

FIGURE **9.16**
Short Answer Problem 4 (b)

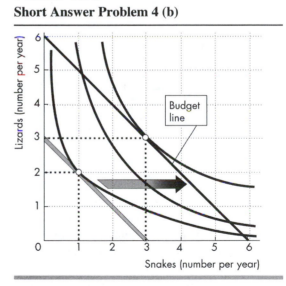

b. The increase in income shifts Igor's budget line, as indicated in Figure 9.16. After his increase in income, Igor buys 3 snakes and 3 lizards. For

Igor, both snakes and lizards are normal goods because he buys more of both when his income increases.

5. a The relative price of curds is the money price of curds divided by the money price of whey: ($1 per unit of curds)/($1.50 per unit of whey) or 2/3 whey per curd.

   b. Let P_c = the price of curds, P_w = the price of whey, Q_c = quantity of curds, Q_w = quantity of whey, and y = income. The budget equation, in general form, is:

   $$Q_w = \frac{y}{P_w} - \left(\frac{P_c}{P_w}\right)Q_c$$

   Because P_c = $1, P_w = $1.50, and y = $12, Ms. Muffet's budget equation is specifically given by:

   $$Q_w = 8 - \frac{2}{3}Q_c$$

   The graph of this budget equation, the budget line, is given in Figure 9.17.

FIGURE **9.17**
Short Answer Problem 5

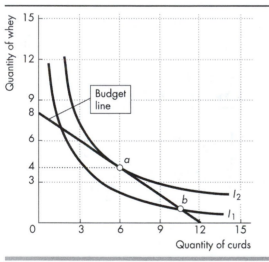

c. Indifference curve I_2 is the indifference curve tangent to the budget line so that Ms. Muffet's best affordable point — that is, her equilibrium point — is point a, with consumption of 6 units of curds and 4 units of whey.

d. The marginal rate of substitution is the magnitude of the slope of the indifference curve at point a. We do not know the slope of the indifference curve directly, but we can easily compute the slope of the budget line and thereby calculate the marginal rate of substitution. At the best affordable point a, the indifference curve and the budget line have the same slope. (The fact that the slope of the indifference curve equals that of the budget line at the best affordable point is the hallmark of the best affordable point.) So we can obtain the marginal rate of substitution of curds for whey by using the slope of the budget line. Because the slope of the budget line is −2/3 the marginal rate of substitution is 2/3. For example, Ms. Muffet is willing to give up 2 units of whey in order to receive 3 additional units of curds.

e. Because indifference curve I_2 lies above the budget line (except at point a), every other point on the budget line is on a lower indifference curve. For example, take point b. Point b lies on indifference curve I_1, which is less preferred than indifference curve I_2. Just like point b, every other point on the budget line lies on a less preferred indifference curve and so every other point is inferior to point a. As a result, point a is the equilibrium point.

FIGURE **9.18**
Short Answer Problem 6 (a)

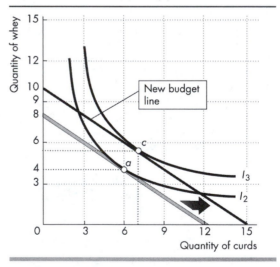

6. a An increase in income causes a parallel rightward shift of the budget line, as shown in Figure 9.18. If both curds and whey are normal goods, Ms. Muffet moves to a point such as c, at which the consumption of both goods has increased.

FIGURE **9.19**
Short Answer Problem 6 (b)

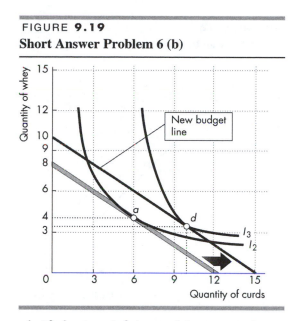

b. If whey is an inferior good, its consumption decreases as income increases, as illustrated in Figure 9.19. Again, the budget line shifts rightward, as in part (a), but Ms. Muffet's preferences are such that her new consumption point is given by a point such as *d*, on indifference curve I_3, where the consumption of whey has declined.

FIGURE **9.20**
Short Answer Problem 7 (a)

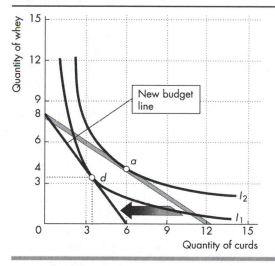

7. a. Ms. Muffet's initial budget line and her initial best affordable point, *a*, are illustrated in Figure 9.20. (The best affordable point is the same point as in Figure 9.17.) Here the new budget line following a rise in the price of curds to $2 is illustrated.

b. After the price rise, point *a* is no longer the best affordable point because now it is no longer affordable.

c. The new best affordable point (labeled *d* in Figure 9.20) indicates a decrease in the consumption of curds. That is as expected because the price of curds rose.

FIGURE **9.21**
Short Answer Problem 7 (d)

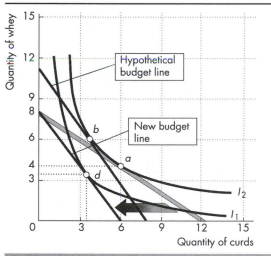

d. The substitution effect is the movement from point *a* to point *b*, and the income effect is the movement from point *b* to point *d*. The key to the substitution effect is that point *b* is on the same indifference curve as point *a*. The hypothetical budget line that determines point *b* has the same slope as the actual new budget line, however Ms. Muffet's income has been (hypothetically) increased along the hypothetical budget line to keep her on the same indifference curve.

The substitution effect *always* leads to a decrease in the consumption of the good whose relative price has risen and an increase in the consumption of a good whose relative price has fallen. In the case at hand, the substitution effect leads to a decrease in the consumption of curds and an increase in the consumption of whey.

FIGURE **9.22**
Short Answer Problem 8 (a)

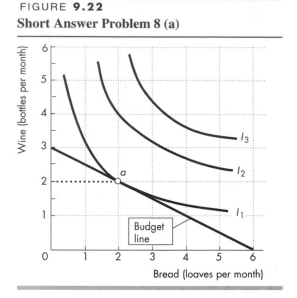

8. a. Figure 9.22 shows Carolyn's budget line. In this figure Carolyn's best attainable point is labeled *a*. She consumes 2 bottles of wine per month.

    b. The fall in the price of a bottle of wine rotates Carolyn's budget line higher, as illustrated in Figure 9.23. Here her best attainable point is *b* and she consumes 4 bottles of wine per month. Note that indifference curve I_3 continues to remain unaffordable.

FIGURE **9.23**
Short Answer Problem 8 (b)

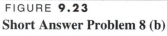
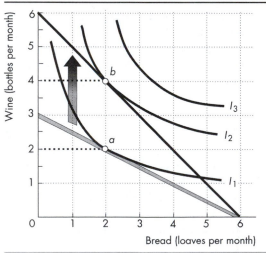

FIGURE **9.24**
Short Answer Problem 8 (c)

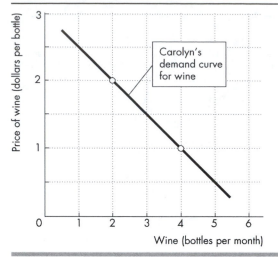

c. When the price of wine is $2 a bottle, part (a) indicates that Carolyn buys 2 bottles of wine. When the price of wine falls to $1 a bottle, part (b) shows that Carolyn buys 4 bottles of wine. These two points on her demand curve are illustrated in Figure 9.24, and her (assumed linear) demand curve is drawn through these points.

■ **You're the Teacher**

1. "It's certainly true that one of the main goals of budget line/indifference curve analysis is deriving the demand curve. There are a couple of reasons for doing so. First, it's 'nice' to see that we can derive a demand curve by just assuming that people consume the best combination of goods and services they can afford. The idea that people make themselves as well off as possible is the hallmark of economics. This idea represents the basic world view of an economist; if you think it's a reasonable assumption, maybe you ought to major in economics!"

    "Second, the indifference curve/budget line approach allows us to think about income and substitution effects. These concepts help clarify some important household choices. For instance, without these ideas, understanding why the quantity of labor people supply has declined as wages rose would be difficult. If we didn't know about the income effect, we'd probably think that people were either irrational or stupid for decreasing the quantity of their labor supplied when wage rates rose. So this approach gives us some new insights into how economists view the world and the factors that affect the choices that people make."

2. "Look, you're wrong about this. I know that both indifference curves and demand curves slope downward, but indifference curves and demand curves really are different. In fact, we use indifference curves to help derive demand curves. But, to see the difference, think about a demand curve. It shows us how the price of a good affects how much we will buy. For instance, your demand curve for frozen yogurt cones tells us how much frozen yogurt you'll buy if a cone is $1.50 or how much you'll buy if one is $2.00. Indifference curves are different. They don't give us the relationship between a good's price and how much you'll buy. Indifference curves show us different combinations of two goods that leave you indifferent. You have indifference curves between frozen yogurt cones and ice cream cones. This type of indifference curve shows us all the combinations of yogurt and ice cream cones such that you don't care which combination you get. So, you see, indifference curves and demand curves aren't the same, so don't make this mistake."

Chapter Quiz

1. Tommy's monthly budget line for street hockey balls and books is plotted with books on the horizontal axis. His budget line shifts rightward and its slope does not change. Hence
   a. the price of a street hockey ball has fallen.
   b. the price of a book has fallen.
   c. Tommy's income has risen.
   d. the price of a street hockey ball has fallen and the price of a book has risen.

2. A household's budget line is determined by
   a. prices and preferences.
   b. income and preferences.
   c. prices and income.
   d. prices, income, and preferences.

3. Emma has weekly income of $200. A textbook costs $50 and a pad of paper $1. When Emma's budget line is drawn with textbooks on the horizontal axis,
   a. the horizontal intercept is 200 pads of paper.
   b. the slope of the budget line is $200.
   c. the horizontal intercept is 4 textbooks.
   d. the budget line shows that Emma cannot buy 3 textbooks.

4. Preferences
   a. do not depend on what the person can afford.
   b. are shown graphically as a budget line.
   c. change when relative prices change.
   d. show feasible consumption combinations.

5. An indifference curve shows all combinations of two goods that
   a. can be purchased with a given income.
   b. have the same marginal rate of substitution.
   c. are preferred to any other combination of the goods.
   d. among which the consumer is indifferent.

6. Right-hand and left-hand gloves are perfect complements. As a result, the corresponding indifference curves
   a. are L-shaped.
   b. intersect each other.
   c. are straight lines.
   d. are vertical.

7. At the best affordable point, the
   a. indifference curve *crosses* the budget line.
   b. marginal rate of substitution exceeds the relative price of the goods by as much as possible.
   c. consumer is on the highest attainable indifference curve.
   d. None of the above.

8. The income effect from a price change
   a. is always greater than the price effect.
   b. is always greater than the substitution effect.
   c. always leads to an increase in the purchase of the good whose relative price has fallen.
   d. None of the above.

9. When the relative price of a normal good falls, the substitution effect results in _____ in the quantity purchased and the income effect results in _____ in the quantity purchased.
   a. an increase; an increase
   b. an increase; a decrease
   c. a decrease; an increase
   d. a decrease; a decrease

10. An increase in the price of any type of food, such as pizza, has
    a. a substitution effect and an income effect.
    b. a substitution effect but does not have an income effect.
    c. an income effect but does not have a substitution effect.
    d. neither a substitution effect nor an income effect.

The answers for this Chapter Quiz are on page 345

■ **Chapter 8**

1. Diminishing marginal utility means that
   a. Ralph will enjoy his first hamburger more than his second.
   b. the utility from one hamburger exceeds the utility from two hamburgers.
   c. the price of two hamburgers is twice the price of one hamburger.
   d. beyond a certain point, total utility falls as income rises.

2. As Sean's consumption of rice decreases, his
   a. average utility from consuming rice falls.
   b. total utility from consuming rice falls.
   c. marginal utility from consuming rice falls.
   d. elasticity of utility from consuming rice falls.

3. Gustov has income of $20. He consumes only jugs of wine, with a price of $4 per jug, and loaves of bread, with a price of $2 per loaf. He currently buys 2 jugs of wine and 6 loaves of bread. Gustov's marginal utility from the second jug of wine is 120 and from the sixth loaf of bread is 60. To maximize his utility, Gustof should
   a. increase his consumption of wine and decrease his consumption of bread.
   b. increase his consumption of bread and decrease his consumption of wine.
   c. increase his consumption of wine and bread, thereby spending all his income.
   d. change nothing because he already is maximizing his utility.

4. Jenny buys sodas and popcorn. Sodas sell for $1 and popcorn sells for $2 a bag. Currently she is in consumer equilibrium with the marginal utility from her last dollar spent on popcorn equal to 50. The marginal utility from her last dollar spent on sodas is
   a. 10.
   b. 15.
   c. 25.
   d. 50.

5. Shaniq's total utility from 2 movies per week is 300 and her marginal utility from a 3rd movie per week is 50. Her total utility if she sees 3 movies is
   a. 250.
   b. 350.
   c. 450.
   d. 1050.

■ **Chapter 9**

6. Inga's graph of her budget line has apples per week on the vertical axis and loaves of bread per week on the horizontal. An increase in the price of apples shifts the
   a. horizontal intercept left.
   b. horizontal intercept right.
   c. vertical intercept down.
   d. vertical intercept up.

7. Movies are $12 a ticket and DVD's are $6 per DVD. With DVDs on the vertical axis, the magnitude of the slope of the budget line is
   a. 0.5.
   b. 2.
   c. 3.
   d. 6.

8. In his consumer equilibrium, Jon equates the relative price of two goods to
   a. his money income.
   b. his real income.
   c. his marginal rate of substitution.
   d. the relative quantities he consumes.

9. For inferior goods, an increase in income
   a. increases the demand.
   b. decreases the demand.
   c. does not change the amount purchased.
   d. changes the slope of the budget line.

10. Compared to diamonds, water has _____ total utility and _____ marginal utility.
    a. higher; higher
    b. higher; lower
    c. lower; higher
    d. lower; lower.

Answers

■ Mid-Term Exam Answers

1. a;   2. b;   3. d;   4. d;   5. b;   6. c;   7. b;   8. c;   9. b;   10. b.

Chapter 10 ORGANIZING PRODUCTION

Key Concepts

The Firm and Its Economic Problem

A **firm** is an institution that hires factors of production and organizes these factors to produce and sell goods and services. The firm's goal is to maximize its (economic) profit, which equals its revenue minus its (opportunity) costs. The *opportunity cost* of any action is the best alternative foregone. Although opportunity cost is the best alternative forgone, opportunity cost is measured in terms of money so that the alternatives can be added up. A firm's opportunity costs can be separated into costs of resources bought in the market, costs of resources owned by the firm, and costs of resources supplied by the owner.

♦ *Cost of capital* — The **implicit rental rate** of capital is the opportunity cost the business incurs by using its own capital rather than renting the capital to another firm. It is equal to the sum of economic depreciation plus foregone interest costs. **Economic depreciation** is the fall in the *market value* of the capital over a given period. The foregone interest is the interest income lost on the funds used to buy the capital.

♦ *Cost of owners' resources* — owners often supply labor *and* entrepreneurship to the business. The return to entrepreneurship is profit. The profit an entrepreneur earns *on average* is called **normal profit.**

Economic profit = Total revenue – Opportunity cost.

A business earning an economic profit is earning a profit that exceeds the normal profit.

Three factors limit a firm's profit:

♦ *Technology constraints* — a **technology** is any method of producing a good or service. Technology limits how a firm can turn resources into output.

♦ *Information constraints* — the future is always uncertain and elements of the present are unknown.

♦ *Marketing constraints* — how much the firm can sell and at what price are limited by its customers' willingness to buy its goods or services and by the prices and marketing efforts of other firms.

Technological and Economic Efficiency

♦ **Technological efficiency** — when the firm produces a given output using the least amount of inputs.

♦ **Economic efficiency** — when the firm produces a given output at the least cost. Economic efficiency depends on the costs of the inputs.

If a business is economically efficient, it must be technologically efficient, but technological efficiency does not necessarily imply economic efficiency. A firm must be economically efficient to maximize its profit.

Information and Organization

Firms must organize production. They can do so using:

♦ **Command system** — organizes production using a managerial hierarchy, so that commands go from managers to workers.

♦ **Incentive system** — organizes production using market-like mechanisms, so that incentives are set up to induce workers to maximize the firm's profit.

The **principal–agent problem** is to set rules for compensation so that agents (people employed by others) act in the best interests of a principal (the individual who employs the agents). Giving managers partial ownership of the company, using incentive pay, and using long-term contracts help overcome the principal-agent problem.

Three forms of business organization are:

♦ *Proprietorship* — a single owner with unlimited liability. Profits are taxed once.

♦ *Partnership* — two or more owners with unlimited liability. Profits are taxed once.

♦ *Corporation* — a business owned by stockholders who have limited liability. Corporate profits are taxed twice. First, the corporation pays taxes on its profits. Second, if the firm pays dividends, its shareholders pay taxes on the amount paid or if the company retains some profit and reinvests it, the price of its stock can rise and shareholders pay taxes on capital gains — the income received when a share of stock is sold for a higher price than was paid for it.

There are more proprietorships than any other type of business, but corporations account for the lion's share of total business revenue.

■ Markets and the Competitive Environment

Economists define four market types:

♦ **perfect competition** — a market with many firms and buyers, each firm sells an identical product, and there are no restrictions on entry of new firms.

♦ **monopolistic competition** — a market structure with a large number of firms. Each firm makes a slightly different product. Making a slightly different product from the product of a competing firm is called **product differentiation.**

♦ **oligopoly** — a market structure in which a small number of firms compete.

♦ **monopoly** — when there is one firm that produces a good or service that has no close substitutes and in which the firm is protected by a barrier preventing the entry of new firms.

Two measures of market concentration are:

♦ **Four-firm concentration ratio** — the percentage of the value of sales accounted for by the four largest firms in an industry.

♦ **Herfindahl–Hirschman Index (HHI)** — the square of the percentage market share of each firm summed over the 50 largest firms in a market.

A low value for either concentration measure indicates the presence of extensive competition. But concentration ratios have limitations:

♦ They are calculated for the national market, but the relevant market for some goods is local and for others is international in scope.

♦ They give no indication of the existence or absence of entry barriers. An industry with a small number of firms may be competitive due to potential entry.

♦ Often the relevant market does not correspond to an industry as defined in the measures and many firms operate in several industries.

Competitive markets account for about 75 percent of the value of goods sold, monopoly accounts for about 5 percent, and oligopoly is near 18 percent.

■ Produce or Outsource? Firms and Markets

Both firms and markets can coordinate product. Firms-rather than markets—coordinate economic activity when they perform the task more efficiently than markets. Firms can have several advantages such as:

♦ *lower transactions costs* — **transactions costs** are the costs of finding someone with whom to do business, of reaching an agreement about the price and other aspects of the exchange, and of ensuring that the terms of the agreement are fulfilled.

♦ **economies of scale** — when the cost of producing a unit of output falls as more output is produced.

♦ **economies of scope** — when specialized resources can be used to produce a variety of products.

♦ *economies of team production* — when individuals specialize in tasks that help support each other's production.

Firms can have lower transactions costs than using a market. Economies of scale, scope, and team production can mean that production within a firm is less expensive than using a market.

Helpful Hints

1. **NORMAL PROFIT AS A COST :** The idea of a normal profit is important. A normal profit is the cost of buying an owner's entrepreneurial ability, say the owner's ability to make sound business decisions.

   Normal profit is part of the firm's opportunity cost of doing business, in the same way that paying workers' wages or paying interest on debt are opportunity costs to the firm. Think of costs as expenses that *must* be paid; if a company fails to meet its expenses, it will (eventually) close. For example, if a business cannot pay its workers their wages or its debt holders the interest due to them, the firm will have to shut down. Similarly, if the firm cannot return at least a normal profit to its owners to compensate them for their talents in running the business, eventually the firm will close as the owners take up other endeavors.

2. **ECONOMIC PROFIT AND NORMAL PROFIT :** Economic profit is revenue minus all opportunity costs. Because a normal profit is already part of the firm's opportunity costs, an economic profit signifies a profit over and above the normal profit; that is, an economic profit is an above-normal profit.

Questions

■ True/False and Explain

The Firm and Its Economic Problem

1. A firm's opportunity costs include resources bought in a market and resources supplied by the owner.

2. Because firms *must* hire workers, the wages paid the workers are not part of the opportunity cost of running the business.

3. A firm's normal profit is part of the opportunity cost of running the business.

4. Technology limits a firm's profits.

Technological and Economic Efficiency

5. By definition, a firm is economically efficient whenever the business *must* increase its use of resources in order to increase the amount it produces.

6. If a firm is economically efficient, it must be technologically efficient.

Information and Organization

7. Using an incentive system of organizing a business means that a manager's commands give the workers the incentive to maximize the firm's profit.

8. A sales associate working in the sportswear department at JCPenney is an example of an "agent."

9. Giving top executives of large corporations stock in the companies is a method of handling a principal-agent problem.

10. If a proprietorship goes bankrupt, the owner is responsible for *all* the firm's debts.

11. A major advantage of the corporate form of business organization is limited liability.

12. A disadvantage of the corporate form of business organization is that its profits are taxed twice.

Markets and the Competitive Environment

13. Monopolistic competition occurs when monopolies compete with each other.

14. The four-firm concentration ratio is the sum of the squared market shares of the four largest firms in an industry.

15. A low concentration ratio indicates a low level of competition.

16. Concentration ratios indicate that most of the nation's goods and services are produced in oligopolistic markets.

Produce or Outsource? Firms and Markets

17. Transaction costs are a reason why firms can be more efficient than markets in coordinating economic activity.

18. Markets — rather than firms — likely will coordinate economic activity in situations where there are economies of scale.

■ Multiple Choice

The Firm and Its Economic Problem

1. A firm's goal is to maximize its
   a. revenue.
   b. costs.
   c. profit.
   d. None of the above.

2. Which of the following is <u>NOT</u> an opportunity cost of operating a business?
   a. The wages paid to the workers.
   b. The salary paid to the owners.
   c. The interest not earned on funds used to buy capital equipment.
   d. ALL of the above are an opportunity cost of running a business.

3. The implicit rental rate of capital includes the _____ and the _____.
   a. normal profit; economic profit
   b. economic profit; economic depreciation
   c. normal profit; economic depreciation.
   d. economic depreciation; forgone interest

4. A normal profit is
   a. the profit the business always earns.
   b. a cost that is always accurately measured by an accountant.
   c. the amount of profit an accountant calculates for a company.
   d. not the same as the company's economic profit.

5. Which of the following constraints limits a firm's profit?
   a. Technology constraints
   b. Information constraints
   c. Market constraints
   d. All of the above limit a firm's profit.

Technological and Economic Efficiency

Use Table 10.1, which shows four methods of producing photon torpedoes, for the next three questions.

TABLE **10.1**

Multiple Choice Questions 6, 7, 8

	Quantities of Resources Used to Produce One Photon Torpedo	
Method	Labor	Capital
1	5	10
2	10	7
3	15	5
4	20	5

6. Which is a technologically inefficient method of making a photon torpedo?
   a. Method 1 only
   b. Method 2 only
   c. Method 3 only
   d. Method 4 only

7. If labor costs $10 per unit and capital $20 per unit, which is an economically efficient method of making a photon torpedo?
   a. Method 1 only
   b. Method 2 only
   c. Method 3 only
   d. All four methods are economically efficient.

8. If labor costs $10 per unit and capital falls to $15 per unit, which is an economically efficient method of making a photon torpedo?
   a. Method 1 only
   b. Method 2 only
   c. Method 3 only
   d. All four methods are economically efficient.

Information and Organization

9. The method of organizing production that uses a managerial hierarchy is
   a. a command system.
   b. an incentive system.
   c. a principal-agent system.
   d. None of the above.

10. The possibility that an employee might not work hard is an example of the
    a. problem of opportunity cost.
    b. principle of scarcity.
    c. limited liability doctrine.
    d. principal-agent problem.

11. Most firms are
    a. proprietorships.
    b. partnerships.
    c. corporations.
    d. nonprofit.

12. A form of business that is simple to set up, whose profits are taxed only once, and is run by a single owner is a
    a. proprietorship.
    b. partnership.
    c. corporation.
    d. either a proprietorship or partnership, depending on other information.

13. A *disadvantage* of the corporate form of business organization is its
    a. limited liability for its owners.
    b. unlimited liability for its owners.
    c. ability to be run by professional managers.
    d. tax liability because retained profits are taxed twice.

For the next two questions, suppose that Tracy and Pat start a business. Because of bad decisions by Tracy, the company goes bankrupt, owing a total of $50,000. Tracy is penniless, but Pat is a multimillionaire.

14. If the company were organized as a partnership, Pat would be responsible for
    a. $100,000 of debt.
    b. $50,000 of debt.
    c. $25,000 of debt.
    d. $0 of debt.

15. If the company were organized as a corporation, Pat would be responsible for
    a. $100,000 of debt.
    b. $50,000 of debt.
    c. $25,000 of debt.
    d. $0 of debt.

Markets and the Competitive Environment

16. What type of industry structure has many firms, each producing a slightly different good, with no barriers to entry or exit?
    a. Perfect competition
    b. Monopolistic competition
    c. Oligopoly
    d. Monopoly

17. The four-firm concentration ratio measures the share of the largest four firms in total industry
    a. profits.
    b. sales.
    c. cost.
    d. capital.

TABLE **10.2**

Market Shares

Firm	Market Share
Sally's Subs	15%
Samantha's Subs	5%
Susan's Subs	30%
Sydna's Subs	20%
Sheryl's Subs	20%
Shirley's Subs	10%

18. In Table 10.2 what is the four-firm concentration ratio in the submarine sandwich industry?
    a. 100 percent
    b. 85 percent
    c. 70 percent
    d. 30 percent

Produce or Outsource? Firms and Markets

19. Which of the following is <u>NOT</u> a reason for the existence of firms?
    a. Lower transactions costs for firms
    b. Principal-agent problem
    c. Economies of scope
    d. Economies of team production

20. Taco Bell can use its equipment and staff to produce and sell tacos, burritos, and drinks less expensively than would be the case if each had to be purchased separately in a market. This situation demonstrates
    a. economies of scale.
    b. economies of scope.
    c. long-term contracts.
    d. none of the above.

■ Short Answer Problems

1. Contrast how an accountant would measure the following with the opportunity cost approach.
   a. depreciation cost
   b. the firm borrowing money to finance purchasing its capital
   c. the firm using its own funds rather than borrowing to purchase its capital
   d. the value of the business owner's inputs

2. Frank decides to start a business manufacturing doll furniture. Frank has two sisters: Angela is an accountant and Edith is an economist. Each of the sisters uses the following information to compute Frank's costs and profit for the first year.
   1) *Revenue* — Frank's revenue for his first year was $100,000.
   2) *Alternative job* — Frank took no income from the firm. He has an offer to return to work full time as a bricklayer for $30,000 per year.
   3) *Rent* — Frank rented his machinery for $9,000 a year.
   4) *Garage* — Frank owns the garage in which he works but could rent it out at $3,000 per year.
   5) *Invested funds* — to start the business, Frank used $10,000 of his own money from a savings account that paid 10 percent per year interest. Frank also borrowed $30,000 at 10 percent per year.
   6) *Employee* — Frank hired one employee at an annual salary of $20,000.
   7) *Materials* — the cost of materials during the first year was $40,000.
   8) *Services* — Frank's entrepreneurial services are worth $20,000 to his business.

   a. Set up a table indicating how Angela and Edith would compute Frank's cost.
   b. What is Frank's profit (or loss) as computed by Angela? By Edith?

3. The standard tip in a restaurant is 15 percent. Restaurants *could* raise their prices 15 percent, set a policy of no tipping, and then give their servers the extra 15 percent. Explain why restaurants do not do so by focusing on the principal-agent problem.

4. Is the principal-agent problem between the owner(s) and manager(s) more severe in proprietorships or corporations? Why?

5. Distinguish between technological efficiency and economic efficiency.

6. Considering the geographic scope of markets, how might a concentration ratio understate the degree of competitiveness in an industry? How might it overstate the degree of competitiveness?

7. Markets and firms are alternative ways of coordinating economic activity. Why do both firms and markets exist?

■ **You're the Teacher**

1. "I don't understand the difference between a 'normal profit' and an 'economic profit'. And, what's more, why should I care? After all, a profit is a profit is a profit!" Explain to your friend the difference and why the difference matters … especially if you own a business!

2. Answer this question posed to you by a classmate: "How can a situation be technologically efficient and not economically efficient?"

ANSWERS

■ True/False Answers

The Firm and Its Economic Problem

1. **T** Opportunity costs include *all* the costs of running a business.

2. **F** The wages are an opportunity cost because the fund used to pay it could have been used to purchase something else.

3. **T** The normal profit is the payment accruing to an owner for the owner's entrepreneurial ability.

4. **T** Other limiting factors are information and marketing constraints.

Technological and Economic Efficiency

5. **F** The question gives the definition of technological efficiency.

6. **T** Economic efficiency means that the firm necessarily is technologically efficient; technological efficiency, however, does not necessarily mean that the firm is economically efficient.

Information and Organization

7. **F** An incentive system sets up incentives, such as paying sales agents by commission, that give workers the incentive to maximize the firm's profit.

8. **T** The sales associate is (indirectly) hired by the shareholders of JCPenney to help sell sportswear. The associate is an agent for the owners, who are the principals.

9. **T** Because the price of a share of stock generally rises when the company increases its profits, giving executives stock in the company gives executives the incentive to maximize the company's profit.

10. **T** The owners of proprietorships and partnerships face unlimited liability for the debts of their companies.

11. **T** Limited liability means that owners of corporations are not liable for its debts if the company goes bankrupt.

12. **T** Corporate profits are taxed once as income to the corporation. The profits are taxed a second time because the shareholders must also pay a tax on them, either as dividends or as capital gains.

Markets and the Competitive Environment

13. **F** Monopolistic competition occurs when many firms, each making a slightly differentiated product, compete with each other.

14. **F** The four-firm concentration is the sum of the market shares of the four largest firms.

15. **F** A low concentration ratio indicates a high degree of competition.

16. **F** Most of the goods and services are produced in competitive markets.

Produce or Outsource? Firms and Markets

17. **T** Doing business with a firm might require only one transaction, whereas conducting the same business in markets might require many transactions.

18. **F** If there are economies of scale (the cost of producing a unit of a good or service falls as more are produced) firms coordinate the activity because they can capture these economies of scale.

■ Multiple Choice Answers

The Firm and Its Economic Problem

1. **c** By maximizing its profit, the firm insures that it has the best chance of surviving and simultaneously makes its owners as well off as possible.

2. **d** The wages paid the workers and the salary paid the owners are opportunity costs of running a business. So, too, is the forgone interest on the funds used to buy capital equipment because this interest could have been used to buy something else.

3. **d** Answer d is the definition of implicit rental rate.

4. **d** Economic profit is any profit over and above normal profit.

5. **d** All of the constraints limit the amount of profit a firm can earn.

Technological and Economic Efficiency

6. **d** Method 4 uses more labor and the same capital as method 3; as a result, it is technologically inefficient.

7. **b** Method 2 costs $240 to produce a photon torpedo, whereas methods 1 and 3 cost $250.

8. **a** With the change in input prices, method 1 costs $200, which is less than method 2 ($205) and method 3 ($225).

Information and Organization

9. **a** The question gives the definition of a command system.

10. **d** By loafing, the agent — the employee — takes an action that is not in the best interests of the principal — the owner.

11. **a** Proprietorships are the most numerous type of business organization.

12. **a** Answers (b) and (d) are incorrect because partnerships (which are easy to set up and whose profits are taxed only once) have more than one owner.

13. **d** The profit is taxed once when the corporation earns it as a profit. It is taxed again when an owner sells his or her stock in the company if the profit was retained by the corporation and led to an increase in the price of the stock.

14. **b** As a partnership, Pat has unlimited liability for all the firm's debts.

15. **d** If the company is a corporation, Pat's liability is limited to the initial amount invested, so Pat has no additional liability for the $50,000 debt.

Markets and the Competitive Environment

16. **b** Monopolistic competition is similar to perfect competition insofar as there are many firms with no barriers to entry or exit. It is dissimilar in that each firm produces a unique but closely related good.

17. **b** Adding the percentage of the industry's sales made by the four largest firms is the definition of the four-firm concentration ratio.

18. **b** Add the market shares of the four largest firms.

Produce or Outsource? Firms and Markets

19. **b** The principal-agent problem is a *difficulty* that firms must overcome.

20. **b** Economies of scope are present when production of a variety of products lowers the cost of producing each unit.

■ Answers to Short Answer Problems

1. a. An accountant measures depreciation using IRS specified rules, under which depreciation cost is computed as a prespecified percentage of the original purchase price of the capital good, with no reference to current market value. The op-

portunity cost approach measures economic depreciation, the change in the market value of the capital good over the period in question.

b. If a firm borrows money, the accountant's cost and the opportunity cost are the same; both include the interest payments because the interest expense is the opportunity cost of the loan.

c. If a firm uses its own funds rather than borrowing, the accountant's cost and the opportunity cost differ. The accounting cost is zero because there are no interest payments being made to someone else. The opportunity cost approach recognizes that those funds could have been loaned and so the interest income forgone is the opportunity cost.

d. If the owner forgoes the opportunity for other employment, this loss of income is not part of the accounting costs even though it is an opportunity cost. If the owner draws a salary, it will be captured as both an opportunity cost and an accounting cost. In addition, whether or not the owner took money from the business, the cost of the entrepreneurial talent the owner provides to the business is always an opportunity cost — the firm's normal profit.

TABLE **10.3**

Short Answer Problem 2

Item	Accounting cost (Angela's costs)	Economic cost (Edith's costs)
1) Revenue	$100,000	$100,000
2) Alternative job	0	30,000
3) Rent	9,000	9,000
4) Garage	0	3,000
5) Invested funds	3,000	4,000
6) Employee	20,000	20,000
7) Materials	40,000	40,000
8) Services	0	20,000

2. a. Table 10.3 shows how Angela, the accountant, and Edith, the economist, calculate Frank's cost and revenue for each item listed.

b. Accounting profit equals revenue minus accounting cost, and economic profit equals revenue minus opportunity cost. The accounting cost is the sum of the accounting costs listed for items 2 to 8, or $72,000, and the opportunity cost is the sum of the economic costs listed for items 2 to 8, or $126,000. Hence Frank's accounting profit is $28,000 and his economic profit actually is an economic loss of –$26,000.

3. Restaurants are faced with a classic principal-agent problem because servers might provide poor service to the customers. Rather than attempt to have the manager closely monitor each server, delegating the monitoring to customers is more efficient. If the server gives good service, the customer might tip the server 15 percent or more; if the server provides poor service, the customer will easily note this fact and might tip less than 15 percent. Hence the server has the incentive to be a good agent and provide prompt, good service, which is precisely what the principal — the restaurant's owner — wants.

4. The principal-agent problem between owners and managers is more severe in corporations. For a proprietorship, the owner is usually the manager. Because the owner and manager are the same person, there is no principal-agent problem. In corporations, however, the owners are the stockholders. For instance, if you own 100 shares of Microsoft, you are one of many owners of Microsoft. But, most stockholders do not manage the company. Hence the managers and owners are different people. The owners must be concerned that the managers act to maximize the firm's profit rather than pursuing their own goals, such as shirking rather than working diligently.

5. A method is technologically efficient if increasing output without increasing inputs is not possible. A method is economically efficient if the cost of producing a given level of output is as low as possible. Technological efficiency is independent of prices, but economic efficiency depends on the prices of inputs. An economically efficient method of production is always technologically efficient, but a technologically efficient method is not necessarily economically efficient.

6. Concentration ratios are calculated from a national geographic perspective. If the actual scope of the market is not national, the concentration ratio will likely misstate the degree of competitiveness in an industry. If the actual market is global, the concentration ratio will understate the degree of competitiveness. A firm might have a concentration ratio of 100 as the only producer in the nation, but might face a great deal of international competition. For

instance, this situation closely resembles the case of certain types of computer memory chips with only one American producer but many producers of the same chip abroad.

When the scope of the market is regional, the concentration ratio will overstate the degree of competitiveness. The concentration ratio includes companies elsewhere in the nation that are not real competitors in the region. Newspapers provide the classic example: A paper published in Maine is hardly a competitor for a newspaper published in San Francisco.

7. As demonstrated by the example in the text, car repair can be coordinated by the market or by a firm. The institution (market or firm) that actually coordinates in any given case is the one that is more efficient. In cases where there are significant transactions costs, economies of scale, or economies of team production, firms are likely to be more efficient and they will dominate the coordination of economic activity. But the efficiency of firms is limited, and there are many circumstances where market coordination of economic activity dominates because it is more efficient. Essentially, if coordination by firms is more efficient, the number of firms increases because doing business with them is cheaper than relying on a market. Conversely, if coordination by the market is more efficient, firms will not be able to compete successfully because doing business with them would be more expensive then relying on a market.

■ You're the Teacher

1. "The difference between a 'normal profit' and an 'economic profit' is important. Every business owner supplies some inputs to the business. One of these inputs is entrepreneurial talent — the decisions, leadership, and possibly insight that the owner provides. Normal profit is the payment for these services. Because this payment (perhaps implicitly) is for services rendered, a normal profit is part of the firm's opportunity costs. Essentially, you should think of the normal profit as the standard — average — payment owed to an owner of a business. An economic profit equals the firm's revenues minus its opportunity costs. Because opportunity costs already include normal profit, an economic profit is a

profit over-and-above a normal profit. Basically, an economic profit is an above-average profit."

2. "Technological efficiency merely reflects a firm's inputs and resulting output. A situation is technologically efficient when producing more output without using more inputs is impossible. The converse is that technological efficiency occurs whenever decreasing the amount of an input used decreases the amount of output produced. In other words, the firm is not wasting resources."

"Economic efficiency occurs when the cost of producing a given amount of output is as low as possible. Clearly, if a firm is wasting resources — so that it is possible to reduce the amount of an input without decreasing the amount produced — the business is not economically efficient because decreasing an input will reduce the firm's costs. Hence, if a firm is economically efficient, it must be technologically efficient, too."

"But a firm can be technologically efficient and not economically efficient if it uses the 'wrong' mix of inputs. For instance, the local McDonald's could hire brain surgeons rather than students to cook its burgers. This move would be technologically efficient because someone is required to cook the burgers. But it would not be economically efficient because the students would work for about $21,000 a year, whereas the brain surgeons command at least $700,000 a year."

Chapter Quiz

1. Which of the following statements is correct?
   a. The firm's goal is to maximize its revenue.
   b. The firm seeks to produce at the lowest possible ratio of labor to capital.
   c. Successful firms have completely overcome the principal-agent problem.
   d. The firm's goal is to maximize its profit.

2. A ____ is an agent and ____ is its principal.
   a. baseball player; a baseball manager
   b. manager of a department at Sears; a sales clerk working in the department at Sears
   c. partnership; a corporation
   d. movie star; an elected official

3. Which of the following is <u>NOT</u> an attempt to overcome a principal-agent problem?
   a. Giving managers long-term contracts.
   b. Paying employees a bonus from the firm's profit.
   c. Granting managers partial ownership of the company.
   d. Granting owners of corporations limited liability.

4. A disadvantage of the corporation over other forms of business organization is that the
   a. owners of a corporation have unlimited liability.
   b. decision-making structure in a corporation is simple.
   c. some profits of the corporation are taxed twice.
   d. corporation can be run by professional managers.

5. As a one-quarter partner in a partnership, Sue is legally responsible for
   a. none of its debts.
   b. one-quarter of its debts.
   c. all of its debts.
   d. a fraction of its debts that depends upon how heavily Sue was involved in running the business.

6. The larger an industry's four-firm concentration ratio, the
   a. more competitive the industry.
   b. less competitive the industry.
   c. larger the industry's total sales.
   d. more firms in the industry.

7. A market with only a few firms competing in it is an example of
   a. a perfectly competitive market.
   b. a monopolistically competitive market.
   c. an oligopoly.
   d. a monopoly.

8. Firms typically incur costs for
   a. only resources that are bought in the market.
   b. only resources that are bought in the market and resources supplied by the owner.
   c. only resources owned by the firm.
   d. resources that are eight bought in the market, owned by the firm, or supplied by the owner.

9. Which of the following describes a situation in which a firm rather than a market coordinates economic activity?
   a. There are only a few, low transactions costs of negotiating the buying and selling for a product.
   b. There are no economies of scale present.
   c. There are substantial economies of team production.
   d. If one producer produced a variety of products, its costs quickly and substantially would increase.

10. Both the four-firm concentration ratio and the Herfindahl-Hirschman index attempt to measure the
    a. number of buyers in a market.
    b. number of sellers in a market.
    c. extent of competition in a market.
    d. total economic profit earned by the firms in an industry.

The answers for this Chapter Quiz are on page 345

Chapter 11 OUTPUT AND COSTS

Key Concepts

■ Decision Time Frames

Firms have two decision time frames:

◆ **Short run** is the time frame in which the quantity of at least one factor of production is fixed. The fixed factors are called the firm's *plant*.

◆ **Long run** is the time frame in which the quantities of *all* factors of production can be varied.

A **sunk cost** is a past cost. Sunk costs do not affect a firm's decisions.

■ Short-Run Technology Constraint

Three product concepts are important:

◆ **Total product** (*TP*) is the maximum output that a given quantity of labor can produce. The total product schedule shows the maximum attainable output with a fixed quantity of capital as the quantity of labor is varied.

◆ **Marginal product** of labor (*MP*) is the increase in the total product resulting from a one-unit increase in the quantity of labor, with all other inputs remaining the same.

◆ **Average product** of labor (*AP*) is equal to the total product divided by the quantity of labor employed.

Figure 11.1 illustrates the *MP* and *AP* curves for labor. The product curves have the shapes shown because production initially has increasing marginal returns (another worker's marginal product is higher than the previous worker's) followed by **diminishing marginal returns** (when an additional worker's marginal product is less than the previous worker's marginal product). The **law of diminishing returns** states that as a firm uses more of a variable factor of production, with a

FIGURE **11.1**

The Average and Marginal Products

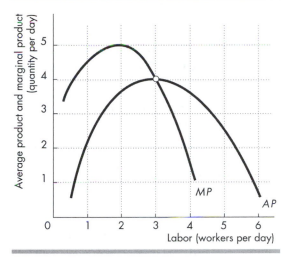

given quantity of fixed factors of production, the marginal product of the variable factor eventually diminishes. This figure also shows the (general) relationship between the marginal product and average product

◆ When the *MP* > *AP*, the *AP* rises.

◆ When the *MP* < *AP*, the *AP* falls.

◆ When *MP* = *AP*, the *AP* is at its maximum.

■ Short-Run Cost

Several important cost concepts are

◆ **Total cost** (*TC*): cost of *all* factors of production used, including the normal profit. **Average total cost** (*ATC*) is total cost per unit of output, $TC \div Q$.

◆ **Total fixed cost** (*TFC*): cost of the firm's fixed factors. **Average fixed cost** (*AFC*) is total fixed cost per unit of output, $TFC \div Q$.

© 2014 Pearson Education, Inc.

♦ **Total variable cost (*TVC*)**: cost of the firm's variable factors. **Average variable cost (*AVC*)** is total variable cost per unit of output, $TVC \div Q$.

♦ **Marginal cost (*MC*)**: the increase in total cost that results from one-unit increase in output or, in terms of a formula, $MC = \Delta TC \div \Delta Q$.

Two relationships between these costs are:

$TC = TFC + TVC$ and $ATC = AFC + AVC$.

Figure 11.2 shows typical *AVC*, *ATC*, and *MC* curves. The *AVC*, *ATC*, and *MC* curves are U-shaped. The *MC* crosses the *AVC* and *ATC* curves where the *AVC* and *ATC* are at their minimums.

♦ As output initially increases, both *AFC* and *AVC* fall, so *ATC* falls.

♦ As output increases still more, returns will diminish. *AVC* increases as output increases, so eventually *ATC* increases when output increases.

The *MC* and *MP* curves are related.

♦ Over the range of output where the *MP* curve slopes upward, the *MC* curve slopes downward.

♦ At the level of output where the *MP* curve is at its maximum, the *MC* curve is at its minimum.

♦ Over the range of output where the *MP* curve slopes downward, the *MC* curve slopes upward.

The *AP* and *AVC* curves have a similar relationship.

An increase in technology that shifts the firm's product curves upward shifts its cost curves downward. A rise in a fixed cost shifts the firm's *TFC*, *AFC*, *TC*, and *ATC* curves upward but does not shift the firm's *TVC*, *AVC*, or *MC* curves. An increase in a variable cost shifts the firm's *TVC*, *AVC*, *TC*, *ATC*, and *MC* curves upward but does not shift the firm's *TFC* or *AFC* curves.

■ Long-Run Cost

The long-run cost is the cost of production when all factors of production are adjusted to their economically efficient levels. There are no fixed costs in the long run.

♦ The production function shows the relationship between the maximum attainable output and the quantities of all factors of production.

In the long run, because all factors can be varied, all costs are variable costs. The **long-run average cost curve (*LRAC*)** is the relationship between the lowest attainable average total cost and output when the firm can change both the size of the plant it uses and the

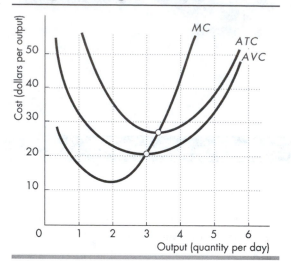

FIGURE **11.2**
Average and Marginal Cost Curves

quantity of labor it employs. The long-run average cost curve is derived from the many different (short-run) average total cost curves that reflect different sized plants. For any quantity the long-run average cost is the point with the lowest average cost of all the (short run) average costs of producing that quantity of output.

The *LRAC* curve is U-shaped. The ranges along the long-run average cost (*LRAC*) curve are:

♦ **Economies of scale** — features of a firm's technology that make long-run average cost fall as output increases. With economies of scale the *LRAC* curve slopes downward. Economies of scale are largely the result of increased specialization of labor and capital as the firm increases its size of operation.

♦ **Diseconomies of scale** — features of a firm's technology that make long-run average cost rise as output increases. With diseconomies of scale the *LRAC* curve slopes upward. Diseconomies of scale reflect the challenges from running a large scale business.

♦ **Constant returns to scale** — features of a firm's technology that make long-run average cost not change as output increases. When a firm has constant returns to scale, the *LRAC* curve is horizontal.

The **minimum efficient scale** is the smallest output at which the long-run average cost reaches its lowest level. The minimum efficient scale in comparison to the market demand plays a role in determining how many firms are in a market.

Helpful Hints

FIGURE **11.3**

Average and Marginal Cost Curves

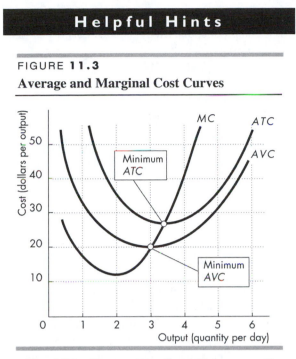

1. **THE MOST IMPORTANT COST CONCEPTS :** Be sure you understand Figure 11.3 thoroughly. Not only is it is the most important graph in the chapter, it is one of the most important graphs in all of microeconomics. You will see it repeatedly in the next several chapters.

   You need to know three important points about Figure 11.3. First, both the *ATC* and *AVC* curves are U-shaped. The *MC* curve also is U-shaped, but the portion that slopes upward is the most important. Second, the *MC* curve intersects the *ATC* and *AVC* curves at their minimum points. In other words, when the *MC* equals the *ATC*, the *ATC* is at its minimum. Third, following the relationship between a marginal and an average, when the *MC* curve is below the *ATC* or *AVC* curves, the *ATC* or *AVC* slope downward. Similarly, when the *MC* curve is above the *ATC* or *AVC* curves, the *ATC* or *AVC* curves slope upward.

2. **MEANING OF THE WORD "MARGINAL" :** Be certain that you understand the difference between "marginal cost" and "average cost." These are *very* different concepts. One way to remember that they are different is to keep in mind that the word "marginal" always means "additional." Economists use the word marginal this way a lot. In this chapter, you already have seen it used in "marginal

product" and "marginal cost". You might also have seen it in Chapter 7 in the discussion of "marginal utility," the additional utility from consuming another unit of a product. In the next few chapters you will encounter the term "marginal revenue," which means additional revenue when output is increased by one unit. In *all* these examples, the word marginal means "additional"!

3. **THE DIFFERENCE BETWEEN ECONOMIES OF SCALE AND DIMINISHING RETURNS :** The last section of the chapter explains the long-run production function and cost function when the plant size — that is, the capital stock, land, and entrepreneurship — varies. As the law of diminishing returns is the key to understanding short-run costs, the concept of economies and diseconomies of scale is the key to understanding long-run costs. In the long run, we explore the change in average cost when *all* factors of production can be changed; in the short run diminishing returns examines what happens to average cost when only *one* factor of production (generally labor) is changed, with the rest of the factors being kept constant.

Questions

■ True/False and Explain

Decision Time Frames

1. The short run is the period of time over which only one factor of production is variable.

2. In the long run, all factors are variable.

Short-Run Technology Constraint

3. If the marginal product of another worker exceeds the marginal product of the previous worker hired, the firm is experiencing economies of scale.

4. The law of diminishing returns implies that the marginal product of a factor of production eventually falls as more of the factor is used.

5. If the marginal product of labor exceeds the average product of labor, the average product of labor rises when more workers are hired.

Short-Run Cost

6. Total cost equals fixed cost plus variable cost.

7. Total costs first fall and then, as diminishing returns sets in, total costs rise as the firm expands its output.

8. Total variable costs are always greater than total fixed costs.

9. Marginal cost equals total cost divided by total output.

10. Marginal cost is always greater than average total cost.

11. The average total cost curve, like the average product of labor curve, has an upside-down U-shape.

12. The *ATC* curve always passes through the minimum point of the *MC* curve.

Long-Run Cost

13. In the long run, all costs are variable costs and no costs are fixed cost.

14. No part of any short-run average total cost curve lies below the long-run average total cost curve.

15. Economies of scale occur when an increase in the number of workers employed increases total output.

16. When the long-run average cost (*LRAC*) curve slopes upward, the firm is experiencing economies of scale.

■ Multiple Choice

Decision Time Frames

1. The short run is a time period in which
   a. one year or less elapses.
   b. all factors of production are variable.
   c. all factors of production are fixed.
   d. there is at least one fixed factor of production and the other factors of production can be varied.

2. In the long run,
   a. only the amount of capital the firm uses is fixed.
   b. all factors of production are variable.
   c. all factors of production are fixed.
   d. a firm must experience diseconomies of scale.

Short-Run Technology Constraint

3. Total product divided by the total quantity of labor employed equals the
   a. average product of labor.
   b. marginal product of labor.
   c. average total cost.
   d. average variable cost.

4. Diminishing marginal returns occurs when
   a. all factors are increased and output decreases.
   b. all factors are increased and output increases by a smaller proportion.
   c. a variable factor is increased and output decreases.
   d. a variable factor is increased and its marginal product falls.

5. The marginal product of labor equals the average product of labor when the
   a. average product of labor is at its maximum.
   b. average product of labor is at its minimum.
   c. marginal product of labor is at its maximum.
   d. None of the above answers are correct because the marginal product of labor never equals the average product of labor.

6. When the marginal product of labor curve is below the average product of labor curve,
   a. the average product of labor curve has a positive slope.
   b. the average product of labor curve has a negative slope.
   c. the total product curve has a negative slope.
   d. the firm experiences diseconomies of scale.

Short-Run Cost

7. Pat's Catering finds that when it caters 10 meals a week, its total cost is $3,000. If, at this level of output, Pat has a total variable cost of $2,500, what is Pat's fixed cost?
   a. $250
   b. $300
   c. $500
   d. $3,000

Use Table 11.1 for the next three questions.

TABLE **11.1**

Multiple Choice Questions 8, 9, 10

Output	Total variable cost	Total cost
3	$15	$21
4	18	24

8. The marginal cost of producing the fourth unit is
   a. $6.
   b. $5.
   c. $3.
   d. $2.

9. The average total cost of the fourth unit is
   a. $6.
   b. $5.
   c. $3.
   d. $2.

10. The average *fixed* cost of the third unit is
    a. $6.
    b. $5.
    c. $3.
    d. $2.

11. If the company produces no output, it must pay
    a. no costs.
    b. a small amount of variable cost.
    c. its fixed cost.
    d. its owners a normal profit.

12. The change in total cost from producing another unit of output equals the
    a. average total cost.
    b. variable cost.
    c. average variable cost.
    d. marginal cost.

13. A farmer discovers that the total cost of growing 50 acres of eggplant is $50,000 and that the total cost of growing 51 acres of eggplant is $52,000. The marginal cost of the 51st acre of eggplant is
    a. $52,000.
    b. $50,000.
    c. $2,000.
    d. $1,000.

Use Figure 11.4 for the next four questions.

FIGURE **11.4**

Multiple Choice Questions 14, 15, 16, 17

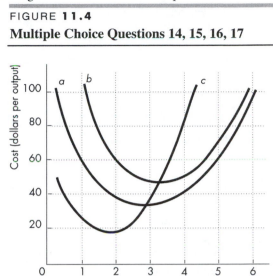

14. In Figure 11.4 the *MC* curve is curve
    a. *a.*
    b. *b.*
    c. *c.*
    d. None of the curves is the *MC* curve.

15. In Figure 11.4 the *ATC* curve is curve
    a. *a.*
    b. *b.*
    c. *c.*
    d. None of the curves is the *ATC* curve.

16. In Figure 11.4 the *AVC* curve is curve
    a. *a.*
    b. *b.*
    c. *c.*
    d. None of the curves is the *AVC* curve.

17. In Figure 11.4 the *AFC* is curve
    a. *a.*
    b. *b.*
    c. *c.*
    d. None of the curves is the *AFC* curve.

18. Which curve intersects the minimum point of the average total cost curve and the average variable cost curve, that is, goes through the minimum points of the *ATC* curve and the *AVC* curve?

    a. The marginal cost (*MC*) curve
    b. The average fixed cost (*AFC*) curve
    c. The marginal product (*MP*) curve
    d. None of the above because no curve goes through the minimum points of the *ATC* and *AVC* curves.

19. If the average total cost (*ATC*) curve slopes downward, then at that level of output the marginal cost (*MC*) curve must be

    a. sloping upward.
    b. sloping downward.
    c. above the *ATC* curve.
    d. below the *ATC* curve.

20. Over the range of output where the *MP* curve slopes upward, the

    a. *MC* curve slopes downward.
    b. *AFC* curve slopes upward.
    c. firm is experiencing economies of scale.
    d. total cost curve slopes downward.

21. A technological advance

    a. shifts the firm's total product curve upward.
    b. does not shift the firm's total product curve.
    c. shifts the firm's total product curve downward.
    d. cannot occur without raising the firm's average total costs and hence shifts the average total cost curve upward.

22. The cost of a variable factor, such as the wage paid to workers, rises. This change shifts the

    a. total fixed cost curve upward.
    b. marginal product of labor curve downward.
    c. average variable cost curve upward.
    d. marginal product of labor curve upward.

Long-Run Cost

23. The concept of diminishing returns

    a. applies to both labor and to capital.
    b. applies to labor but does not apply to capital.
    c. applies to capital but does not apply to labor.
    d. does not apply to either labor or capital.

24. The *LRAC* curve

    a. equals the minimum points on all the short-run *ATC* curves.
    b. equals the lowest possible marginal cost of producing the different levels of output.
    c. equals the lowest attainable average total cost for all levels of output when all factors can be varied.
    d. generally lies above the short-run *ATC* curves.

25. The *LRAC* curve generally is

    a. shaped as an upside-down U.
    b. U-shaped.
    c. upward sloping.
    d. downward sloping.

26. When a firm is experiencing economies of scale,

    a. the *MP* curve slopes upward.
    b. the *LRAC* curve slopes downward.
    c. diminishing returns to labor have been suspended.
    d. the *MC* curve slopes downward.

27. Constant returns to scale means that as production is increased,

    a. total output remains constant.
    b. average total cost rises.
    c. average total cost rises at the same rate as the factors.
    d. total output increases in the same proportion as the factors.

■ Short Answer Problems

1. Where does the marginal product curve intersect the average product curve? Why?

2. a. Table 11.2 (on the next page) gives the total weekly product of turkeys at Al's Turkey Town. Complete this table. (The marginal product is entered midway between rows to emphasize that it is the result of changing factors — moving from one row to the next. Average product corresponds to a fixed quantity of labor and so is entered on the appropriate row.)

   b. In Figure 11.5 (on the next page) label the axes and draw a graph of the total product curve (*TP*).

   c. In Figure 11.6 (on the next page) label the axes and draw a graph of the marginal product (*MP*) and the average product (*AP*). (As in Table 11.2,

TABLE 11.2
Short Answer Problem 2 (a)

Labor	Quantity (turkeys per week)	Average product of labor (AP)	Marginal product of labor (MP)
0	0	XX	
			100
1	100	100	
			___
2	300	___	
			___
3	450	___	
			110
4	___	___	
			___
5	630	___	
			___
6	___	110	

FIGURE 11.5
Short Answer Problem 2 (b)

plot the marginal products midway between the units of labor and the average products directly above the units of labor.) Where do the *AP* and *MP* curves cross?

FIGURE 11.6
Short Answer Problem 2 (c)

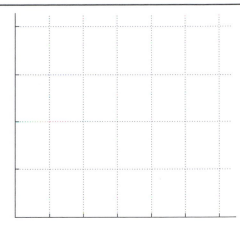

3. a. Let's examine Al's short-run cost of growing turkeys. The first two columns of Table 11.2 are reproduced in the first two columns of Table 11.3. The cost of 1 worker (the only variable factor) is $2,000 per month. Total fixed cost is $4,000 per month. Complete Table 11.3 by using your answers from Table 11.2 and by computing total variable cost and total cost.

TABLE 11.3
Total Cost of Growing Turkeys

Labor	Quantity (turkeys per week)	Total variable cost (TVC)	Total cost (TC)
0	0	___	$4,000
1	100	2,000	___
2	300	___	___
3	450	___	___
4	___	___	12,000
5	630	___	___
6	___	12,000	___

FIGURE **11.7**
Short Answer Problem 3 (b)

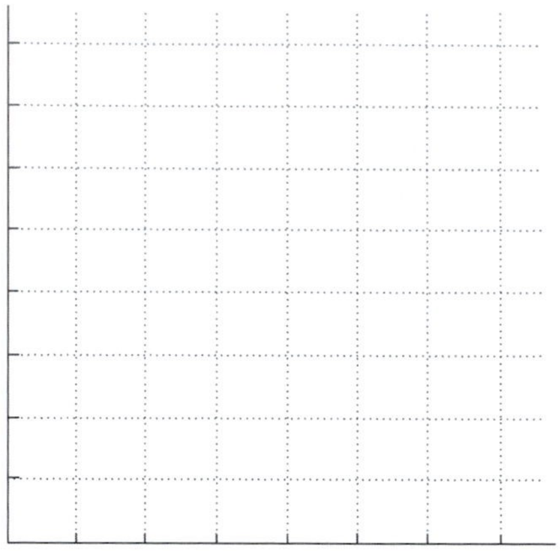

FIGURE **11.8**
Short Answer Problem 3 (d)

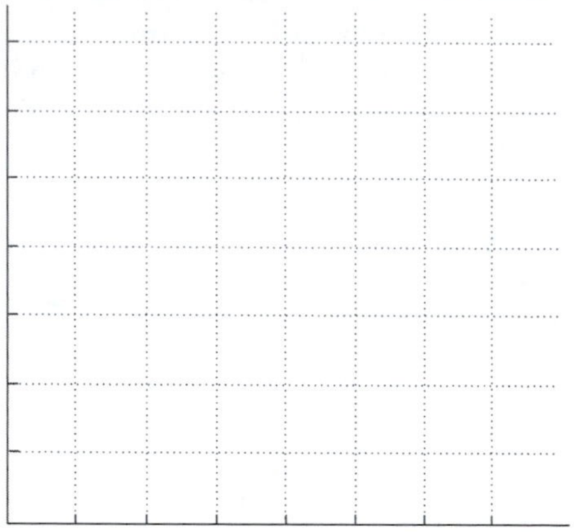

b. In Figure 11.7 label the axes and draw the *TC* and *TVC* curves. What is the relationship between these two curves?

c. Table 11.4 contains spaces for some of Al's other costs, the average total cost (*ATC*), average variable cost (*AVC*), and marginal cost (*MC*). Complete this table by using your answers from Table 11.3 and calculating the new costs called for in Table 11.4.

d. In Figure 11.8 label the axes and draw the *ATC*, *AVC*, and *MC* curves. Be sure to plot the values for the *MC* between the relevant levels of output. What is the relationship between the *ATC* and *AVC* curves? Between the *MC* and *AVC* curves?

4. a. Suppose Al discovers new technology that boosts the productivity of his workers so that more turkeys can be grown than before. Complete Table 11.5, which presents production data with the new technology.

TABLE **11.4**

Other Costs of Growing Turkeys

Quantity (turkeys per week)	Average variable cost (AVC)	Average total cost (ATC)	Marginal cost (MC)
0	XX	XX	
			$20.00
100	$20.00	___	
			___
300	___	___	
			___
450	___	___	
			___
___	___	21.43	
			___
630	___	___	
			66.67
___			

TABLE **11.5**

New Technology

Labor	Quantity (turkeys per week)	Average product of labor (AP)	Marginal product of labor (MP)
0	0	XX	
			120
1	120	120	
			___
2	360	___	
			___
3	540	___	
			___
4	672	___	
			___
5	756	___	
			___
6	792	___	

b. Al's fixed cost remains at $4,000 and he can continue to hire workers at a wage rate of $2,000. Use the new technology production data to complete Table 11.6, which has the total cost, and Table 11.7, which has (some of) the average costs and the marginal cost.

TABLE 11.6

New Technology and Total Costs

Labor	Quantity (turkeys per week)	Total variable cost (TVC)	Total cost (TC)
0	0	____	____
1	120	____	____
2	360	____	____
3	540	____	____
4	672	____	____
5	756	____	____
6	792	____	____

TABLE 11.7

New Technology and Other Costs

Quantity (turkeys per week)	Average variable cost (AVC)	Average total cost (ATC)	Marginal cost (MC)
0	XX	XX	
			____
120	____	____	
			____
360	____	____	
			____
540	____	____	
			____
672	____	____	
			____
756	____	____	
			____
792	____	____	

c. In Figure 11.9, plot the *ATC* and *MC* curves you have just entered in Table 11.7. Also draw the *ATC* and *MC* curves you have already plotted in Figure 11.8 (before the technology changed). Label the old *ATC* curve *ATC*$_1$ and the old *MC* curve *MC*$_1$ label the new *ATC* curve *ATC*$_2$ and the new *MC* curve *MC*$_2$. How do the

old and new *ATC* curves compare? The old and new *MC* curves?

FIGURE 11.9

Short Answer Problem 4 (c)

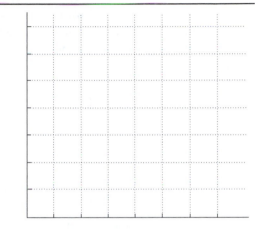

5. a. Return to the old technology for growing turkeys, which you studied and worked out in problems 2 and 3. Suppose that the cost of Al's fixed factors remain at $4,000. Now the cost of his variable factor, labor, rises. Specifically, suppose that a worker now receives $3,000 per month. Complete Table 11.8. For the two missing quantities, copy your answers from Table 11.2.

TABLE 11.8

A Change in Variable Costs

Labor	Quantity (turkeys per week)	Total variable cost (TVC)	Total cost (TC)
0	0	____	$4,000
1	100	3,000	____
2	300	____	____
3	450	____	____
4	____	____	16,000
5	630	____	____
6	____	18,000	____

TABLE **11.9**
Comparison of Costs

Quantity	Before increase		After increase	
	Average total cost (ATC)	Marginal cost (MC)	Average total cost (ATC)	Marginal cost (MC)
0	XX		XX	
		____		____
100	____		____	
		____		____
300	____		____	
		____		____
450	____		____	
		____		____
____	____		____	
		____		____
630	____		____	
		____		____
____	____		____	

b. To compare the effect of the rise in the variable cost on the average total cost and marginal cost, complete Table 11.9. (Hint: As before, copy the "before increase" *ATC* and *MC* values from Table 11.4; work out the "after increase" *ATC* and *MC* values from Table 11.8.) From Table 11.9, how did the rise in variable costs affect the average total cost? The marginal cost?

6. What is the difference between diminishing returns and diseconomies of scale?

■ You're the Teacher

1. "This chapter has a lot to say about firms: production, costs, and stuff like that. But I don't really see the purpose. In real life, businesses are a lot more complicated than this chapter says. Workers are different, different companies make different goods, Intel's factory sure isn't the same as what we see at Krispy Kreme and what have you. What's the use of this chapter?" This student is missing an essential point about economic theories. Can you help straighten out the student?

2. "I get the idea that marginal cost is important, but I don't know why. You have any ideas about it?" Your friend is asking you for your ideas; you have a chance to help your friend, so explain why you think marginal cost is important.

Answers

■ True/False Answers

Decision Time Frames

1. **F** In the short run, at least one factor or production is *fixed*.

2. **T** The question presents the definition of the long run.

Short-Run Technology Constraint

3. **F** The firm has increasing *marginal* returns because only *one* factor has been changed.

4. **T** The question presents the definition of diminishing returns.

5. **T** This result is a reflection of the relationship between marginals and averages.

Short-Run Cost

6. **T** Total cost is the sum of fixed cost and variable cost.

7. **F** As output increases, total cost always rises.

8. **F** The amount of variable cost and the amount of fixed cost are not necessarily related, except that in the long run all costs are variable costs.

9. **F** Marginal cost equals the *additional* total cost divided by the *additional* output.

10. **F** Marginal cost usually starts below the average total cost and then rises above it.

11. **F** The average total cost curve has a "right-side-up" U shape.

12. **F** The *MC* curve always passes through the minimum point of the *ATC* curve.

Long-Run Cost

13. **T** In the long run, all factors of production can be varied so all costs are variable costs.

14. **T** The long-run average cost curve shows the least possible cost to produce any level of output.

15. **F** Economies of scale occur when an increase in output leads to a fall in the average cost.

16. **F** When the *LRAC* curve slopes upward, average cost increases when output increases, so over this range of output the firm is experiencing diseconomies of scale.

■ Multiple Choice Answers

Decision Time Frames

1. **d** This is the definition of the short run.

2. **b** The long run is the amount of time until all factors of production become variable.

Short-Run Technology Constraint

3. **a** The average product of labor is total product (output) per worker.

4. **d** Answer (d) is the definition of diminishing returns.

5. **a** When $MP > AP$, the average product rises when employment increases; when $MP < AP$, the average product falls; and when $MP = AP$, the average product is at its maximum.

6. **b** This answer reflects the average/marginal relationship that when the marginal is below the average, the average falls.

Short-Run Cost

7. **c** Total cost equals fixed cost plus variable cost, so fixed cost equals total cost minus variable cost.

8. **c** The marginal cost equals the difference in total cost ($24 − $21 = $3) divided by the change in output (4 − 3 = 1) so the marginal cost is $3.

9. **a** Average total cost equals total cost divided by total output, that is, $24 ÷ 4, or $6.

10. **d** Because total cost equals total fixed cost plus total variable cost, total fixed cost equals $6. Then, average fixed cost is total fixed cost divided by total output, so average fixed cost equals $6 ÷ 3 = $2.

11. **c** Fixed cost remains the same regardless of the level of output, that is, whether the firm produces a million units of output or no units of output.

12. **d** Marginal cost shows the added cost from producing an added unit of output.

13. **c** The marginal cost equals the change in total cost ($52,000 − $50,000, or $2,000) divided by the change in output (51 acres of eggplant − 50 acres of eggplant, or 1 acre of eggplant). Therefore the marginal cost equals $2,000 per acre of eggplant.

FIGURE **11.10**

Multiple Choice Questions 14, 15, 16, 17

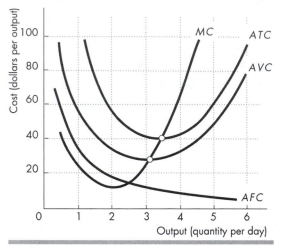

14. **c** Figure 11.10 identifies the *MC* curve. Note that it goes through the minimum points of both the *ATC* and *AVC* curves.

15. **b** Again, Figure 11.10 identifies the *ATC* curve.

16. **a** Figure 11.10 shows that the *AVC* curve is the U-shaped curve that lies below the U-shaped *ATC* curve.

17. **d** None of the curves in the original figure was the *AFC* curve, but Figure 11.10 shows the *AFC* curve.

18. **a** The *MC* curve intersects both the *ATC* and the *AVC* curves at their minimums.

19. **d** When the marginal cost is less than the average cost, the average cost falls as output expands.

20. **a** When the *MP* curve slopes upward, each additional unit of the variable factor produces more additional output than the previous unit of the factor. So the added cost of producing the added units falls — that is, the *MC* curve slopes downward — because each variable factor has the same additional cost as the previous factor, but each produces more additional output.

21. **a** By shifting the total product curve upward, the technological advance generally shifts the average total cost curve downward.

22. **c** Wages are a variable cost, so a rise in the wage rate shifts the average variable cost curve upward.

Long-Run Cost

23. **a** *All* factors are subject to diminishing returns.

24. **c** The long-run average cost curve, or *LRAC* curve, shows the lowest possible average total cost for producing any level of output.

25. **b** The *LRAC* curve has a U shape: When output increases, at first the *LRAC* falls but as output increases still more, the *LRAC* rises.

26. **b** Economies of scale means that increases in output lower the firm's long-run average costs.

27. **d** This is the definition of constant returns to scale.

■ Answers to Short Answer Problems

FIGURE **11.11**

Short Answer Problem 1

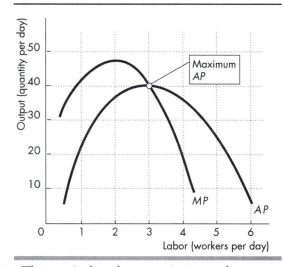

1. The marginal product curve intersects the average product curve where the average product is at its maximum. To understand why, look at Figure 11.11. To the left of the maximum point of 3 workers, *MP* > *AP*. That means that an additional worker produces more additional output than the average of the previously employed workers. As a result, the average product increases. So, as long as the *MP* exceeds the *AP*, the average product must be increasing. Now look to the right of the maximum point. Here *MP* < *AP*. Each new worker produces less additional output than the average of the previously employed workers, so the average product falls. As long as the *MP* is less than the *AP*, the average product must decrease. That means that when-

ever the marginal product exceeds the average product, which is the case at any point left of the intersection point, the average product increases with output; whenever the marginal product is less than the average product, which is true for any point right of the intersection point, the average product falls. Hence when the marginal product equals the average product, the average product does not change. Left of this point the average product is rising and right it is falling. Therefore at this point the average product is at its maximum.

2. a. Table 11.10 completes Table 11.2. The average product of labor column is calculated by dividing the total product by the total amount of labor; that is, $APL = Q \div L$. So, the AP when 2 workers are employed is $300 \div 2$, or 150. The marginal product of labor is the extra output produced by an extra worker. In terms of a formula, the MP equals the change in total product divided by the change in labor, so that $MP = \Delta Q \div \Delta L$. So, between 2 and 1 workers the MP is $(300 - 100) \div (2 - 1) = 200$. Because the MP equals the additional output when another unit of labor is employed, the quantity of output produced when 4 workers are employed equals the total quantity produced when 3 workers are employed (450) plus the additional amount the 4th worker produces, 110, or 560.

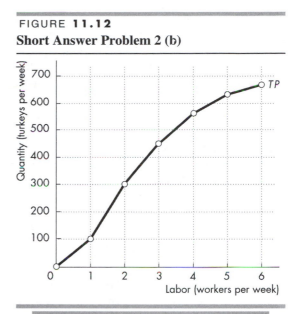

FIGURE **11.12**

Short Answer Problem 2 (b)

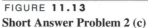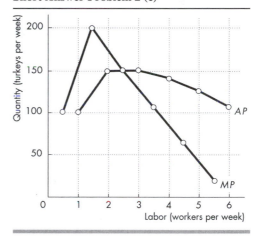

FIGURE **11.13**

Short Answer Problem 2 (c)

Finally, for the total quantity when 6 workers are used, multiply the average product of labor, 110, by the total number of workers employed, 6, to get the total product of 660.

b. Figure 11.12 shows the graph of the firm's total product curve.

c. Figure 11.13 shows the firm's AP and MP curves. The MP curve crosses the AP curve when the AP is at its maximum.

TABLE **11.10**

Short Answer Problem 2 (a)

Labor	Quantity (turkeys per week)	Average product of labor (AP)	Marginal product of labor (MP)
0	0	XX	
			100
1	100	100	
			200
2	300	150	
			150
3	450	150	
			110
4	560	140	
			70
5	630	126	
			30
6	660	110	

3. a. Table 11.11 shows the total cost for each quantity of labor. Total variable cost equals the number of workers (the variable factor) multiplied by $2,000 per worker. Total cost then equals the total variable cost plus the total fixed cost, which is given in the problem as $4,000.

lated by dividing total cost by the total quantity produced. Finally, marginal cost equals the change in total cost divided by the change in quantity, that is, $MC = \Delta TC \div \Delta Q$. Hence the MC between 300 and 100 turkeys per week is ($8,000 − $6,000) ÷ (300 − 100), or $10.00.

TABLE 11.11
Short Answer Problem 3 (a)

Labor	Quantity (turkeys per week)	Total variable cost (TVC)	Total cost (TC)
0	0	$0	$4,000
1	100	2,000	6,000
2	300	4,000	8,000
3	450	6,000	10,000
4	560	8,000	12,000
5	630	10,000	14,000
6	660	12,000	16,000

b. Figure 11.14 shows the firm's total cost (TC) and total variable cost (TVC) curves. The TC curve always lies $4,000 above the TVC curve.

TABLE 11.12
Short Answer Problem 3 (c)

Quantity (turkeys per week)	Average variable cost (AVC)	Average total cost (ATC)	Marginal cost (MC)
0	XX	XX	
			$20.00
100	$20.00	$60.00	
			10.00
300	13.33	26.67	
			13.33
450	13.33	22.22	
			18.18
560	14.29	21.43	
			28.57
630	15.87	22.22	
			66.67
660	18.18	24.24	

FIGURE 11.14
Short Answer Problem 3 (b)

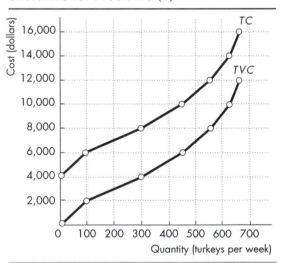

FIGURE 11.15
Short Answer Problem 3 (d)

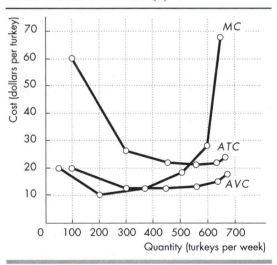

c. Table 11.12 completes Table 11.4. In Table 11.12 the average variable cost column was calculated by dividing total variable cost by the total quantity produced. So the AVC when 300 turkeys are produced is $4,000 ÷ 300 = $13.33. Similarly, the average total cost column is calcu-

d. Figure 11.15 shows the ATC, AVC, and MC curves. The AVC curve lies below the ATC curve, but the vertical distance between the two (which equals AFC) shrinks as output expands. The MC curve crosses the AVC curve where the

AVC is at its minimum. (It also crosses the ATC curve where the ATC is at its minimum.)

4. a. Table 11.13 shows the new APs and MPs. These answers were calculated in the same way as the answers for short answer problem 2 (a).

TABLE **11.13**

Short Answer Problem 4 (a)

Labor	Quantity (turkeys per week)	Average product of labor (AP)	Marginal product of labor (MP)
0	0	XX	
			120
1	120	120	
			240
2	360	180	
			180
3	540	180	
			132
4	672	168	
			84
5	756	151.2	
			36
6	792	132	

b. Tables 11.14 and 11.15 show the firm's new costs after the advance in technology. The answers in Table 11.16 are calculated similarly to those in Table 11.13 for short answer problem 3 (a); the answers in Table 11.17 correspond to the those in Table 11.14 for short answer problem 3 (c).

TABLE **11.14**

Short Answer Problem 5 (b)

Labor	Quantity (turkeys per week)	Total variable cost (TVC)	Total cost (TC)
0	0	$0	$4,000
1	120	2,000	6,000
2	360	4,000	8,000
3	540	6,000	10,000
4	672	8,000	12,000
5	756	10,000	14,000
6	792	12,000	16,000

TABLE **11.15**

Short Answer Problem 5 (b)

Quantity (turkeys per week)	Average variable cost (AVC)	Average total cost (ATC)	Marginal cost (MC)
0	XX	XX	
			$16.67
120	$16.67	$50.00	
			8.33
360	11.11	22.22	
			11.11
540	11.11	18.52	
			15.15
672	11.90	17.86	
			23.81
756	13.23	18.52	
			55.55
792	15.15	20.20	

FIGURE **11.16**

Short Answer Problem 4 (c)

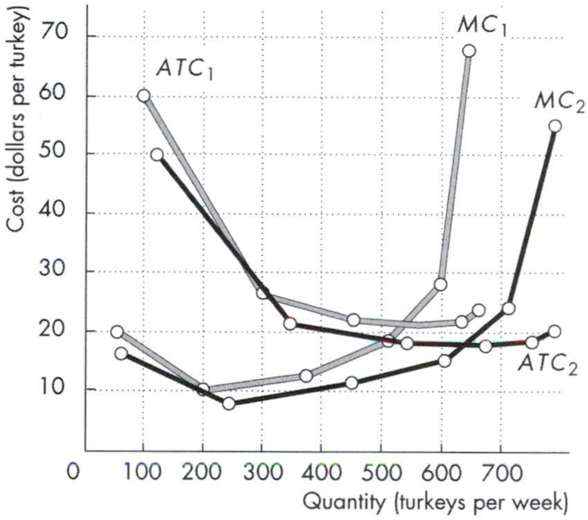

c. Figure 11.16 shows the old and new ATC and MC curves. The new ATC curve appears generally to lie beneath the old ATC curve. Actually, the new curve *always* lies below the old curve, but the large discrete changes in output that are plotted make the new ATC curve appear to lie a little above the old ATC curve at low levels of output. The new MC curve is below the old MC curve. Technological advances shift the firm's average and marginal cost curves downward.

TABLE 11.16

Short Answer Problem 5 (a)

Labor	Quantity (turkeys per week)	Total variable cost (TVC)	Total cost (TC)
0	0	$0	$4,000
1	100	3,000	7,000
2	300	6,000	10,000
3	450	9,000	13,000
4	560	12,000	16,000
5	630	15,000	19,000
6	660	18,000	22,000

5. a. Table 11.16 completes Table 11.10 and shows Al's total variable cost and total cost after the variable factor, labor, and rises in cost. The rise in the cost of the variable factor raises both the total variable cost and the total cost.

TABLE 11.17

Short Answer Problem 5 (b)

Quantity	Before increase Average total cost (ATC)	Before increase Marginal cost (MC)	After increase Average total cost (ATC)	After increase Marginal cost (MC)
0	XX		XX	
		$20.00		$30.00
100	$60.00		$70.00	
		10.00		15.00
300	26.67		33.33	
		13.33		20.00
450	22.22		28.88	
		18.18		27.27
560	21.43		28.57	
		28.57		42.86
630	22.22		30.16	
		66.67		100.00
660	24.24		33.33	

b. Table 11.17 shows the firm's average total cost and marginal cost after the variable cost has risen. The rise in variable cost raises both the average total cost and the marginal cost. In other words, at any level of output, both the average total cost and marginal cost are greater after the rise in variable cost than before. In a diagram,

the rise in Al's variable cost would shift both the firm's *ATC* and *MC* curves upward.

6. The law of diminishing returns states that as a firm uses additional units of a variable factor of production, while holding constant the quantity of fixed factors, the marginal product of the variable factor will eventually diminish. Diseconomies of scale occur when a firm increases all of its factors of production, both its plant and its labor, and its long-run average cost rises. Diminishing (marginal) returns is a short-run concept because there is a fixed factor of production, the size of the firm's plant. Diseconomies of scale is a long run concept because all factors of production are variable factors.

■ **You're the Teacher**

1. "Look, we've talked about this before. Economic theories are abstract on purpose; that is, they deliberately do not include all the nitty-gritty detail of the real world. Instead they focus only on the most important issues. Sure, all companies employ lots of different types of labor — skilled labor, unskilled labor, blue collar workers, white collar workers, sales representatives, and so on. So what? Including this fact in a theory would just give us a bunch more details that don't tell us anything."

"You know, consumers are different too. That didn't stop us from developing useful theories about the factors that affect their demand curves."

"The whole idea is that economic theory looks for qualities that are the same. That is what we're doing with firms. For instance, *all* firms hire labor and use capital. And these factors are different when we think about how rapidly the firm can change the amounts that it uses. So all firms have to face the difference between fixed and variable factors. I don't care if you're talking about Intel building chips or that Krispy Kreme store we both like. The point is that the theory we're learning can be applied to all types of firms, which gives the theory its power."

2. "You're lucky because I've been reading ahead in the book. Remember the discussion of marginal analysis in one of the earlier chapters? You know, where people looked at the effects from making small changes and then compared the additional costs from the change to the additional benefits? Well, that's what we'll be using marginal cost for. When we want to know how much a firm will pro-

duce, we can ask whether it wants to increase its production. By increasing its production, the firm will incur some additional costs — its marginal cost. We'll then compare this cost to the added benefit from increasing production. So you're right: Marginal cost really is important because it's basically half the marginal analysis we'll be doing in the chapters ahead."

Chapter Quiz

1. In the short run,
   a. at least one factor is fixed.
   b. all factors are fixed.
   c. at least one factor is variable.
   d. all factors are variable.

2. In the long run,
   a. at least one factor is fixed.
   b. all factors are fixed.
   c. at least one factor is variable.
   d. all factors are variable.

3. The marginal product of labor is the
   a. inverse of the marginal product of capital when the firm is in the long run.
   b. slope of the curve showing the average product of labor.
   c. change in total product divided by the change in labor.
   d. total product divided by total labor.

4. The average product of labor curve is at its maximum when the
   a. marginal product of labor curve is below it.
   b. marginal product of labor curve crosses it.
   c. marginal product of labor curve is above it.
   d. level of output is at its maximum.

5. The more shallow is a firm's total product curve, the
   a. greater is the marginal product of labor.
   b. smaller is the marginal product of labor.
   c. lower is the total cost curve.
   d. lower is the variable cost curve.

6. Variable cost is sum of all the
   a. costs associated with variable factors.
   b. costs associated with the production of the product.
   c. explicit costs but not all the implicit costs.
   d. costs that do not change when the amount produced increases.

7. A firm's average variable cost is $10, its total fixed costs are $50 and the firm produces 25 units of output. Hence its average total cost is
   a. more than $50.
   b. $12.
   c. $4.
   d. $2.

8. When producing 99 units, the total cost is $595. The marginal cost of the 100th unit is $5. The total cost of producing 100 units is
   a. $600.
   b. $590.
   c. $6.
   d. an amount that cannot be calculated without additional information.

9. The average total cost curve is lowest when the
   a. marginal cost curve is below it.
   b. marginal cost curve crosses it.
   c. marginal cost curve is above it.
   d. level of output is at its maximum.

10. When long-run average costs increase when output increases, there definitely are
    a. economies of scale.
    b. diseconomies of scale.
    c. diminishing returns.
    d. constant returns to scale.

The answers for this Chapter Quiz are on page 346

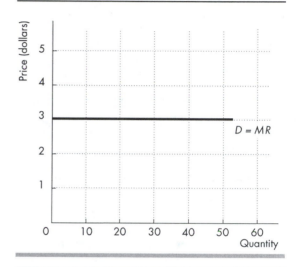

Chapter **12** **PERFECT COMPETITION**

Key Concepts

■ What is Perfect Competition?

Perfect competition is a market with many firms selling identical products to many buyers; no restrictions on entry into the industry; no advantage for existing firms over new firms; and, sellers and buyers are well informed about prices.

Perfect competition occurs when the minimum efficient scale of a firm is small relative to demand.

◆ Each perfectly competitive firm is a **price taker,** that is, the firm cannot influence the market price because its production is an insignificant part of the total market. Price takers set their price equal to the market price.

Economic profit equals total revenue minus total opportunity cost. Part of the opportunity cost is a normal profit, the return the firm's entrepreneur can obtain in an alternative business. **Total revenue** equals the price of the output multiplied by the number of units sold, $TR = P \times Q$.

◆ **Marginal revenue,** *MR*, equals the change in total revenue from a one-unit increase in the quantity sold. In terms of a formula, $MR = \Delta TR \div \Delta Q$.

◆ In perfect competition $P = MR$. As illustrated in Figure 12.1, a perfectly competitive firm's *MR* curve is horizontal at the market-determined price.

◆ The *market* demand curve slopes downward but each *firm* faces a perfectly elastic demand. A firm's demand curve is horizontal at the going price and, as illustrated in Figure 12.1, is the same as the *MR* curve.

■ The Firm's Output Decision

To maximize its profit in the short run, the firm produces the quantity of output at which $MR = MC$. This result is illustrated in Figure 12.2, in which the firm maximizes its profit by producing 40 units. The firm's price is $3, the same as the (given) market price.

FIGURE 12.1

Perfectly Competitive Firm's Demand Curve

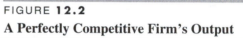

FIGURE 12.2

A Perfectly Competitive Firm's Output

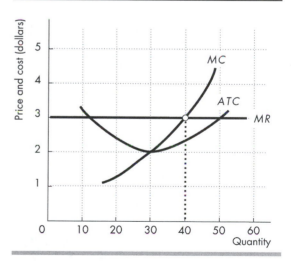

Maximizing profit by setting $MR = MC$ is an example of marginal analysis: As long as $MR > MC$, producing an extra unit of output adds to the firm's total profit.

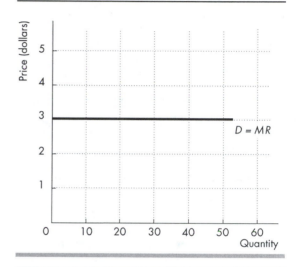

When the firm in Figure 12.2 produces 40 units, it has produced all the profitable units, the units for which $MR > MC$, and none of the non-profitable units, the units for which $MR < MC$.

Figure 12.2 shows that the higher the market price of a good, the greater is the quantity supplied of the good.

A firm incurring economic losses must decide whether to shut down temporarily:

♦ If $P < AVC$, the firm shuts down temporarily. The **shutdown point** is the price and quantity at which the firm is indifferent between producing and shutting down. At that point the firm's total revenue just equals its total variable cost. The shutdown point is reached when P equals the minimum AVC.

♦ If $P > AVC$, the firm continues to produce.

A perfectly competitive firm's supply curve is its MC curve above the minimum AVC.

■ Output, Price, and Profit in the Short Run

The equilibrium market price and equilibrium market quantity of output are determined by the market demand and supply curves. The number of firms in the industry, and their size, is fixed in the short run.

The **short-run market supply curve** shows the quantity supplied by all the firms in the market at each price when each firm's plant and the number of firms remains the same. At every price, the short-run market supply curve is the sum of the amounts supplied by each firm in the market at that price.

When the demand for the good increases, the market price rises. Each firm moves up along its supply curve and increases the quantity it produces.

In the short run, perfectly competitive firms can make an economic profit, break even (make a zero economic profit), or an economic loss:

♦ $P > ATC$ — the firm makes an economic profit. (This case is illustrated in Figure 12.2.)

♦ $P = ATC$ — the firm makes zero economic profit. (The firm breaks even.)

♦ $P < ATC$ — the firm incurs an economic loss.

■ Output, Price, and Profit in the Long Run

In the long run, the number of firms in the market can adjust.

When firms in a perfectly competitive market are making an economic profit, as time passes new firms enter the market; when the firms are incurring an economic loss, as time passes some existing firms exit. When firms make zero economic profit, there is no incentive to enter or exit.

♦ Economic profit brings entry by new firms. The market supply curve shifts rightward and reduces the market price. The fall in price reduces economic profit and decreases the incentive to enter the industry. New firms enter until it is no longer possible to make an economic profit.

♦ Economic losses lead to exit by existing firms, which shifts the market supply curve leftward. The price rises, and the higher price reduces economic losses. Firms exit until no firms incur an economic loss.

♦ In the long run, economic profit and economic loss have been eliminated by entry and exit. With a normal profit, entry and exit cease.

♦ In the long run perfectly competitive firms make zero economic profit.

■ Changes in Demand and Supply as Technology Advances

Changes in demand lead to adjustments. An increase in demand:

♦ Initially raises the price. Each firm increases its output, so the market output increases.

♦ Firms make an economic profit, so new firms enter the market. Entry shifts the market supply curve rightward, so the price falls and the market quantity increases.

♦ The price eventually falls to eliminate the economic profit. At this point, firms no longer enter the market and long-run equilibrium is established.

A decrease in demand:

♦ Initially lowers the price. Each firm decreases its output, so the market output decreases.

♦ Firms incur economic losses, so some exit the market. Exit shifts the market supply curve leftward, so the price rises and the market quantity decreases.

♦ The price eventually rises to eliminate economic losses. At this point, firms no longer exit and long-run equilibrium is established.

Technological change also creates adjustments:

♦ New technology lowers firms' costs and increases their supply. The market supply curve shifts rightward, lowering the price and increasing market output.

♦ Firms that do not adopt the new technology incur economic losses and exit the industry.

♦ In the long run, all firms use the new technology and make zero economic profit.

■ Competition and Efficiency

Resources are used efficiently when we produce the goods and services people value most highly. When resources are used efficiently, no one can be made better off without making someone else worse off.

♦ Consumers' demands reflect their actions to get the most value from their incomes. The demand curve is consumers' marginal benefit curve. If consumers gain all the benefits of consumption, the market demand curve is the marginal social benefit curve.

♦ Competitive firms produce the quantity that maximizes their profit. The supply curve is producers' marginal cost curve. If producers pay all the costs of production, the market supply curve is the marginal social cost curve.

FIGURE 12.3
The Efficient Level of Output

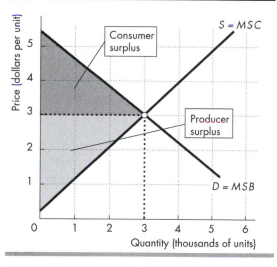

Figure 12.3 shows how perfect competition is efficient. In Figure 12.3, 3,000 units is the equilibrium quantity and is also the efficient quantity because 3,000 units sets the marginal social benefit equal to the marginal social cost. Firms are producing at the lowest possible average cost so the good cannot be produced at a lower cost. The price equals this lowest possible average cost so consumers are as well off as possible.

Helpful Hints

1. **WHY STUDY PERFECT COMPETITION ?** Although perfectly competitive markets are rare in the real world, there are three important reasons for developing a thorough understanding of their behavior.

   First, many markets closely *approximate* perfect competition. This chapter gives direct and useful insights into the behavior of these markets.

   Second, the theory of perfect competition allows us to isolate the effects of competitive forces that are at work in all markets, even in those that do not match the assumptions of perfect competition.

   Third, the perfectly competitive model serves as a useful benchmark for evaluating the efficiency of different market structures.

2. **THE PROFIT MAXIMIZATION RULE, *MR = MC* :** A firm maximizes its *total* economic profit. To meet this objective, the firm produces any unit of output for which the revenue from the unit exceeds the cost of producing the unit. Why? If the revenue from the unit (the marginal revenue, *MR*) is greater than the cost of producing it (the marginal cost, *MC*) the unit adds to the firm's *total* economic profit. Some units add more to the profit — those with *MR* much greater than *MC* — and others add less — those with *MR* only slightly larger than *MC* — but as long as producing the unit of output adds to the total profit, the firm produces it. Comparing the additional revenue from a unit to its additional costs (using marginal analysis) shows that the firm passes up profit if it produced so that *MR > MC*. Only by producing the quantity that sets *MR = MC* does the firm insure that it is producing *all* the profitable units, so only at this level of output does the firm maximize its total economic profit.

3. **THE PROFIT MAXIMIZATION RULE, REVISITED :** It might seem odd that the firm produces the unit of output for which *MR = MC* because this unit adds nothing to the firm's total economic profit. But think about this unit: when the firm produces it, the firm has produced *all* the profitable units, that is, all the units for which *MR > MC*. And the firm has produced *none* of the losing units, the units for which *MR < MC*. If the firm produced fewer units, it would forgo profitable units and would have a smaller profit; if the firm produced more units, it would produce some losing units and

would have a smaller profit. By producing the unit for which *MR* equals *MC*, the firm maximizes its economic profit by producing *all* of the profitable units and *none* of the losing units.

4. **WHY OPERATE WITH ZERO ECONOMIC PROFIT?** Why does a firm continues to operate even though its economic profit is zero? The key to this result rests in the definition of cost. Recall that the company's total costs are all its *opportunity* costs, which includes the normal profit, the return the owners can earn on the average in an alternative business. When total revenue equals total cost, the firm makes zero economic profit, that is, the firm's owners earn a normal profit. In this situation the owners are earning the same profit they could obtain elsewhere. As the phrase "normal profit" implies, a normal profit is the amount of profit that could normally be made in any other industry. Even though the economic profit is zero, by earning a normal profit the firm's owners are earning just as much profit as they could anywhere else, which leaves them content to continue producing.

Questions

■ True/False and Explain

What is Perfect Competition?

1. In a perfectly competitive industry many firms produce very similar but slightly different products.

2. The minimum efficient scale of a firm is the smallest level of output at which the long-run average total cost is at its minimum.

3. In a perfectly competitive industry, no single firm can significantly affect the price of the good.

4. The market demand curve in a perfectly competitive industry is horizontal.

5. A perfectly competitive firm can charge whatever price it wants for its goods.

The Firm's Output Decision

6. If it does not shut down, to maximize its profit a perfectly competitive firm produces the level of output that sets *MR* = *MC*.

7. If the price is less than a perfectly competitive firm's minimum *ATC*, to maximize its profit the

firm immediately shuts down.

8. A perfectly competitive firm's supply curve shows the quantities of output supplied at all prices that enable the firm to earn an economic profit.

9. A perfectly competitive firm's supply curve is its *ATC* curve.

Output, Price, and Profit in the Short Run

10. The short-run market supply curve is upward sloping.

11. A perfectly competitive firm can make an economic profit, zero economic profit, or incur an economic loss in the short run.

12. If *P* > *ATC*, a perfectly firm incurs an economic loss.

Output, Price, and Profit in the Long Run

13. When firms enter a market, the market demand increases.

14. Firms exit a market whenever they cannot make an economic profit.

15. When firms are incurring persistent economic losses, some firms exit the market and the price rises.

Changes in Demand and Supply as Technology Advances

16. Firms in a competitive market make a short-run economic profit if demand increases.

17. Firms in a competitive market make a long-run economic profit if demand increases.

18. If demand decreases, then some firms in a competitive market exit the market.

19. New technology raises firms' costs, which causes all firms to incur an economic loss in the short run.

Competition and Efficiency

20. Efficient use of resources occurs when making one person better off must make someone else worse off.

21. At the efficient quantity, the total producer surplus must equal the total consumer surplus.

22. In the long run, in a perfectly competitive market consumers pay the lowest possible price that allows the firms to earn zero economic profit.

■ Multiple Choice

What is Perfect Competition?

1. Which of the following is <u>NOT</u> a characteristic of a perfectly competitive industry?
   a. A downward-sloping market demand curve.
   b. A perfectly elastic demand for each firm.
   c. Each firm decides its quantity of output.
   d. Each firm produces a good slightly different from that of its competitors.

2. Of the following, which is a perfect competitor?
   a. AT&T, one of the three major providers of land-based long distance telephone service in the United States.
   b. The company that provides your local cable TV service.
   c. A tomato grower living in Florida.
   d. DeBeers, the provider of more than 70 percent of the rough diamonds in the world.

Use Table 12.1 for the next question.

TABLE **12.1**
Multiple Choice Question 3

Quantity	Price (dollars)
100	5.00
101	5.00

3. Using Table 12.1, what is the marginal revenue from selling 101 units of output rather than 100?
   a. $5
   b. $500
   c. $505
   d. $0

4. For a perfectly competitive firm, MR always equals
   a. ATC.
   b. P.
   c. AVC.
   d. none of the above because MR is not always equal to the same thing.

The Firm's Output Decision

5. Paul runs a shop that sells printers. Paul's business is a perfect competitor and can sell each printer for a price of $200. The marginal cost of selling one printer an hour is $100, the marginal cost of selling a second printer is $100, and the marginal cost of selling a third printer is $250. To maximize his profit, Paul should sell
   a. one printer an hour.
   b. two printers an hour.
   c. three printers an hour.
   d. more than three printers an hour.

6. Which of the following is necessarily true when a perfectly competitive firm is in short-run equilibrium?
   a. $MR = MC$.
   b. P = minimum $LRAC$.
   c. $P = ATC$.
   d. All of the above are true at short-run equilibrium.

7. A perfectly competitive firm marginal costs rise. But its demand curve does not change. As a result, the firm _____ the amount it produces and _____ its price.
   a. decreases; raises
   b. increases; lowers
   c. decreases; does not change
   d. increases; raises

8. If a perfectly competitive firm incurs an economic loss, it
   a. always shuts down immediately.
   b. continues to operate until either the price rises or its costs fall so that it no longer has an economic loss.
   c. shuts down if $P > AVC$.
   d. shuts down if $P < AVC$.

9. For prices below the minimum average variable cost, a perfectly competitive firm's supply curve is
   a. horizontal at the market price.
   b. vertical at zero output.
   c. the same as its marginal cost curve.
   d. the same as its average variable cost curve.

Output, Price, and Profit in the Short Run

10. The short-run market supply curve is
    a. the sum of the quantities supplied by all the firms.
    b. undefined because the number of firms is constant in the short run.
    c. vertical at the total level of output being produced by all firms.
    d. horizontal at the current market price.

11. In the short run, a perfectly competitive firm can
    a. make an economic profit.
    b. make zero economic profit.
    c. incur an economic loss.
    d. All of the above answers are possible.

12. A perfectly competitive firm is definitely incurring an economic loss when
    a. $MR < MC$.
    b. $P > ATC$.
    c. $P < ATC$.
    d. $P > AVC$.

FIGURE **12.4**

Multiple Choice Questions 13 and 14

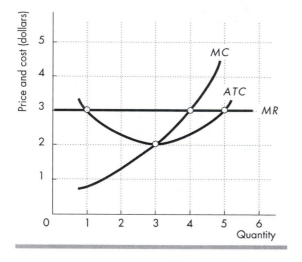

13. The firm illustrated in Figure 12.4 will produce how much output?
    a. 1 unit
    b. 3 units
    c. 4 units
    d. 5 units

14. The firm illustrated in Figure 12.4 is
    a. making an economic profit.
    b. making zero economic profit.
    c. incurring an economic loss.
    d. in long-run equilibrium.

15. In the short run, which of the following is <u>FALSE</u>?
    a. Perfectly competitive firms can possibly make an economic profit.
    b. The number of firms is fixed.
    c. To maximize its profit, a perfectly competitive firm produces enough output so that $MR = MC$.
    d. Perfectly competitive firms always produce at the minimum ATC.

Output, Price, and Profit in the Long Run

16. When will new firms want to enter a market?
    a. When $MR = MC$ for the existing firms in the market.
    b. Any time the price of the good has risen.
    c. When the new firms can make economic profits.
    d. When the firms in the market are not maximizing profit.

17. Suppose that firms in a perfectly competitive market are making economic profits. Over time,
    a. other firms enter the market so that the price rises and economic profits fall.
    b. some firms leave the market so that both the price and economic profits rise.
    c. other firms enter the market so that both price and economic profits fall.
    d. nothing happens because there are no incentives for change.

18. In the long run, a perfectly competitive firm can
    a. make an economic profit.
    b. make zero economic profit.
    c. incur an economic loss.
    d. All of the above are possible.

19. If firms in a market are incurring an economic loss, then as some exit, the price _____ and the surviving firms' economic losses _____.
    a. rises; do not change
    b. rises; become smaller
    c. falls; become larger
    d. falls; become smaller

Changes in Demand and Supply as Technology Advances

20. In the short run, after an increase in demand firms ____ and in the long run, after an increase in demand firms ____.
    a. incur an economic loss; make zero economic profit
    b. make an economic profit; make an economic profit
    c. make an economic profit; make zero economic profit
    d. make zero economic profit; make zero economic profit

21. If demand for a good decreases, in the short run the price
    a. falls and each firm produces more output to make up for the lower price.
    b. falls and, as long as the price remains above the firms' average variable cost, each firm produces less output.
    c. does not change, but some firms shut down because less is demanded.
    d. does not change because each firm produces less output.

22. Following a decrease in demand, the price falls more in the ____ and the quantity decreases more in the ____.
    a. short run; short run
    b. short run; long run
    c. long run; short run
    d. long run; long run

23. New technology in an industry means that
    a. all firms in the industry permanently make an economic profit regardless of whether they adopt the technology.
    b. firms that adopt the new technology permanently make an economic profit.
    c. firms that do not adopt the new technology permanently make an economic profit.
    d. firms that adopt the new technology temporarily make an economic profit.

Competition and Efficiency

24. Which of the following statements is true?
    a. A competitive market cannot use its resources efficiently.
    b. Resource use is efficient when marginal social benefit exceeds marginal social cost by as much as possible.
    c. When demand is the same as marginal social benefit and supply is the same as marginal social cost, a perfectly competitive market is efficient.
    d. A perfectly competitive market cannot be efficient in the long run because the firms cannot make an economic profit.

25. In the long-run equilibrium in a perfectly competitive market, the firms produce at the ____ possible average total cost and the price equals the ____ possible average total cost.
    a. highest; highest
    b. highest; lowest
    c. lowest; highest
    d. lowest; lowest

FIGURE **12.5**
Multiple Choice Question 26

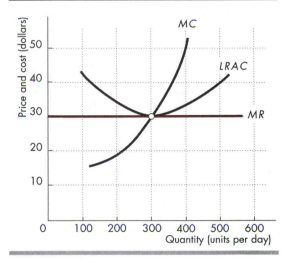

26. In Figure 12.5, producing 300 units per day is not the firm's long-run equilibrium because the firm is
    a. making zero economic profit.
    b. making an economic profit.
    c. incurring an economic loss.
    d. None of the above answers is correct because producing 300 units *is* the long-run equilibrium.

■ Short Answer Problems

1. Why will a firm in a perfectly competitive market choose not to charge a price either above or below the equilibrium market price?

TABLE **12.2**

Igor's Total Cost and Revenue

Quantity (tons)	Total cost (dollars)	Total revenue (dollars)
1	1,000	2,000
2	2,500	4,000
3	5,000	6,000
4	8,500	8,000
5	13,000	10,000
6	18,500	12,000

2. Igor runs a mushrooms farm. Igor relishes the idea of maximizing his profit, so he must decide how many acres to farm. He receives a price of $2,000 per ton of mushrooms grown. Table 12.2 shows Igor's total cost and total revenue for different amounts of tons grown.

   a. Based on Table 12.2, how many tons of mushrooms should Igor farm? What is his total economic profit?

TABLE **12.3**

Igor's Marginal Cost and Revenue

Quantity (tons)	Marginal cost (dollars)	Marginal revenue (dollars)
1	____	____
2	____	____
3	____	____
4	____	____
5	____	____
6		

   b. Complete Table 12.3, which gives Igor's marginal cost and marginal revenue schedules. Note that both marginal costs and marginal revenues relate to changes in production, so they are located between the quantities of tons grown. That is, the first marginal cost and marginal revenue figures apply to the cost and revenue of

changing from 1 ton grown to 2 tons.

   c. Based on Table 12.3, in Figure 12.6, draw Igor's marginal cost and marginal revenue curves. Using this table and figure, how many tons should Igor grow? Why?

   d. Are your answers to parts (a) and (c) different?

FIGURE **12.6**
Igor's MC and MR

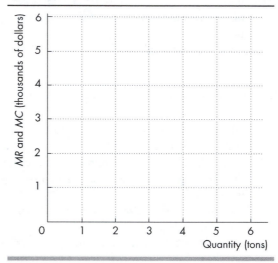

3. a. More people decide that they like French fried mushrooms. As a result, the price of mushrooms rises to $4,000 a ton. Igor's costs do not change from those in Table 12.2. Draw Igor's new MC and MR curves in Figure 12.7.

FIGURE **12.7**
Igor's New MC and MR

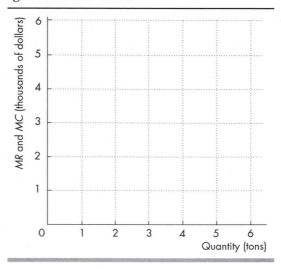

b. How does Igor respond to the rise in the price of mushrooms?

c. If all mushroom farmers have the same cost schedule as Igor, does your answer in part (b) represent the long-run equilibrium? Why?

TABLE **12.4**
Samantha's Sweater Shop

Quantity (sweaters sold per day)	Total variable cost (dollars)	Total cost (dollars)
1	40	100
2	60	120
3	90	150
4	130	190
5	180	240
6	240	300

TABLE **12.5**
Samantha's Average and Marginal Costs

Quantity (sweaters sold per day)	Average variable cost (dollars)	Average total cost (dollars)	Marginal cost (dollars)
1	____	____	
			____
2	____	____	
			____
3	____	____	
			____
4	____	____	
			____
5	____	____	
			____
6	____	____	

4. a. Table 12.4 presents total costs at Samantha's Sweater Shop, a perfectly competitive firm. Use these cost figures to complete Table 12.5.

   b. In Figure 12.8 draw Samantha's *MC* curve.

   c. Use the costs from Table 12.5 and the graph in Figure 12.8 to determine Samantha's supply schedule in Table 12.6.

   d. Draw Samantha's supply curve in Figure 12.8.

5. a. Draw a diagram illustrating the case of a perfectly competitive firm that is making an economic profit. In the diagram, show the amount of the economic profit.

   b. In a diagram, show the case of a perfectly competitive firm that is breaking even (earning a normal profit), that is, it is not incurring an economic loss nor making an economic profit.

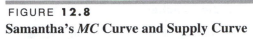

FIGURE **12.8**
Samantha's *MC* Curve and Supply Curve

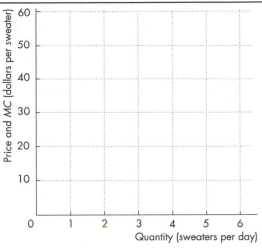

TABLE **12.6**
Samantha's Supply Curve

Price (dollars per sweater)	Quantity (sweaters per day)
25	____
35	____
45	____
55	____

c. Draw a diagram to illustrate the case of a perfectly competitive firm that is incurring an economic loss but is continuing to operate. Be sure to include the *AVC* curve. Show the amount of the economic loss.

6. A perfectly competitive market is at long-run equilibrium. Then there is a decrease in demand for the market's good. How does the market adjust to its new long-run equilibrium? Be sure to discuss what happens to the companies' profits and the number of firms in the market. Also draw two diagrams showing what happens to the price and quantity during the adjustment process.

7. Why will economic profit be zero at long-run equilibrium in a perfectly competitive market? Be sure to mention the roles played by economic profits and losses.

■ You're the Teacher

1. "I really don't get why a perfectly competitive firm wants to produce so that $MR = MC$. I mean, the goal of the firm is to make the most profit possible. Why does it produce so that $MR = MC$? I think that it ought to want to produce so that $MR > MC$; that is, so that revenues exceed costs and it makes a profit." This student is making a fundamental error. Correct the student's analysis.

2. "You know, one thing that seems weird about this chapter is the claim that a business will operate even though it's losing money. I'd think that the moment a business started to incur an economic loss, unless there was some chance that the loss would be reversed in the future, the business would shut down." This student is right: A business operating even though it incurs an economic loss *does* seem weird. Can you explain why this situation happens?

Answers

■ True/False Answers

What is Perfect Competition?

1. **F** In a perfectly competitive industry, each of the many firms produces an identical product.

2. **T** The question gives the definition of the minimum efficient scale.

3. **T** Each firm is a price taker.

4. **F** The *firm's* demand curve is horizontal, but the *market* demand curve slopes downward.

5. **F** A perfectly competitive firm is a price taker, for instance, a wheat farmer who can charge only the going price for the wheat grown.

The Firm's Output Decision

6. **T** The rule to maximize profit is to produce the level of output at which $MR = MC$.

7. **F** If $P < AVC$, the firm shuts down (if $P < ATC$ the firm suffers an economic loss).

8. **F** The firm's supply curve shows the amount that will be produced regardless of whether or not the firm earns an economic profit.

9. **F** The firm's supply curve is its MC curve above its AVC curve.

Output, Price, and Profit in the Short Run

10. **T** The short-run market supply curve is the sum of the quantities supplied by all the firms in the market.

11. **T** In the short run, depending on market demand and the firm's costs, a perfectly competitive firm can make an economic profit, incur an economic loss, or make zero economic profit.

12. **F** If $P < ATC$, the firm incurs an economic loss.

Output, Price, and Profit in the Long Run

13. **F** When firms enter a market, the market *supply* increases.

14. **F** Even if they do not make an economic profit, firms remain in the industry as long as they break even, that is, make zero economic profit.

15. **T** The higher price decreases the surviving firms' economic losses.

Changes in Demand and Supply as Technology Advances

16. **T** The increase in demand raises the price of the product, thereby allowing the firms producing it to make an economic profit.

17. **F** The short-run economic profit from the increase in demand attracts new firms. The new firms produce more output, the price falls, and the economic profit is eliminated.

18. **T** A decrease in demand lowers the price and the firms incur an economic loss. The economic loss will lead some firms to exit the market.

19. **F** Firms that adopt the new technology lower their costs and make a temporary economic profit.

Competition and Efficiency

20. **T** The statement conveys the meaning of efficiency.

21. **F** The sum of the producer surplus plus consumer surplus is maximized but there is no necessary reason for them to equal each other.

22. **T** In the long run, the price equals the lowest possible average total cost.

■ Multiple Choice

What is Perfect Competition?

1. **d** In perfect competition, each firm produces a good identical to that of its competitors.

2. **c** The other possibilities describe industries with only a few firms, so they cannot be perfectly competitive firms.

3. **a** $MR = \Delta TR \div \Delta Q$, so in this case $MR = (\$505 - \$500) \div (101 - 100) = \$5$. More directly, for a perfectly competitive firm, marginal revenue equals price.

4. **b** Because a perfectly competitive firm can always sell another unit of output at the market price, the market price is the firm's marginal revenue.

The Firm's Output Decision

5. **b** Selling the second printer adds $50 to Paul's total profit, so it will be sold; however selling the third printer lowers Paul's total profit by $50, so it will not be sold.

6. **a** The condition $MR = MC$ is necessary for the firm to be maximizing its profit.

7. **c** When the marginal costs rise, the MC curve

shifts upward. In response, the firm decreases the amount it produces. The firm's demand curve did not change, which indicates that the (market) price is constant.

8. **d** As long as $P > AVC$, the firm's losses are smaller if it operates than if it shuts down.

9. **b** At prices below the minimum average variable cost, the firm shuts down and produces zero.

Output, Price, and Profit in the Short Run

10. **a** At any price, the market quantity supplied is the sum of the quantities that all the firms supply.

11. **d** In the short run, any type of profit or loss is possible: the firm might make an economic profit, zero economic profit, or incur an economic loss.

12. **c** When $P < ATC$, the firm incurs an economic loss.

13. **c** The firm produces the level of output so that $MR = MC$, 4 units of output.

14. **a** The price, $3, exceeds the average total cost of producing 4 units of output, so the firm makes an economic profit.

15. **d** In the long run, perfectly competitive firms produce at the minimum ATC, but that is not necessarily the case in the short run.

Output, Price, and Profit in the Long Run

16. **c** The possibility of making an economic profit leads to entry into the industry.

17. **c** The entry of new firms lowers the price and the economic profit, thereby driving the industry toward its long-run equilibrium.

18. **b** Free entry and exit mean that only zero economic profit is possible in the long run.

19. **b** Firms continue to exit as long as they incur an economic loss, thereby driving the price higher and reducing the survivors' economic losses.

Changes in Demand and Supply as Technology Advances

20. **c** In the short run, the price rises and the firms make an economic profit but in the long run the price falls to eliminate the economic profit.

21. **b** When the price falls, each firm moves down its MC curve and produces less. This response — each firm producing less — accounts for the reduction in the quantity supplied along the market supply curve when the price falls.

22. **b** In the short run, both the price and quantity fall, and firms incur an economic loss. The economic loss means that firms exit the industry and the supply decreases. Thus the price rises from its initial fall, but the amount of the industry output continues to decrease.

23. **d** New technology creates economic profits, giving firms the incentive to adopt the technology. The increased competition from these firms ultimately eliminates the economic profit.

Competition and Efficiency

24. **c** Efficiency is achieved when $MSB = MSC$.

25. **d** In the long-run, perfectly competitive firms produce at the minimum average total cost and the price equals this lowest possible average total cost.

26. **d** Figure 12.5 shows the long-run equilibrium for a perfectly competitive firm producing 300 units.

■ Answers to Short Answer Problems

1. If a firm in a perfectly competitive market charged a price higher than the market price, it will lose all of its sales. So, it will not charge a price above the market price. Because the firm can sell all it wants at the going price, it will not increase its sales by lowering its price. So, the firm will not set its price below the market price because the lower price will decrease its profit.

2. a. Table 12.2 shows that Igor's profit-maximizing quantity of mushrooms is 2 tons. Igor's economic profit when growing 2 tons of mushrooms is $1,500 (Igor's total revenue of $4,000 minus his total cost of $2,500). This amount exceeds his economic profit at any other level of production.

   b. Table 12.7 (on the next page) shows the marginal cost and marginal revenue schedules. Marginal cost is equal to $\Delta TC \div \Delta Q$, with ΔTC the change in total cost and ΔQ the change in quantity. The marginal cost from 1 to 2 tons grown equals ($2,500 − $1,000) ÷ (2 − 1), or $1,500. Marginal revenue can be calculated two ways. First, for a perfectly competitive firm, marginal revenue equals price, so marginal revenue is $2,000. Alternatively, the definition of marginal revenue is $\Delta TR \div \Delta Q$, where ΔTR is the change in total revenue. Using this formula, the marginal revenue from 1 to 2 tons is ($4,000 − $2,000) ÷ (2 − 1) = $2,000.

TABLE **12.7**

Short Answer Problem 2 (b)

Quantity (tons)	Marginal cost (dollars)	Marginal revenue (dollars)
1		
	1,500	2,000
2		
	2,500	2,000
3		
	3,500	2,000
4		
	4,500	2,000
5		
	5,500	2,000
6		

FIGURE **12.9**

Short Answer Problem 2 (c)

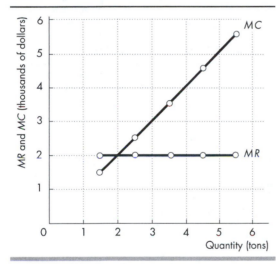

c. Figure 12.9 shows the *MC* and *MR* curves. Table 12.7 shows that Igor should grow 2 tons of mushrooms. The marginal cost between 1 ton and 2 tons is $1,500 and the marginal cost between 2 tons and 3 tons is $2,500, so the marginal cost of 2 tons is the average, $2,000. This marginal cost equals Igor's marginal revenue, the price of a ton of mushrooms, or $2,000. This result means that Igor must produce 2 tons of mushrooms to maximize his profit. Similarly, Figure 12.9 shows that the marginal revenue and marginal cost curves intersect at 2 tons, also indicating that Igor should grow 2 tons of mushrooms.

d. The answers in parts (a) and (c) are the same:

Igor grows 2 tons of mushrooms. Note the important point that the analysis based on *marginal* revenue and *marginal* cost, in part (c), gives the same answer as the analysis based on *total* revenue and *total* cost, in part (a).

FIGURE **12.10**

Short Answer Problem 3 (a)

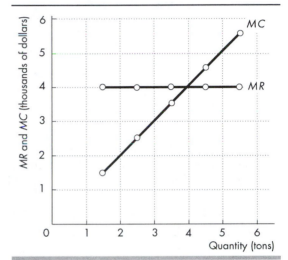

3. a. Figure 12.10 shows Igor's new *MR* curve. The marginal cost curve does not change from before. Igor's marginal revenue equals the price of a ton of mushrooms. The rise in the price to $4,000 shifts Igor's *MR* curve (which is the same as Igor's demand curve) upward to $4,000.

b. As Figure 12.10 shows, with the higher price for a ton of mushrooms, Igor increases the quantity of mushrooms he grows to 4 tons.

c. The answer in part (b) cannot be the long-run equilibrium. When Igor grows 4 tons of mushrooms, his total revenue is $16,000 and his total cost (from Table 12.2) is $8,500. Igor is earning an economic profit of $7,500. The presence of an economic profit attracts new farmers to the mushroom market. As new farmers begin to grow mushrooms, the market supply curve for these fungi shifts rightward, lowering the price of a ton of mushrooms and eliminating some of the economic profit. New farmers continue to enter and the price of a mushroom continues to fall as long as an economic profit exists. Only when the economic profit is entirely eliminated does entry stop so that the long-run equilibrium is attained.

TABLE **12.8**

Short Answer Problem 4 (a)

Quantity (sweaters sold per day)	Average variable cost (dollars)	Average total cost (dollars)	Marginal cost (dollars)
1	40.00	100.00	
			20.00
2	30.00	60.00	
			30.00
3	30.00	50.00	
			40.00
4	32.50	47.50	
			50.00
5	36.00	48.00	
			60.00
6	40.00	50.00	

4. a. Table 12.8 contains Samantha's average costs and marginal cost. Average variable cost equals $TVC \div Q$, where TVC is total variable cost and Q is quantity.

   Average total cost is computed in a similar fashion, namely $TC \div Q$ with TC total cost.

   Finally, marginal cost is $\Delta TC \div \Delta Q$. So the marginal cost of going from 2 to 3 sweaters sold per day is ($150 − $120) ÷ (3 − 2) or $30.

   b. Figure 12.11 shows the MC curve.

   c. Table 12.9 has Samantha's supply schedule. The supply curve is the same as her marginal cost curve above the average variable cost curve. When the price of a sweater is $25, Figure 12.11 shows that Samantha would supply 2 sweaters *except* for the fact that this price is below the average variable cost. If Samantha supplied 2 sweaters her loss would be greater than if she shut down. When the price is $25, Samantha shuts down and does not supply any sweaters. At $35, Figure 12.11 shows that Samantha supplies 3 sweaters. Because this price is above her average variable cost, Samantha supplies 3 sweaters. The rest of Samantha's supply curve is obtained from Figure 12.11 in a similar manner.

   d. Figure 12.12 shows Samantha's supply curve. At prices above $30, that is, at prices above the minimum average variable cost, the supply curve is identical to Samantha's marginal cost curve. For prices below $30, Samantha supplies no sweaters.

FIGURE **12.11**

Short Answer Problem 4 (b)

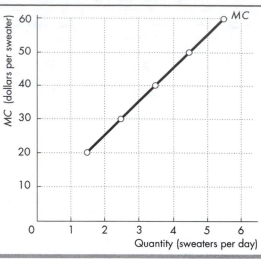

TABLE **12.9**

Short Answer Problem 4 (c)

Price (dollars per sweater)	Quantity supplied (sweaters per day)
25	0
35	3
45	4
55	5

FIGURE **12.12**

Short Answer Problem 4 (d)

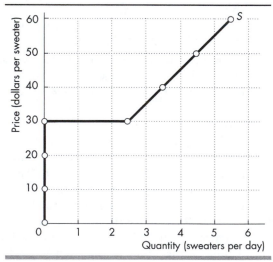

FIGURE **12.13**

Short Answer Problem 5 (a)

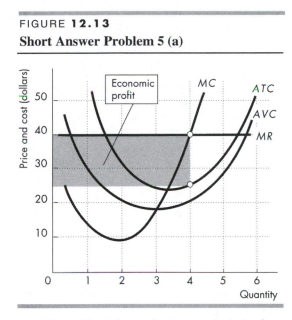

FIGURE **12.15**

Short Answer Problem 5 (c)

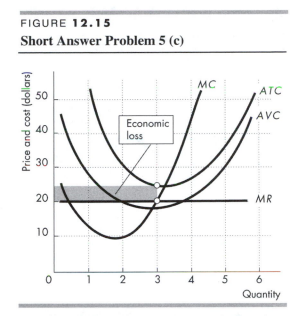

5. a. Figure 12.13 shows the case in which the firm makes an economic profit. To maximize its profit, the firm produces the level of output such that $MR = MC$. Because $P > ATC$, the firm is making an economic profit, as shown in the figure.

FIGURE **12.14**

Short Answer Problem 5 (b)

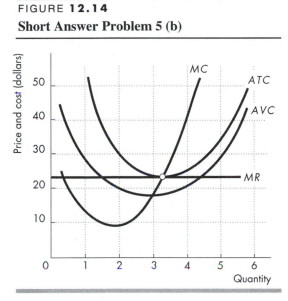

b. A perfectly competitive firm making zero economic profit is illustrated in Figure 12.14. To maximize its profit the firm produces q, the level of output that makes $MR = MC$. Because $P = ATC$, the firm is making zero economic profit.

c. Figure 12.15 illustrates the case of a firm that incurs an economic loss but continues to operate. The firm incurs an economic loss because, at the profit-maximizing (loss-minimizing) level of output q, $P < ATC$. But the firm minimizes its loss by operating because $P > AVC$.

6. In the short run, the decrease in demand means the price falls. In response to the fall in price, each firm produces less (some firms might even shut down if the price falls below their minimum average variable cost), so the market quantity also decreases.

In the initial situation, before the decrease in demand, each business was making zero economic profit. The fall in price now means that firms incur economic losses. These losses induce some firms to leave the market. This exit shifts the market supply curve leftward, thereby raising the market price. The rising price reduces the economic losses for the remaining firms. But as long as firms are incurring economic losses, some firms exit and the price continues to rise. The price rises until the economic losses are totally eliminated, at which time firms no longer exit the market.

The price continues to rise until it equals the average total cost because at that point the firms are breaking even, making zero economic profit. Costs have not been affected by the decrease in demand. So the price continues rising until it equals the (unchanged) average total cost.

FIGURE **12.16**
Short Answer Problem 6

FIGURE **12.16**
Short Answer Problem 6

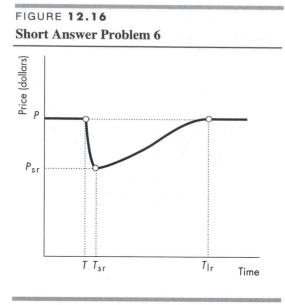

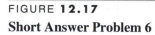

FIGURE **12.17**
Short Answer Problem 6

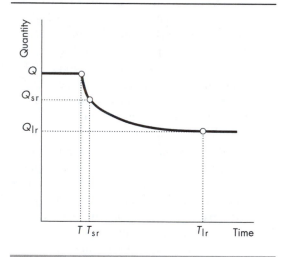

Figures 12.16 and 12.17 illustrate these changes. In the short run the price falls from P to P_{sr} and the market quantity decreases from Q to Q_{sr} at time T_{sr}. Exit now takes place and the supply decreases. As shown in Figure 12.16, the decrease in supply starts to raise the price until in the long run, at time T_{lr}, the price returns to its original level. At that time the price equals the firms' (unchanged) average total cost so the firms are breaking even. In the long run each firm produces as much as it did originally. But as shown in Figure 12.17, the equilibrium quantity produced by the total market is less than what was initially produced (Q versus Q_{lr}) because the number of firms in the market has decreased.

7. In a perfectly competitive market, the existence of economic profit attracts the entry of newcomers. Entry of new firms shifts the market supply curve rightward, causing the price to fall and firms' economic profit to decline. However, entry continues as long as there are economic profits. Similarly, the existence of economic losses results in firms exiting the market. Exit shifts the market supply curve leftward, causing the price to rise and (surviving) firms' economic loss to decline. Exit continues as long as economic losses are being incurred. Only when economic profits and losses are zero, so that the firms are breaking even, is there no tendency for firms to enter or exit the industry. The market is in long-run equilibrium only when economic profit is zero because an economic profit or an economic loss are the signals to enter or exit a market.

■ **You're the Teacher**

1. "Look, you're making just one mistake. It's an easy mistake to make, but it's a *big* one! The idea is that a firm wants to maximize its *total* profit. That is, it wants to maximize the difference between its total revenue and its total costs. You're confusing these terms with marginal revenue and marginal cost. Remember that the word 'marginal' means 'additional'. So, marginal revenue means additional revenue, and marginal cost means additional cost."

"Now, suppose that *MR* is larger than *MC*. For instance, suppose that a wheat farmer finds that the marginal revenue from growing an additional acre of wheat is $5,000 and that the marginal cost of doing so is only $3,000. Then, growing the additional acre of wheat adds more to the farmer's revenue than it adds to the cost, so this acre will add to the farmer's total profit. In particular, this acre adds $2,000 (marginal revenue of $5,000 minus marginal cost of $3,000) to the farmer's total profit. The farmer will want to grow this additional acre of wheat."

"The next acre still has a marginal revenue of $5,000, but suppose that it has a marginal cost of $4,000. *MR* still is larger than *MC*, so this acre will continue to add to the farmer's total profit. Yeah, it adds less (only $1,000), but the key point is that it adds. So the farmer will plant this acre, too."

"Now look, I know that the added profit from the second acre isn't as much as the added profit from the first acre. But who cares? As long as the acre adds to the profit, the farmer, who wants to get the maximum possible total profit, will still grow the second acre of wheat. The deal is that as long as another acre adds to total profit, the farmer will grow more wheat. In other words, as long as $MR > MC$, the additional acre adds additional profit, so the farmer will put the acreage into production. Only when $MR = MC$ does the additional acre not add to profit. So the farmer simply stops adding acres when $MR = MC$."

2. "At first thought, it does seem weird that a business would continue to produce even though it's losing money. I couldn't get the point, either, until I thought about it a bit. Here's the idea: Whenever the price of output falls below the break-even point (the minimum average total cost) but remains above the shutdown point (the minimum average variable cost), the firm continues to produce even though it's incurring an economic loss. The key here is that the firm's owner wants to make the loss as small as possible."

"If the owner shuts down, the firm still must pay its fixed costs. Remember that fixed costs are independent of output; whether the firm produces 10 million units or 0 units, fixed costs remain the same. So if the owner shuts down, the total loss will equal the total fixed cost. The owner compares this loss to the loss incurred by operating. If the price exceeds the average variable cost, the owner loses less by operating the business. When $P > AVC$, by staying open the firm makes enough revenue to pay all its variable costs and have some revenue left over to cover part of its fixed costs. In this case, by operating the business, the owner loses less than the total amount of the fixed costs. The loss is smaller than would be incurred by shutting down, so the owner will operate the business as long as $P > AVC$. But, if $P < AVC$, the loss from running the business exceeds the total fixed cost because the business's revenue isn't sufficient to cover all of the variable costs. Hence when the average variable costs exceed the price, the owner will close the business."

Chapter Quiz

1. In perfect competition, the product of a single firm
   a. has an infinite elasticity of demand.
   b. is sold under many different brand names.
   c. is unique to that firm and cannot be copied by others.
   d. has many perfect complements.

2. A perfectly competitive firm faces a
   a. downward sloping demand curve.
   b. downward sloping marginal revenue curve.
   c. horizontal marginal revenue curve.
   d. downward sloping marginal cost curve.

3. In the case of a perfectly competitive firm, as the firm sells more output, the price of the product _____ and the marginal revenue _____.
   a falls; falls
   b. falls; does not change
   c. does not change; falls
   d. does not change; does not change

4. When a perfectly competitive firm is making zero economic profit, the owner is
   a. going to close the business in the long run.
   b. earning an accounting loss.
   c. earning the same profit he or she could obtain elsewhere on the average.
   d. will boost output to earn a larger profit.

5. Even though it is incurring an economic loss, a firm will stay open if price is
   a. above minimum average variable cost.
   b. below minimum average variable cost.
   c. above total variable cost.
   d. below total variable cost.

6. A perfectly competitive firm is producing at the point where its marginal cost equals price. If the firm decreases its output, total revenue will _____ and total profit will _____.
   a. rise; rise
   b. rise; fall
   c. fall; rise
   d. fall; fall

7. The supply curve for a perfectly competitive firm is the same as its marginal cost curve
   a. above the horizontal axis.
   b. above the minimum average variable cost.
   c. below the minimum average variable cost.
   d. below the average total cost.

8. The market supply curve is the sum of the
   a. supply curves of all the firms.
   b. average variable cost curves of all the firms.
   c. average total cost curves of all the firms.
   d. average fixed cost curves of all the firms.

9. In a perfectly competitive industry, a permanent increase in demand creates a temporary economic _____ and _____ by some firms.
   a. profit; entry
   b. profit; exit
   c. loss; exit
   d. loss; entry

10. A perfectly competitive firm _____ make an economic profit in the short run and _____ make an economic profit in the long run.
    a. can; can
    b. can; cannot
    c. cannot; can
    d. cannot; cannot

The answers for this Chapter Quiz are on page 346

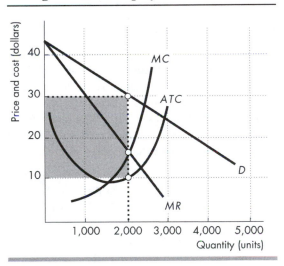

Chapter 13 MONOPOLY

Key Concepts

■ Monopoly and How It Arises

A **monopoly** is a market with a single firm that produces a good or service with no close substitute and that is protected by a barrier that prevents other firms from entering that market. A **barrier to entry** is a constraint that protects a firm from potential competitors. Barriers to entry include:

- Natural barriers to entry, which can lead to **natural monopoly**, a market in which economies of scale (which create a downward sloping *LRAC* curve) enable one firm to supply the entire market at the lowest possible cost.

- Ownership control over a key resource.

- Legal barriers to entry (public franchise, government license, or patent) create **legal monopolies**.

Monopolists can sell a larger quantity only by charging a lower price. Monopolies can charge a single price or price discriminate.

- **Single-price monopoly** — a firm that sells each unit of its output at the same price to all its customers.

- **Price-discrimination** —selling different units of a good for different prices, so some customers pay a lower price than others for the good or an individual consumer pays a lower price for additional units.

■ A Single-Price Monopoly's Output and Price Decision

- The monopoly firm's demand curve is the market demand curve.

- At each level of output, marginal revenue for a monopoly is less than its price (*MR* < *P*).

In moving down the monopoly's demand curve:

- when demand is elastic, *MR* is positive and total revenue rises when output increases.

- when demand is unit elastic, *MR* is zero and total revenue is at its maximum.

- when demand is inelastic, *MR* is negative and total revenue falls when output increases.

A monopoly's cost curves are similar to those of a competitive firm. A profit-maximizing monopoly produces the output at which *MR* = *MC*. (The same rule used by a perfectly competitive firm.) The monopoly uses the demand curve to determine the maximum price that consumers are willing to pay for this quantity of output. Figure 13.1 shows a profit maximizing level of output, 2,000, and price, $30.

FIGURE 13.1
A Single-Price Monopoly

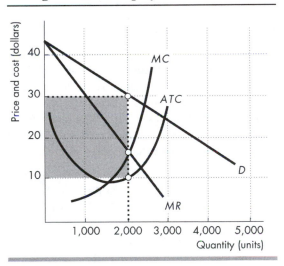

- Figure 13.1 shows that *P* exceeds *MC* for a monopoly.

- Because *P* > *ATC*, the single-price monopoly in the figure makes an economic profit equal to the area of the shaded rectangle, $20 × 2,000, or $40,000.

- Barriers to entry prevent new companies from entering the market, so a monopoly's economic profit can last indefinitely.

■ **Single-Price Monopoly and Competition Compared**

Compared to a perfectly competitive market, a single-price monopoly with the same costs:

♦ charges a higher price.

♦ produces a smaller output.

FIGURE **13.2**

A Single-Price Monopoly's Deadweight Loss

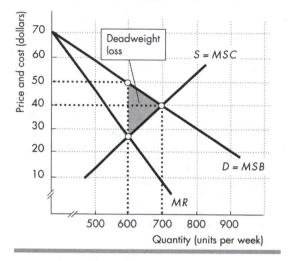

Figure 13.2 illustrates these results. If the market is perfectly competitive, 700 units are produced and the price is $40. (The price and quantity are determined by where the demand and supply curves cross.) In comparison, if the market is a single-price monopoly with the same costs, 600 units are produced (where the *MR* and *MC* curves cross) and the price is $50.

Perfect competition can be efficient because it produces where *MSB* = *MSC*. Because its output is less than that of a competitive market, a single-price monopoly creates a deadweight loss. Figure 13.2 illustrates the deadweight loss from a single-price monopoly.

Economic rent is any surplus—consumer surplus, producer surplus, or economic profit. **Rent seeking** is the pursuit of wealth by capturing an economic rent. Rent seekers try to buy or create a monopoly. Resources used in rent seeking are a cost to society. In equilibrium, rent seeking continues until the economic profit from the monopoly is eliminated by the costs of acquiring the economic rent.

■ **Price Discrimination**

Price discrimination occurs when a firm charges different prices for a good. Price discrimination can occur among groups of buyers, so that some buyers pay a lower price, or among units of a good, so that larger orders get a discount. Price discrimination increases the firm's producer surplus and hence its economic profit.

With price discrimination among groups of people, the group with the higher willingness to pay pays a high price and the group with the lower willingness to pay pays a low price.

♦ **Perfect price discrimination** occurs if a firm is able to sell each unit of output for the highest price anyone is willing to pay for it. Perfect price discrimination extracts the entire consumer surplus and gives the firm the largest possible economic profit.

The more perfectly a monopoly can price discriminate, the closer its output is to the competitive amount and the more efficient is the outcome. A perfectly price-discriminating monopoly eliminates the *entire* consumer surplus. However it does not result in a deadweight loss, so it is efficient.

■ **Monopoly Regulation**

A natural monopoly can produce at lowest possible cost than could two or more firms but as a monopoly, operating in its self-interest, it will create a deadweight loss. Regulation is a potential solution to this conflict.

♦ **Regulation** consists of rules administered by a government agency that determine prices, quantities, entry, and other aspects of economic activity.

♦ **Deregulation** is the process of removing regulation of prices, quantities, entry, and other aspects of economic activity.

Regulation can follow two approaches:

♦ **Social interest theory** — predicts that the political and regulatory process seeks out inefficiency. Regulation eliminates deadweight loss and allocates resources efficiently.

♦ **Capture theory** — predicts that regulation serves the self-interest of the producer, who captures the regulator and maximizes economic profit.

Natural monopolies can be regulated using different regulatory schemes. Figure 13.3 (on the next page) shows a natural monopoly.

FIGURE **13.3**

A Natural Monopoly

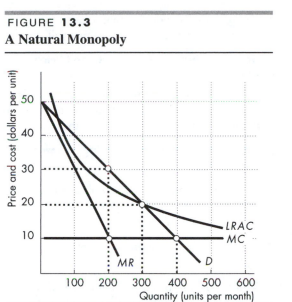

- Left unregulated, the firm in Figure 13.3 maximizes its profit by producing 200 units, where *MR=MC*, and setting a price of $30 per unit.

- A **marginal cost pricing rule** requires the firm to set its price equal to its marginal cost. In Figure 13.3, the firm sets a price of $10 per unit and produces 400 units. The firm produces the efficient amount of output so this type of regulation is efficient. But the firm incurs an economic loss so the government might need to subsidize the firm or the firm might price discriminate.

- An **average cost pricing rule** requires the firm to set its price equal to its average cost. In Figure 13.3, the firm sets a price of $20 per unit and produces 300 units. The firm produces an inefficient amount of output and makes zero economic profit.

Determining the firm's average total cost is difficult. So regulators use one of two practical rules:

- **Rate of return regulation** — a firm justifies its price by showing that its return on its capital does not exceed a specified target rate. But the firm's managers have no incentive to operate efficiently because spending on unnecessary costs does not lower the firm's profit.

- **Price cap regulation** — a price ceiling that specifies the highest price the firm is permitted to set. Compared to an unregulated natural monopoly, a price cap lowers the price the firm charges and increases the quantity the firm produces.

1. **WHY STUDY PERFECT COMPETITION AND MONOPOLY?** The opposite extreme from perfect competition is monopoly. In perfect competition there are many firms that can decide only the quantity they produce but not the price to be charged. In contrast, a monopoly is a single firm that sets both its quantity and price. Understanding the differences between perfect competition and monopoly is valuable because these two industry structures are the ends of the competition spectrum. If competition within an industry heats up, the industry moves closer to behaving like a perfectly competitive industry; if competition dries up, the industry's output and price approach those of a monopoly.

2. **UNDERSTANDING MARGINAL REVENUE FOR A MONOPOLY:** In a monopoly, there is only one firm, so the downward sloping market demand curve is also the firm's demand curve. If a single-price monopoly wants to sell one more unit of output, it must lower its *price*. Selling another unit thus has two effects on revenue:

   - First, the sale of the additional unit raises revenue by the amount of the (new, lower) price. If this effect was the sole effect, the marginal revenue would equal the price. (This effect is the only one for a perfectly competitive firm, so for these firms marginal revenue equals the price.)

   - Second, because the firm also lowers the price on all the units it had previously sold, revenue from these units falls. (This effect is absent from a perfectly competitive firm because it does not need to lower its price in order to sell an additional unit of output.)

By itself, the first effect yields marginal revenue equal to the price, but the second effect subtracts from the first. Hence marginal revenue is less than the price. Therefore, for a monopoly, the marginal revenue curve lies below the demand curve.

3. **WHICH MARKETS SHOULD BE REGULATED?** According to the social interest theory, regulations will be designed to make markets behave more competitively. The ultimate goal is a perfectly competitive market because it maximizes the total surplus (the sum of consumer surplus plus producer surplus) enjoyed by society. Markets that behave like monopolies lead to economic inefficiency by

creating deadweight losses. However, there are fewer reasons to regulate markets that are already competitive.

4. **NATURAL MONOPOLY :** In a diagram, the defining characteristic of a natural monopoly is that its *LRAC* curve slopes downward until it crosses the demand curve. When the *LRAC* curve falls until it crosses the demand curve, why can one company supply the market at a lower cost than two or more? Suppose that the *LRAC* crosses the demand curve at 100 units of output, that the *LRAC* of 50 units of output is $15, and that the *LRAC* of 100 units is $10. If one firm produced 100 units of output, the total cost is 100 × $10 = $1,000. To have two firms produce 100 units, say each produces 50 units. Then, each firm's total cost is 50 × $15 = $750. The total cost of having 100 units produced by these two firms is $750 + $750, or $1,500. The total cost of having two firms produce 100 units of output — $1,500 — exceeds the total cost of having only one firm produce 100 units.

Because one company can supply the market at a lower cost than two or more firms, a tension is created from society's point of view. Having one firm in the industry and thereby reducing costs is good; the lower the cost of producing a product, the more resources available to produce other goods and services. However, monopolies restrict the level of their output in order to raise their prices and earn economic profits. The restriction of output creates economic inefficiency and harms society. The result from these countervailing forces is regulation: The government grants the right to one firm to have a monopoly, but in exchange the government regulates it. In this way, society attempts to gain the advantage of lower costs and side step the disadvantage of monopoly behavior. The capture theory of regulation, however, reminds us that this effort might not be successful.

Questions

■ True/False and Explain

Monopoly and How it Arises

1. Barriers to entry are essential to a monopoly.

2. Patents grant the patent owner a legal monopoly.

3. A single-price monopoly charges each consumer the highest single price the consumer will pay.

A Single-Price Monopoly's Output and Price Decision

4. A difference between a perfectly competitive firm and a monopoly is that the monopolist's decisions about how much to produce affect the good's price.

5. For a single-price monopoly, marginal revenue, *MR*, equals price, *P*.

6. To maximize their profits, both monopolies and perfectly competitive firms produce the level of output that sets *MR* = *MC*.

7. When a single-price monopoly is maximizing its profit, *P* > *MC*.

8. A monopoly can make an economic profit indefinitely.

Single-Price Monopoly and Competition Compared

9. Monopolies decrease the deadweight loss from perfectly competitive industries.

10. In moving from perfect competition to single-price monopoly, the monopoly captures as economic profit the entire consumer surplus lost by consumers.

11. Rent seeking is a cost to society of monopoly.

Price Discrimination

12. Price discrimination is an attempt by a monopolist to capture the producer surplus.

13. If a monopoly can successfully price discriminate, it can increase its economic profit.

14. A firm's producer surplus equals its economic profit.

15. Compared to a single-price monopoly, a perfectly price-discriminating monopoly reduces the amount of consumer surplus.

Monopoly Regulation

16. A marginal cost pricing rule imposed on a natural monopoly creates an efficient use of resources.

17. A natural monopoly regulated using an average cost pricing rule produces an inefficient level of output.

18. Rate of return regulation gives producers a strong incentive to minimize their costs.

■ Multiple Choice

Monopoly and How it Arises

1. Suppose that one taxi company in your city is granted a license by the city so that it is the only cab company that may operate within the city limits. Granting this license is an example of a
   a. natural barrier to entry.
   b. case in which a single firm controls a resource necessary to produce the good.
   c. price-discriminating monopoly.
   d. legal barrier to entry.

2. Which of the following is a *natural* barrier to the entry of new firms in an industry?
   a. Licensing
   b. Economies of scale
   c. Issuing a patent
   d. Granting a public franchise

3. In order to sell more output, a single-price monopoly must _____ its price and a price-discriminating monopoly must _____ its price.
   a. raise; raise
   b. raise; lower
   c. lower; raise
   d. lower; lower

A Single-Price Monopoly's Output and Price Decision

4. Max's Christmas tree lot has a monopoly on sales of Christmas trees. To increase his sales from 100 trees to 101 trees, he must drop the price of all his trees from $28 to $27. What is Max's marginal revenue when he lowers his price and increases his sales from 100 to 101 trees?
   a. $2,800
   b. $28
   c. $27
   d. −$73

5. A monopolist finds that when it produces 20 units of output, its demand is elastic. At this level of output, its marginal revenue necessarily is
   a. positive.
   b. zero.
   c. negative.
   d. none of the above is correct because the marginal revenue and the elasticity of demand are unrelated.

6. A monopolist finds that the marginal revenue from producing another unit of output exceeds the marginal cost of the unit. To increase its profit the monopolist will
   a. produce the unit.
   b. not produce the unit, but not cut back its production at all.
   c. not produce the unit and cut back its production by at least one unit.
   d. do none of the above.

7. Which of the following is true for a single-price monopoly?
   a. Price always equals marginal cost, that is, $P = MC$ at all levels of output.
   b. For all levels of output, price equals marginal revenue, that is, $P = MR$.
   c. In the short run, the monopoly might make zero economic profit or incur an economic loss.
   d. None of the above because all the statements are false.

FIGURE **13.4**

Multiple Choice Questions 8 and 9

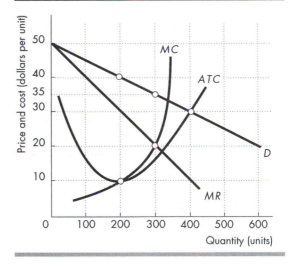

8. In Figure 13.4, a profit-maximizing single-price monopoly will produce _____ units.
   a. 200
   b. 300
   c. 400
   d. None of the above.

9. In Figure 13.4, a profit-maximizing single-price monopoly will set a price of

a. $10.
b. $20.
c. $35.
d. $40.

10. Because of an increase in labor costs, a monopoly finds that its *MC* and *ATC* have risen. Presuming that the monopoly does not shut down, it will _____ its price and _____ the quantity it produces.

a. raise; increase
b. raise; decrease
c. lower; increase
d. lower; decrease

11. In the short run a monopoly can make

a. only an economic profit.
b. only an economic profit or zero economic profit.
c. only zero economic profit.
d. an economic profit, zero economic profit, or incur an economic loss.

12. A monopoly can make an economic profit

a. only in the short run.
b. only in the long run.
c. indefinitely, that is, in both the short run and the long run.
d. The premise of the question is wrong because a monopoly can never make an economic profit.

Single-Price Monopoly and Competition Compared

13. Compared to a perfectly competitive industry with the same cost, the amount of output produced by a single-price monopoly is

a. more than the competitive industry.
b. the same as the competitive industry.
c. less than the competitive industry.
d. not comparable to the competitive industry.

14. Compared to a perfectly competitive industry, the price charged by a single-price monopoly with the same costs is

a. more than the competitive industry.
b. the same as the competitive industry.
c. less than the competitive industry.
d. not comparable to the competitive industry.

Figure 13.5 illustrates a single-price monopoly. Use it for the next three questions

FIGURE **13.5**
Multiple Choice Questions 15, 16, and 17

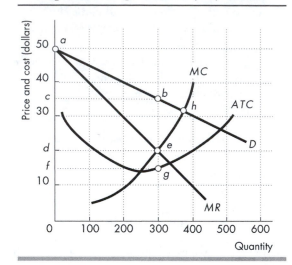

15. The deadweight loss in Figure 13.5 is the area

a. *abc.*
b. *bcde.*
c. *bcfg.*
d. *beh.*

16. The consumer surplus in Figure 13.5 is the area

a. *abc.*
b. *bcde.*
c. *bcfg.*
d. *beh.*

17. The economic profit in Figure 13.5 is the area

a. *abc.*
b. *bcde.*
c. *bcfg.*
d. *beh.*

18. If a perfectly competitive industry becomes a single-price monopoly and costs do not change, the producer _____, demanders _____, and society _____.

a. benefits; are harmed; is harmed
b. is harmed; benefit; is harmed
c. is harmed; are harmed; is harmed
d. is harmed; benefit; benefits

19. Activity for the purpose of creating a monopoly in order to earn an economic profit is

    a. not legal in the United States.
    b. called rent seeking.
    c. called price discrimination.
    d. called legal monopoly.

Price Discrimination

20. Price discrimination allows a monopoly to

    a. lower its marginal cost.
    b. reduce its producer surplus.
    c. increase its economic profit.
    d. charge all customers a higher price.

21. A monopoly that is able to perfectly price discriminate

    a. charges everyone the lowest price that they want to pay for each unit purchased.
    b. produces less output than it would were it a single-price monopoly.
    c. eliminates consumer surplus.
    d. creates a larger deadweight loss than it would if it were a single-price monopoly.

22. A monopoly movie theater discovers that viewers who watch movies at 8 P.M. are willing to pay more than viewers who watch 5 P.M. As a result, if the movie theater owner wants to price discriminate and earn a larger economic profit, the owner sets

    a. a higher price at 8 P.M.
    b. the same price at 5 P.M. as at 8 P.M.
    c. a lower price at 8 P.M.
    d. There is not enough information given to answer the question.

23. Business travelers usually pay higher airline fares than families on a vacation. So,

    a. business travelers aren't maximizing their wellbeing.
    b. business travelers have a greater willingness to pay for air travel than do vacation travelers.
    c. the MC of serving vacation travelers is lower than that of serving business travelers.
    d. vacation travelers have a greater willingness to pay for air travel than do business travelers.

Monopoly Regulation

24. The capture theory of intervention predicts that government regulation will maximize

    a. economic profit.
    b. consumer surplus.
    c. deadweight loss.
    d. total surplus.

Use Figure 13.6 for the next three questions.

FIGURE **13.6**

Multiple Choice Questions 25, 26, and 27

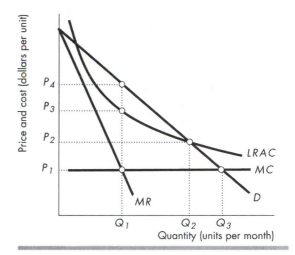

25. In Figure 13.6, if the firm is regulated using a marginal cost pricing rule it produces _____ units per month and sets a price of _____.

    a. Q_1; P_4
    b. Q_1; P_3
    c. Q_2; P_2
    d. Q_3; P_1

26. In Figure 13.6, if the firm is left unregulated and maximizes its profit, it produces _____ units per month and sets a price of _____.

    a. Q_1; P_4
    b. Q_1; P_3
    c. Q_2; P_2
    d. Q_3; P_1

27. In Figure 13.6, if the firm is regulated using an average cost pricing rule it produces ____ units of output and sets a price of ____.

    a. Q_1; P_4
    b. Q_1; P_3
    c. Q_2; P_2
    d. Q_3; P_1

28. If a natural monopoly is required to set its price equal to its marginal cost,
    a. the company makes an economic profit.
    b. the company incurs an economic loss.
    c. competitors will enter the market.
    d. the company will produce more than the efficient level of output.

29. A natural monopoly under rate of return regulation has an incentive to
    a. inflate its costs.
    b. produce more than the efficient quantity of output.
    c. charge a price equal to marginal cost.
    d. maximize consumer surplus.

■ Short Answer

1. Why is marginal revenue less than price for a single-price monopoly?

2. In a small college town, Laura's Bookstore has a monopoly in selling textbooks. Laura's fixed costs are $100, and her total costs are shown in Table 13.1.

    a. Complete Table 13.1 by computing average total cost and marginal cost.

    b. Table 13.2 lists points on the demand curve facing Laura's Bookstore. Copy the marginal costs from Table 13.1 and complete the table.

    c. What is Laura's profit-maximizing quantity of output? At what price will she sell her books? What is her total economic profit?

    d. In Figure 13.7 (on the next page), plot the demand curve and the *MR*, *ATC*, and *MC* curves corresponding to the data in parts (a) and (b). Show the equilibrium output and price. On your diagram, illustrate the area that equals Laura's economic profit.

TABLE **13.1**

Short Answer Problem 2 (a)

Quantity (books per hour)	Total cost (dollars)	Average total cost (ATC)	Marginal cost (MC)
9	247.00	27.44	
			9.00
10	256.00	____	
11	267.00	____	____
12	280.00	____	____
13	295.00	____	____
14	312.00	____	____
15	331.00	____	____
16	352.00	____	____
17	375.00	____	____
18	400.00	____	____
19	427.00	____	____
20	456.00	____	____
21	487.00	____	____

TABLE **13.2**

Short Answer Problem 2 (b)

Quantity demanded (books per hour)	Price (dollars per book)	Total revenue (dollars)	Marginal revenue (MR)	Marginal cost (MC)
9	57.00	513.00		
			47.00	9.00
10	56.00	____		
11	55.00	____	____	____
12	54.00	____	____	____
13	53.00	____	____	____
14	52.00	____	____	____
15	51.00	____	____	
16	50.00	____	____	____
17	49.00	____	____	____
18	48.00	____	____	____
19	47.00	____	____	____
20	46.00	____	____	____
21	45.00	____	____	

FIGURE **13.7**
FIGURE **13.7**
Short Answer Problem 2

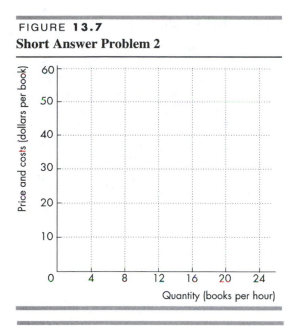

FIGURE **13.8**
Short Answer Problem 3

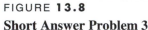

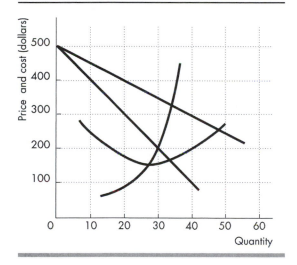

3. In Figure 13.8 label the curves. What amount will this single-price monopolist produce and what price will it charge? Indicate the firm's economic profit and show the deadweight loss created.

4. Why can a monopoly, but not a perfectly competitive firm, make an economic profit in the long run?

5. Explain why the output of a perfectly competitive industry is greater than the output of the same industry if it is a single-price monopoly.

6. Derek is the owner of the only movie theater in town. By hiring several well-trained economists,

Derek learns that the people watching movies after 8 P.M. have a much higher willingness to pay to watch a movie than people watching at 5 P.M. The costs of showing a movie are identical at 5 P.M. and 8 P.M. To maximize his profit, what should Derek do? Give him some specific advice, including drawing him a diagram or two. (Derek can get his economists to interpret your diagrams as long as you label all the axes and all the curves.)

7. Suppose that your city grants one pizza delivery service a legal monopoly to deliver pizzas; all other pizza delivery services must close.
   a. What happens to the price and quantity of delivered pizzas?
   b. What happens to the economic profit of the owner who has been granted the monopoly?
   c. Suppose that the owner offers to sell the pizza delivery company to you. Would you be able to make an economic profit? Be careful when you answer this question; think about the price the previous owner will charge you for the business.

8. Three industries have the same market demand and identical cost curves. Industry A is perfectly competitive, industry B is a single-price monopoly, and industry C is a monopoly able to perfectly price discriminate.
   a. Draw a figure showing the (downward sloping) market demand curve (label it D); the marginal revenue curve (label it MR); the marginal cost curve (label it MC); and the average total cost curve (label it ATC).
      In the figure, identify how much each industry produces by labeling the outputs as Q_A, Q_B, and Q_C for industry A, B, and C, respectively.
   b. In which industry or industries is consumer surplus the largest? The smallest?
   c. In the long run, in which industry or industries is the total economic profit the largest? The smallest?
   d. Which industry structure(s) are efficient?

9. a. How is rate of return regulation of a natural monopoly implemented? What incentive do companies have to reduce their costs?
   b. What is price cap regulation? With this type of regulation, what incentive do companies have to reduce their costs?

FIGURE **13.9**
Short Answer Problem 10

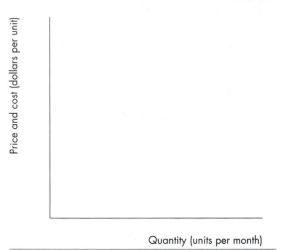

10. In Figure 13.9 draw a diagram illustrating a natural monopoly. Suppose the company is regulated using an average cost pricing rule. Show the amount of production, the price, and the deadweight loss.

■ **You're the Teacher**

1. "I don't really understand how monopoly firms decide how much to produce and what price to charge. Can you give me some help? I'd really like just a rule or two to remember." Because you have studied this material, you are in a position to help this student. Offer a couple of rules that this student can use to determine, first, how much is produced, and second, what price is charged.

2. "How can price discrimination ever reduce the amount of consumer surplus? I mean, by price discriminating the company charges some people a lower price, so how can this ever reduce consumer surplus?" These questions are short and to the point, so give a similar answer to them!

Answers

■ True/False Answers

Monopoly and How It Arises

1. **T** Without barriers to entry, other firms will enter the industry so that it no longer is a monopoly.

2. **T** Patents legally prohibit anyone else from producing the same good.

3. **F** A single-price monopoly charges each consumer the same price.

A Single-Price Monopoly's Output and Price Decision

4. **T** The monopolist is the only producer in the market, so the monopolist's decisions about how much to produce determine the market price.

5. **F** For a single-price monopoly, $P > MR$.

6. **T** No matter its industry type, a firm producing so that $MR = MC$ earns the maximum profit.

7. **T** A single-price monopoly produces at $MR = MC$. Because $P > MR$, the equality between MR and MC means that $P > MC$.

8. **T** Barriers to entry limit the competition faced by the monopoly, so it is able to make an economic profit indefinitely.

Single-Price Monopoly and Competition Compared

9. **F** A monopoly creates deadweight loss; it does not reduce it.

10. **F** Single-price monopolists capture only part of the consumer surplus. They create deadweight loss, part of which is the consumer surplus lost to everyone in society.

11. **T** Rent seeking refers to the use of resources to establish a monopoly.

Price Discrimination

12. **F** Price discrimination captures consumer surplus, not producer surplus.

13. **T** This motivation lies behind price discrimination.

14. **F** Economic profit = producer surplus – fixed cost.

15. **T** A perfectly price-discriminating monopolist converts the entire consumer surplus into additional economic profit for itself.

Monopoly Regulation

16. **T** A marginal cost pricing rule means that the firm produces the efficient quantity but the firm incurs an economic loss.

17. **T** With an average cost pricing rule, the natural monopoly produces less than the efficient amount of output.

18. **F** If the costs rise, the producer knows that the regulators will allow the company to hike its price to offset the higher costs.

■ Multiple Choice Answers

Monopoly and How It Arises

1. **d** The taxi company has been granted a legal monopoly.

2. **b** The other possibilities are legal barriers to entry.

3. **d** *All* monopolies must lower their price in order to sell more output.

A Single-Price Monopoly's Output and Price Decision

4. **d** Total revenue when 100 trees are sold is $2,800; when 101 trees are sold, it is $2,727. Hence the marginal revenue from the 101st tree is –$73.

5. **a** When demand is elastic, MR is positive; when demand is inelastic, MR is negative.

6. **a** As long as MR exceeds MC, producing the unit adds to the firm's total profit because it adds more to revenue than to cost.

7. **c** If the demand for a monopoly's good declines or its costs rise, a monopoly, like any firm, might make zero economic profit or incur an economic loss.

8. **b** The firm produces the level of output that sets $MR = MC$.

9. **c** The firm produces 300 units of output. The highest price the firm can charge and sell this amount of output is $35 per unit.

10. **b** The rise in marginal costs shifts the MC curve up, which leads the firm to decrease the quantity it produces and raise the price it charges.

11. **d** In the short run, depending on demand and cost, any firm can make an economic profit, zero economic profit, or incur an economic loss.

12. **c** A monopoly can make an economic profit and, because of the barriers to entry, the economic profit can last indefinitely.

Single-Price Monopoly and Competition Compared

13. **c** A single-price monopoly creates a deadweight loss because it produces less than a competitive industry.

14. **a** Because it produces less output, the monopoly is able to boost the price it charges.

15. **d** The deadweight loss is created because a single-price monopoly produces less than a perfectly competitive industry.

16. **a** The consumer surplus is the area between the demand curve and the price.

17. **c** The economic profit is the area of the rectangle with its height the difference between P and ATC and its length the quantity produced.

18. **a** The producer benefits because the monopoly can make an economic profit; consumers lose because of the reduction in consumer surplus; and society loses due to the deadweight loss.

19. **b** The question defines rent seeking.

Price Discrimination

20. **c** By price discriminating, a monopoly increases its economic profit, which is the incentive to price discriminate.

21. **c** Prefect price discrimination eliminates all consumer surplus by converting it into producer surplus.

22. **a** Customers who are willing to pay more are charged a higher price.

23. **b** Airlines price discriminate and charge business travelers, who are willing to pay more, a higher price than vacation travelers, who are not willing to pay a high price.

Monopoly Regulation

24. **a** The capture theory predicts that regulation benefits the interest of producers, who have managed to "capture" the regulator.

25. **d** A marginal cost pricing rule means that the firm produces the amount of output where the marginal cost curve intersects the demand curve and then sets its price equal to the marginal cost of producing that amount of output.

26. **a** This answer reflects the monopoly level of output and price, which is the combination of output and price that maximizes economic profit.

27. **c** An average cost pricing rule means that the firm produces the amount of output where the average cost curve intersects the demand curve and then sets its price equal to the average cost of producing that amount of output.

28. **b** Because the company incurs an economic loss, it needs to be subsidized or allowed to price discriminate in order to breakeven (make zero economic profit).

29. **a** The firm's incentive to inflate its costs is a drawback of rate-of-return regulation.

■ **Answers to Short Answer Problems**

1. To sell an additional unit of output, a single-price monopoly must lower its price. The additional unit sold at the lower price adds an amount equal to the (lower) price to the firm's revenue. But now previous customers pay the new, lower price whereas before they had been paying a higher price. Marginal revenue equals the new revenue, the new (lower) price, minus the loss of revenue from previous customers, so marginal revenue is less than the price.

TABLE **13.3**
Short Answer Problem 2 (a)

Quantity (books per hour)	Total cost (dollars)	Average total cost (ATC)	Marginal cost (M C)
9	247.00	27.44	
			9.00
10	256.00	25.60	
			11.00
11	267.00	24.27	
			13.00
12	280.00	23.33	
			15.00
13	295.00	22.69	
			17.00
14	312.00	22.29	
			19.00
15	331.00	22.07	
			21.00
16	352.00	22.00	
			23.00
17	375.00	22.06	
			25.00
18	400.00	22.22	
			27.00
19	427.00	22.47	
			29.00
20	456.00	22.80	
			31.00
21	487.00	23.19	

2. a. Table 13.3 shows the average total costs and
        marginal costs. The average total costs are calcu-
        lated by dividing the total costs by the total out-
        puts. For instance, the average total cost when
        10 books are sold is $256 ÷ 10, or $25.60. The
        rest of the *ATC*s are calculated similarly. Mar-
        ginal cost equals the change in the total cost di-
        vided by the change in output. For example, the
        marginal cost going from 10 to 11 units of out-
        put is ($267 − $256) ÷ (11 − 10), which equals
        $11.00. The remaining *MC*s are calculated in
        the same way.

TABLE **13.4**

Short Answer Problem 2 (b)

Quantity demanded (books per hour)	Price (dollars per book)	Total revenue (dollars)	Marginal revenue (MR)	Marginal cost (MC)
9	57.00	513.00		
			47.00	9.00
10	56.00	560.00		
			45.00	11.00
11	55.00	605.00		
			43.00	13.00
12	54.00	648.00		
			41.00	15.00
13	53.00	689.00		
			39.00	17.00
14	52.00	728.00		
			37.00	19.00
15	51.00	765.00		
			35.00	21.00
16	50.00	800.00		
			33.00	23.00
17	49.00	833.00		
			31.00	25.00
18	48.00	864.00		
			29.00	27.00
19	47.00	893.00		
			27.00	29.00
20	46.00	920.00		
			25.00	31.00
21	45.00	945.00		

b. Table 13.4 gives the total revenue and marginal
    revenue. Total revenue is Quantity × Price. For
    example, the total revenue at the quantity of 10
    books is 10 × $56 = $560. Once the total reve-
    nue is calculated, the marginal revenue can be
    calculated as the change in total revenue divided
    by the change in output. For instance, take the

marginal revenue going from 10 to 11 books
sold per hour as an example. This marginal revenue equals ($605 − $560) ÷ (11 − 10), or $45.
The rest of the marginal revenues are computed
the same way.

c. To maximize her profit, Laura produces at *MR* =
    MC. Between 18 and 19 books the marginal
    revenue is $29 and between 19 and 20, it is $27.
    So, at 19 books the marginal revenue is $28.
    Similarly, the marginal cost is $27 between 18
    and 19 books and $29 between 19 and 20
    books, which indicates that at 19 books the
    marginal cost is $28. Marginal revenue equals
    marginal cost at an output of 19 books, so this
    quantity is the profit-maximizing level of out-
    put.

    The data for the demand curve show that Laura
    can sell 19 books at a price per book of $47, so
    the monopoly price is $47 per book. (Note that
    the price, $47, is greater than the marginal cost,
    $28.) Laura's economic profit equals her total
    revenue minus her total cost. From Table 13.4,
    the total revenue when selling 19 books is $893,
    and, from Table 13.3, the total cost of selling 19
    books is $427. Laura's total economic profit is
    $893 − $427 = $466.

FIGURE **13.10**

Short Answer Problem 2 (d)

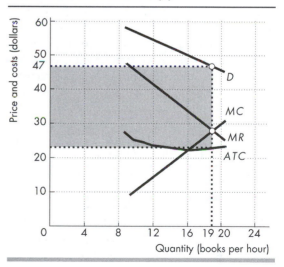

d. Figure 13.10 shows the demand, *MR*, and cost
    curves. The area of the darkened rectangle equals
    Laura's economic profit.

FIGURE **13.11**
Short Answer Problem 3

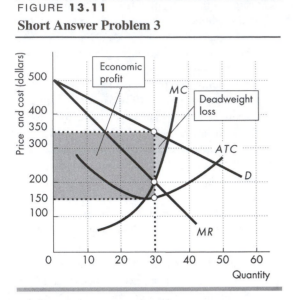

FIGURE **13.12**
Short Answer Problem 6

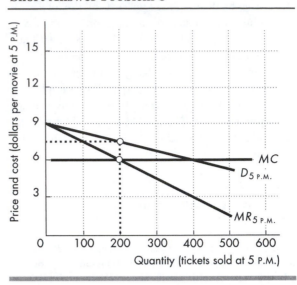

3. The curves are labeled in Figure 13.11. The monopoly produces 30 and sets a price of $350. The economic profit the monopoly makes is the darker rectangle and the deadweight loss is the lighter triangular area.

4. The fundamental reason that monopolies are able to make an economic profit in the long run is because they are protected from competition by barriers to entry. When the monopolist is making an economic profit, other firms would like to enter that market. However, they are unable to enter because of the existence of barriers to entry — some feature of the market, be it economies of scale or perhaps a patent, which prevents new firms from entering the industry. Perfectly competitive firms are not protected by barriers to entry. If they are making an economic profit, new competitors *will* enter the market and, by so doing, compete away the economic profit. It is the barriers to entry that allow a monopoly to indefinitely make an economic profit.

5. A perfectly competitive industry produces the level of output at which the industry's marginal cost curve (which is the same as the industry's supply curve) intersects the industry's demand curve. A single-price monopoly produces the level of output at which the monopoly's marginal cost curve intersects its marginal revenue curve. Because the marginal revenue curve lies below the demand curve, the monopoly produces less than a perfectly competitive market.

FIGURE **13.13**
Short Answer Problem 6

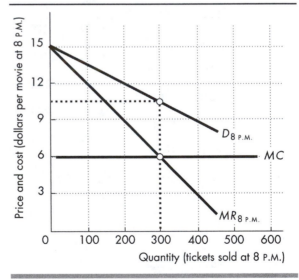

6. In order to maximize his profit, Derek should charge a lower price for his 5 o'clock movies and a higher price for his 8 o'clock movies. In other words, Derek should price discriminate because by so doing, Derek increases his economic profit.

Why does price discrimination increase Derek's profit? Figures 13.12 and 13.13 shed light on this question. The marginal cost of showing a movie at 5 P.M. or at 8 P.M. is assumed to be constant. In order to maximize his profit in the 5 o'clock market, Derek equates *MR* to *MC* and sells 200 tickets by charging $7.50 per ticket. In the high demand, 8 P.M. market, Derek sells 300 tickets by charging $10.50 per ticket. By charging a lower price at 5 P.M. and a higher price at 8 P.M., Derek is able to increase his economic profit because he is maximizing his profit in both markets. If he charged the same price in both markets, he would not be maximizing his profit.

7. a. When the one firm is granted a monopoly for pizza delivery, it boosts its price and reduces its output. The price of a pizza delivery will rise, the quantity of pizzas delivered will decrease, and so the quantity of pizzas consumed decreases as fewer pizzas are delivered.

   b. The owner of the (new) monopoly pizza delivery service earns an economic profit.

   c. Perhaps surprisingly, though you might be rent seeking by offering to buy the delivery service, once you buy the pizza deliverer, you will not be able to make an economic profit. Why not? Think of the selling price the pizza owner will charge to buy the pizza delivery company and its monopoly. The selling price must compensate the owner for all the economic profit that he or she will lose in the future by not owning the business. Hence the price of the business will rise to reflect the economic profit that it is making, both now and in the future. The fact that the price of the business rises means that in this rent-seeking equilibrium, once you own the firm, you will be able to make only a normal profit on the funds that you use to buy the business. The moral is that if your firm wants to make an economic profit, it must be in on the ground floor.

8. a. Figure 13.14 shows the demand, marginal revenue, average total cost, marginal cost curves and the level of output for each industry structure. The single-price monopoly produces the least, 300 units, labeled Q_B. Both the perfectly competitive industry and the perfectly price discriminating monopoly produce the same amount, 400 units, labeled $Q_A = Q_C$. A perfectly competitive industry and a perfectly price discriminating monopoly produce more output than the amount produced by a single-price monopolist.

FIGURE **13.14**

Short Answer Problem 8

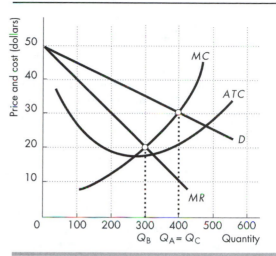

   b. The consumer surplus is largest in the perfectly competitive industry; it is smallest (zero) with the perfectly price-discriminating monopoly.

   c. The total economic profit is largest for the monopoly able to perfectly price discriminate because this monopoly converts the entire potential consumer surplus to economic profit. It is smallest for the perfectly competitive industry because in the long run firms in this industry cannot make economic profits.

   d. Both the perfectly competitive industry and the perfectly price-discriminating monopoly produce the efficient amount.

9. a. Rate of return regulation is related to an average total cost price rule. Regulators determine a fair rate of return on the company's capital. This rate of return is then multiplied by the total amount of the firm's capital to determine the total "profit" that the regulators consider fair. (If the company has, say, $10 million in capital and the rate of return is 15 percent, the total amount of "profit" is $1.5 million, $10 million times 15 percent.) This total profit is added to the firm's other costs and the amount becomes the regulators' "target" for the firm's total revenue. Then, the regulators determine a price that will enable the firm to earn this amount of revenue. Companies have very little incentive to reduce their costs; if costs rise, the regulators will raise the price that the company can charge, thus allow-

ing the company to recoup the increased costs. Similarly, companies have an incentive to use more capital than necessary because the regulators will increase the company's total return when its capital increases.

b. Price cap regulation sets a price ceiling and then allows the company to charge whatever price it wishes as long as the price remains under the ceiling. Typically there is an earnings sharing provision so that if the company's profit rises above a certain level, the profit must be shared with consumers by reducing the price the company charges. These methods give the company more incentive to control its costs because if the business can lower its costs and hence increase its profit, the company will be allowed to keep (at least part of) the higher profit.

FIGURE **13.15**
Short Answer Problem 10

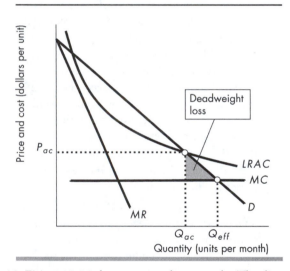

---

10. Figure 13.15 shows a natural monopoly. The distinguishing characteristic of a natural monopoly is that its *LRAC* curve falls until after it crosses the demand curve. Under an average cost pricing rule, the company must set its price equal to its average cost, which means that the price that will be charged is P_{ac} and the level of output is Q_{ac}. (To buy Q_{ac}, consumers are willing to pay P_{ac}, and this

price equals the average cost of producing output Q_{ac}.) The deadweight loss equals the loss of consumer and producer surplus on the difference between the efficient level of output Q_{eff} — where the demand (the marginal social benefit) and the marginal cost (the marginal social cost) curves cross — and the amount of output actually produced, which is Q_{ac}. The deadweight loss is illustrated by the shaded triangle.

■ **You're the Teacher**

1. "A couple of mechanical rules might be helpful when we're studying how a monopoly selects its output and determines its price. First, decide how much the firm produces. Second, determine the price charged."

"To find the profit-maximizing quantity, use the *MR* and *MC* curves. The equilibrium quantity is where these curves cross: Draw a vertical line down to the horizontal axis and read the quantity. Then, to find the profit-maximizing price, continue this vertical line up to the demand curve. From the intersection of the demand curve and your vertical quantity line, draw a horizontal line over to the price axis. Where this line meets the price axis is the profit-maximizing price. Use these rules and you'll be okay."

2. "Look, the whole idea of price discrimination is that a monopoly wants to charge you a price for the good that more closely reflects how much you value it. If you value it a lot, the monopoly wants to stick you with a really high price; if you don't value it too much, the monopoly will let you buy it for a lower price. Now, the idea behind consumer surplus is that it measures the difference between how much you value a good and how much you have to pay for it. By price discriminating, the monopoly can reduce this difference: Customers who value it a lot, pay a lot, and customers who don't value it as much don't pay as much. So, a price-discriminating monopoly moves the price closer to how much the good is valued, which means that the monopoly can reduce consumer surplus."

Chapter Quiz

1. Which of the following is a feature of a monopoly?
   a. Monopoly has no barriers to entry.
   b. Monopolies produce a product with a very close substitute.
   c. A monopoly is the only supplier of the product.
   d. A monopoly faces a perfectly elastic demand for its product.

2. A patent is a _____ barrier to entry and a public franchise is a _____ barrier to entry.
   a. natural; natural
   b. natural; legal
   c. legal; natural
   d. legal; legal

3. For a single-price monopoly, the marginal revenue curve lies
   a. above the demand curve.
   b. on top of the demand curve.
   c. below the demand curve.
   d. sometimes above, sometimes on top of, and sometimes below the demand curve depending on the marginal cost curve.

4. The more perfectly a monopoly can price discriminate, the _____ its output and the _____ its profit.
   a. larger; higher
   b. larger; lower
   c. smaller; higher
   d. smaller; lower

5. The social interest theory of regulation predicts that _____ will be eliminated and the capture theory predicts that _____ will be maximized.
   a. consumer surplus; deadweight loss
   b. consumer surplus; economic profit
   c. deadweight loss; economic profit
   d. deadweight loss; deadweight loss

6. Which of the following occurs with *both* a perfectly competitive market and a perfectly price discriminating monopoly?
   a. The amount of output is inefficient.
   b. The amount of output is efficient.
   c. Deadweight loss is created.
   d. All consumer surplus is lost to the firm(s).

7. A single-price monopolist will shut down if price is
   a. less than average fixed cost.
   b. less than the minimum average variable cost.
   c. greater than the minimum average total cost.
   d. greater than minimum average variable cost but less than minimum average total cost.

8. A perfectly competitive market is more efficient than a single-price monopoly because the perfectly competitive market
   a. has higher total costs.
   b. produces more output.
   c. has a market demand that is more elastic.
   d. None of the above.

9. Compared to a perfectly competitive market, a single-price monopoly produces _____ output and sets a _____ price.
   a. more; higher
   b. more; lower
   c. less; higher
   d. less; lower

10. For a regulated natural monopoly, setting an average cost pricing rule
    a. means the firm produces the allocatively efficient quantity.
    b. means the firm makes zero economic profit, that is, the firm breaks even.
    c. maximizes producer surplus.
    d. maximizes consumer surplus.

The answers for this Chapter Quiz are on page 346

Chapter 14 MONOPOLISTIC COMPETITION

Key Concepts

■ What Is Monopolistic Competition?

The market structure of most industries lies between the extremes of perfect competition and monopoly. Monopolistic competition is one such "intermediate" industry structure. **Monopolistic competition** is a market structure in which:

◆ A large number of firms compete. Because there are a large number of firms, each firm has a small market share so no one firm can dictate the price. Collusion amongst the firms is impossible.

◆ Each firm produces a differentiated product (**product differentiation** occurs when a firm makes a product that is slightly different from the products of competing firms).

◆ Firms compete on product quality, price, and marketing. Brand-name products advertise their superiority to generics and generics advertise their low price.

◆ Firms are free to enter or exit the industry.

A monopolistically competitive firm faces a downward sloping demand curve because it produces a differentiated product. As a result, a monopolistically competitive firm's marginal revenue curve lies below its demand curve.

■ Price and Output in Monopolistic Competition

In the short run:

◆ The firm maximizes its profit by producing the level of output such that $MR = MC$.

◆ The firm might make an economic profit. If it does, free entry means that competitors will enter the industry. Alternatively, the firm might incur an economic loss. If it does incur an economic loss, it (or other firms) eventually exits the industry.

In the long run:

◆ The firm maximizes its profit by producing the amount of output that sets $MR = MC$.

◆ The firm breaks even, that is the firm makes zero economic profit, so $P = ATC$.

Figure 14.1 shows the long-run equilibrium for a monopolistically competitive firm.

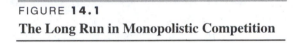

FIGURE **14.1**

The Long Run in Monopolistic Competition

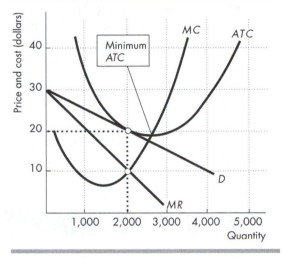

A firm has **excess capacity** if it produces less than its **efficient scale**, the level of output for which its ATC is at its minimum. Firms in monopolistic competition have excess capacity because, as Figure 14.1 shows, in the long run they do not produce at the minimum ATC. Firms in perfect competition do not have excess capacity because they produce at the minimum ATC.

A firm's **markup** is the amount by which price exceeds marginal cost. In Figure 14.1, the markup is $10 (the price, $20, minus the marginal cost, $10). Firms in monopolistic competition have a markup while firms in perfect competition do not have a markup.

Firms in monopolistic competition produce less than the efficient quantity, so on this count monopolistic competition is not efficient. But firms in monopolistic competition produce a large variety of differentiated products and consumers value variety. So compared to the alternative of total uniformity from perfect competition, monopolistic competition might be efficient.

■ Product Development and Marketing

Monopolistically competitive firms constantly strive to differentiate their products and (temporarily) earn an economic profit. The extent of innovation and product development is determined by the marginal cost and marginal revenue of innovation and development.

Monopolistically competitive firms spend huge amounts on marketing. Such selling costs are fixed costs, which shift the firm's *ATC* curve upward. Because all firms advertise, the effect of advertising on the demand for any particular firm's product is ambiguous. If all firms advertise, a firm's demand can become more elastic. If the demand becomes elastic enough, even though the costs have risen, the price and markup might fall.

A **signal** is an action taken by an informed person (or firm) to send a message to uninformed people. Some advertising, such as brand names, signals the high quantity of the product.

The efficiency of monopolistic competition is unclear. In some cases, the gains from product variety exceed the selling costs and extra cost from excess capacity. In other situations, the gains fall short of the costs.

Helpful Hints

1. **BARRIERS TO ENTRY AND LONG-RUN ECONOMIC PROFIT :** Free entry leads to zero long-run economic profits (that is, a normal profit) both in perfect competition and monopolistic competition. If a monopoly is earning an economic profit, other firms would like to enter the monopoly's industry, but barriers to entry keep them out. Whether a business can make an economic profit in the long run revolves around the presence or absence of barriers to entry. The presence makes a long-run economic profit possible; the absence makes a long-run economic profit impossible.

Questions

■ True/False and Explain

What Is Monopolistic Competition?

1. Monopolistic competition is similar to perfect competition because there are a large number of firms in both market structures.

2. Product differentiation gives each monopolistically competitive firm a downward sloping demand curve.

3. Monopolistically competitive firms compete only on price.

Price and Output in Monopolistic Competition

4. To maximize its profit, in the short run a monopolistically competitive firm produces the level of output that sets $P = ATC$.

5. Monopolistically competitive firms incur an economic loss if they produce the level of output that sets $MR = MC$.

6. Monopolistically competitive firms can make an economic profit in the short run and in the long run.

7. Free entry is the reason that monopolistically competitive firms have excess capacity.

8. In monopolistic competition, price exceeds marginal cost.

9. Monopolistic competition leads to more product variety than perfect competition.

Product Development and Marketing

10. A monopolistically competitive firm can make an economic profit if it develops new products.

11. Monopolistically competitive firms have large marketing and selling costs.

12. Advertising by monopolistically competitive firms must increase their markups.

13. Advertising can signal product quality.

■ Multiple Choice

What Is Monopolistic Competition?

1. A monopolistically competitive firm is like a *monopoly* firm insofar as
   a. both face perfectly elastic demand.
   b. both make an economic profit in the long run.
   c. both have *MR* curves that lie below their demand curves.
   d. neither is protected by high barriers to entry.

2. A monopolistically competitive firm is like a *perfectly competitive* firm insofar as
   a. both face perfectly elastic demand.
   b. both can make an economic profit in the long run.
   c. both have *MR* curves that lie below their demand curves.
   d. neither is protected by high barriers to entry.

3. Product differentiation
   a. means that monopolistically competitive firms can compete on quality and marketing.
   b. occurs when a firm makes a product that is slightly different from that of its competitors.
   c. makes a monopolistically competitive firm's demand curve downward sloping.
   d. All of the above answers are correct.

4. Monopolistically competitive firms compete on all of the following <u>EXCEPT</u>
   a. quality.
   b. price.
   c. quantity.
   d. marketing.

5. Taco Bell is a monopolistically competitive firm. Taco Bell's demand curve is _____ and its marginal revenue curve is _____.
   a. downward sloping; downward sloping
   b. horizontal; horizontal
   c. upward sloping; downward sloping
   d. downward sloping; upward sloping

Price and Output in Monopolistic Competition

Figure 14.2 shows a monopolistically competitive restaurant in the short run. Use it for the next four questions.

FIGURE **14.2**

Multiple Choice Questions 6, 7, 8, and 9

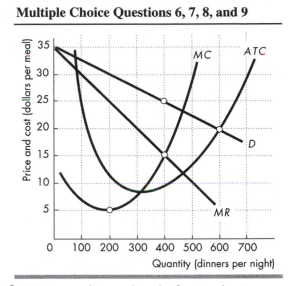

6. How many dinners does the firm produce?
   a. 200
   b. 400
   c. 600
   d. None of the above

7. What price does the firm charge per meal?
   a. $5
   b. $15
   c. $20
   d. $25

8. The firm in the figure is
   a. making an economic profit.
   b. breaking even (making zero economic profit).
   c. incurring an economic loss.
   d. incurring an accounting loss.

9. In the long run,
   a. new restaurants will enter and each existing restaurant's demand decreases.
   b. new restaurants will enter and each existing restaurant's demand increases.
   c. existing restaurants will leave and each remaining restaurant's demand decreases.
   d. existing restaurants will leave and each remaining restaurant's demand increases.

10. A monopolistically competitive firm has excess capacity because in the
   a. short run $MR = MC$.
   b. short run the firm does not produce at the minimum marginal cost.
   c. long run the firm does not produce at the minimum average total cost.
   d. long run the firm earns an economic profit.

11. In the long run, a monopolistically competitive firm's economic profit is zero because of
   a. product differentiation.
   b. the lack of barriers to entry.
   c. excess capacity.
   d. the downward-sloping demand curve of each firm.

Product Development and Marketing

12. Monopolistically competitive firms constantly develop new products in an effort to
   a. make the demand for their product more elastic.
   b. increase the demand for their product.
   c. increase the marginal cost of their product.
   d. None of the above answers is correct.

13. When deciding upon how much to spend on product development, a firm will consider
   a. only the marginal revenue from product development.
   b. only the marginal cost of product development.
   c. both the marginal revenue and marginal cost of product development.
   d. the price and average total cost of product development.

14. Which of the following statements about monopolistically competitive firms is correct?
   a. In the long run, they have deficient capacity.
   b. They have high selling costs.
   c. They produce the efficient amount of output.
   d. They rarely advertise.

15. Brand names
   a. are an unnecessary expense.
   b. mean a firm does not need to advertise.
   c. provide no value to consumers.
   d. give firms an incentive to maintain consistent quality.

■ Short Answer Problems

FIGURE 14.3
Short Answer Problem 1

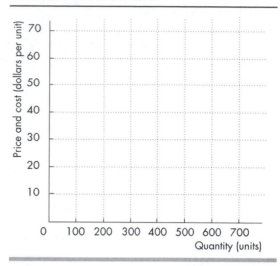

1. In Figure 14.3 draw a diagram illustrating a monopolistically competitive firm that is making an economic profit in the short run. Identify the area that equals the economic profit.

FIGURE 14.4
Short Answer Problem 2

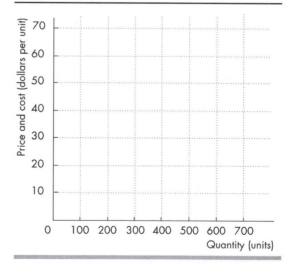

2. In Figure 14.4 draw the long-run equilibrium for a monopolistically competitive firm. What conditions must be satisfied for long-run equilibrium?

FIGURE **14.5**

Short Answer Problem 3

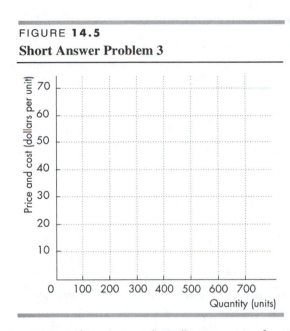

3. Suppose that a monopolistically competitive firm is initially in long-run equilibrium and it succeeds in further differentiating its product. As a result, the demand for its product increases. In Figure 14.5 show what happens to this firm in the short run. Without drawing a diagram, describe what happens in the long run.

4. Compare the advantages and disadvantages of perfect competition and monopolistic competition in terms of how they benefit society.

5. Explain why advertising might actually lead to monopolistically competitive firms charging lower prices.

6. How can advertising brand names send a signal to consumers?

■ **You're the Teacher**

1. "You know, I've really been studying the book and this study guide and now a lot of this stuff is making sense. I like the fact that firms in perfect competition, monopolistic competition, and monopoly actually have only one profit-maximization rule, the *MR = MC* rule. It sure makes it easy if we don't have to memorize different rules for different industries! Can you think of any other rules that are the same across all industries?" This student is correct: Common rules ease your work. Perhaps more importantly, common rules also show you that there are factors in common to firms in perfect competition, monopolistic competition, and monopoly. There is another rule that is common; it deals with when a firm makes an economic profit. With this hint, explain the other rule to the eager student.

Answers

■ True/False Answers

What Is Monopolistic Competition?

1. **T** A competitive industry has a large number of firms.

2. **T** By making its product different from those of its competitors, each monopolistically competitive firm has a unique product and hence a downward-sloping demand curve.

3. **F** Because its product is differentiated, monopolistically competitive firms compete on product quality and marketing, as well as on price.

Price and Output in Monopolistic Competition

4. **F** Monopolistically competitive firms use the same rule as all firms: to maximize their profit, produce so that MR equals MC.

5. **F** By producing the quantity that sets $MR = MC$, a firm maximizes its profit.

6. **F** The firms cannot make an economic profit in the long run because there are no barriers to entry.

7. **F** Monopolistically competitive firms have excess capacity because they produce differentiated goods.

8. **T** The firm sets $MR = MC$, but because $P > MR$, it is the case that $P > MC$. The difference between P and MC is the markup.

9. **T** The increased product variety from monopolistic competition is a benefit of monopolistic competition relative to perfect competition.

Product Development and Marketing

10. **T** Monopolistically competitive firms constantly try to further differentiate their products, and developing new products is one method they use.

11. **T** Marketing and advertising play key roles in monopolistically competitive firms' efforts to differentiate their products.

12. **F** If firms advertise, then the demand for each firm's product can become more elastic, which reduces the firm's makeup.

13. **T** Advertising can be used to signal to consumers that the product is high quality.

■ Multiple Choice Answers

What Is Monopolistic Competition?

1. **c** Both have downward-sloping demand curves, so both have MR curves that lie below their demand curves.

2. **d** The absence of high barriers to entry accounts for the large number of firms in each industry.

3. **d** Answer b is the definition of product differentiation and answers a and c are results of product differentiation.

4. **c** The firms compete on all the factors listed except quantity.

5. **a** The downward sloping demand curve and the resulting downward sloping marginal revenue curve are the result of product differentiation.

Price and Output in Monopolistic Competition

6. **b** The monopolistically competitive firm maximizes its profit by producing so that $MR = MC$.

7. **d** With the firm producing 400 meals, the demand curve shows that the price of $25 per dinner is the highest price that can be charged and still sell all that is produced.

8. **a** The restaurant makes an economic profit because, at output of 400 meals, $P > ATC$.

9. **a** New restaurants enter because they, too, want to make an economic profit. As these firms enter, they decrease the demand for the existing restaurant's meals, which reduces the economic profit.

10. **c** The firm produces less output than that which minimizes its long-run ATC.

11. **b** If firms in the industry are making an economic profit, the absence of barriers to entry means that new firms enter the industry and compete away the economic profit.

Product Development and Marketing

12. **b** If the firm can increase the demand for its product, it can temporarily make an economic profit.

13. **c** For virtually all business decisions, a firm compares the marginal revenue and marginal cost resulting from the decision.

14. **b** Monopolistically competitive firms incur large selling costs trying to differentiate their products.

15. **d** To preserve their valuable brand names, firms must maintain consistent quality.

■ Answers to Short Answer Problems

Short Answer Problem 1

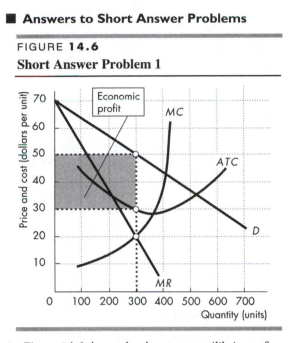

Short Answer Problem 2

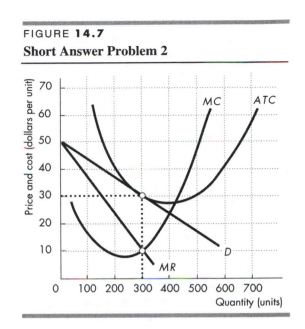

the case if $P > ATC$. But for the market to be in long-run equilibrium, the equality condition is required.) Both conditions — production at $MR = MC$ and $P = ATC$ — are met in Figure 14.7 so Figure 14.7 illustrates the long-run equilibrium.

Short Answer Problem 3

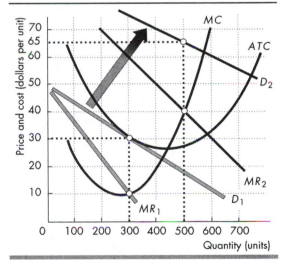

1. Figure 14.6 shows the short-run equilibrium of a monopolistically competitive firm. To maximize its profit, the firm produces 300 units because that is the quantity for which $MR = MC$. At this level of output, the price is $50 per unit and the average total cost is $30 per unit, so $P > ATC$, and the firm makes an economic profit, as illustrated by the darkened rectangle. This diagram is identical to that of a monopoly firm making an economic profit. Both monopoly and monopolistically competitive firms face downward-sloping demand curves, both produce so that $MR = MC$, and, as long as $P > ATC$, both firms make an economic profit.

2. Figure 14.7 shows the long-run equilibrium for a monopolistically competitive firm. Two conditions must be satisfied for this diagram to show the long-run equilibrium. Think of these requirements as a *firm condition* and a *market condition*. For the firm to be satisfied, it must maximize its profit, which requires that it be producing the amount of output so that $MR = MC$. In Figure 14.7, the firm must produce 300 units of output. Then, for there to be long-run equilibrium in the market, firms must have no incentive either to enter or exit the industry. As a result, the firms must make zero economic profit, so $P = ATC$. In the figure, both the P and ATC equal $30 per unit. (This second condition is not what the firm would choose. The firm would rather make an economic profit, which would be

3. Figure 14.8 shows the effect when a monopolistically competitive firm succeeds in further differentiating its product. The demand for the firm's good increases, thereby shifting the demand curve and the MR curve rightward. With the increase in demand,

the firm increases its output from 300 units to 500 units and raises its price from $30 per unit to $65 per unit. The firm makes an economic profit.

In the long run, other firms copy its product by making their own differentiated version. As they do so, the demand for the initial firm's good decreases; that is, the demand curve and *MR* curve shift leftward. Ultimately, demand decreases enough that the pioneering firm — and all other new entrants — no longer make an economic profit. At this point, other firms do not have an incentive to copy the good and the market is in long-run equilibrium.

4. An advantage of perfect competition is that it produces at minimum average total cost, while monopolistic competition produces at a higher average total cost because of its excess capacity. Another advantage is that a perfectly competitive market is efficient; it produces the level of output that sets marginal social benefit equal to marginal social cost. A monopolistically competitive industry, however, is not efficient because the price of the product (which equals the marginal social benefit) exceeds the marginal social cost (which equals the marginal cost).

The advantage of monopolistic competition is that product differentiation leads to greater product variety, an outcome consumers value. In addition, monopolistically competitive firms have a greater incentive to innovate new and improved products and methods of production. Monopolistically competitive firms must do more advertising and sales promotion than perfectly competitive firms. To the extent that these activities provide valued services to consumers, they benefit society.

The loss in efficiency and the higher *ATC* that occurs in monopolistic competition must be weighed against the gain of greater product variety, greater incentives to innovate, and potentially valuable promotional activity.

5. Advertising by a monopolistically competitive firm aims to increase the demand for its good or service. But if *all* firms advertise then the demand for each firm's good or service might become more elastic because consumers become aware of all possible substitutes. If the demand becomes elastic, then even though the firm's costs are higher because of the advertising expense, the profit-maximizing price the firm sets might fall.

6. Brand names send a signal to consumers because they are costly to create and maintain. Pepsi and Coke, for instance, both advertise to maintain their brand names. Consumers know that if Pepsi or Coke started to sell low-quality products, then the expenditures on brand-name advertising would be wasted. Because Pepsi and Coke do not want to incur costs for no purpose, consumers can be certain that Pepsi and Coke products will be high quality. By this means, Pepsi and Coke use their brand-name advertising to signal the high quality of their products.

■ You're the Teacher

1. "One other rule works for a firm in perfect competition, monopolistic competition, and monopoly. In particular, if $P > ATC$, the firm makes an economic profit; if $P = ATC$, the firm makes zero economic profit; and if $P < ATC$, the firm incurs an economic loss. Let's take the case of $P > ATC$ and find out why it means that the firm makes an economic profit. If we multiply both sides of the inequality by q, the amount of output the firm produces, we get $P \times q > ATC \times q$. Now, $P \times q$ (the price multiplied the amount produced) equals the firm's total revenue. And $ATC = TC \div q$, so multiplying ATC by q gives TC, the firm's total cost. So when $P > ATC$, total revenue > total cost. Because the owners' normal profit is already included in its total cost, the fact that the firm's total revenue exceeds its total cost means that the 'extra' profit is an economic profit."

"But look, the main point of what I am saying is that we do have it easy: Here's another case where we don't have to memorize a bunch of different rules. If a firm finds that P exceeds ATC, it's making an economic profit."

Chapter Quiz

1. Pizza Hut, a monopolistically competitive firm, _____ likely to advertise extensively and _____ likely to innovate new products.
   a. is not; is not
   b. is not; is
   c. is; is not
   d. is; is

2. In the long run, a firm in monopolistic competition _____ excess capacity and _____ a markup of price over marginal cost.
   a. has; has
   b. has; does not have
   c. does not have; has
   d. does not have; does not have

3. Which of the following statements about advertising is FALSE?
   a. Advertising shifts the *ATC* curve upward.
   b. Advertising can be used to signal quality.
   c. Advertising might increase the number of firms in an industry.
   d. If all firms in an industry advertise, the advertising makes each firm's demand less elastic.

4. A distinction between a monopolistically competitive industry and a perfectly competitive industry is that firms in a monopolistically competitive industry
   a. produce identical products.
   b. are protected by high barriers to entry.
   c. produce at the minimum *ATC* in the long run.
   d. produce a product that is different from those produced by its competitors.

5. If firms in a monopolistically competitive industry make an economic profit,
   a. other firms will enter the industry.
   b. some firms will leave the industry.
   c. firms will neither enter nor exit.
   d. The premise of the question is wrong because monopolistically competitive firms cannot make an economic profit.

6. A firm in which type of industry *always* has excess capacity in the long run?
   a. Perfect competition
   b. Monopolistic competition
   c. Monopoly
   d. Perfect competition, monopolistic competition, and monopoly

7. Advertising _____ the firm's average total cost and _____ the firm's marginal cost.
   a. does not change; raises
   b. raises; does not change
   c. raises; raises
   d. raises; lowers

8. In the long run, a monopolistically competitive firm ___ make an economic profit and a monopoly _____ make an economic profit.
   a. can; can
   b. can; cannot
   c. cannot; can
   d. cannot; cannot

9. In the long run, a firm in monopolistic competition can
   a. make an economic profit.
   b. incur an economic loss.
   c. break even, that is, make zero economic profit.
   d. make either an economic profit or zero economic profit.

10. To maximize its profit, a firm in monopolistic competition produces so that
    a. $MR = MC$.
    b. $P = MC$.
    c. $P = MR$.
    d. $MR = ATC$.

The answers for this Chapter Quiz are on page 346

15 OLIGOPOLY

Key Concepts

■ What Is Oligopoly?

Oligopoly is a market structure in which natural or legal barriers prevent the entry of new firms and in which a small number of firms compete. A **duopoly** is an oligopoly market with two firms.

♦ Because there are a small number of firms, the firms are interdependent. Each firm's actions have a large effect on its profit and the profits of the other firms.

The firms in an oligopoly can increase their profit if they form a cartel and act as a monopoly.

♦ A **cartel** is a group of firms acting together—colluding—to limit output, raise price, and increase economic profit. Cartels are illegal but even if they were legal, they would tend to break down.

A market in which the Herfindahl-Hirschman Index exceeds 1,000 is usually an oligopoly.

■ Oligopoly Games

Game theory is a tool for studying *strategic behavior*—behavior that takes into account the expected behavior of others and the recognition of mutual interdependence. Games have rules, strategies, payoffs, and an outcome:

♦ *Rules* specify permissible actions by players.

♦ **Strategies** are all the possible actions of each player, such as raising or lowering price, advertising, or changing product quality.

♦ *Payoffs* are the profits and losses of the players. A **payoff matrix** is a table that shows the payoffs for every possible action by each player for every possible action taken by the other player.

♦ The *outcome* is determined by the players' choices. In a **Nash equilibrium**, Player *A* takes the best possible action given the action of Player *B*, and *B* takes the best possible action given the action of *A*.

Prisoners' Dilemma Payoff Matrix

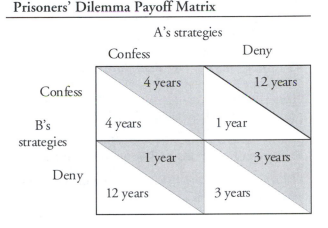

A "prisoners' dilemma" is a two-person game. The payoff matrix above gives a typical prisoners' dilemma game in which the players are being interrogated about their participation in a crime. In a one-time prisoners' dilemma game, each player's best strategy is to confess regardless of the other player's action. The Nash equilibrium is for each player to confess. This outcome is a **dominant-strategy equilibrium** because each player has the same best strategy (confess) regardless of the other player's action. The Nash equilibrium is *not* the best equilibrium for the prisoners because each end up doing more time than if both denied involvement.

In an oligopoly, the firms might have a **collusive agreement,** an agreement between the producers to form a cartel to restrict their output, raise their price, and thereby increase their profits. Such an agreement is illegal in the United States. In a price-fixing game, each firm can comply with the agreement by raising its price and restricting its output or can cheat by lowering its price and increasing its output. Each firm knows that if it *and all other* firms comply with the agreement, it will make a large economic profit. But each firm also knows that if it *and it alone* cheats, its economic profit is higher than if it complies with the agreement. In a one-time game, a prisoners' dilemma Nash equilibrium emerges, in which each firm's strategy is to cheat and the outcome is not the best equilibrium for the firms.

Some games have a unique equilibrium; others do not. A game of chicken does not have a unique equilibrium. One example of a game of chicken is two drivers who race toward each other to see who "chickens." The Nash equilibrium is for one driver to "chicken" but it is not possible to predict which driver will chicken. R&D (research and development) sometimes can be analyzed as a game of chicken. In the case in which R&D benefits not only the firm that pays for the R&D but also its competitors, the situation is a game of chicken in which each firm wants the other firm to pay for the R&D. The Nash equilibrium is for one firm to conduct the R&D (to "chicken") but it is not possible to predict which firm undertakes the R&D.

■ Repeated Games and Sequential Games

In a *repeated game*, other strategies can lead to a **cooperative equilibrium,** an equilibrium in which the players cooperate and so make and share the monopoly profit.

♦ A *tit-for-tat strategy* consists of taking the same action (cheating or not cheating) the other player took last period.

♦ A *trigger strategy* cooperates until the other player cheats and then plays the Nash equilibrium strategy (cheating) forever after.

In a repeated game the players might be able to attain the cooperative equilibrium because the long-run profit from colluding is greater than the short-run profit from cheating. But price wars can occur when new firms enter an industry and the industry finds itself in a prisoners' dilemma game. It becomes more difficult for firms to maintain a cartel agreement as the number of firms gets larger.

In a *sequential game*, one firm makes a decision at the first stage of the game and the other makes a decision at the second stage. A sequential game can occur in a contestable market. A **contestable market** is a market in which one firm (or a small number) operates but in which entry and exit are easy, so the existing firm faces competition from potential entrants. At the first stage, the existing firm sets its price and at the second stage potential entrants decide whether to enter or not. The firm in the market can play an entry-deterrence game:

♦ In an entry-deterrence game the firm in the market sets a competitive price (rather than a monopoly price) and makes zero economic profit in order to keep potential competitors from entering the market.

♦ **Limit pricing** refers to the situation in which the existing firm sets the price at the highest level that inflicts an economic loss on an entrant. This price might allow the existing firm to make an economic profit. But the prospect of incurring an economic loss keeps potential competitors out of the market.

♦ Limit pricing and competitive behavior depend on the assumption that the existing firm cannot change its price from what it set in the first stage.

■ Antitrust Law

Antitrust law is the law that regulates oligopolies and prevents them from becoming monopolies or behaving like monopolies. The two major antitrust laws are:

♦ *Sherman Act* — the first federal antitrust law, passed in 1890. Section 1 prohibits restrictions of trade; Section 2 outlaws "attempts to monopolize."

♦ *Clayton Act* — passed in 1914, prohibited certain business practices "*only if* they substantially lessen competition or create monopoly." (if the practices do not substantially lessen competition or create monopoly, the actions are legal.) Made illegal are: price discrimination, tying arrangements, requirements contracts, exclusive dealing, territorial confinement, acquiring a competitors shares or assets, and becoming a director of a competing firm.

Price fixing by competitors is *always* illegal. If horizontal price fixing can be proven, there is no acceptable defense; the firms are guilty.

♦ **Resale price maintenance** occurs when a manufacturer agrees with a distributor to resale the product at or above a certain price. A resale price maintenance agreement is legal provided it is not anticompetitive. Resale price maintenance is inefficient if it enables dealers to charge the monopoly price; it can be efficient if it allows manufacturers to induce its dealers to provide the efficient standard of service.

♦ A **tying arrangement** is an arrangement to sell one product only if the buyer agrees to buy another, different product. Sometimes a tying arrangement allows the producer to increase its market power and make more profit, albeit at the cost of creating inefficiency.

- **Predatory pricing** is setting a low price to drive competitors out of business with the intention of setting a monopoly price when the competition is gone. Predatory pricing is illegal under Section 2 of the Sherman Act. Economists doubt that predatory pricing occurs frequently because it trades a high and certain loss for a temporary an uncertain gain.

Mergers, when two or more firms agree to combine, and acquisitions, when one firm buys another, are subject to the merger guidelines used by the Federal Trade Commission. These guidelines include:

- If the initial Herfindahl-Hirschman Index (HHI) is less than 1,000, a merger will be unopposed.

- If the initial HHI is between 1,000 and 1,800, a merger that raises the HHI by 100 or more will be contested.

- If the initial HHI is larger than 1,800, a merger that increases the HHI by 50 or more will be challenged.

Helpful Hints

1. **HOW TO DETERMINE THE EQUILIBRIUM IN A PRISONERS' DILEMMA GAME :** Learning how to find the equilibrium of a prisoners' dilemma-type game is important. Take the example of Chris and Loren in a prisoner's dilemma. Each player has to choose between two strategies, confess or deny. First, set up the payoff matrix. Then look at the payoff matrix from Chris's point of view. Chris does not know whether Loren is going to confess or deny, so Chris asks two questions: (1) Assuming that Loren confesses, do I get a better payoff if I confess or deny? (2) Assuming that Loren denies, do I get a better payoff if I confess or deny? Notice that Chris twice asks "What if Loren does this?" Chris's "what if" questions concern Loren's choices. If Chris's best strategy is to confess, regardless of whether Loren confesses or denies, confessing is Chris's dominant strategy.

Next, look at the payoff matrix from Loren's point of view. Let Loren ask the equivalent two questions. That is, let Loren ask "What if Chris does this or what if Chris does that?" Use Loren's answers to determine whether Loren has a dominant strategy. The combination of Chris's strategy and Loren's strategy comprises the equilibrium outcome of the game.

2. **THE PRISONERS' DILEMMA GAME AND THE REAL WORLD :** The key insight of the prisoners' dilemma game is the tension between the equilibrium outcome (in which both players' best strategy is to confess because they can't trust each other) and the fact that both players could make themselves better off if only they would cooperate. In a prisoners' dilemma game, the invisible hand breaks down because it is neither player's *self-interest* to cooperate if the other one cooperates This tension helps explain events in the real world. In particular, it is not uncommon for cartels to break apart, as individual producers cheat, and then reform, when all producers realize that being in the cartel is in their joint interest, only to break apart once again as yet another producer cheats. A cartel that can persist for years is without defections and failures is the exception not the rule!

Questions

■ True/False and Explain

What Is Oligopoly?

1. There are no barriers to entry in oligopoly.

2. An oligopolist will consider the reactions of its competitors before it decides to cut its price.

Oligopoly Games

3. In a one-time only prisoners' dilemma game, the best strategy for a prisoner is to confess only if the prisoner believes that the other player will confess.

4. If oligopolistic firms are able to sustain an output-restricting, price-increasing collusive agreement, they will produce the efficient level of output.

5. If two firms' decisions about whether to conduct R&D can be characterized as a game of chicken, the Nash equilibrium is for neither to conduct R&D.

Repeated Games and Sequential Games

6. Repeated games are more likely to have a cooperative equilibrium than one-time only games.

7. Price wars can break out when a small number of new firms enter an industry.

8. A single firm in a contestable market might be unable to make an economic profit.

9. Limit pricing refers to attempts by firms to set their price at the highest possible limit.

Antitrust Law

10. The Sherman Act prohibits conspiracies that restrict interstate trade.

11. The only situation in which price fixing among competitors is legal is if it is necessary to prevent a firm from going bankrupt.

12. Resale price maintenance might create efficiency if it induces dealers to provide the efficient standard of service when selling a product.

13. The larger the initial Herfindahl-Hirschman Index, the more likely the Federal Trade Commission is to allow a merger to take place.

■ Multiple Choice

What Is Oligopoly?

1. Suppose the efficient scale of production is such that a market has only three firms in it. This market is
   a. a three-firm monopoly.
   b. an economies-of-scale oligopoly.
   c. a cost-based oligopoly.
   d. a natural oligopoly.

2. Because an oligopoly has a small number of firms,
   a. each firm can act as a monopoly.
   b. the firms are interdependent.
   c. the firms may legally form a cartel.
   d. the HHI for the industry is small.

Oligopoly Games

3. In the prisoners' dilemma game with a Nash equilibrium,
   a. only one prisoner confesses.
   b. neither prisoner confesses.
   c. both prisoners confess.
   d. any confession is thrown out of court.

4. In a duopoly with a collusive agreement, when is the *industry-wide* economic profit as large as possible?
   a. When both firms comply with the collusive agreement.
   b. When one firm cheats on the cartel and the other firm does not.
   c. When both firms cheat on the collusive agreement.
   d. The answer is indeterminate because it depends on the industry's *MR* curve.

5. In a duopoly with a collusive agreement, when can *one firm* have the maximum possible economic profit?
   a. When both firms comply with the collusive agreement.
   b. When one firm cheats on the agreement and the other firm does not cheat.
   c. When both firms cheat on the agreement.
   d. The answer is indeterminate because it depends on the firm's *MR* curve.

Firms A and B are in a duopoly game, so they can either comply with a cartel agreement or cheat on the agreement. The cartel agreement calls for each firm to boost its price and restrict the amount it produces. For the next 4 questions, use the following payoff matrix that shows the firms' economic profits.

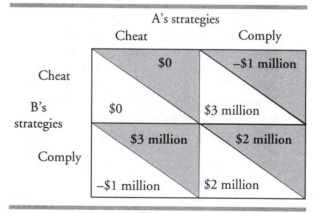

6. If firm A cheats on the cartel and firm B complies with the agreement, firm A's economic profit is
   a. $3 million.
   b. $2 million.
   c. zero.
   d. −$1 million.

7. If firm A cheats on the cartel and firm B complies with the agreement, firm B's economic profit is
   a. $3 million.
   b. $2 million.
   c. zero.
   d. −$1 million.

8. If this game is played only once,
   a. both firms A and B will cheat.
   b. firm A will cheat and firm B will not cheat.
   c. firm A will not cheat and firm B will cheat.
   d. neither firm A nor firm B will cheat.

9. The equilibrium in the previous question is called a
   a. credible strategy equilibrium.
   b. Nash equilibrium.
   c. duopoly equilibrium.
   d. cooperative equilibrium.

10. If an R&D game between two firms is a game of chicken, then the equilibrium has
    a. both firms conducting the R&D.
    b. neither firm conducting the R&D.
    c. one of the two firms conducting the R&D.
    d. a flaw because R&D *must* be done but the game's equilibrium is that it *might* be done.

Repeated Games and Sequential Games

11. A strategy in which a firm takes the same action that the other firm did in the last period is a
    a. dominant strategy.
    b. trigger strategy.
    c. tit-for-tat strategy.
    d. wimp's strategy.

12. Price wars can be the result of
    a. a cooperative equilibrium.
    b. a firm playing a tit-for-tat strategy in which last period the competitors complied with a collusive agreement.
    c. new firms entering the industry and immediately agreeing to comply with a collusive agreement.
    d. new firms entering an industry and all firms then finding themselves in a prisoners' dilemma.

13. Limit pricing refers to
    a. the fact that a monopoly firm always sets the highest price possible.
    b. a situation in which a firm might set a low price to keep potential competitors from entering its market.
    c. how the price is determined in a Nash equilibrium.
    d. none of the above.

Antitrust Law

14. Which of the following statements about the Sherman Act is correct?
    a. The Sherman Act was the second federal antitrust law.
    b. The Sherman Act legalized monopolization.
    c. The Sherman Act outlawed natural monopolies.
    d. The Sherman Act made restriction of interstate trade illegal.

15. All of the following are prohibited if they substantially lessen competition <u>EXCEPT</u>
    a. price discrimination.
    b. cutting prices to meet competition.
    c. contracts that prevent a firm from selling competing items (exclusive dealing).
    d. acquiring a competitor's shares or assets.

16. Tying arrangements are _____ illegal and _____ increase the firm's profit.
    a. always; always
    b. always; do not always
    c. not always; always
    d. not always; do not always

17. The Herfindahl-Hirschman index (HHI) in an industry is 900. A merger is proposed that will raise the HHI to 980. In this case, the
    a. Sherman Act will prohibit the merger.
    b. Federal Trade Commission will challenge the merger.
    c. Federal Trade Commission will not challenge the merger.
    d. rule of reason will prevent the merger if it is a merger among competitors.

■ **Short Answer Problems**

1. Explain why firms in oligopoly are interdependent while firms in perfect competition, monopolistic competition, and monopoly are not.

Payoff Matrix for Short Answer Problem 2

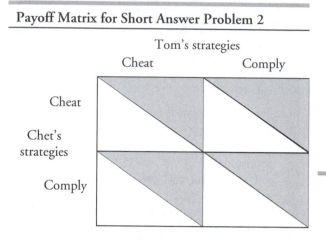

2. Two firms — Tom's Taxis and Chet's Cabs — are the only two taxicab companies in a small college town. These firms are engaged in a duopoly game. If they both adhere to a collusive agreement to restrict the number of their cabs and raise their price, each can make an economic profit of $2 million. However, if one company cheats on the agreement — by shading its price a bit and perhaps quietly acquiring some more taxis — and the other complies with the agreement, the cheater makes an economic profit of $2.5 million and the compiler incurs an economic loss of $1 million. If both cheat, both make $0 economic profit; that is, both make zero economic profit.

  a. Use the description of the situation to complete the payoff matrix above. Put Tom's payoffs in the darker triangles and Chet's in the other triangles.

  b. If this game is played only once, what is Tom's best strategy? What is Chet's best strategy? What will be the equilibrium outcome?

  c. When is the *joint* total profit the largest? When is Tom's profit the largest? Chet's profit?

3. Suppose that the taxi firm duopoly game played in problem 3 changes: The payoffs are the same as before except when one firm cheats and the other does not. Now the cheating firm makes an economic profit of $2.5 million, and the firm com-

Payoff Matrix for Short Answer Problem 3

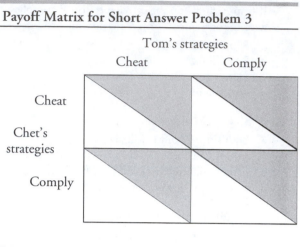

plying with the agreement makes an economic profit of $0.5 million.

  a. Complete the second payoff matrix for Problem 3 for the new taxi firm duopoly game.

  b. Does Tom have a clear-cut best strategy? Does Chet? Is there a clear equilibrium outcome in this game?

Payoff Matrix for Short Answer Problem 4

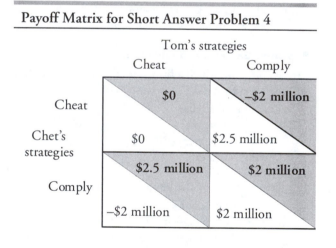

4. The taxi market changes again and the new payoff matrix is above. Chet and Tom now see that they will be playing a repeated game. Chet knows that Tom has adopted a tit-for-tat strategy. Last period Chet did not cheat on the cartel agreement.

  a. If Chet cheats this period, what is his economic profit? If he cheats this period, what is the maximum profit he can earn next period? What is his maximum two-period profit if he cheats?

b. If Chet complies with the agreement, what is the maximum economic profit he earns this period? If he complies next period, what will be his economic profit? If he does not cheat in either period, what is the two-period total economic profit he earns?

c. Is Chet likely to cheat this period? Why?

5. How can a price war that eliminates profits be explained with game theory?

6. We've met Igor in some past chapters. Igor has quit his job with his old master and now works for a new master: the Federal Trade Commission. Igor is overseeing a merger in the snake market. Currently, the snake market comprises 5 firms of equal size; that is, each firm has a 20 percent market share. Two firms are considering a merger so that after the merger the market will have 4 firms, one with a 40 percent share and 3 with 20 percent shares. Will Igor challenge the merger or will he allow it to slither through? Why or why not?

7. The two surviving producers of blank CDs agree to raise the price of their discs.

a. If both firms were breaking even (making zero economic profit) before they entered into this agreement, is the agreement legal?

b. If one of the firms would close in the absence of this agreement, is the agreement legal?

c. Under what conditions is the agreement legal? Why?

■ You're the Teacher

1. "I think our teacher sometimes says that efficiency means that helping someone without hurting someone else is impossible. I seem to remember this comment from our book. But does this mean that when there is inefficiency, we can take actions that help everyone?" This student is close to seeing an important point. If you already see the insight, explain it; if you don't quite see it, sneak a look at the answer...

Answers

■ True/False Answers

What Is Oligopoly?

1. **F** Oligopoly has only a small number of firms competing because barriers to entry prevent new firms from entering the market.

2. **T** This mutual interdependence makes oligopoly a difficult industry structure to analyze.

Oligopoly Games

3. **F** In a prisoners' dilemma game, the Nash equilibrium is for each player to confess.

4. **F** The collusive agreement described in the problem decreases output below its efficient level.

5. **F** In a game of chicken, the Nash equilibrium is for one firm to conduct R&D but it is not possible to predict which firm undertakes the R&D.

Repeated Games and Sequential Games

6. **T** Repeated games have strategies that are unavailable in games played only once, such as the tit-for-tat strategy. These new strategies often can result in the cooperative equilibrium. So, repeated games are more likely to have a cooperative equilibrium.

7. **T** When a small number of new firms enter a market, the firms might find themselves in a prisoners' dilemma in which competition forces the price of the product down.

8. **T** In a contestable market, if the firm sets its price so that it makes an economic profit, competitors enter the market.

9. **F** Limit pricing refers to the situation in which an established firm sets a low price in order to keep new competitors out of the market.

Antitrust Law

10. **T** Conspiracies that restrain trade are outlawed in the first section of the Sherman Act.

11. **F** Price fixing is automatically and always illegal.

12. **T** Resale price maintenance can lead to efficiency, as described in the question, but it can also lead to inefficiency if it enables dealers to operate as a cartel and charge the monopoly price.

13. **F** The *lower* the initial HHI, the more likely the Federal Trade Commission will not challenge a merger.

■ Multiple Choice Answers

What Is Oligopoly?

1. **d** A natural oligopoly occurs when the efficient scale of production is large enough so that the market can support only a small number of firms.

2. **b** The firms are interdependent because each firm's actions will affect its profit as well its competitors' profits.

Oligopoly Games

3. **c** Both players confess even though it is in their joint interest for neither to confess.

4. **a** The interest of the industry as a whole is to maintain the cartel.

5. **b** Each firm's individual interest is to be the lone cheater on the cartel agreement. Compare this answer to the previous answer.

6. **a** Firm A's profits are in the darkened triangle in the square at the lower left.

7. **d** Firm B's profits are in the white triangle in the square at the lower left.

8. **a** Both firms adopt the strategy of cheating.

9. **b** A Nash equilibrium occurs when each player takes the best action possible, given the action of the other player.

10. **c** In the Nash equilibrium, one firm conducts the R&D, even though the firm that does not conduct the R&D has a higher profit.

Repeated Games and Sequential Games

11. **c** Tit-for-tat implies that "I'll do to you what you did to me last time."

12. **d** Neither the new firms nor the old ones want a price war, but a prisoners' dilemma game might make a price war inevitable.

13. **b** Limit pricing can occur in contestable markets when the firm plays an entry deterrence game.

Antitrust Law

14. **d** The Sherman Act was the first federal antitrust law and outlawed restriction of interstate trade.

15. **b** Cutting prices to meet competition is legal and is a hallmark of competitive markets.

16. **d** Tying arrangements are illegal under the Clayton action *only if* they substantially lessen competition or create monopoly. Whether a tying arrangement allows a firm to increase its profit depends on the demand for the two products.

17. **c** Whenever the initial HHI is below 1,000, the U.S. Department of Justice will not contest a merger in the industry.

■ Answers to Short Answer Problems

1. Firms in oligopoly are interdependent because an oligopoly has only a small number of firms in the market. In this case, each firm's actions will affect its competitors' profits. In perfect competition and monopolistic competition, there are so many firms that any one firm's actions have no effect on its competitors. In monopoly, the firm has no competitors, so it is not interdependent with any other firm.

Short Answer Problem 2 (a)

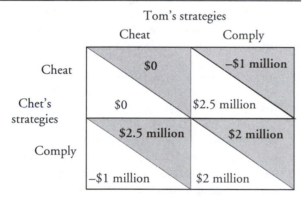

2. a. The payoff matrix is given above.
   b. Tom's best strategy is to cheat without regard to what Chet does. If Chet adheres to the agreement and does not cheat, Tom will cheat because his profit when cheating ($2.5 million) exceeds his profit when he does not cheat ($2 million). And, if Chet cheats, Tom also will cheat because his profit ($0) is higher than the loss he would incur by not cheating (–$1 million). Tom has a dominant strategy: cheat.
   In exactly the same way, Chet's profits are higher if he cheats regardless of what Tom does. So, Chet also has a dominant strategy of cheating. The Nash equilibrium outcome is for both Tom and Chet to cheat on the cartel agreement.

c. The industry's total profits are highest ($4 million) when neither Tom nor Chet cheat. Tom's profit is largest if he cheats and Chet does not. Similarly, Chet's profit is greatest if he alone cheats. Though each player's *individual* interest is to cheat, their *joint* interest is to comply.

Short Answer Problem 3 (a)

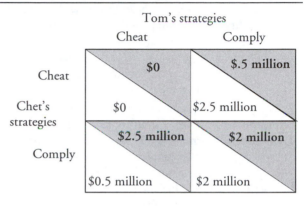

3. a. The new payoff matrix is given above.
   b. Tom and Chet no longer have a dominant strategy. In particular, if Chet complies with the agreement, Tom wants to cheat because in this case his profit by cheating ($2.5 million) exceeds his profit by complying ($2 million). But, if Chet cheats on the agreement, Tom will want to comply. If Chet is cheating, Tom earns a profit of $0.5 million by complying but $0 by cheating. Hence Tom's best strategy depends on what Chet does. Chet is in the same situation: His best strategy depends on what Tom does. Unlike the situation in problem 2, the outcome is not clear-cut. The equilibrium depends on which strategy Chet and Tom decide to pursue.

4. a. Last period Chet did not cheat, so Tom's tit-for-tat strategy means that Tom will not cheat this period. Because Tom will comply with the cartel agreement, Chet's profit this period by cheating is $2.5 million. Next period Tom will cheat because Chet cheated this period. Therefore next period the most profit that Chet can earn is $0 by also cheating. (If Chet complied with agreement and Tom cheated, Chet loses –$2 million.) Over the two periods, Chet's total profit if he cheats in the first period is $2.5 million.

b. If Chet does not cheat this period, this period he will earn $2 million. Because Chet complied with the agreement this period, Tom's tit-for-tat strategy means that next period Tom will comply with the agreement. Then, if Chet also complies next period, he will earn $2 million. By complying each period Chet earns a total of $4 million over the two periods.

c. Chet is not likely to cheat. If he does, his total profits over the two periods are significantly less than if he complies over the two periods. So players in a repeated game are more likely to reach the cooperative equilibrium than players in a one-time game.

5. Game theory explains price wars as the consequence of firms in a colluding industry responding to the cheating of a firm or as the response to new firms entering the industry. If one firm cheats by cutting its price, all other firms will cut their prices, and a price war ensues. After the price has fallen sufficiently (perhaps so the firms make zero economic profit), they have an incentive to rebuild their collusion. Alternatively, if new firms (or even just one) enter an industry, the old and new players might find themselves playing a prisoners' dilemma game. Neither set of firms wants the price to fall and profits to shrink, but they might be unable to collude successfully to keep the price and profit high.

6. Igor's decision whether to challenge the merger depends on the initial Herfindahl–Hirschman index (HHI) and the effect of the merger on the HHI.

Before the merger, HHI = 2,000, calculated from $20^2 + 20^2 + 20^2 + 20^2 + 20^2$. If the merger occurs, the HHI = 2,800, or $40^2 + 20^2 + 20^2 + 20^2$. This merger would increase the HHI by 800. If the initial HHI exceeds 1,800, any merger that raises it by 50 or more might be contested by the Federal Trade Commission. Consequently Igor will challenge this merger.

7. a. The agreement is illegal.

b. The agreement is illegal.

c. The agreement is *always* illegal. Section 1 of the Sherman Act makes price fixing among competitors *always* illegal without consideration of the firms' profits or losses.

■ You're the Teacher

1. "Yeah, you're right: When there is inefficiency, we can take actions that help everyone! The idea is that inefficiency means a deadweight loss. When we remove the inefficiency, we eliminate the deadweight loss. That serves as a bonus — something that we can spread around and make everyone better off."

"Look, a numerical example will make this point a lot clearer. Take some industry. Suppose that consumer surplus would be $200 and producer surplus would be $100, for a total surplus of $300 if this industry is perfectly competitive. However, suppose that this industry is a monopoly. Then consumer surplus is, say, $80 and producer surplus is $150. In this case, the total surplus is $230 and the deadweight loss (the difference between the two total surpluses) is $70."

"Now, if we broke up the monopoly and made the industry perfectly competitive, we'd get a total surplus of $300. It would include a consumer surplus of $200 (so that consumers would gain $120, the new consumer surplus of $200 minus the current consumer surplus of $80) and a producer surplus of $100 (so that producers would lose $50, the difference between the current producer surplus of $150 minus the new producer surplus of $100). But suppose that we took away, say, $75 of the gain from consumers and gave it to producers. Then consumers would still be better off because their new consumer surplus would be $125, as compared to only $80 when the industry was a monopoly. And producers would also be better off because their producer surplus would be $175 versus only $150 as a monopoly. You see, with this redistribution, *both* consumers and producers can be better off when the industry is perfectly competitive!"

"Okay, I'll agree that this outcome is unrealistic because we've assumed that we can redistribute the gain as we want. If we didn't do any redistribution and just broke up the monopoly, consumers would gain ($120) and producers would lose ($50). But what this story shows is important anyway: Whenever there is inefficiency, it can be eliminated and *everyone* made better off. You know, now that I think about it, it's my guess that this is why our teacher likes the idea of efficiency so much!"

Chapter Quiz

1. In a duopoly game that is repeated many times, each player tries to
   a. maximize the industry's total profit.
   b. minimize the other player's profit.
   c. maximize its market share.
   d. maximize its profit.

2. Which of the following is <u>NOT</u> a feature possessed by *all* games?
   a. Nash equilibrium
   b. rules
   c. strategies
   d. payoffs

3. Which of the following firms is best described as an oligopoly?
   a. New Balance, one of many shoe manufacturing firms.
   b. Tampa Electric, the only distributor of electricity in Tampa, Florida.
   c. Doria's Dairy, one of the thousands of dairy farmers.
   d. Intel, one of the only two producers of CPU chips used in computers.

4. Which of the following statements about oligopoly is correct?
   a. The prisoners' dilemma shows that the Nash equilibrium is the best outcome for both players.
   b. In an R&D game of chicken, the equilibrium has both firms conducting the R&D.
   c. Oligopoly is similar to monopolistic competition because each firm's actions affect only its profit and have no effect on its competitors' profits.
   d. A repeated game makes it more likely for the players to reach the cooperative equilibrium.

5. To cheat on a collusive agreement, a firm
   a. exits the market.
   b. sets the same price as would a monopoly.
   c. does not raise its price as high as agreed upon.
   d. produces less output than agreed upon.

6. In a prisoners' dilemma game, the Nash equilibrium is that
   a. both prisoners deny involvement.
   b. both prisoners confess.
   c. one prisoner confesses and the other prisoner denies involvement.
   d. None of the above answers is correct because there is no Nash equilibrium for a prisoners' dilemma game.

7. If one firm and only that firm in a cartel cheats on a collusive agreement, its profits _____ and the profits of the other firms _____.
   a. rise; rise
   b. rise; fall
   c. fall; rise
   d. fall; fall

8. If two firms in a duopoly enter into a collusive agreement, the firms agree to _____ their outputs and _____ their prices.
   a. increase; lower
   b. increase; raise
   c. decrease; raise
   d. decrease; lower

9. When each player selects his or her best strategy taking as given what the other player will do, the resulting equilibrium is called a
   a. cooperative equilibrium.
   b. tit-for-tat equilibrium.
   c. Nash equilibrium.
   d. trigger strategy equilibrium.

10. A strategy in which a player cooperates in the current period if the other player cooperated in the previous period, but cheats in the current period if the other player cheated in the previous period is called a
    a. tit-for-tat strategy.
    b. trigger strategy.
    c. duopoly strategy.
    d. dominant firm strategy.

The answers for this Chapter Quiz are on page 346

Mid-Term Examination

■ **Chapter 10**

1. Partners in a partnership have _____ liability and shareholders in a corporation have _____ liability.
   a. limited; limited
   b. limited; unlimited
   c. unlimited; unlimited
   d. unlimited; limited

2. An economically efficient method of production
   a. is always technologically efficient.
   b. lies below the production function.
   c. lies below the supply curve.
   d. may not always be technologically efficient.

3. An electrician quits her current job, which pays $30,000 per year. She can take a job with another firm for $40,000 per year or work for herself. The opportunity cost of working for herself is
   a. $10,000.
   b. $30,000.
   c. $40,000.
   d. $70,000.

4. In their relation to a firm's managers, shareholders act
   a. as agents.
   b. as principals.
   c. in loco parentis.
   d. as a cabinet for advice.

5. If the cost of producing a unit of a good falls as more is produced, there are are said to _____ and in this case it is likely that _____ will coordinate economic activity.
   a. economies of scale; firms
   b. lower transactions costs; markets
   c. lower transactions costs; firms
   d. economies of scope; markets

■ Chapter 11

6. If a firm's marginal product of labor is greater than its average product of labor, then an increase in its use of labor necessarily will

   a. reduce its total product.
   b. raise its average product of labor.
   c. raise its marginal product of labor.
   d. not change its average product of labor.

7. The additional cost of producing an additional unit of output is the firm's

   a. *MC.*
   b. *ATC.*
   c. *AVC.*
   d. *AFC.*

8. In general, diseconomies of scale occur

   a. as output expands at low levels of production.
   b. through the entire range of production.
   c. as output expands at high levels of production.
   d. whenever the slope of the total product curve is positive.

9. The intersection of the *MC* and *ATC* curves is the point at which

   a. average total cost is minimized.
   b. average variable cost is minimized.
   c. average fixed cost is minimized.
   d. total product is maximized.

10. A firm's average total cost, *ATC,* is $30, its fixed cost, *FC,* is $200, and its production, *Q,* is 10. What is its variable cost, *VC?*

    a. $400
    b. $100
    c. $20.
    d. More information is needed to determine the firm's variable cost.

■ Chapter 12

11. In perfect competition, which is the case?

    a. A firm can influence the price of the good.
    b. There are many sellers.
    c. There are restrictions on entry.
    d. All firms sell a slightly different product.

12. To increase its profit, a firm will decrease its output as long as its

    a. average total revenue exceeds its average total cost.
    b. average total revenue exceeds its average variable cost.
    c. marginal cost exceeds its marginal revenue.
    d. marginal revenue exceeds its marginal cost.

13. At a firm's shutdown point, its minimum average variable cost equals its
    a. average total cost.
    b. average fixed cost.
    c. price.
    d. None of the above.

14. A perfectly competitive firm finds that at its current output, $MR = MC$ and $P > ATC$. Then this firm will
    a. expand its output and lower its price.
    b. reduce its output and raise its price.
    c. shut down.
    d. not change its output nor its price.

15. A perfectly competitive firm _____ earn an economic profit in the short run and _____ earn an economic profit in the long run.
    a. can; can
    b. can; cannot
    c. cannot; can
    d. cannot; cannot

■ **Chapter 13**

16. Public franchises are _____ barriers to entry and patents are _____ barriers to entry.
    a. legal; legal
    b. legal; natural
    c. natural; natural
    d. natural; legal

17. The demand curve for a monopoly
    a. lies above its marginal revenue curve.
    b. lies on its marginal revenue curve.
    c. lies below its marginal revenue curve.
    d. is horizontal.

18. When a single-price monopoly is maximizing its profit, then the level of output it produces is
    a. efficient because profit is maximized.
    b. inefficient.
    c. efficient because $MR = MC$.
    d. efficient because costs are minimized.

19. If a natural monopoly is regulated using an average cost pricing rule, the firm _____ and _____ the efficient quantity of output.
    a. earns an economic profit; produces
    b. earns an economic profit; does not produce
    c. incurs an economic loss; produces
    d. earns a normal profit; does not produce

20. A monopoly _____ earn an economic profit in the short run and _____ earn an economic profit in the long run.

    a. can; can

    b. can; cannot

    c. cannot; can

    d. cannot; cannot

■ Chapter 14

21. An industry with many firms, each making a differentiated product is _____ industry.

    a. a perfectly competitive

    b. a monopolistically competitive

    c. an oligopoly

    d. a monopoly

22. When firms in a monopolistically competitive industry incur economic losses, firms will

    a. enter the industry, and demand will increase for the original firms.

    b. exit the industry, and demand will increase for the remaining firms.

    c. exit the industry, and demand will decrease for the remaining firms.

    d. enter the industry, and demand will decrease for the original firms.

23. To maximize its profit, a firm in monopolistic competition produces so that

    a. $P > ATC$.

    b. $MR = MC$.

    c. $P = ATC$.

    d. $MR > MC$.

24. Advertising expenditures are fixed costs. Advertising can wind up lowering the markup and the price.

    a. Both sentences are correct.

    b. The first sentence is correct and the second is incorrect.

    c. The first sentence is incorrect and the second is correct.

    d. Both sentences are incorrect.

15. A monopolistically competitive firm _____ earn an economic profit in the short run and _____ earn an economic profit in the long run.

    a. can; can

    b. can; cannot

    c. cannot; can

    d. cannot; cannot

■ Chapter 15

26. A cartel is a group of firms which agree to

    a. behave competitively.

    b. decrease their production and raise the price of their good.

    c. increase their production and lower the price of their good.

    d. decrease their production and lower the price of their good.

27. The cooperative strategy in the prisoners' dilemma game results in
    a. both players winning.
    b. both players losing.
    c. the first player to take an action winning.
    d. the last player to take an action winning.

28. In a prisoners' dilemma, oligopoly game in which the two firms have the choice to comply with a collusive cartel agreement or cheat on the agreement, in the Nash equilibrium _____ and the equilibrium outcome _____ the best outcome for the players.
    a. both players comply with the agreement; is
    b. both players comply with the agreement; is not
    c. one player complies with the agreement and the other player cheats on the agreement; is not
    d. both players cheat on the agreement; is not

29. Which of the following activities is *always* illegal?
    a. attempts to monopolize by any firm
    b. price discrimination
    c. acquiring a competitor's assets
    d. price fixing by competing firms

30. Which of the following is *always* illegal?
    a. Coke lowers the price of a case of its soda to $4.75 in order to meet Pepsi's price of $4.75 for a case.
    b. Coke lowers the price of a case of its soda to $4.50 in order to beat Pepsi's price of $4.75 for a case.
    c. Pepsi and Coke agree to charge $6 for a case of soda.
    d. Pepsi signs a deal with Burger King that only Pepsi products will be sold at Burger King.

Answers

■ Mid-Term Exam Answers

1. d;   2. a;   3. c;   4. b   5. a;   6. b;   7. a;   8. c;   9. a;   10. b;
11. b;   12. c;   13. c;   14. d   15. b;   16. a;   17. a;   18. b;   19. d;   20. a;
21. b;   22. b;   23. b;   24. a;   25. b;   26. b;   27. a;   28. d;   29. d;   30. c.

Chapter 16 PUBLIC CHOICES AND PUBLIC GOODS

Key Concepts

■ Public Choices

All economic choices are made by individuals but some are private choices and some are public choices. Private choices affect only the person making the choice. **Public choices** affect many people and perhaps the entire society. Decisions made by people in the government are often public choices.

Market failure occurs when the market produces an efficient amount of output. Sometimes public choices can correct that inefficiency. But **government failure**, a situation in which government actions lead to inefficiency, can also occur.

To analyze choices made by people in the government, economists have developed a public choice theory of the political marketplace. Four groups of decision makers interact in the political marketplace: Voters, firms, politicians, and bureaucrats. Some voters and forms lobby politicians for policies that benefit the voter or the firm. Politicians seek votes in order to remain in office. Bureaucrats try to maximize the budgets of their agencies. In the political equilibrium the choices of voters, firms, politicians, and bureaucrats are all compatible and no group can see a way of improving its position by making a different choice.

A good, service, or resource can be classified as either

♦ **Excludable** — it is possible to prevent someone from enjoying the good's benefit, or

♦ **Nonexcludable** — it is impossible (or extremely costly) to prevent anyone from benefiting from the good.

and as either

♦ **Rival** — one person's use of the good decreases the quantity available for someone else, or

♦ **Nonrival** — one person's use of the good does not decrease the quantity available for someone else.

A **private good** is rival and excludable; a **public good** is nonrival and nonexcludable. a **common resource** is rival and nonexcludable; and, a natural monopoly is nonrival, so the marginal cost of another person using it is zero, and excludable.

Another type of good is a mixed good. A **mixed good** is a private good the production or consumption of which creates an externality. An **externality** is a cost (external cost) or a benefit (external benefit) that arises from the production or consumption of a private good and that falls on someone other than its producer or consumer.

Public goods, mixed goods, common resources, and natural monopoly goods all require public choices to overcome inefficiency problems. The market economy underprovides public goods and goods with external benefits. It overprovides goods with external costs and overuses common resources.

■ Providing Public Goods

A free rider is a person who consumes a good or service without paying for it. Because public goods are nonexcludable, they create a **free-rider problem**, that the economy would provide an inefficiently small quantity of a public good.

Just as the case for a private good, a person's marginal benefit from a public good decreases as more of the good is consumed. Because everyone consumes the same units of a public good, the marginal social benefit of a public good is the sum of the marginal benefits of all individuals at *each quantity*. Hence the marginal social benefit curve from a public good is equal to the *vertical* sum of each person's marginal benefit curve. (This construction contrasts with the marginal social benefit curve for a private good. Because each unit of a private good is consumed by one person, the marginal social benefit curve is constructed by adding the quantities each person consumes at each marginal social benefit. That is, the marginal social benefit curve is the *horizontal* sum of each person's marginal benefit curve.)

The *efficient quantity* of a public good is the amount that sets the marginal social benefit of another unit equal to the marginal social cost of supplying it.

♦ With private provision, free riding limits the amount produced and results in an inefficiently low level of output.

♦ Government provision can attain efficiency because free riding is prevented by imposing taxes to finance production of the good.

Politicians often follow the principle of minimum differentiation:

♦ **Principle of minimum differentiation** — the tendency for competitors (political parties) to make themselves similar in order to appeal to the maximum number of clients or voters.

FIGURE **16.1**
A Public Good

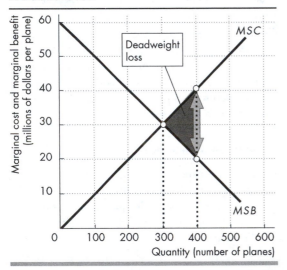

♦ If voters are well informed, politicians won't allow bureaucrats to expand expenditure beyond the efficient level. In Figure 16.1, the efficient quantity, 300 airplanes, is provided.

♦ Voters might be rationally ignorant by deciding *not* to acquire information because the (personal) cost of acquisition is larger than the (personal) expected benefit from the information. If voters are rationally ignorant, politicians, influenced by bureaucrats and lobbyists representing special interests, might inefficiently overprovide the public good. In Figure 16.1, 400 airplanes might be provided even though, as the grey arrow shows, $MSB < MSC$ and a deadweight loss is created.

■ Positive Externalities: Education and Health Care

Most of the goods and services provided by the government are mixed goods not public goods.

♦ **Marginal private benefit** (*MB*) — the benefit that the consumer of a good or service receives from an additional unit of it.

♦ **Marginal external benefit** — the benefit from an additional unit of a good or service that people other than its consumer enjoy.

♦ **Marginal social benefit** (*MSB*) — the marginal benefit enjoyed by the entire society, both by the consumer and by everyone else. In an equation, $MSB = MB +$ Marginal external benefit.

FIGURE **16.2**
A Mixed Good With an External Benefit

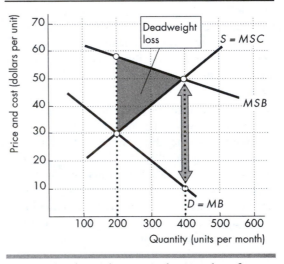

Figure 16.2 shows the marginal private benefit curve, which is the demand curve and is labeled $MB = D$. The marginal social benefit curve is labeled *MSB*. The marginal external benefit is the vertical distance between the two curves, equal at 400 units to the length of the double headed arrow, $40 per unit. The supply curve is the same as the marginal social cost curve and is labeled $S = MSC$. The efficient quantity is 400 units, where the *MSC* and *MSB* curves intersect. The equilibrium quantity is 200 units, where the *D* and *S* curves intersect. A deadweight loss is created because less than the efficient quantity is produced.

The government has three methods it can use to attain a more efficient outcome when external benefits exist:

♦ **Public provision** — a public authority that receives

its revenue from the government can produce the good or service. An example if a state university that provides education. In Figure 16.2, the government can produce the efficient quantity, 400. It then sets the price equal to $10 per unit to insure that demanders buy 400 units.

- Private subsidies — a **subsidy** is a payment from the government to the private producers. A subsidy decreases producers' costs and thereby increases the quantity produced.

- Vouchers — a **voucher** is a token that the government provides to households, which they can use when they buy specified goods or services. In Figure 16.2, a voucher equal to the length of the double headed arrow, $40 per unit, would shift the demand curve so that the equilibrium quantity is the same as the efficient amount, 400 units.

Though all three methods can be used to overcome the market failure with a mixed good, not all three necessarily will work equally well. Public provision has the problem that the bureaucrats in charge have the same incentive to maximize their budget and overprovide the good or service. A private subsidy means that a bureaucrat must decide how much of a given budget will be devoted to the subsidy and how much to administrative costs. Economists generally favor vouchers: there is little incentive to and bureaucratic budgets; there is little incentive for consumers to lobby for larger vouchers; and if there is competition among producers, there is large incentive for the producers to provide a quality product to attract the consumers.

Health care comprises two different products: Health insurance and health-care services. Health care has external benefits: health care, such as a flu shot, help limit the spread of infectious diseases; healthy neighbors and co-workers are more pleasant to deal with; and, for many people living in a society that gives older and poorer people access to health care is desirable. In the United States, In the United States, there is both underprovision of health care services (because private choices do not reflect the external benefits) and overprovision (because private health-care providers decide how much to produce and then the government pays them for the quantity of services they have produced). Compared to the systems in Canada and the United Kingdom, the U.S. system is more costly but health outcomes are comparable.

Helpful Hints

1. **THE MARGINAL SOCIAL BENEFIT FROM A PUBLIC GOOD :** The properties of nonrivalry and nonexcludability associated with public goods imply that the marginal social benefit curve for a public good is constructed differently from that for private goods.

A private good is rival in consumption. To obtain the marginal social benefit curve, we sum the individual marginal benefit curves *horizontally*. For instance, at a price of $8 you demand 5 units and I demand 5 units. Because the goods are rival in consumption, none of the 5 units you consume can be the same as any of the 5 units I consume. So, we sum the *quantities* and at $8, in total we demand 10 units—5 for you and 5 for me. Therefore for 10 units the *MSB* is $8.

For the economy's marginal social benefit curve for a public good, we sum the individual marginal benefit curves *vertically*. For instance, for the 5th unit you are willing to pay $8 and I am willing to pay $8. If 5 units are provided, because the public good is nonrival, the 5 units that you consume are precisely the same as the 5 units that I consume. So, we sum the *prices* at 5 units. In total we are willing to pay is $16—you p[ay $8 and I pay $8. So for this public good, for 5 units the *MSB* is $16.

The key difference — that for a public good we consume the same units but for a private good we must consume different units — is the reason that the marginal social benefit curve for a public good is derived differently than the marginal social benefit curve for a private good. However, while the curves are derived differently, they both show the benefit to society of an additional unit of the good.

2. **PUBLIC GOODS AND GOVERNMENT PROVIDED GOODS :** Not all goods provided by the government are public goods. A public good is defined by the characteristics of nonrivalry and nonexcludability, not by whether it is publicly provided. For example, some cities and communities provide swimming pools; others provide utility services such as electricity. None of these are public goods even though they are provided by the government because they are all excludable. Indeed, in many other communities, the same services are provided by the private sector.

Questions

■ True/False and Explain

Public Choices

1. Because you are a member of the public, your decision to buy a pizza is a public choice.

2. In the political marketplace, voters and firms demand policies.

3. A public good is nonexcludable and nonrival.

4. A movie shown in an uncrowded movie theater is both nonexcludable and nonrival.

5. A fish in the middle of the ocean is a common resource.

6. Externalities can arise from both production and consumption.

7. Flu vaccination is an example of a good with an external benefit.

Providing Public Goods

8. Public goods face the free-rider problem.

9. A person's marginal benefit from a public good increases as more of the good is consumed.

10. The marginal social benefit curve for a public good is obtained the same way as the marginal social benefit curve for a private good.

11. A private market produces less than the efficient quantity of pure public goods.

12. Government failure generally leads to underprovision of public goods.

13. Rational ignorance is the situation wherein politicians are uninformed about certain voters' desires.

Positive Externalities: Education and Health Care

14. Any good supplied by government is a public good.

15. If a good has an external benefit, the marginal social benefit exceeds the marginal private benefit.

10. The private market produces more than the efficient amount of a good having an external benefit.

11. A subsidy can be the appropriate public policy for a good or service with an external benefit.

12. Taxing *private* producers of education helps overcome the inefficiency in the market for education.

19. A problem with vouchers is that each consumer who receives a voucher has a strong incentive to lobby for overprovision of the good.

20. Even though health care is a mixed good, most nations leave the delivery of health care services to the private market.

■ Multiple Choice

Public Choices

1. Public choices _____ lead the government to produce more than the efficient quantity of a good, a situation which, when it occurs, is called _____.
   a. can; market failure
   b. can; government failure
   c. cannot; market failure
   d. cannot; government failure

2. In the political marketplace, which of the following groups lobby for policies that will help them?
   i.   politicians
   ii. voters
   iii. firms
   iv. bureaucrats
   a. iii only
   b. ii and iv
   c. i and iv
   d. ii and iii.

3. If one person's consumption of a good does not decrease the quantity available for everyone else, the good is
   a. excludable.
   b. nonexcludable.
   c. rival.
   d. nonrival.

4. Which of the following is rival and nonexcludable?
   a. A public good
   b. A common resource
   c. A private good
   d. A natural monopoly

5. Which of the following is rival and excludable?
   a. A public good
   b. A common resource
   c. A private good
   d. A natural monopoly

6. Of the following, which an example of public good?
   a. The defense services provided by a new stealth bomber
   b. A pair of pants
   c. A cable television system
   d. An uncrowded theme park such as Walt Disney World

7. An externality can be a cost or benefit arising from the production of a good that falls upon
   a. consumers but not producers.
   b. producers but not consumers.
   c. the consumer and the producer both.
   d. someone other than the consumer or producer.

8. Of the following, which is the best example of mixed good or service?
   a. A fast food taco
   b. Education
   c. A dam
   d. An uncrowded public beach

Providing Public Goods

9. A free rider is someone who
   a. does not pay taxes.
   b. cannot be excluded from consuming a public good even though he or she did not pay for the good.
   c. paid more than his or her fair share for the provision of a public good.
   d. cannot be forced to pay for his or her consumption of a private good.

10. The economy's marginal social benefit curve for a public good is obtained by summing the individual
    a. marginal cost curves horizontally.
    b. marginal cost curves vertically.
    c. marginal benefit curves horizontally.
    d. marginal benefit curves vertically.

11. The efficient amount of a public good
    a. is as much as the public demands.
    b. cannot be provided unless the tragedy of nonexcludability is overcome.
    c. is the amount that has the marginal social benefit exceeding the marginal social cost by as much as possible.
    d. is such that the marginal social benefit equals the marginal social cost.

12. Suppose that the marginal social benefit from another unit of a public good exceeds the marginal social cost of producing it. The quantity produced
    a. equals the efficient quantity.
    b. exceeds the efficient quantity.
    c. is less than the efficient quantity.
    d. might exceed, be less than, or equal to the efficient quantity but because the good is a public good, more information is needed.

13. Governments often provide public-goods such as national-defense because
    a. governments know how to produce these goods.
    b. of the free-rider problems that result in underproduction by private markets.
    c. people do not value national defense very highly.
    d. of the potential that private firms will make excess profits.

14. The idea that political parties will have similar policy proposals reflects
    a. free riding.
    b. rational ignorance.
    c. government failure.
    d. the principle of minimum differentiation.

15. Amy realizes that her personal benefit from becoming an expert on welfare reform is limited, so she does not learn about this issue. Amy's decision reflects
    a. the rival nature of information.
    b. the nonexcludability principle.
    c. the principle of minimum differentiation.
    d. rational ignorance.

16. The efficient quantity of a public good is likely to be provided if
    a. voters are well informed.
    b. rational ignorance is combined with special interest lobbying.
    c. politicians are well informed.
    d. bureaucrats are rationally ignorant.

Positive Externalities: Education and Health Care

17. The marginal private benefit from a good is $24 and marginal external benefit is $6. The *MSB* equals
    a. $30.
    b. $18.
    c. $4.
    d. None of the above answers are correct.

Use Table 16.1 for the next four questions.

TABLE **16.1**

Multiple Choice Questions 18, 19, 20, 21

Quantity	Marginal private cost (dollars)	Marginal private benefit (dollars)	Marginal social benefit (dollars)
500	$5	$9	$11
550	6	8	10
600	7	7	9
650	8	6	8
700	9	5	7

18. Table 16.1 represents the market for a good with
    a. only an external cost.
    b. only an external benefit.
    c. both external costs and benefits.
    d. no externalities.

19. With no government policy, the equilibrium quantity is
    a. 550.
    b. 600.
    c. 650.
    d. 700.

20. The efficient level of output is
    a. 550.
    b. 600.
    c. 650.
    d. 700.

21. What can the government do so that the efficient amount is produced?
    a. Subsidize suppliers $8 per unit.
    b. Subsidize suppliers $2 per unit.
    c. Tax suppliers $2 per unit.
    d. Tax suppliers $8 per unit.

22. If the government is making a payment to the private producers of a mixed good with an external benefit, the government is
    a. engaged in public production of the good.
    b. giving the producers a voucher.
    c. taxing the private producers.
    d. giving the private producers a subsidy.

23. A problem with public provision of a mixed good with an external benefit is that
    a. the cost of the production might be inefficiently too high.
    b. the producers might demand a larger subsidy.
    c. the producers are likely to lobby the consumers to buy more of the good.
    d. the producer has the incentive to produce at the minimum cost.

24. Vouchers _____ the demand for the good and _____ each individual consumer the incentive to lobby for overprovision of the good.
    a. increase; give
    b. increase; do not give
    c. decrease; give
    d. decrease; do not give.

■ **Short Answer Problems**

1. What is the difference between a private choice and a public choice?

2. What is market failure? What is government failure?

3. Explain the nonrivalry and nonexcludability features of a public good. Why are both necessary for the good to be a public good?

4. What is the free-rider problem? For what type of goods is the free-rider problem particularly acute? Why does free riding hinder private firms from producing the efficient amount (or any amount!) of a public good?

TABLE **16.1**

Security at Parkin Springs Apartments

Number of guards	Total cost of guards (dollars)	Marginal benefit per resident (dollars)	Marginal social benefit to all residents (dollars)
1	$300	$10	$____
2	600	4	____
3	900	3	____
4	1,200	2	____

5. Parkin Springs Apartments has 100 residents who all are concerned about security. Table 16.1 gives the total cost per day of hiring a 24-hour security

guard service and the marginal benefit per day to each of the residents.

  a. Why is a security guard a public good for the residents of Parkin Springs Apartments?

  b. Why will no guards be hired if each of the residents must act individually?

  c. Complete the last column of Table 16.1 by computing the marginal social benefit of security guards to all the residents combined.

6. Continuing problem 5, suppose that the residents form an Apartment Council that acts as a governing body to address the security issue.

  a. What is the efficient number of guards?

  b. How might the Apartment Council pay for the guards it will hire?

7. The ships of 10 companies must navigate a treacherous section of coastline. Each year each shipping line incurs $200,000 in shipping costs from ships running aground there. If a lighthouse was built, these costs would fall to zero. Building and maintaining the lighthouse would cost $1,900,000 a year. If it was constructed, *all* the ships that pass that way would benefit from the lighthouse and none would run aground. The ships do not dock anywhere nearby so they cannot be charged for using the lighthouse.

  a. From society's point of view, is building the lighthouse efficient?

  b. From a company's point of view, if each company pays ¹/10 the total cost of building a lighthouse, is building it profitable?

  c. Suppose that the lighthouse was constructed but that one company did not help pay for it. What is the company's profit from the lighthouse?

  d. Based on your answers to parts (b) and (c), what incentive does each company have?

8. Explain why voter ignorance might be rational.

9. At public colleges and universities, governments provide education at a price (tuition) less than cost. What economic argument supports the policy of charging students at public universities less than the full cost of their education?

10. Vaccination creates an external benefit and has no external costs. Use Figure 16.3 to illustrate the market for chicken pox vaccination. In the figure, arrange your curves so that 50 million doses will be taken in the absence of any government intervene

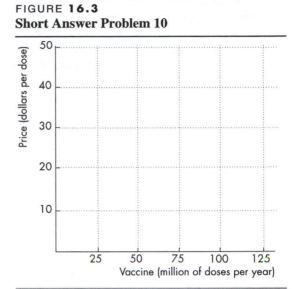

FIGURE 16.3
Short Answer Problem 10

tion and 75 million doses is the efficient number of doses. Illustrate the deadweight loss in the figure. How can the government move this market toward efficiency?

TABLE 16.2
Education in Transylvania

Quantity (number of students)	Marginal private benefit (dollars)	Marginal private cost (dollars)	Marginal social benefit (dollars)
1	$500	$200	$800
2	400	250	700
3	300	300	600
4	200	350	500
5	100	400	400
6	0	450	300

11. The first two columns of Table 16.2 give the demand schedule, the marginal private benefit, for education in Transylvania and the third column gives the marginal private cost. Education generates external benefits so the marginal social benefit shown in the last column is greater than marginal private benefit. Education creates no external costs.

  a. What equilibrium price and quantity would result if the market for education is unregulated?

  b. What is the efficient quantity of students in Transylvania?

c. In an attempt to address the inefficient level of education in his nation, Igor — the newly appointed minister of education — has decided to provide a low-cost public university, Igor Omphesus (Igor's middle name is Omphesus) University. To attain the efficient level of schooling, what must tuition be at the new university, I.O.U.?

d. What is the marginal cost of schooling the last student at this university?

■ You're the Teacher

1. "I heard my bio teacher talking about 'herd immunity,' when a bunch of people or animals are immune to disease. That sure sounded a lot like some of the stuff we are talking about but I just can't get the connection." Can you help out your friend by relating the concept of herd immunity to the concept of an external benefit?

Answers

■ True/False Answers

Public Choices

1. **F** Your decision to buy a pizza is a private choice because it affects only you not the public at large.

2. **T** On the other side of political marketplace, politicians and bureaucrats supply policies.

3. **T** The question gives the definition of a public good.

4. **F** The movie is nonrival but not nonexcludable because a theater can easily exclude people who do not pay to see the movie.

5. **T** The fish is rival, because if one person catches it another cannot, and nonexcludable, because the people cannot prevent the other from trying to catch it.

6. **T** Externalities can arise from both production and consumption and can be either benefits or costs.

7. **F** Flu vaccination is a good example of good with an external benefit.

Providing Public Goods

8. **T** Public goods are nonexcludable and therefore face a severe free-rider problem.

9. **F** Like the marginal benefit from a private good, the marginal benefit from a public good decreases as more of the good is consumed.

10. **F** The marginal social benefit curve for a public good is derived by adding *vertically* each individual's marginal benefit curve; the marginal social benefit curve for a private good is derived by adding *horizontally* each person's marginal benefit curve.

11. **T** Because of the free-rider problem, a private unregulated market produces less than the efficient amount of a public good.

12. **F** Government failure leads to the *overprovision* of public goods.

13. **F** Rational ignorance occurs when a voter is uninformed about an issue because the benefit to the voter of becoming informed is less than the cost to the voter.

Positive Externalities: Education and Health Care

14. **F** Public goods are characterized by nonrivalry and nonexcludability *not* by government supply. Most goods supplied by the government are mixed goods.

15. **T** The marginal social benefit equals the marginal private benefit plus the marginal external benefit.

16. **F** The private market produces *less* than the efficient amount of a good with an external benefit.

17. **T** Left alone, the private market would produce less than the efficient amount of the good. A subsidy will increase the amount produced.

18. **F** Education has an external benefit, so the right policy is to subsidize, not tax, education.

19. **F** Because vouchers are generally spread over many consumers, any one consumer does *not* have the incentive to lobby to overprovide the good.

20. **F** Health care is a mixed good, but most nations do not leave its provision to the private market.

■ Multiple Choice Answers

Public Choices

1. **b** Public choices are frequently made by the government and in some situations can lead to inefficient overprovision of a good or service, that is, can create government failure.

2. **d** Voters and firms lobby politicians and bureaucrats for policies that help them.

3. **d** The good is nonrival because many people can simultaneously consume the same unit of the good.

4. **b** A common resource, such as fish in the ocean, is rival and nonexcludable.

5. **c** Private foods are rival and excludable; most goods are private goods.

6. **a** The defense services are nonrival and nonexcludable and so are a public good.

7. **d** Answer (d) is correct because an externality falls upon someone who is neither the producer nor consumer of the good or service.

8. **b** Education is a mixed good because people other than the educated student gain from that student's education so education has an external benefit.

Providing Public Goods

9. **b** This answer is the definition of a free rider.

10. **d** Vertical summation shows the price everyone in total is willing to pay for any particular quantity.

11. **d** If the marginal social benefit from *any* good equals the marginal social cost, the efficient amount is produced.

12. **c** If one more unit is produced, the gain to society (the marginal social benefit) exceeds the cost to society (the marginal social cost), so total surplus increases if another unit is produced.

13. **b** The free-rider problem limits the private market's ability to produce the efficient amount of public goods.

14. **d** Both parties want to appeal to a majority of voters in order to be elected. So to appeal to voters, both present similar proposals, which is the principle of minimum differentiation.

15. **d** Amy is pursuing her own self-interest and rationally decides not to become an expert on welfare reform.

16. **a** If voters are well informed, they can ensure that politicians force bureaucrats to provide the efficient amount of the public good.

Positive Externalities: Education and Health Care

17. **a** $MSB = MB$ + Marginal External Benefit, so MSB is $24 + $6 = $30.

18. **b** At any level of output, the marginal social benefit exceeds the marginal private benefit, which indicates that there must be an external benefit.

19. **b** The private market produces the level of output that equalizes the marginal private cost (the private supply curve) and the marginal private benefit (the private demand curve).

20. **c** Efficiency requires that the amount of the good produced equalize the marginal social cost and the marginal social benefit. In this case, efficiency requires that output be 650.

21. **b** If suppliers are granted a $2 per unit subsidy, the marginal private cost schedule drops by $2 at every unit of output. Hence to produce 650 units of output, the new marginal private cost becomes $6. This equals the marginal private benefit of 650 units, so the (new) equilibrium price is $6 and the quantity produced is the efficient amount, or 650 units.

22. **d** This question defines what a subsidy is.

23. **a** For example, the cost per student when education is publicly provided at public colleges is much higher than the comparable cost at private colleges.

24. **b** Vouchers help pay part of the price of the good and thereby increase the demand for it. But because vouchers are spread out over millions of consumers, no one consumer has a strong financial interest in lobbying for overprovision of the good.

■ Answers to Short Answer Problems

1. A private choice is a choice made by an individual that affects that person only. A public choice is a choice that affects many people, perhaps the entire economy.

2. Market failure occurs when an unregulated private market fails to produce the efficient quantity of output, thereby creating a deadweight loss. Government failure occurs when government actions lead to an inefficient quantity of production, thereby also creating a deadweight loss.

3. A good has the nonrivalry feature if its consumption by one person does not reduce the amount available for others. The nonexcludability feature means that if the good is produced and consumed by one person, others cannot be excluded from consuming it. Both characteristics are necessary for the good to be a public good. The nonrivalry feature of a public good means that everyone can consume the good simultaneously. Limiting the consumption to one person at a time would be inefficient because others can consume the product without denying it to anyone else. In addition, private goods are sold by firms so that the firms' owners can earn an income and thereby purchase goods and services for themselves. Public goods are nonexcludable, which means that anyone can consume the product regardless of the amount paid. This fact gives people the incentive to free ride. Free riding makes the provision of such goods by private companies unlikely because the firm will not be able to collect any revenue from selling the product.

4. The free-rider problem is that people will try to avoid paying for a public good. In unregulated markets the free-rider problem results in the production of too little of a public good because there is little

incentive for individuals to pay for it. The free rider will not pay because that payment will likely have no perceptible effect on the amount the person will be able to consume. Hence avoiding payment is rational. This incentive creates a problem for the private sector when it attempts to provide the product. In particular, suppliers — firms — produce goods in exchange for payments because the suppliers want to use their income to buy goods and services for themselves. If people do not pay for the goods, suppliers receive no income and hence have no incentive to produce the goods.

5. a. A security guard is a public good because the guard's services are nonrival and nonexcludable. Employment of the guard involves nonrivalry because one resident's consumption of the security provided does not reduce anyone else's security. Nonexcludability is involved because, once a security guard is in place, all residents enjoy the increased security and none can be excluded.

    b. If each resident must act individually to hire a security guard none will be hired because each resident receives only $10 in benefit from the first guard, who costs $300 per day.

TABLE 16.2

Short Answer Problem 5

Number of guards	Total cost of guards (dollars)	Marginal benefit per resident (dollars)	Marginal social benefit to all residents (dollars)
1	$300	$10	$1,000
2	600	4	400
3	900	3	300
4	1200	2	200

    c. The entries in the last column of Table 16.2 show the marginal social benefit. These answers are obtained by multiplying the marginal benefit per resident by the number of residents, 100. This multiplication is the numerical equivalent of summing the individual marginal private benefit curves vertically for each quantity of guards.

6. a. If the apartment council hires the number of guards that sets the marginal social benefit equal to the marginal social cost, it will hire the efficient number of guards. The marginal social benefit of the third guard, $300, equals the mar-

ginal social cost, $300, so the efficient number of guards is 3.

    b. The apartment council might pay for the guards by collecting a security fee of $9 per day from each of the 100 residents in order to hire two security guards.

7. a. Yes, building the lighthouse is efficient. The marginal social benefit from the lighthouse is the saving in shipping costs because of its existence. Each firm would save $200,000 annually, so society as a whole would save $2,000,000 annually. The marginal social cost of building and running the lighthouse is $1,900,000 annually, so, on balance, society would be better off by $100,000 a year if the lighthouse was constructed.

    b. Yes, building the lighthouse would be profitable. The company would incur a cost of $190,000, its $1/10$ share of the cost. But the company would save $200,000 in shipping costs. So, on balance, each company comes out $10,000 ahead.

    c. After the lighthouse is built, the company would save $200,000 in shipping costs. If the company did not help pay for the lighthouse, its profit would increase by $200,000.

    d. Each company has the incentive to free ride, that is, to not pay for the lighthouse. If the company can avoid payment, its profit increases by $200,000, but if it must pay its $1/10$ share of the cost, its profit increases by only $10,000.

8. Most issues have only a small and indirect effect on most voters. So for a voter to spend much time and effort to become well informed about such issues would be irrational because the additional cost incurred *by the voter* would exceed any additional benefit enjoyed *by the voter*. Only if the voter is significantly and directly affected by an issue does becoming well informed pay. As a result, most voters will be rationally ignorant about any specific issue.

9. The economic argument is that education generates external benefits. In particular, when individuals are educated, society at large receives benefits beyond the private benefits that accrue to those choosing how much education to obtain. The presence of the external benefit means that in the absence of government intervention, the private sector would provide too little education. To attain efficiency in the market for education, the government provides below-cost education at public colleges and universities.

FIGURE **16.4**
Short Answer Problem 10

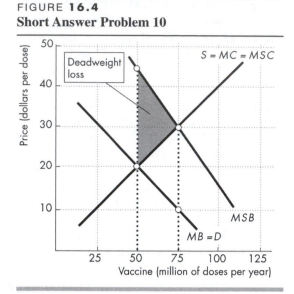

10. Figure 16.4 shows the market for chicken pox vaccine. Because there are no external costs, the marginal social cost curve equals the marginal private cost curve, which is the same as the supply curve. This curve is labeled $S = MC = MSC$ in the figure. It also is the private supply curve. However, the presence of the external benefit means that the marginal social benefit (MSB) curve lies right of the marginal private benefit curve, which is the same as the private demand curve (labeled $MB = D$). The vertical distance between the curves equals the marginal externality; that is, it is the additional (external) benefit to society over and above the benefit to the consumer. In the absence of government intervention, 50 million doses of vaccine are produced but the efficient amount is 75 million doses. To move this market closer to the efficient level of output, the government might subsidize production. This policy could take the form of subsidizing producers $20 per does. The aim is to lower the costs of the private producers so that the efficient quantity of vaccines, 75 million doses, is produced. Consumers would pay a price $10 per dose and the remainder of the producers' costs, $20 per does, is covered by the subsidy. Alternatively, the government might buy 75 million doses and then resell them to consumers below cost at $10 per dose, the price necessary to induce consumers to buy 75 million doses.

11. a. In an unregulated market, the equilibrium price and quantity are determined by the intersection of the marginal private benefit and marginal private cost curves because these are the market's demand and supply curves, respectively. Thus the equilibrium price is $300, and the equilibrium quantity is 3 students.

b. The efficient quantity is determined by the intersection of the marginal social cost and marginal social benefit curves. Because there are no external costs, the marginal private cost equals the marginal social cost. As a result, efficiency is attained at a quantity of 5 students attending college.

c. Igor wants 5 students to attend his new university, I.O.U. Five students will attend only when the tuition is $100.

d. When 5 students attend the university, the marginal cost of the 5th student is $400. By charging the student only $100 in tuition, Igor apparently is losing money on this student. However, the loss is only apparent: Five students are the efficient level of education because the *total* marginal social benefit from the 5th student is $400, which equals the marginal cost of educating this student.

■ **You're the Teacher**

1. "The idea of 'herd immunity' means that someone is less likely to get sick if he or she associates with people who are immune to the disease. Herd immunity is actually what vaccinations try to create: If enough people get vaccinated against a disease, it makes it a lot less likely that anyone else will catch the disease. And that's the basic idea of the external benefit behind vaccinations. If you get, say, vaccinated against polio, you won't be giving polio to me and that's the external benefit of your polio vaccination. And if enough of us all get vaccinated against polio, it becomes really unlikely that *any* of us will get polio because of the external benefit."

Chapter Quiz

1. An example of mixed good or service is
   a. a new purse, which was imported from another country.
   b. electricity whose generation emits pollution.
   c. watching a movie in a non-crowded theater.
   d. an economics textbook.

2. If a good has an external benefit, a market left unregulated will produce
   a. more than the efficient amount.
   b. the efficient amount.
   c. less than the efficient amount.
   d. an amount that may be more than, less than, or equal to the efficient amount depending on how large the external benefit is relative to the private benefit.

3. The relationship between marginal private benefit (MB), marginal external benefit, and marginal social benefit (MSB) is
   a. $MB = MSB$ + marginal external benefit.
   b. marginal external benefit = $MB + MSB$.
   c. $MSB = MB$ + marginal external benefit.
   d. None of the above answers is correct.

4. Which of the following goods is nonexcludable?
   a. a lighthouse
   b. pay-per-view television
   c. a restaurant meal
   d. a college education

5. A public good is necessarily
   a. nonrival and nonexcludable.
   b. nonrival and excludable.
   b. rival and nonexcludable.
   d. rival and excludable.

6. Of the goods and activities listed below, the best example of a public good is
   a. a tuna in the ocean.
   b. national defense.
   c. building a large apartment for low-income families.
   d. producing paper for use in newspapers.

7. When a student makes a decision about how much schooling to acquire, the student considers only the
   a. private marginal benefits and private marginal costs.
   b. social marginal benefits and social marginal costs.
   c. marginal external benefits and marginal external costs.
   d. private marginal benefits and social marginal costs.

8. What characteristic of a public good makes free riding possible?
   a. The nonrival characteristic.
   b. The rival characteristic.
   c. The nonexcludable characteristic.
   d. The excludable characteristic.

9. The free-rider problem for a public good means that
   a. a private market provides less than the efficient amount of the good.
   b. a private market provides more than the efficient amount of the good.
   c. the good is rival.
   d. the good is excludable.

10. Who might opt to be rationally ignorant?
    a. Special interest groups
    b. Voters
    c. Politicians
    d. Bureaucrats

The answers for this Chapter Quiz are on page 346

Chapter 17 EXTERNALITIES AND THE ENVIRONMENT

■ Negative Externalities: Pollution

Air pollution is an example of environmental problems. The trends in air pollution show decreasing pollution.

The costs of producing a good or service that creates pollution can be divided into the costs paid by the (private) producers and the costs paid by everyone else.

♦ **Marginal private cost** (*MC*) — the cost of producing an additional unit of a good or service that is borne by the producer of the good or service.

♦ **Marginal external cost** — the cost of producing an additional unit of a good or service that falls on people other than the producer.

♦ **Marginal social cost** (*MSC*) — the marginal cost incurred by the society, that is, by the producer and by everyone else on whom the cost falls.

In an equation, *MSC* = *MC* + Marginal external cost.

Figure 17.1 shows the marginal cost curve, which is the private supply curve, labeled *MC* = *S,* and the marginal social cost curve, labeled *MSC*. The marginal external cost is the vertical distance between the two curves equal at 300 units per day to the length of the grey arrow. The demand curve is the same as the marginal social benefit curve and is labeled *D* = *MSB*.

In the figure, the efficient quantity is 200 units per day, where the *MSC* and *MSB* curves intersect, and the equilibrium quantity is 300 units per day, where the *D* and *S* curves intersect. A deadweight loss is created because more than the efficient amount is produced.

The inefficiency from an external cost can be reduced by establishing a property right; by mandating use of clean technology; or by taxing or pricing pollution.

♦ **Property rights** — legally established titles to the ownership, use, and disposal of factors of production and goods and services.

When property rights are established and enforced, the private producers face the pollution cost they create.

FIGURE **17.1**
A Good With an External Cost

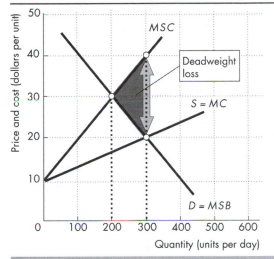

Firms can respond by using an **abatement technology** (a production technology that reduces or prevents pollution) or by producing less and thereby polluting less.

♦ **Coase theorem** — the proposition that if property rights exist, if only a small number of parties are involved, and transactions costs are low, then private transactions are efficient. **Transactions costs** are the opportunity costs of conducting a transaction. The Coase theorem implies that, regardless to whom the property right is given (the polluter or the victim), as long as a property right is granted, the efficient level of pollution results.

Regulation by mandating limits on pollution or mandating the abatement technology that must be used is a common government response to pollution. Economists point out that abatement is not always the least-cost solution to the external cost produced by pollution.

Governments can also impose taxes or use cap-and-trade:

♦ Taxes — the government can levy a tax on producers equal to the marginal external cost. Such a tax is called a **Pigovian tax.** Imposing a tax equal to the marginal external cost increases firms' costs and shifts the private supply curve so that it is the same as the marginal social cost curve, *MSC*.

♦ Cap-and-Trade — each polluter is given a pollution limit. If it reduces its pollution below this limit, it can sell the "excess" reduction to other firms who, once they own the permit, then do not need to reduce their pollution by the amount of the permit. Marketable permits provide a sharp incentive to find technologies that reduce pollution.

■ The Tragedy of the Commons

Common resources create the **tragedy of the commons**, the overuse of a common resource because its users have to incentive to conserve the resource and use it sustainably and efficiently. The decline in fishing stocks is an example of the tragedy of the commons.

The sustainable catch of fish (or of any renewable resource) is the quantity that can be caught so that the stock either grows or remains constant. Figure 17.2 illustrates that as the fish stock initially increases the sustainable catch increases but eventually as the stock increases still more, food for the fish becomes scarce so the sustainable catch decreases. If more than the sustainable catch is caught, the stock decreases.

Use of a common resource has an external cost.

♦ Each fisher's marginal private cost, *MC*, is the costs paid by the fisher. The *MC* increases as more fish are caught. These costs determine the fisher's supply and the fishers' supplies together determine the market supply, *S* in Figure 17.3.

♦ Each fisher imposes an external cost on other fishers because each fisher's catch decreases the stock of fish and makes it more difficult for other fishers to catch fish. This marginal external cost increases as more fish are caught.

♦ The marginal social cost, *MSC*, is the sum of the private *MC* plus the marginal external cost. In Figure 17.3, the *MSC* curve lies above the *MC* curve by the amount of the marginal external cost,

♦ The marginal social benefit from fish is equal to the marginal private benefit, so the *MSB* curve is the same as the demand curve.

The unregulated market equilibrium is the quantity at which the marginal private cost equals the marginal social benefit, *MC* = *MB*. In Figure 17.3, the unregulated catch is 30 thousand tons per year.

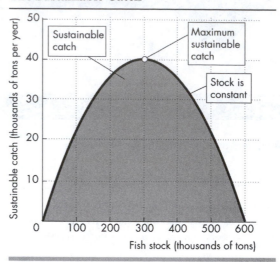

FIGURE 17.2
The Sustainable Catch

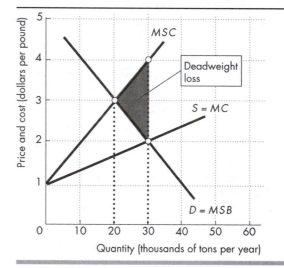

FIGURE 17.3
A Common Resource

The efficient quantity is the amount that sets the *MSC* equal to the *MSB*, which in Figure 17.3 is 20 thousand tons per year. The resource is over-used and, as illustrated, there is a deadweight loss from the overuse.

Three main methods can be used to bring about the efficient use of a common resource:

♦ *Property rights* — By assigning a property right to the resource, so that someone owns it, the owner will use the resource efficiently. The owner takes account of the fact that an additional user increases the costs of all the previous users, so that the owner's *MC* is the same as the *MSC*. In this situation the market supply curve is the same as the *MSC* curve and the market equilibrium is efficient. Assigning property rights has worked in some cases, such as with the frequency spectrum. But it is difficult to assign property rights to some common resources, such as air or fish.

♦ *Production quotas* — A production quota is an upper limit to the quantity of the resource that may be used. The government can set a quota for use of the resource at the efficient quantity. Quotas have two drawbacks: first, everyone wants to cheat on the quota; and, second, the marginal costs of the different users are different, so more efficient producers might not receive a larger share of the quota.

♦ *Individual transferable quotas*— The government could grant **individual transferable quotas** (**ITQ**), which are production limits assigned to individuals who are free to transfer the quota to someone else. The market price of an ITQ equals the marginal private benefit at the quota quantity minus the marginal cost of using the resource. In Figure 17.3, if the quota is 20 thousand tons of fish, the market price of an ITQ is $1.33 per pound − $3.00 per pound minus $1.67 per pound. Producers still have the incentive to cheat on the quota with ITQs.

Helpful Hints

1. **OIL AS A COMMON RESOURCE :** Oil is generally found in pools underground. The oil is a common resource: Anyone who owns ground above the pool can drill as many wells as wished, so the resource is nonexcludable. But if one user extracts a barrel of oil, there is less available for the others, so the resource is rival. If the oil in a pool is extracted too rapidly, the maximum amount of oil that can ultimately be recovered is reduced. The tragedy of the commons can occur if all the users pump as rapidly as possible from as many wells as possible. In this case, the total amount of oil recovered will be lower than if the oil is pumped more slowly. One solution to this commons problem is to give one land owner, or a group of land owners, a property right to the oil. In this case, just as the Coase theorem predicts, the oil is withdrawn from the ground at the rate that maximizes the total amount of oil that will be recovered.

Questions

■ True/False and Explain

Negative Externalities: Pollution

1. The costs imposed by pollution are examples of external costs.

2. If the production of a good involves an external cost, the marginal social cost exceeds the marginal private cost.

3. The vertical distance between the *MSC* curve and the *MC* curve is equal to the marginal external cost.

4. When external costs are present, the private market produces less than the efficient level of output.

5. The Coase theorem states that if property rights exist and transactions costs are low, there will be no externalities regardless of who owns the property rights.

6. The inefficiency created by a negative production externality can be overcome if the government subsidizes production of the good.

7. Taxes and a cap-and-trade policy can be used by the government to cope with the problem of pollution.

The Tragedy of the Commons

8. The tragedy of the commons is that people use an inefficiently small quantity of the common resource.

9. As additional people use a common resource, the marginal private benefit for the initial users decreases.

10. For a common resource, the marginal private benefit from using the resource exceeds the marginal social benefit.

11. The efficient use of a common resource requires using the resource to the point where the *MSC* of using the resource equals the *MSB* of the resource.

12. Assigning a property right is a potential method that can lead to the efficient use of a common resource.

13. The price of an ITQ equals the difference between the marginal private benefit at the quota quantity minus the marginal cost of using the resource.

■ Multiple Choice

Negative Externalities: Pollution

1. The marginal cost of the 100th ton of paper is $80 and the marginal external cost is $30. The marginal social cost is
   a. $110.
   b. $50.
   c. $2,400.
   d. None of the above answers are correct.

Use Figure 17.4 for the next five questions.

FIGURE **17.4**
Multiple Choice Questions 2, 3, 4, 5, 6

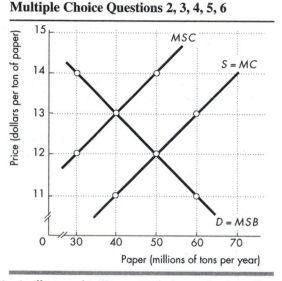

2. As illustrated in Figure 17.4, the production of paper creates
   a. only an external benefit.
   b. only an external cost.
   c. both external benefits and costs.
   d. no externalities.

3. The amount of the externality in Figure 17.4 is
   a. $14 per ton.
   b. $12 per ton.
   c. $2 per ton.
   d. $0 per ton because no externality is produced.

4. In the absence of any government intervention, how many tons of paper are produced in a year?
   a. 60 million tons
   b. 50 million tons
   c. 40 million tons
   d. 30 million tons

5. The efficient amount of paper produced in a year is
   a. 60 million tons.
   b. 50 million tons.
   c. 40 million tons.
   d. 30 million tons.

6. What amount of tax is necessary to lead to production of the efficient amount of paper?
   a. $14 a ton
   b. $12 per ton
   c. $2 per ton
   d. Zero because the efficient amount is produced without any government intervention.

7. A copper ore refiner pollutes the water upstream from a brewery. The transactions costs of reaching an agreement between the two are low. When will the amount of copper refining be at its efficient level?
   a. If the property right to the stream is assigned to the ore refiner but not if it is assigned to the brewery.
   b. If the property right to the stream is assigned to the brewery but not if it is assigned to the ore refiner.
   c. Whenever the property right to the stream is assigned to *either* the refiner or the brewer.
   d. None of the above because there is no such thing as the efficient level of copper refining since refining copper creates pollution.

8. Economists point out that direct regulation of pollution by the government
   a. is the most efficient way to deal with the external costs from pollution.
   b. is almost always combined with the assignment of property rights.
   c. can require that firms use abatement even if the technology is not the least-cost solution.
   d. None of the above answers are correct.

9. Production of rubber for sneakers creates an external cost of $2 per ton of rubber. What government tax or subsidy program will lead to the efficient amount of rubber being produced?
   a. A subsidy of more than $2 per ton of rubber.
   b. A subsidy of $2 per ton of rubber.
   c. A tax of more than $2 per ton of rubber.
   d. A tax of $2 per ton of rubber.

The Tragedy of the Commons

10. The tragedy of the commons is the absence of incentives to
    a. correctly measure the marginal cost.
    b. prevent under use of the common resource.
    c. prevent overuse and depletion of the common resource.
    d. discover the resource.

11. For a common resource such as fish, the marginal private cost of an additional fisher is _____ the marginal social cost of an additional fisher.
    a. less than
    b. equal to
    c. greater than
    d. not comparable to

12. For a common resource, the equilibrium with no government intervention is such that _____ equals _____.
    a. marginal private benefit; marginal social cost
    b. marginal social benefit; marginal social cost
    c. marginal private benefit; marginal social benefit
    d. marginal social benefit; marginal private cost

13. For a common resource, efficiency requires that the _____ equals the _____.
    a. marginal private benefit; marginal private cost
    b. marginal social benefit; marginal social cost
    c. marginal private benefit; marginal social benefit
    d. marginal social cost; marginal private cost

14. For a common resource, unregulated equilibrium quantity is _____ the efficient quantity and _____ deadweight loss is created.
    a. greater than; a
    b. equal to; no
    c. less than; a
    d. greater than; no

15. If the government assigns private property rights to a common resource, then the
    a. resource is under-utilized.
    b. marginal private cost becomes equal to the marginal social cost.
    c. government needs to set a quota to achieve efficiency.
    d. None of the above answers is correct.

16. When individual transferable quotas are used in the market for a common resource, the market price of an ITQ is equal to the
    a. marginal private benefit at the quota quantity.
    b. marginal social benefit at the quota quantity.
    c. marginal private benefit at the quota quantity minus the marginal private cost.
    d. marginal social benefit at the quota quantity minus the marginal private cost.

■ **Short Answer Problems**

FIGURE 17.5
Short Answer Problem 1

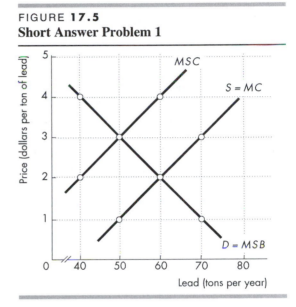

1. Figure 17.5 shows the market for lead. The production of lead creates pollution. What is the efficient quantity? If the market is left unregulated, what is the equilibrium quantity? How much is the deadweight loss and illustrate it in the figure.

2. Farmer Dave's and farmer Mark's farms are next to each other. They get along well so transactions costs are low. The only problem in their existence is Dave's pig, Riblet, who occasionally gets into Mark's corn field and eats the corn. If Riblet did not get into the corn, he would eat valueless garbage, not the corn. A fence can keep Riblet out of the corn. Suppose that Riblet eats $350 of corn per year and that to erect a fence to keep Riblet off Mark's farm costs $250 per year. Either Dave or Mark can erect the fence and, once the fence is in place, Riblet eats none of the corn.

Property rights that allow Riblet to roam free, or, alternatively, that keep Mark's farm free from Dave's pig, have yet to be assigned

a. Suppose that the property right is given to Dave, so that Riblet can roam free any time he desires. Will Mark erect a fence?

b. Now suppose that the property right is given to Mark, so that he can charge Dave whenever Riblet shows up on Mark's farm and eats the corn. Will Dave erect a fence?

c. What general proposition is illustrated in this question?

3. Explain how a tax can be used to achieve efficiency in the face of external costs.

4. In a small town two factories — factory A and factory B — each produce 10 units of pollution so that the total pollution is 20 units. Factory A can decrease its pollution at a constant marginal cost of $50 per unit; factory B can reduce its pollution at a constant marginal cost of $100 per unit.

a. If both factories A and B decrease their pollution by 5 units, what is the total amount of pollution in the town and what is the total cost of reaching this level of pollution?

b. If factory A decreases its level of pollution by 10 units and factory B does not decrease its pollution, what is the total amount of pollution in the town and what is the total cost of achieving this level of pollution?

c. From a social standpoint, to reach a total of 10 units of pollution, which is more desirable: both factories cutting back by 5 units each or A cutting back by 10 units and B not cutting back? Why?

d. Suppose that the EPA determines that the efficient level of pollution is 10 units. The EPA introduces a cap-and-trade policy and grants each firm 5 marketable permits. Each permit allows the firm to produce 1 unit of pollution. What is likely to occur? In particular, will factory A or B want to sell its permits to the other factory and is the other factory willing to buy them? If there is a potential buyer and seller of the permits, what is the price range in which the permits will trade?

e. From a social standpoint, what has the cap-and-trade policy accomplished?

6. What is the tragedy of the commons and why does it occur? Give an example of how the tragedy of the commons affects the world's fisheries.

7. Why are some common resources, such as fish, subject to the tragedy of the commons while other common resources, such as a gold mine, are not? In your answer be certain to use the term "property rights."

8. For a common resource, why does the marginal private cost not equal the marginal social cost? Which is larger?

FIGURE **17.6**
Short Answer Problem 9

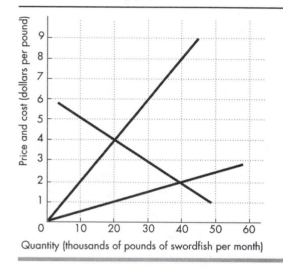

Quantity (thousands of pounds of swordfish per month)

9. Figure 17.6 shows the marginal social cost, marginal private cost, and marginal social benefit curves for swordfish, which are a common resource. Label each curve.

a. What is the equilibrium quantity of swordfish caught? What is the efficient quantity of swordfish caught? Illustrate the deadweight loss.

b. If the government sets a production quota, what quota achieves the efficient outcome? At this quota amount, what is the profit margin on a pound of swordfish? What incentive does this profit margin create?

c. If the government issues individual transferable quotas (ITQ) and limits the catch to the efficient quantity, what is the market price of an ITQ?

■ **You're the Teacher**

1. "I just don't understand some of this stuff. I mean, even after the government taxes a product with pollution, there's still an external cost. I mean, that's

got to mean that there's some pollution, right? I mean, come on, pollution is bad; we don't want any of it. I mean, the best level of pollution has to be zero, right?" Aside from having a severe "I mean" problem, this student also has a severe prob-lem understanding that the efficient level of pollu-tion is not zero. You probably can't do anything about the "I mean" problem, but you should be able to help the student grasp why zero pollution is not desirable.

Answers

■ True/False Answers

Negative Externalities: Pollution

1. **T** The costs of pollution are external costs because they are costs of production that are not paid by the producers.

2. **T** The marginal social cost equals the marginal private cost plus the marginal external cost. If there is a marginal external cost then the marginal social cost exceeds the marginal private cost.

3. **T** At any quantity, the difference between the marginal social cost and the marginal private cost is the marginal external cost.

4. **F** The existence of external costs means that the private market produces *more* than the efficient amount of the good.

5. **T** The question essentially is the definition of the Coase theorem.

6. **F** If production of a good creates an external cost, to attain efficiency its production needs to be taxed, not subsidized.

7. **T** Both Pigovian taxes and cap-and-trade are methods the government can use to overcome the inefficiency from a negative production externality such as pollution.

The Tragedy of the Commons

8. **F** The tragedy of the commons is that an inefficiently *large* quantity of the common resource is used.

9. **T** For instance, as more people fish in an area, the catch of all the initial fishers decreases.

10. **T** The marginal social benefit takes account of the fact that an additional user of a resource decreases the quantity that all previous users of the resource obtain.

11. **T** Efficient use of *any* resource requires that the *MSC* equal the *MSB*.

12. **T** Assigning a property right, establishing a quota, and assigning individual transferable quotas are three methods that can lead to the efficient use of a common resource.

13. **T** Because the ITQ can be sold, less efficient users will sell their ITQs to more efficient users, which leads to the efficient use of a common resource.

■ Multiple Choice Answers

Negative Externalities: Pollution

1. **a** The *MSC* equals the *MC* plus the marginal external cost.

2. **b** Because the *MSC* curve is above the *MC* curve, the figure shows that paper production creates an external cost.

3. **c** The vertical distance between the *MSC* curve and the *MC* curve is the marginal external cost, which in this case is $2 per ton for every ton.

4. **b** In the absence of any intervention, the private market produces where the demand curve (which is the same as the marginal private benefit curve) intersects the supply curve (which is the same as the marginal private cost curve).

5. **c** Efficiency requires that production be the amount for which marginal social cost, *MSC*, equals marginal social benefit, *MSB*.

6. **c** The tax must shift the private *MC* curve until it is the same as the *MSC* curve. Imposing a $2 tax shifts the *MC* curve by the amount of the tax, $2, which is the amount desired. By imposing a tax equal to the marginal external cost, the new marginal private cost, which includes the tax, is the same as the marginal social cost.

7. **c** The Coase theorem shows that when transactions costs are low and the number of parties involved is small, to whom a property right is assigned makes no difference: The externality will be eliminated and the efficient level of production will result.

8. **c** Government agencies often do not have the knowledge necessary to choose the least-cost solution to the problems created by pollution.

9. **d** Imposing a tax equal to the marginal external cost sets the marginal private cost, *including* the tax, equal to the marginal social cost, thereby ensuring that the efficient amount of rubber will be produced.

The Tragedy of the Commons

10. **c** The tragedy of the commons is that common resources are used too intensively.

11. **a** Each additional fisher decreases the stock of fish, thereby making it more costly for the other fishers to catch fish. The increased cost imposed on the other fishers is an external cost.

12. **d** An unregulated equilibrium is the quantity that sets the marginal private benefit, which equals the marginal social benefit, equal to the marginal private cost, which does *not* equal the marginal social cost.

13. **b** The efficient quantity sets the marginal *social* benefit equal to the marginal *social* cost.

14. **a** The unregulated equilibrium for a common resource is that the resource is over used. The equilibrium quantity is greater than the efficient quantity and hence a deadweight loss is created.

15. **b** Once property rights are assigned, the marginal private cost equals the marginal social cost and the efficient quantity of the common resource is used.

16. **c** The price equals the value of the ITQ, the marginal private benefit at the quota quantity minus the cost of using the resource, which is the marginal private cost.

■ Answers to Short Answer Problems

FIGURE **17.7**
Short Answer Problem 1

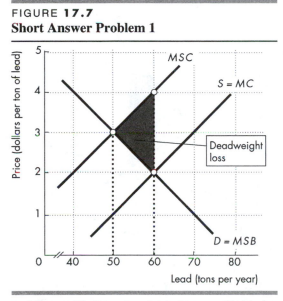

1. The equilibrium quantity is 60 tons of lead, determined by the intersection of the demand and supply curves. The efficient quantity is 50 tons of lead, determined by the intersection of the marginal social benefit and marginal social cost curves. The deadweight loss is the triangle illustrated in Figure 17.7. The area of the triangle is ½ × base × height. The base is 10 tons of lead. The height is $2 per ton

of lead, the difference between the marginal social cost of another ton of lead and the marginal social benefit from another ton. So the deadweight loss is equal to ½ × 10 tons × $2 per ton = $10 million.

2. a. Farmer Mark will erect the fence. Doing so costs him $250 a year, but it saves him the $350 Riblet would otherwise eat.

   b. Farmer Dave will erect the fence. If he did not do so, Riblet would eat $350 worth of corn, and Mark would bill Dave for the corn. Thus erecting the fence costs Dave $250 a year, but saves him $350 for a net gain of $100.

   c. These answers illustrate the Coase theorem. Erecting the fence is efficient because the cost to society of the fence, $250, is less than the benefit to society of the fence, $350 saved by preventing the pig from eating the corn. As the Coase theorem points out, regardless of whether Dave or Mark is given the property right, the fence is erected and Riblet dines on valueless garbage rather than valuable corn.

3. The existence of external costs means that producers do not take into account all costs when deciding how much to produce. If a tax is levied that is exactly the amount of the external cost, the cost is no longer external. As a result, the producer takes it into account and so is induced to produce the efficient quantity.

4. a. The total amount of pollution is 10 units, 5 remaining units from factory A and 5 remaining units from factory B. The total cost of achieving this level of pollution is $750, the cost of $250 incurred by factory A plus the cost of $500 incurred by factory B.

   b. The total amount of pollution (again) is 10 units, comprising no pollution from factory A and 10 units from factory B. The total cost of attaining this level of pollution is $500, all incurred by factory A.

   c. From a social standpoint, having factory A decrease its pollution by 10 units and factory B do nothing is the most efficient because it has the lowest total social cost, $500 versus $750 for an equal reduction at each factory. Eliminating the 10 units of pollution by having only A cut back has inflicted the lowest possible total cost on society, which is a desirable outcome.

   d. Factory A will sell its permits to factory B. This

transaction will occur because decreasing its pollution is less expensive for factory A than it is for factory B. In particular, the price of a permit for a unit of pollution will range between $50 and $100. For any price greater than $50, factory A is willing to sell its permits and reduce its pollution because this transaction is profitable: The cost to A is $50 per unit of pollution eliminated but, as long as the price exceeds $50, factory A profits. Factory B is willing to buy permits for any price less than $100 because buying permits at this price reduces B's costs. For each permit that B can buy, it saves $100 by not having to decrease its pollution. As long as the price of a permit is less than $100, buying the permits reduces B's costs.

  e. With a cap-and-trade policy only factory A decreases its pollution. Factory B does not lower its pollution but instead buys permits from factory A. With a cap-and-trade policy we obtain, as in part (c), the socially desirable outcome: Factory A decreases its pollution and factory B does not.

6. The tragedy of the commons is that there is no incentive to prevent the overuse and depletion of a commonly used resource. For instance, as more boats fish, the stock of fish is decreased so that the cost to the other boats of catching fish increase. But no individual fisher takes account of the increase in the costs for the other fishers because each person is concerned about what he or she catches As a result, additional fishers continue to fish until their marginal private cost equals the marginal (social) benefit of fishing. Each fisher considers only his or her marginal private cost. With this many people fishing, the marginal social cost is greater than marginal social benefit and the fish stock is depleted. In other words, the tragedy of the commons strikes the world's fishing stocks.

7. The marginal private cost of using a common resource does not equal the marginal social cost because the marginal private cost does not take account of the (external) effect that using the resource has on others. As a common resource is used more intensively, each additional person's use increases everyone else's cost of using the resource. But the marginal private cost ignores the increase in other people's costs. The marginal social cost takes account of both the added cost to the new user (the marginal private cost) *and* the increase in everyone

else's cost. So the marginal social cost is greater than the marginal private cost.

8. The tragedy of the commons applies to common resources, which are resources that are nonexcludable but rival. Fish are a good example of a common resource: They are rival because one person's catch of a fish decreases the amount available for other people. But fish are non excludable because no one can be prevented from trying to catch the fish. Gold mines, on the other hand, are not a common resource. They are rival—one miner's extraction of a ton of ore decreases the amount available for other people—but the mine is excludable—the mine has an owner who determines who is allowed to mine the ore. The essential reason the gold mine is excludable is because the owner has the property right to the mine. And the essential reason the fish are nonexcludable is because no one has the property right to the fish.

FIGURE **17.8**
Short Answer Problem 9

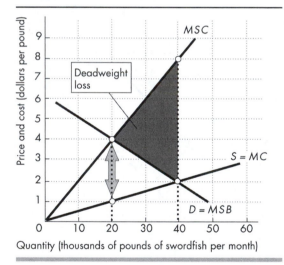

9. Figure 17.8 labels the curves.

  a. The equilibrium quantity of swordfish is determined by the intersection of the marginal private cost curve, $S = MC$, and the marginal social benefit curve, $D = MSB$. The equilibrium quantity of fish is 40,000 pounds of swordfish per month. The efficient quantity of swordfish is determined by the intersection of the marginal social cost curve and the marginal social benefit curve, so the efficient quantity of swordfish is 20,000 pounds per month. The deadweight loss from the overuse of swordfish is equal to the area of the grey triangle in the figure.

b. If the government sets the production quota at the efficient quantity, the quota for total production is set at the quantity at which marginal social benefit equals marginal social cost. Here that quantity is what 20,000 pounds of swordfish per month. At this quantity, the price of swordfish is $4 per pound and the marginal cost of catching a pound is $1. There is a $4 − $1 profit margin of $3 on another pound of swordfish. This large profit margin creates an incentive for each fisher to cheat on the quota by catching more than the quota quantity.

c. The market price of an individual transferable quota, ITQ, equals the marginal social benefit (the price of a pound of swordfish) minus the marginal private cost at the quota level of fish. The government issues ITQs so that 20,000 pounds of swordfish per month can be caught. At this quantity the price of an ITQ is $4 − $1, which equals a market price for an ITQ of $3 per pound of swordfish.

■ You're the Teacher

1. "I agree with you that pollution is bad, but clearly to totally eliminate it isn't optimal because it would cost way too much. Think about it this way: Society could get rid of all air pollution by outlawing all cars, all trains, all planes, shutting down all factories, and eliminating all cows. (Cows produce methane you know.) But, come on, you know we won't do this and we don't want to do it. The reason is immediate: It's just too expensive."

"Sure, we'd like less pollution, but the cost to get to zero pollution is prohibitive — a whole lot more than the benefit! So, anyone that says 'Zero pollution is best' hasn't thought through the issue. In fact, some pollution is good. We get to drive rather than walk, we get to have pizza delivered rather than doing without, we get to air condition our homes rather than perspire, and we get to heat our homes rather than freeze."

Chapter Quiz

1. If production of a good creates an external cost, to move the economy closer to efficiency the government might
   a. subsidize production of the good.
   b. regulate the firms to use abatement technology.
   c. remove the offending property right.
   d. None of the above actions move the economy closer to efficiency.

2. An example of a common resource is a
   a. bridge.
   b. non-crowded movie theater.
   c. tuna in the ocean.
   d. None of the above answers is correct.

3. The production of steel creates pollution with a marginal external cost of $4 per ton. To eliminate the deadweight loss, the government could
   a. sell ITQs to the steel firms for $4 per ton.
   b. subsidize the steel firms $4 per ton.
   c. impose a tax on the steel firms of $4 per ton.
   d. buy ITQs from the steel firms for $4 per ton.

4. When the government sets a production quota for a common resource, the producers have the incentive to produce _____ than the quota because
   a. more; they will be able to buy more ITQs.
   b. less; a tax might also be imposed.
   c. more; efficiency requires that more be produced.
   d. more; additional units are profitable.

5. Potential solutions to the external cost created by pollution include
   a. subsidizing the production of the good or using emissions charges.
   b. taxing the production of the good or using cap-and-trade.
   c. using cap-and-trade or issuing patents or copyrights.
   d. public provision by the government or using vouchers.

6. The tragedy of the commons arises because _____ exceeds _____ at the unregulated equilibrium quantity.
   a. marginal social benefit; marginal private benefit
   b. marginal private benefit; marginal social benefit
   c. marginal private benefit; marginal social cost
   d. marginal social cost; marginal social benefit

7. If production of a good creates an external cost, resource use definitely is efficient when production is such that
   a. marginal external cost equals marginal external benefit.
   b. marginal private cost equals marginal private benefit.
   c. marginal social cost equals marginal social benefit.
   d. marginal external cost is zero and marginal external benefit is as large as possible.

8. Which of the following illustrates the concept of external cost?
   a. Bad weather decreases the size of the wheat crop.
   b. An increase in the demand for cheese raises the price paid by consumers of pizza, thereby harming these consumers.
   c. Smoking harms the health of the smoker.
   d. Smoking harms the health of nearby non-smokers.

9. To achieve the efficient amount of use of a common resource, the use should be such that _____ equals _____.
   a. marginal social cost; marginal private cost
   b. marginal social cost; marginal social benefit
   c. marginal private benefit; marginal social cost
   d. marginal private cost; marginal private benefit

10. A policy of cap-and-trade means that the government
   a. imposes a tax equal to the marginal cost of pollution.
   b. issues to firms marketable permits, each allowing a certain amount of pollution.
   c. caps the amount of trading (production) polluting firms are allowed to do.
   d. None of the above are correct.

The answers for this Chapter Quiz are on page 346

5 MARKET FAILURE AND GOVERNMENT

Mid-Term Examination

■ **Chapter 16**

1. A common resource is
   a. rival and excludable.
   b. rival and nonexcludable.
   c. nonrival and excludable.
   d. nonrival and nonexcludable.

2. Nonrivalry is a feature of
   a. external goods.
   b. common resources.
   c. private goods.
   d. public goods.

3. The free rider problem is most serious for
   a. private goods.
   b. public goods.
   c. common resources.
   d. natural monopolies.

4. The Coase theorem applies when transactions costs are
   a. low and property rights have been assigned.
   b. low and property rights do not exist.
   c. high and property rights have been assigned.
   d. high and property rights do not exist.

5. Rational ignorance on the part of voters can lead to the government providing
   a. less than the efficient quantity of a good with an external benefit.
   b. more than the efficient quantity of a good with an external benefit.
   c. less than the efficient quantity of a public good.
   d. more than the efficient quantity of a public good.

■ **Chapter 17**

6. Compared to the efficient quantity, an unregulated market produces too ____ of a good or service with an external cost and use too ____ of a common resource.

    a. much; much
    b. much; little
    c. little; much
    d. little; little

7. ITQs can be used for the case of a ____ and ITQs ____ firms' incentives to cheat on the quota.

    a. good with an external cost; eliminate
    b. good with an external cost; do not eliminate
    c. common resource; eliminate
    d. common resource; do not eliminate

8. If production of a good creates a marginal external cost, then the

    a. *MC* curve lies above the *MSC* curve.
    b. *MSC* curve lies above the *MC* curve.
    a. *MB* curve lies above the *MSB* curve.
    a. *MSB* curve lies above the *MB* curve.

9. The tragedy of the commons is that common resources

    a. have too much free riding.
    b. are under-utilized by society.
    c. are inefficiently provided by the government.
    d. are overused and depleted.

10. Using a common resource ____ a marginal private cost and ____ a marginal external cost.

    a. creates; creates
    b. creates; does not create
    c. does not create; creates
    d. does not create; does not create

Answers

■ Mid-Term Exam Answers

1. b;   2. d;   3. b;   4. a;   5. d   6. a;   7. d;   8. b;   9. d;   10. a

Chapter 18 MARKETS FOR FACTORS OF PRODUCTION

Key Concepts

■ The Anatomy of Factor Markets

Factors of production (*labor*, *capital*, *land*, and *entrepreneurship*) are used to produce output.

- Labor services are the physical and mental efforts people supply. Most labor markets are competitive but in some labor markets a labor union organizes the workers and introduces some market power.

- Capital is the tools, instruments, machines, and buildings that help produce goods and services. Capital services are paid a rental rate.

- Land is all the gifts of nature—natural resources. The services of land are paid rental rate. Most natural resources are reusable but **nonrenewable natural resources** are resources, such as coil and oil, which can be used only once.

- Entrepreneurship is not traded in markets. Entrepreneurs receive profit or bear the loss from their business.

For most factors of production, demand and supply in factor markets determine their prices.

■ The Demand for a Factor of Production

A firm's demand for a factor of production is a **derived demand**, stemming from the demand for the goods and services produced by the factor. A firm hires the quantities of factors of production that maximize its profit. The cost of hiring an additional unit of a factor is the factor price. The value to the firm from hiring one more unit of a factor is the factor's value of marginal product.

- **Value of marginal product** (*VMP*) equals the price of a unit of output multiplied by the marginal product of the factor, $P \times MP$. The *VMP* is the change in total revenue from employing one more unit of the factor. As more workers are hired, the *VMP* diminishes.

The *VMP* of labor tells the worth to the firm from hiring an additional worker. A firm hires an additional worker if the wage, *W*, paid the worker is less than the worker's *VMP*. To maximize its profit, a firm hires the quantity of workers such that the wage rate equals the value of marginal product.

Because the firm hires the quantity of workers that sets *VMP* = *W*, the *VMP* curve shows how many workers a firm hires. Therefore the *VMP* curve is the firm's demand for labor curve.

- If the wage rate rises, the firm decreases the quantity of workers it demands.

A firm's demand for labor increases when:

- the price of the firm's output rises.

- the prices of other factors of production rise.

- technological change increases the marginal product of labor.

■ Labor Markets

The market demand for labor is the sum of the quantities of labor demanded by all the firms at each wage rate.

The supply of labor is determined by decisions made by households. Households allocate time between labor supply and leisure. A household's supply of labor depends on the reservation wage and also the household's income and substitution effects.

- At wage rates above a household's *reservation wage*, the household supplies labor.

All wage changes have both a substitution effect and an income effect.

- The *substitution effect* from a higher wage rate increases the quantity of labor supplied.

- The *income effect* from a higher wage rate decreases the quantity of labor supplied and increases the amount of time spent at leisure.

FIGURE **18.1**

An Individual's Supply of Labor Curve

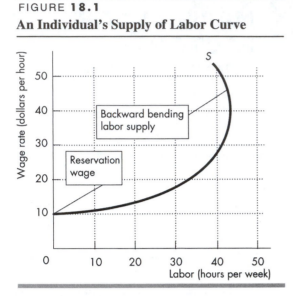

- An individual's labor supply curve bends backward, as Figure 18.1 shows. The illustrated curve bends backward for wages higher than $40 per hour because at these wage rates the income effect from a higher wage rate outweighs the substitution effect.

The market supply of labor curve is the sum of all individual supply of labor curves and slopes upward over the normal range of wage rates.

The labor market equilibrium between the demand for labor and the supply of labor determines the wage rate and employment.

Over the years, wage rates have increased because the demand for labor has increased. Technological change and the accumulation of capital both increase the demand for labor. In markets that do not enjoy productivity gains, the demand for labor still increases if the demand for the product produced by these workers increases so that the price of the good or service rises. Over the past years the demand for skilled workers has increased more than the demand for low-skilled workers, so the wages paid skilled workers have increased relative to the wages paid low-skilled workers.

A **labor union** is an organized group of workers that aims to increase wages and influence other job conditions. Unions attempt to raise their members' wage rates. They do so by influencing the supply and demand for labor. Unions attempt to:

- *restrict the supply of labor.* If the supply of labor decreases, the wage rate rises. If there is an abundant

supply of non-union labor, the union cannot decrease the supply of labor.

- *increase the demand for union labor.* Unions try to increase the demand for their members' labor by raising the marginal product of their members, encouraging import restrictions, encouraging consumers to buy the goods and services produced by the union members, supporting minimum wage laws, and supporting immigration restrictions.

If a competitive labor market becomes unionized, the increased demand and decreased supply raise union members' wages and incomes. If the supply decreases more than the demand increases, the quantity of employment falls.

A **monopsony** is a market in which there is a single buyer. A firm that is the only employer in town is a monopsonist in the labor market.

- A monopsony determines what wage it will pay and pays the lowest wage that lets it hire the number of workers it wants to employ.

FIGURE **18.2**

A Monopsony Labor Market

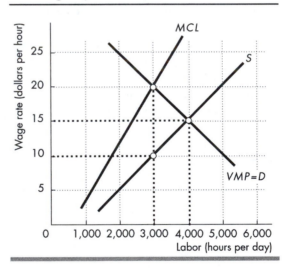

To hire more labor, a monopsony must pay a higher wage to *all* its workers. Because a monopsony raises the wage it pays all workers, the marginal cost of labor exceeds the wage paid the new worker. As illustrated in Figure 18.2, the marginal cost of labor curve (*MCL*) for the monopsony lies above the supply curve (*S*) of labor.

To maximize profit, a monopsony (1) hires the quantity of labor determined by the intersection of the *MCL* curve and the *VMP* (= *D*) curve, and (2) then uses the labor supply curve to offer the lowest wage rate possible that allows it to hire the quantity of labor it wants. In Figure 18.2, the monopsony hires 3,000 hours of labor and pays a wage rate of $10 per hour.

♦ With a monopsony, employment and the wage rate are lower than in a competitive labor market. In Figure 18.2 a competitive labor market results in employment of 400 hours of labor and a wage rate of $12 per hour versus employment of 300 and a wage rate of $8 for a monopsony.

♦ If the monopsonist faces a union, the labor market is characterized as a **bilateral monopoly**, a situation in which a monopoly seller (the union) faces a monopsony buyer (the firm). In this case the wage rate is determined by the relative bargaining strengths of the firm and the union.

♦ A minimum wage law can affect the outcome in a monopsony market. The minimum wage makes labor supply perfectly elastic at the minimum wage so that the *MCL* falls so it equals the minimum wage. In response, the monopsonist hires more labor and pays a higher wage rate.

■ Capital and Natural Resource Markets

Capital and natural resource markets also depend on demand and supply.

CAPITAL RENTAL MARKETS

♦ The demand for capital is determined by firms' profit-maximizing choices and is based on the value of marginal product of capital. Firms hire the quantity of capital services that makes the value of marginal product of capital equal to the rental rate of capital. When the rental rate of capital rises, the quantity of capital demanded decreases.

♦ When the rental rate of capital increases, the quantity of capital supplied increases.

The equilibrium rental rate of capital makes the quantity of capital demanded equal to the quantity supplied.

♦ Firms that buy capital implicitly rent the capital to themselves. To determine if it should buy or rent the capital, the firm must compare a cost incurred in the present (buy the capital) with a series of costs incurred in the future (rent the capital). The present value is the *current* worth of the future flows of rental payments. The Mathematical Note covers present value in detail. The firm will choose to buy or rent depending on whichever is cheaper

LAND RENTAL MARKETS

♦ The demand for land is based on the value of marginal product of land. Firms rent the quantity of land that sets the value of marginal product of land equal to the rental rate of land. When the rental of land rises, the quantity of land demanded decreases.

♦ The quantity of land is fixed so its supply is perfectly inelastic and its supply curve is vertical.

The equilibrium rental rate of land makes the quantity of land demanded equal to the quantity supplied. Because the supply of land is perfectly inelastic, changes in demand change the rental rate for land but do not change its quantity.

NONRENEWABLE NATURAL RESOURCE MARKETS

Nonrenewable natural resources are resources that can be used only once and cannot be replaced, such as coal, natural gas, and oil.

♦ The demand for a nonrenewable natural resource, say oil, depends in the value of marginal product of oil (the *fundamental* influence) and the expected future price of oil (the *speculative* influence). The fundamental influence is similar to other resources: the higher the price of oil, the smaller the quantity demanded. The speculative influence occurs because oil can be stored and sold in the future. If the price of oil is expected to rise more rapidly than the interest rate, traders demand oil to store and sell in the future.

♦ The supply of oil depends on the known oil reserves, the scale of current oil production facilities (the *fundamental* influence), and the expected future price of oil (the *speculative* influence). If known oil reserves increase, the supply increases but this effect is small and indirect. The current scale of oil production facilities affects the marginal cost of producing oil. Because the marginal cost, *MC*, increases with the production of oil, the higher the price of oil, the greater is the quantity supplied. If the price of oil is expected to rise more rapidly than the interest rate, producers decrease the supply of oil in order to store it and sell it in the future.

The market fundamentals price of oil is based on the *VMP*, the fundamental influence on demand, and the *MC*, the fundamental influence on supply. If the expected future price also is based on the market fundamentals, then the equilibrium price is the market fundamentals price. But if the future expected price diverges from the price based on fundamentals, then speculation makes the equilibrium price differ from the fundamental price.

The **Hotelling principle** is the idea that traders expect the price of a nonrenewable natural resource to rise at a rate equal to the interest rate. This expected price rise is the only expectation for which oil inventories do not shrink to zero or expand indefinitely.

Helpful Hints

1. **PROFIT MAXIMIZATION AND FIRMS' DEMANDS FOR FACTORS :** This chapter discusses characteristics that are common to the demand for factors of production. In particular, firms hire each factor up to the point at which the value of marginal product equals the cost of the factor. With the exception of the speculative demand for some nonrenewable natural resources, this result holds regardless of whether the factor is labor, land, or capital. Why? When deciding whether to hire another unit of a factor, profit-maximizing firms compare the added revenue the factor would generate (the *VMP*) to the cost of hiring the factor. As long as the additional revenue from hiring the factor exceeds the additional cost, hiring the factor is profitable. However, if the added revenue falls short of the added cost, hiring the factor reduces the firm's profit. This result holds true for *any* factor: land, labor, or capital. This result also holds for *any* firm—a competitive firm or a monopsony firm— so that the maximum profit is reached by hiring the amount of the factor necessary to equalize the value of marginal product and the factor's cost. Of course, a competitive firm hires so that the *VMP* equals the factor's price while a monopsony firm hires so that the *VMP* equals the marginal cost of the factor.

2. **THE LABOR DEMAND CURVE :** The most important graph in this chapter demonstrates that a firm's demand curve for labor is the same as its value of marginal product curve of labor.

   Why is the *VMP* curve the same as a firm's demand curve for labor? We construct the demand curve for labor by asking the question: "How much labor is a firm willing to hire at alternative wage rates?" Because firms are profit maximizers, they hire labor up to the point at which the value of marginal product of labor equals the wage rate. For example,

if the wage rate is $10 per hour and the value of marginal product is $10 when three workers are hired, the firm hires three workers. As a result, the demand curve for labor is the *VMP* curve.

Questions

■ True/False and Explain

The Anatomy of Factor Markets

1. In most labor markets, firms unilaterally determine the wage rate that workers receive.

2. Some natural resources are renewable and others are nonrenewable.

The Demand for a Factor of Production

3. The value of marginal product of labor is the same as the marginal product of labor.

4. If the price of a firm's output is $50 per unit and the marginal product of capital is 10 units, the value of marginal product of capital is $500.

5. A firm's demand for labor curve is the same as its value of marginal product of labor curve.

6. A firm's demand for labor curve shifts rightward when the wage rate falls.

Labor Markets

7. A household supplies no labor when the wage rate is above its reservation wage rate.

8. An individual's labor supply curve bends backward when the substitution effect is larger than the income effect.

9. Unions support minimum wage laws in part because they raise the cost of low-skilled labor, a substitute for high-skilled union labor.

10. Unions try to increase the demand for their members' labor.

11. For a monopsony, the marginal cost of hiring another worker is less than the wage it must pay.

12. A monopsony determines the amount of labor it hires by where the *MCL* curve crosses the labor supply curve.

13. A monopsony pays a higher wage rate than would be paid in a perfectly competitive labor market.

Capital and Natural Resource Markets

14. The higher the interest rate, the greater the quantity of capital demanded.

15. An increase in the value of marginal product of capital increases the demand for capital.

16. A unique feature of the market for land is the result that the demand for land is perfectly inelastic.

17. All natural resources can be used only once and cannot be replaced.

18. Nonrenewable natural resources do not have a value of marginal product.

19. For a nonrenewable natural resource such as oil, the market fundamentals price and the equilibrium price cannot differ.

20. The Hotelling principle states that the price of a nonrenewable natural resource is expected to fall at a rate equal to the interest rate.

■ Multiple Choice

The Anatomy of Factor Markets

1. Natural gas is an example of
   a. capital.
   b. a nonrenewable natural resource.
   c. a renewable natural resource.
   d. a casual resource.

2. Which of the factors of production is not traded in markets?
   a. labor
   b. capital
   c. land
   d. entrepreneurship

The Demand for a Factor of Production

3. An example of derived demand is the demand for
   a. sweaters derived by an economics student.
   b. sweaters produced by labor and capital.
   c. labor used in the production of sweaters.
   d. sweater brushes.

4. The change in total revenue resulting from employing an additional worker is the
   a. marginal product of labor.
   b. marginal revenue of labor.
   c. marginal cost of labor.
   d. value of marginal product of labor.

5. Renting another acre of land increases the corn a farm can grow by 4,000 bushels. The price of a bushel of corn is $5. What is the value of marginal product of an acre of land?
   a. $800
   b. $4,005
   c. $20,000
   d. None of the above answers is correct.

6. A company finds that when it hires the next worker, the worker's value of marginal product exceeds the cost of hiring the worker. In this case the company should
   a. definitely hire the worker.
   b. perhaps hire the worker, depending on the relationship between the worker's marginal product and the cost of hiring the worker.
   c. definitely not hire the worker.
   d. None of the above answers is correct.

7. A firm's value of marginal product of labor curve is the same as its
   a. labor supply curve.
   b. labor demand curve.
   c. marginal cost curve.
   d. marginal revenue curve.

8. The price of the good produced by a perfectly competitive firm falls. As a result, the labor
   a. supplied to the firm decreases.
   b. supplied to the firm increases.
   c. demanded by the firm increases.
   d. demanded by the firm decreases.

9. A technological change that increases the marginal product of labor shifts the
   a. demand curve for labor rightward.
   b. demand curve for labor leftward.
   c. supply curve of labor leftward.
   d. supply curve of labor rightward.

Labor Markets

10. A worker's reservation wage is the
    a. highest wage rate before the income effect starts to dominate the substitution effect.
    b. lowest wage rate before the income effect starts to dominate the substitution effect.
    c. the lowest wage rate for which the worker will supply labor.
    d. wage rate paid to head waiters, who are involved in taking reservations at fine restaurants.

11. If the wage rate rises, the substitution effect gives a household the incentive to
    a. raise its reservation wage.
    b. increase its time spent at leisure and decrease its time spent supplying labor.
    c. increase its time spent supplying labor and decrease its time spent at leisure.
    d. increase both the time spent at leisure and at supplying labor.

12. If the wage rate rises, the income effect gives a household the incentive to
    a. raise its reservation wage.
    b. increase its time spent at leisure and decrease its time spent supplying labor.
    c. increase its time spent supplying labor and decrease its time spent at leisure.
    d. increase both the time spent at leisure and at supplying labor.

13. In a supply and demand model of the labor market, the equilibrium wage rate is the wage rate
    a. at which the labor supply curve starts to bend backwards.
    b. at which the labor demand curve starts to bend backwards.
    c. at which the labor demand and labor supply curves intersect.
    d. that equals the reservation wage rate.

14. Which of the following would unions be most likely to support?
    a. Decreasing the legal minimum wage.
    b. Encouraging immigration.
    c. Restricting imports.
    d. Decreasing demand for the goods that their workers produce.

15. If a union formed in a competitive labor market cannot affect the firms' demand for labor but can affect the supply of labor, then the union _____ the wage rate and _____ employment.
    a. lowers; decreases
    b. lowers; increases
    c. raises; decreases
    d. raises; increases

16. In order to hire an additional worker, a monopsony must pay
    a. a higher wage rate than it paid before.
    b. the same wage rate it paid before.
    c. a lower wage rate than it paid before.
    d. a wage rate that is sometimes higher, sometimes lower, and sometimes the same as before, depending on its labor supply curve.

17. For a monopsony, the *MCL* curve
    a. lies above the labor supply curve.
    b. is the same as the labor supply curve.
    c. lies below the labor supply curve.
    d. is the same as the labor demand curve.

Use Figure 18.3 for the next four questions.

FIGURE **18.3**

Multiple Choice Questions 18, 19, 20, and 21

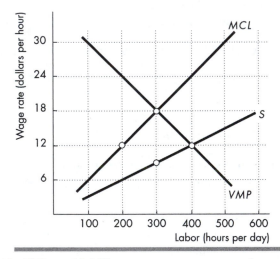

18. If Figure 18.3 illustrates a monopsony, employment is _____ hours per day.
    a. 200
    b. 300
    c. 400
    d. None of the above.

19. If Figure 18.3 illustrates a monopsony, the wage rate is _____ per hour
    a. $9.00
    b. $12.00
    c. $18.00
    d. None of the above.

20. If Figure 18.3 illustrates a perfectly competitive labor market, employment is _____ hours per day.
    a. 200
    b. 300
    c. 400
    d. None of the above.

21. If Figure 18.3 illustrates a perfectly competitive labor market, the wage rate is _____ per hour.
    a. $9.00
    b. $12.00
    c. $18.00
    d. None of the above.

22. A minimum wage can lead a monopsony to
    a. lower its wage rate and lower its level of employment.
    b. increase employment.
    c. lower its wage rate and increase its level of employment.
    d. none of the above.

23. Technological change that increases workers' marginal product _____ the wage rate and _____ employment.
    a. raises; increases
    b. raises; decreases
    c. lowers; increases
    d. lowers; decreases

Capital and Natural Resource Markets

24. An increase in the marginal product of capital shifts the
    a. supply of capital curve rightward.
    b. supply of capital curve leftward.
    c. demand for capital curve leftward.
    d. demand for capital curve rightward.

25. If the demand for land increases, the rental rate for land _____ and the quantity of land _____.
    a. rises; increases
    b. does not change; increases
    c. falls; increases
    d. rises; does not change

26. An example of a nonrenewable natural resource is
    a. coal.
    b. land.
    c. water.
    d. a river.

27. Which of the following increases the *fundamental* supply of oil?
    a. An increase in the expected future price of oil.
    b. An increase in current oil production facilities.
    c. An increase in the value of marginal product of oil.
    d. A decrease in the expected future price of oil.

28. For a nonrenewable natural resource, such as oil, the equilibrium price _____ the market fundamentals price.
    a. is always the same as
    b. can be greater than but not less than
    c. can be less than but not greater than
    d. can be less than, greater than, or equal to

29. If people suddenly start to expect the price of oil to rise more rapidly than the interest rate, the demand for oil _____ and the supply of oil _____.
    a. increases; increases
    b. increases; decreases
    c. decreases; increases
    d. decreases; decreases

30. If the price of a barrel of oil is $100 this year and the interest rate is 5 percent, then the price next year is expected to be _____ per barrel.
    a. $95
    b. $100
    c. $105
    d. None of the above answers is correct.

■ Short Answer Problems

Quantity of labor (L)	Marginal product of labor (MP)
3	20
4	12
5	6
6	3
7	1

TABLE **18.2**

Christopher's Value of Marginal Product

Quantity of labor (L)	Cookies @ $1.00 Value of marginal product (VMP)	Cookies @ $2.00 Value of marginal product (VMP)
3	____	____
4	____	____
5	____	____
6	____	____
7	____	____

1. Table 18.1 shows the marginal product of labor schedule for Christopher's Cookies, a perfectly competitive store that, unsurprisingly, sells cookies.

   a. Based on Table 18.1, if Christopher can sell a cookie for $1.00, complete the first *VMP* column of Table 18.2.

   b. If Christopher must pay workers $6 an hour, how many workers does Christopher hire? If the wage rate rises to $12 an hour, how many workers will Christopher employ?

   c. The price of a cookie rises to $2.00. Complete the second *VMP* column in Table 18.2.

   d. If Christopher must pay workers $6 an hour, how many workers does Christopher hire now? If the wage rate rises to $12 an hour, how many workers does he hire?

   e. In Figure 18.4, draw Christopher's demand for labor curve when the price of a cookie is $1.00 and when the price is $2.00. What is the effect of the rise in the price of a cookie?

2. Why does the labor supply curve bend backward? In your answer, be sure to discuss the role played by the substitution and income effects.

FIGURE **18.4**

Short Answer Problem 1 (e)

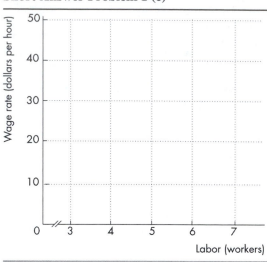

3. Most members of labor unions earn wages well above the minimum wage. Why, then, do unions support raising the legal minimum wage?

TABLE **18.3**

Towne Hospital

Wage rate (dollars per day)	Labor demand (workers)	Labor supply (workers)	Marginal cost of labor, MCL (dollars per hour)
$20	10	2	
30	9	3	____
40	8	4	____
50	7	5	____
60	6	6	____
70	5	7	____
80	4	8	____
90	3	9	____

4. Table 18.3 shows the supply of nurses facing Towne Hospital, the only employer of nurses in a town.

   a. Calculate the values for the *MCL* column and complete the table.

   b. Plot the labor demand, labor supply, and *MCL* schedules in Figure 18.5 (on the next page).

FIGURE **18.5**
Short Answer Problem 4 (b)

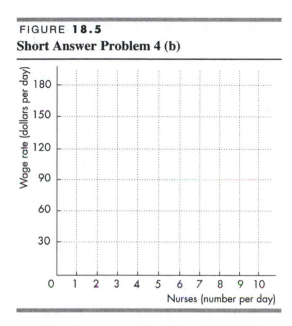

FIGURE **18.6**
Short Answer Problem 5

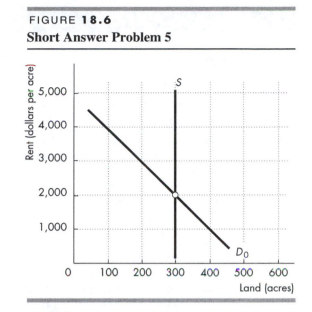

c. How many nurses does Towne hire? What wage rate does Towne pay?

d. Suppose the hospital market for nurses is competitive rather than a monopsony. Based on the supply and demand schedules in Table 18.3, how many nurses would be hired and what wage rate would be paid?

e. How does the wage rate that Towne pays when it is a monopsony compare with the wage rate paid if the market was perfectly competitive? How does the number of nurses hired compare in the two cases?

5. A new shopping center on the outskirts of town doubles the *VMP* of the surrounding land. Figure 18.6 shows the market for this land before the shopping center. Use the figure to show the effect of the shopping center. What was the initial rental rate and quantity of land and the rent and quantity of land after the shopping center is built?

6. Figure 18.7 shows the market fundamentals for oil. Suppose that demanders and suppliers come to expect that the price of oil will rise more rapidly than previously believed. In Figure 18.7, show the effect of this change in beliefs. How does the equilibrium price compare to the market fundamentals price?

FIGURE **18.7**
Short Answer Problem 6

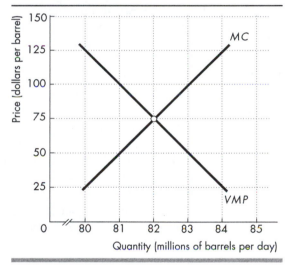

■ **You're the Teacher**

1. "I really don't get the whole idea about the supply of labor. People don't have a choice about how much labor to supply: Once you get out of school, you either work 40 hours a week or you don't work. But the book talks like people have got a choice about how many hours to work. That really seems silly." While your friend is laughing over this point, take a moment to explain to your friend why it's not a laughing matter at all!

Answers

■ True/False Answers

The Anatomy of Factor Markets

1. **F** Wages in most labor markets are determined by the demand for labor and the supply of labor.

2. **T** A river is an example of a renewable natural resource; coal is an example of a nonrenewable natural resource.

The Demand for a Factor of Production

3. **F** The value of marginal product of labor equals the price of the good or service produced multiplied by the marginal product of labor.

4. **T** The value of marginal product of capital equals the price multiplied by the marginal product of capital, or $10 per unit × 50 units, or $500.

5. **T** The firm's demand curve for any factor is the same as the factor's *VMP* curve.

6. **F** A fall in the wage rate leads to a movement along the demand for labor curve *not* a shift of the curve.

Labor Markets

7. **F** The household supplies labor whenever the wage rate exceeds its reservation wage.

8. **F** The supply curve bends backward when the income effect — which encourages an increase in leisure, thereby reducing the quantity of labor supplied whenever the wage rate rises— is larger than the substitution effect.

9. **T** By raising the cost of substitute inputs, such as low-skilled workers, unions increase the demand for their members' labor.

10. **T** To raise their members' wages, unions try to increase the demand for their members' labor.

11. **F** The marginal cost of hiring another worker *exceeds* the wage rate that must be paid.

12. **F** The level of employment is determined where the *MCL* curve crosses the *MRP* curve.

13. **F** A monopsony exploits its market power by paying a lower wage rate.

Capital and Natural Resource Markets

14. **F** A rise in the interest rate *decreases* the quantity of capital demanded.

15. **T** An increase in the value of marginal product of capital increases the demand for capital and shifts the capital demand curve rightward.

16. **F** It is the *supply* of land that is perfectly inelastic not the demand for land.

17. **F** Nonrenewable resources can be used only once, but renewable resources can be used any number of times or else can be replaced.

18. **F** All factors of production have a value of marginal product; indeed, firms are willing to hire a factor only because the factor increases the firm's revenue and this increase is the factor's value of marginal product.

19. **F** When the prices differ, speculative factors are affecting the demand and supply of the resource and thereby affecting the equilibrium price.

20. **F** The Hotelling principle states that the price of a nonrenewable natural resource is expected to *rise* at the same rate as the interest rate.

■ Multiple Choice Answers

The Anatomy of Factor Markets

1. **b** Natural gas is nonrenewable because once a cubic foot of natural gas is used, that cubic foot is gone forever.

2. **d** Land, labor, and capital are traded in markets; entrepreneurship is not traded in a market.

The Demand for a Factor of Production

3. **c** The demand for a factor is derived from the demand for the final goods and services that the factor produces.

4. **d** The a answer defines the value of marginal product of labor.

5. **c** The value of marginal product of land equals the price of corn, $5 a bushel, multiplied by the number of bushels grown, 4,000 bushels, or $20,000. Basically if the farm rents this acre, its revenue increases by $20,000.

6. **a** The worker will add to the firm's total profit (because the additional revenue, the *VMP*, exceeds the additional cost) and should be hired.

7. **b** The *VMP* of labor curve shows how many workers a firm hires for any wage rate, so it is the same as the firm's demand for labor curve.

8. **d** The demand for labor decreases when the price falls because the fall in price decreases the value

of marginal product.

9. **a** By raising the marginal product from workers, the value of marginal product increases which means that the demand for labor increases.

Labor Markets

10. **c** The answer defines the reservation wage.

11. **c** By increasing the opportunity cost of leisure, the substitution effect of a higher wage rate encourages households to substitute away from leisure and toward labor supply.

12. **b** By raising a household's income, the income effect of a higher wage rate encourages a household to "buy" more normal goods, such as leisure, and thereby decrease its labor supply.

13. **c** Like any other competitive market, the labor market is in equilibrium at the wage rate where the demand curve intersects the supply curve.

14. **c** Imports are produced by foreign labor, which is a substitute for domestic, union labor. Hence unions try to restrict imports.

15. **c** Unions decrease the supply of labor, thereby raising the wage rate that must be paid their members but also decreasing employment in the unionized industry.

16. **a** The monopsony must pay the higher wage to *all* the workers it employs, so the marginal cost of hiring another worker exceeds the wage rate.

FIGURE **18.8**
Multiple Choice Question 17

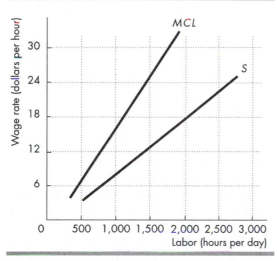

17. **a** As Figure 18.8 shows, the *MCL* curve lies above

the labor supply curve.

18. **b** A monopsony sets its employment so that the marginal cost of labor (the *MCL*) equals the value of marginal product of labor (the *VMP*). In Figure 18.3, the firm hires 300 hours of labor.

19. **a** The monopsony hires 300 hours of labor. The supply curve indicates that the lowest wage rate it can pay and hire this amount of labor is $9 per hour.

20. **c** In a perfectly competitive labor market, the equilibrium quantity of labor is determined by the intersection of the supply curve and demand curve, which is the same as the *VMP* curve.

21. **b** The wage rate is determined by the equilibrium between the demand for labor and the supply of labor and is $12 per hour in Figure 18.3. The last four answers show that a monopsony pays a lower wage rate and hires fewer workers then in a perfectly competitive labor market.

22. **b** In a competitive labor market, a minimum wage decreases employment, but might increase employment in a monopsony labor market.

23. **a** The increase in the marginal product increases the demand for labor, thereby raising the wage rate and increasing employment.

Capital and Natural Resource Markets

24. **d** An increase in the marginal product of capital increases the value of marginal product of capital, which increases the demand for capital.

25. **d** Because the supply curve of land is vertical, an increase in demand raises the rental rate but does not change the equilibrium quantity of land.

26. **a** Once a ton of coal is burned, it is gone forever.

27. **b** An increase in current oil production facilities lowers the marginal cost of producing oil, which is the key factor determining the fundamental supply of oil.

28. **d** Speculation about the future price of oil can cause the equilibrium price of oil to differ from its fundamentals price.

29. **b** The demand increases as traders want to buy the oil to store and the supply decreases as current owners want to hold the oil to sell in the future.

30. **c** The price is expected to rise at the same rate as the interest rate, in this case, to rise 5 percent (which is $5) over the next year.

■ **Answers to Short Answer Problems**

FIGURE **18.9**
Short Answer Problem 1 (e)

TABLE **18.4**

Short Answer Problem 1

Quantity of labor (L)	Cookies $1.00 Value of marginal product, VMP (dollars)	Cookies $2.00 Value of marginal product, VMP (dollars)
3	20..00	40.00
4	12.00	24.00
5	6.00	12.00
6	3.00	6.00
7	1.00	2.00

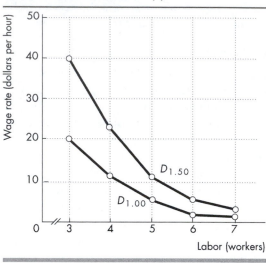

1. a. Table 18.4 has the value of marginal products. To calculate these answers, recall that the value of marginal product equals the price multiplied by the marginal product. The price is $1.00, so using this value, the *VMP* of the 4th workers is $1.00 × 12, or $12. The rest of the value of marginal product schedule is computed in the same way.

    b. If the wage rate is $6 an hour, Christopher will hire 5 workers. Hiring a 5 workers maximizes Christopher's profit because 5 workers sets Christopher's value of marginal product, $6, equal to the wage rate, also $6. If the wage rate rises to $12 an hour, Christopher maximizes his profit by hiring 4 workers.

    c. The *VMPs* are calculated the same way as outlined for part (a), using a price of $2.00 per cookie rather than $1.00.

    d. At a wage rate of $6 an hour, Christopher will now hire 6 workers. If the wage rate rises to $12 an hour, Christopher will now hire 5 workers.

    e. The labor demand curves are the same as the value of marginal product schedules. Figure 18.9 shows both demand curves. The labor demand curve when cookies are $1.00 is labeled $D_{1.00}$ and when cookies are $2.00 is labeled $D_{2.00}$. The rise in the price of a cookie shifts Christopher's demand for labor curve rightward.

2. Suppose that the wage rate rises. As a result, the opportunity cost of leisure increases so individuals have a tendency to shift from leisure to work. This change is the substitution effect, which leads to an

FIGURE **18.10**
Short Answer Problem 2

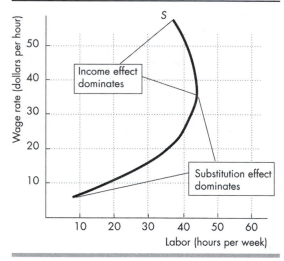

increase in the quantity of labor supplied. In addition, the higher wage rate increases the individual's income so the person increases his or her demand for leisure (and other normal goods). This result is the income effect, which leads to a decrease in the quantity of labor supplied. As Figure 18.10 shows, at low wage rates, the substitution effect dominates the income effect, so the labor supply curve slopes upward. At high wage rates, the income effect is larger and the labor supply curve bends backward.

3. A rise in the minimum wage boosts the cost of hiring low-skilled labor. Low-skilled labor can substi-

tute — to an extent — for high-skilled union labor. Hence the rise in the cost of low-skilled labor increases the demand for high-skilled labor and makes sustaining its higher wage easier for the union.

TABLE **18.5**

Short Answer Problem 4 (a)

Wage rate (dollars per day)	Labor demand (workers)	Labor supply (workers)	Marginal cost of labor, *MCL* (dollars per hour)
$20	10	2	
			$50
30	9	3	
			70
40	8	4	
			90
50	7	5	
			110
60	6	6	
			130
70	5	7	
			150
80	4	8	
			170
90	3	9	

4. a. Table 18.5 shows the marginal cost of labor, the *MCL*. To calculate these values, consider the *MCL* between 2 and 3 workers. The marginal cost of labor is $(\Delta\text{total wages})/\Delta L$. Total wages equals the number of workers employed multiplied by the wage rate, so for 2 nurses it is $20 × 2 workers, or $40 and for 3 nurses it is $90. So the *MCL* between 2 and 3 workers is equal to $($90 − $40)/(3 − 2) = 50. The rest of the *MCLs* in the table are calculated similarly.

b. Figure 18.11 shows the labor demand curve, labor supply curve, and *MCL* curve.

c. As Figure 18.11 illustrates, Towne hires 4 nurses because employing this number of nurses sets the marginal cost of labor equal to the value of marginal product of labor, given by the demand curve. This number of nurses, 4, is determined by the intersection of Towne's *MCL* curve and its labor demand curve. The labor supply curve shows that 4 nurses will work for $40 a day, so Towne pays a wage rate of $40 a day.

d. If the labor market was perfectly competitive, the intersection of the demand curve for labor and

FIGURE **18.11**

Short Answer Problem 4 (b)

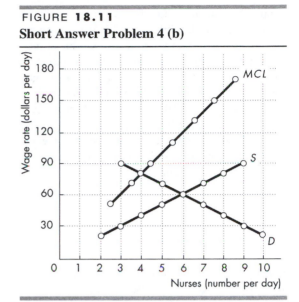

the supply curve of labor shows the quantity of labor employed. Figure 18.11 indicates that 6 nurses would be the equilibrium level of employment and that the equilibrium wage rate would be $60 a day.

e. Towne hires fewer workers and pays them a lower wage when it is a monopsony.

FIGURE **18.12**

Short Answer Problem 5

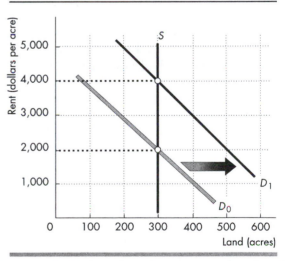

5. Figure 18.12 shows how the increase in the value of marginal product affects the market for this land. The initial demand curve is the same as the initial value of marginal product curve for the land. The

value of marginal product for any quantity of land is equal to the height of the demand curve. Because the new shopping center doubles the value of marginal product, the demand for labor curve shifts upward so that at each quantity of land the height of the new curve is twice the height of the old curve. The initial rent is $2,000 per acre and the initial quantity of land is 300 acres. After the shopping center is built, the new rent is $4,000 per acre. Because the supply of land is perfectly inelastic, the quantity of land remains 300 acres.

FIGURE **18.13**
Short Answer Problem 6

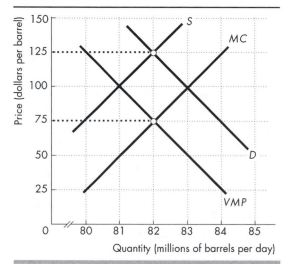

6. The new expectation of the more rapid rise in the price of oil increases the demand for oil and decreases the supply. The demand increases because traders demand oil to store and sell in the future. The supply decreases because producers who have oil also want to store it to sell it in the future. Figure 18.13 shows the impact of these changes: The de-

mand curve shifts rightward from the fundamentals demand curve, *VMP* to *D*, and the supply curve shifts leftward from the fundamentals supply curve, *MC*, to *S*. As shown in the figure, these speculative elements force the current equilibrium price upward. (In the figure, the quantity does not change because the curves change by the same amount. This outcome is an assumption and does not always need to be the case.) The equilibrium price, $125 per barrel, is higher than the market fundamentals price, $75 per barrel.

■ **You're the Teacher**

1. "You're missing the point, so quit laughing and listen up. First, a lot of jobs don't require 40 hours of work per week; think about my part-time job at JCPenney, where I'm working 20 hours a week. When I've graduated from law school and I'm an attorney, I'll work a whole lot more than 40 hours a week. I understand that attorneys working for large firms often put in 60 or 70 hours a week! There are also jobs like in construction where you might work 40 hours a week some weeks but not at all in others. Some jobs have 2 weeks of vacation, others 4 or 5 weeks. Still other jobs offer a lot of overtime at various times in the year. So the whole idea that you either work 40 hours or not at all is nonsense. I was talking with our economics teacher and I found out that nowadays the average person in the United States works about 34 hours a week! So, it makes sense to think about a supply of labor because people can decide what sort of jobs they want to look for and can decide how many hours they will be putting in at work."

Chapter Quiz

1. A decrease in the demand for a factor normally _____ the factor's price and _____ the quantity employed of the factor.
   a. raises; increases
   b. raises; decreases
   c. lowers; increases
   d. lowers; decreases

2. Which supply curve can "bend-backwards"?
   a. The supply curve of capital.
   b. The supply curve of land.
   c. The supply curve of labor.
   d. None of the above.

3. The value of marginal product of a factor is the
   a. additional output produced by using an additional unit of the factor.
   b. total revenue divided by the total amount of the factor used.
   c. additional revenue gained by employing an additional unit of the factor.
   d. additional revenue gained by selling one more unit of output.

4. A firm's value of marginal product of labor curve is
   a. upward sloping.
   b. the same as the firm's supply of labor curve.
   c. the same as the firm's demand for labor curve.
   d. the same as the firm's marginal cost curve.

5. If a new technology increases the marginal product of capital, the firm's demand for capital curve
   a. shifts rightward.
   b. does not shift.
   c. shifts leftward.
   d. becomes steeper.

6. A firm's demand for labor increases when
   a. the wage rate rises.
   b. the price of a substitute for labor falls.
   c. the price of the firm's output rises.
   d. the wage rate falls.

7. The demand for the services of labor _____ a derived demand and the demand for the services of capital _____ a derived demand.
   a. is; is
   b. is; is not
   c. is not; is
   d. is not; is not

8. Compared to a perfectly competitive labor market, a monopsony firm pays a _____ wage rate and hires _____ labor.
   a. higher; more
   b. high; less
   c. lower; more
   d. lower; less

9. For a nonrenewable natural resource, the price of the resource is expected to rise over time at a rate equal to the
   a. rate at which the resource is being used.
   b. rate of increase of known reserves.
   c. interest rate.
   d. growth rate of the value of marginal product of the resource.

10. In the _____ market, the supply is perfectly inelastic.
    a. labor
    b. capital
    c. land rental
    d. nonrenewable natural resource

The answers for this Chapter Quiz are on page 346

PRESENT VALUE AND DISCOUNTING

Key Concepts

■ Comparing Current and Future Dollars

A firm must decide whether to buy a piece of capital equipment or rent it. If it buys the item, it pays for it immediately while if it rents, it makes payments in the future. The firm must compare an expenditure made today with expenditures made in the future.

The **present value** of a future amount of money is the amount of money that, if invested today, will grow to be as large as the future amount when the interest it will earn is taken into account. **Discounting** is converting a future amount of money to a present value. (Calculating a present value means that the value of money to be received in the future must be decreased ("discounted") to express it in terms of today's worth.)

■ Compound Interest

The future amount of money equals the present amount (present value) plus the interest it will earn in the future:

Future amount = Present value + Interest income

The interest income is equal to the present value, multiplied by the interest rate, r, so:

Amount after 1 year = Present value + ($r \times$ Present value)

- ◆ Rearranging this formula yields:
  Amount after 1 year = Present value $\times (1 + r)$.
- ◆ The amount of money 2 years in the future equals
  Amount after 2 years = Present value $\times (1 + r)^2$.
- ◆ The amount of money n years in the future equals
  Amount after n years = Present value $\times (1 + r)^n$.

■ Discounting a Future Amount

The equations giving the amounts at times in the future can be rearranged to *discount* the future amount of money into its present value.

- ◆ The present value of money to be received 1 year in the future is:
$$\text{Present value} = \frac{\text{Amount 1 year in the future}}{(1+r)}$$
- ◆ The present value of money to be received n years in the future is:
$$\text{Present value} = \frac{\text{Amount } n \text{ years in the future}}{(1+r)^n}$$

■ Present Value of a Sequence of Future Amounts

If money payments are to be received at several times in the future, the present value of this stream of payments is equal to the sum of the present value of each money payment.

■ The Decision

To determine whether to rent or buy the capital equipment, the firm compares the present value of the rent payments it will make in the future to the current cost of buying the equipment. The firm will rent or buy, depending on which amount is lower.

Helpful Hints

1. **PRESENT VALUE :** The concept of present value is especially important in finance classes. For instance, when a company or government borrows by issuing a bond, the company or government promises to make fixed interest payments of money at specified times in the future and to repay the amount borrowed at some time in the future. *Today's* value of these payments is their present value. So *today's* value, which is the price of the bond, is the present value of the payments it promises to make. Combine this observation with one more: When the interest rate rises, the present value of

the future payments decreases. (Look at the formula for the present value to see this fact.) From these results we can see an important fact: When the interest rate rises, the present value of each of these future payments falls, which means that their sum—the price of the already issued bonds—falls. Similarly, when the interest rate falls, the price of already issued bonds rises. In other words, there is an inverse relationship between the interest rate and the price of bonds!

Questions

■ True/False and Explain

Present Value and Discounting

1. Money to be received in the future is worth less than the same amount of money received today.

2. If the interest rate is 10 percent a year, the present value of $100 received in one year is $110.

3. To determine whether to rent or buy a piece of capital equipment, the firm compares the cost of buying the item to the present value of the stream of rental payments and selects whichever is the smaller.

■ Multiple Choice

Present Value and Discounting

1. The present value of $100 to be received in a year is
   a. less the lower the interest rate.
   b. less the higher the interest rate.
   c. not at all related to the interest rate.
   d. related, though in an inconsistent manner, to the interest rate.

2. If the interest rate is 5 percent, the present value of $100 to be received in one year is
   a. $105.00.
   b. $100.00.
   c. $95.24.
   d. $95.00.

3. If the interest rate is 10 percent, the present value of $100 to be received in one year is
   a. $110.00.
   b. $100.00.
   c. $90.91.
   d. $90.00.

4. If the interest rate is 10 percent, the present value of $100 to be received in two years is
   a. $121.00.
   b. $120.00.
   c. $100.00.
   d. $82.64.

5. Which of the following statements is correct?
   a. Profit-maximizing firms almost always buy capital equipment because they do not want to incur rental costs that extend into the future.
   b. The higher the interest rate, the larger the present value of payments made in the future.
   c. The present value of $100 to be paid in a year is less than $100.
   d. None of the above statements is correct.

■ Short Answer Problems

1. Explain present value by discussing why $110 received one year from now has a present value of $100 if the interest rate is 10 percent per year.

2. Larry, the owner of Larry's Lawn Care Company, is considering the purchase or rental of another lawn mower. The lawn mower has a life of two years and costs $240 to buy. Alternatively Larry can rent the mower for two years and pay $130 each year.
   a. If the interest rate is 5 percent, will Larry buy or rent the mower?
   b. If the interest rate is 10 percent, will Larry buy or rent the mower?

3. How does an increase in the interest rate affect a business's decision whether to buy or rent a piece of capital equipment?

■ You're the Teacher

1. "I really don't get this 'present value' thing. I mean, a dollar is a dollar, right? Why is it worth less if I get it sometime in the future than if I get I right now?" Explain to your friend why a dollar received in the future is worth less than a dollar received now.

Answers

■ True/False Answers

Present Value and Discounting

1. **T** Money received in the present can be *immediately* saved and earn additional interest, an opportunity not available with money received in the future.

2. **F** The present value equals $100/(1.10) = $90.91.

3. **T** This calculation is the fundamental calculation that must be made to determine whether to rent or buy the capital equipment.

■ Multiple Choice Answers

Present Value and Discounting

1. **b** The present value is $100/(1+r)$ with r the interest rate, so the higher is r, the lower is the present value.

2. **c** The present value equals $100/(1+r)$ with r the interest rate, which equals $100/(1+0.05) = $95.24.

3. **c** Comparing this answer with the previous answer shows that the higher the interest rate, the lower the present value of funds to be received in the future.

4. **d** The present value is $100/(1.10)^2$.

5. **c** The present value of an amount to be paid in the future is *always* less than the amount itself because the future payment must be discounted to make it equal its present value.

■ Answers to Short Answer Problems

1. The present value of $110 received one year from now is the amount that, if saved today at the market interest rate, would grow to be $110 in one year. The interest rate is 10 percent, so $100 saved grows to $110 in one year. As a result, $100 is the present value of $110 in one year.

2. a. The decision to rent or buy depends on whichever is less expensive. The cost of buying the lawn mower is $240. The present value of renting the lawn mower when the interest rate is 5 percent is:

$$\frac{\$130}{(1+0.05)} + \frac{\$130}{(1+0.05)^2} = \$123.81 + \$117.91$$

= $241.72. The cost of buying the lawn mower is less then renting it, so Larry buys the mower.

b. If the interest rate is 10 percent, the present value of renting the mower is:

$$\frac{\$130}{(1+0.10)} + \frac{\$130}{(1+0.10)^2} = \$118.18 + \$107.44$$

= $225.62. The cost of renting the lawn mower is less then buying it, so Larry rents the mower.

3. An increase in the interest rate makes the business more likely to rent the item of capital. When the interest rate increases, the present value of the rental payments decreases, which lowers the cost of renting the equipment.

■ You're the Teacher

1. "Look, the deal is that if you get the dollar now, you have an option that is not open to you if you get it, say, one year in the future. In particular, you can save the dollar that you get now for this next year. The dollar that you get next year you can't save for this year. The fact that you have this extra option makes the dollar you get now worth more than the dollar you get in a year. Think about it this way: If you get the dollar now, you can save it and earn some interest income. If the interest rate is, say, r, then the interest income you would earn is $1 \times r$ or r of interest income. A dollar received today can grow to be $1 + r$ dollars in a year. The dollar you receive in one year is going to be worth only $1 in a year. So you can see why a dollar received in a year is worth less than a dollar received now—the dollar you get now can grow because it can be saved immediately! Think that 'discounting' means 'shrinking.' With this idea, you can see that we discount or shrink the value of a dollar that we get in the future because it's worth less than a dollar we receive now!"

Chapter 19 ECONOMIC INEQUALITY

■ Economic Inequality in the United States

Money income equals market income plus cash payments to households by the government. **Market income** equals wages, interest, rent, and profit earned in factor markets before paying income taxes. In 2011,

♦ the mode (most common) household income was between $20,000 to $25,000;

♦ the median (the income for which 50 percent of families have higher incomes and 50 percent have lower) household income was $50,054, and

♦ the mean (or average) household income was $69,677.

The distribution of income is positively skewed, so that a relatively few people make very high incomes.

♦ The poorest 20 percent of families received 3.2 percent of the total income; the richest 20 percent received 51.1 percent of the total income.

Inequality in income and wealth is illustrated by a Lorenz curve. A **Lorenz curve** for income (wealth) graphs the cumulative percentage of income (wealth) against the cumulative percentage of households. Figure 19.1 illustrates a Lorenz curve for income.

♦ The "line of equality" shows the (hypothetical) distribution of income (wealth) if everyone had the same income (wealth).

♦ The farther the Lorenz curve is from the line of equality, the more unequal is the distribution.

Income is the amount of earnings received by a household over a period of time while **wealth** is the value of things the household owns at a point in time. Measured wealth is more unequally distributed than income.

♦ The data used to construct the wealth distribution do not include human capital and therefore overstate wealth inequalities.

FIGURE 19.1
The Lorenz Curve

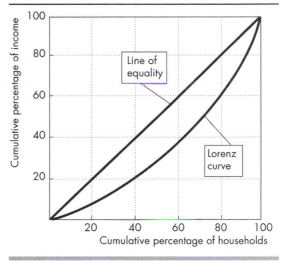

♦ The distribution of *annual* income is more unequal than distribution of *lifetime* income.

The distribution of income can be measured by the **Gini ratio**, which equals the ratio of the area between the line of equality and the Lorenz curve to the entire area beneath the line of equality. Over the last three decades the Gini ratio has risen, which indicates that the distribution of income in the United States has become more unequal over this time period. On the average, households with more education and married couples have higher incomes than the average.

Poverty exists when a household cannot buy the quantities of food, shelter, and clothing that are deemed necessary. In 2012, 46 million Americans, or 15 percent of the population, had incomes below the official poverty level, $23,050 for a four-person household. A disproportionate number of these households were of Hispanic origin or were black. More than 28 percent of households in which householder is female and no husband is present are below the poverty level.

■ Inequality in the World Economy

Among the world's nations, the distribution of income in Brazil and South Africa are among the most unequal and the distribution of income in Finland and Sweden are among the most equal. The United States falls between these extremes.

In the world as a whole, 50 percent of the population lives on an income of $2.50 per day or less; 80 percent live on an income of $10 a day or less. The world distribution of income is less equally distributed than that in the United States. However, since 1970 the world distribution of income has moved toward greater equality of income even though the distribution of income within most nations has become less equal.

■ The Sources of Economic Inequality

Differences in wages and earnings are partly a result of differences in human capital. High-skilled labor, with high human capital, has higher wages because:

♦ Demand — the demand for high-skilled labor exceeds the demand for low-skilled labor.

♦ Supply — skills are costly to acquire, so the supply of high-skilled labor is less than the supply of low-skilled labor.

FIGURE 19.2
High-skilled and Low-skilled Labor

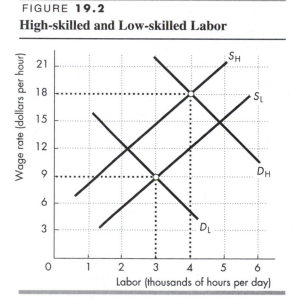

Figure 19.2 illustrates the demand and supply for high-skilled and low-skilled labor. As the figure shows, high-skilled labor is paid a higher wage rate ($18 per hour) than low-skilled labor ($9 per hour) because the demand for skilled labor is greater and the supply is smaller.

Human capital differences create differences in income. Workers with more human capital receive higher wages.

♦ Technological changes, such as computers and laser scanners, are substitutes for low-skilled labor and complements for high skilled labor. Technological change has increased the demand for high-skilled workers and decreased the demand for low-skilled workers, thereby increasing the difference in wages between high-skilled and low-skilled workers.

♦ Globalization has decreased the demand for low-skilled labor and increased the demand for high-skilled labor, so globalization also has increased the differences in wages.

Discrimination can lead to differences in income. Those discriminated against receive lower wages than others. Economists point out that the higher wages paid more favored workers boosts firms' costs and thereby makes it hard for firms to sustain this discrimination.

Differences in degree of specialization can affect income differences. Specializing in market production increases productivity and hence wages. Social conventions have led men to specialize in market activities and women to divide their time between market activities and non-market activities, such as household production.

Contests among superstars have lead to extremely high incomes for the winners. "Contests" also include competitions amongst job prospects for top positions within corporations: the executives who "win" the contest are paid extremely large salaries. Globalization has increased the size of the talent pool for top executives and so the "prize"—the salary—has increased.

Unequal wealth also leads to differences in incomes. Inequalities can be passed to future generations through bequests (gifts to the next generation) and assortative mating (marrying within one's socioeconomic class).

■ Income Redistribution

Income is redistributed by governments through income taxes, income maintenance programs, and provision of goods and services below cost.

An income tax can be a:

♦ **Progressive income tax** — the average tax rate increases when income increases.

♦ **Regressive income tax** — the average tax rate decreases when income increases.

♦ **Proportional income tax** — the average tax rate does not change when income increases.

Income maintenance programs include social security, unemployment compensation, and welfare. Taxes and income maintenance programs reduce the degree of inequality in the United States. In addition to transferring income to poorer households, government provided subsidized services also redistribute income.

The **big tradeoff** is the tradeoff between equity and efficiency. It points out that redistribution which makes incomes more equal creates less efficiency because redistribution weakens the incentive to work.

Young women who have not completed high school, have at least one child, and live without a partner are a major welfare challenge. More education and job training are the long-term solutions to removing these people from poverty. Support payments and welfare provide income. The current welfare program for this group is the Temporary Assistance for Needy Families (TANF) program, which requires an adult member of the family work or perform community service and generally has a 5-year limit for receiving assistance.

Helpful Hints

1. **HOW TO CALCULATE A LORENZ CURVE :** If you are ever called upon to construct a Lorenz curve, the crucial point to recall is that it measures *cumulative* percentages. In other words, along the horizontal axis is the cumulative percentage of households and along the vertical axis is, say, the cumulative percentage of income. *Cumulate* is just a fancy word for *sum* or *add*, so the cumulative percentage of income means the total (the "added up") income received by *all* households up to the point under consideration in the income distribution.

   To construct a Lorenz curve, obtain a summary of the incomes of all the households. Calculate the income of the 20 percent having the lowest incomes, which in recent years is 3.5 percent of the nation's total income. Plot this point. Then determine the income for the next 20 percent, which in recent years is 8.8 percent of the nation's total income. Add these two to obtain the cumulative percentage, in this case 12.3 percent. Then plot another point representing the cumulative percentage of households, 40 percent, and the cumulative percentage of income, 12.3 percent. Continue until you reach 100 percent of the households. Connect the points that you have plotted to get the Lorenz curve.

Questions

■ True/False and Explain

Economic Inequality in the United States

1. Income in the United States is distributed normally; that is, it has the common bell shape.

2. The poorest 20 percent of American families receive about 15 percent of the nation's total income; the richest 20 percent receive about 25 percent of the nation's total income.

3. The farther the Lorenz curve is from the line of equality, the more equal is the distribution of income.

4. The larger the Gini ratio, the more equally incomes are distributed.

5. Income in the United States is distributed less equally today than forty years ago.

Inequality in the World Economy

6. The distribution of income in the United States is less equal than in other countries.

7. Since 1970, the world distribution of income has become more equally distributed.

The Sources of Economic Inequality

8. The demand for low-skilled workers is less than the demand for high-skilled workers.

9. More years of schooling and more years of work experience both will increase human capital.

10. If males on average earn more than females, there must be discrimination in the labor market.

11. Globalization has increased the salary received by the "winner" of a contest to become the top executive of large multinational company.

12. Inheritances generally make the income distribution more equal.

Income Redistribution

13. A progressive income tax is one whose average tax rate falls as income increases.

14. Government redistribution makes the income distribution more equal.

15. The big tradeoff is the idea that equalizing the distribution of income reduces economic efficiency.

■ Multiple Choice

Economic Inequality in the United States

1. The mean (average) U.S. family income in 2011 was approximately
   a. $13,000.
   b. $70,000.
   c. $93,000.
   d. $150,000.

2. In a Lorenz diagram for income, the line of equality shows
   a. the most equitable income distribution.
   b. how unequally incomes are distributed.
   c. how much redistribution occurs.
   d. the income distribution if everyone received the same income.

Use Figure 19.3 for the next two questions.

FIGURE **19.3**

Multiple Choice Questions 3 and 4

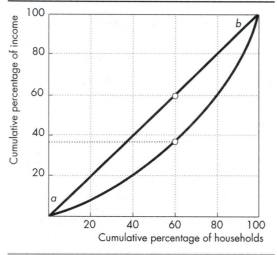

3. In Figure 19.3 the straight line labeled *ab* is the
   a. Lorenz curve.
   b. line of equality.
   c. line of poverty.
   d. line of distribution.

4. In Figure 19.3 the poorest 60 percent of households have what percent of the nation's total income.
   a. About 23 percent
   b. About 37 percent
   c. About 60 percent
   d. About 63 percent

5. The farther away a Lorenz curve for income is from the line of equality, the
   a. more equally wealth is distributed.
   b. more equally income is distributed.
   c. less equally income is distributed.
   d. None of the above.

6. The measured annual distribution of wealth
   a. understates inequality because it does not take into account the family's stage in its life cycle.
   b. understates inequality because it does not take into account the distribution of human capital.
   c. overstates inequality because it takes into account the family's stage in its life cycle.
   d. overstates inequality because it does not take into account the distribution of human capital.

7. Which of the following would show the <u>LEAST</u> amount of inequality?
   a. Measured annual income
   b. Measured annual wealth
   c. Lifetime income
   d. Measured annual income and annual wealth are equally distributed and are more equally distributed than lifetime income.

8. On average, which families have the highest incomes?
   a. Black households
   b. Households of Hispanic origin
   c. White households
   d. Households of Hispanic origin and white households are tied for the highest income

9. Of the approximate total population of 300 million people in America, about how many have incomes below the official poverty level?
   a. Approximately 13 million
   b. Approximately 46 million
   c. Approximately 73 million
   d. Approximately 104 million

Inequality in the World Economy

10. The world distribution of income is _____ the U.S. distribution of income.
    a. less equal than
    b. equal to
    c. more equal than
    d. not comparable to

11. Over the past several decades, the distribution of income within most countries has become _____ equal and the distribution of income in the world has become _____ equal.
    a. more; more
    b. more; less
    c. less; more
    d. less; less

The Sources of Economic Inequality

12. The higher the cost of acquiring skills, the _____ are the high-skilled and low-skilled labor _____ curves.
    a. closer together; demand
    b. farther apart; demand
    c. closer together; supply
    d. farther apart; supply

13. Which of the following is a reason why the wage rate paid high-skilled workers exceeds the wage rate paid low-skilled workers?
    a. The market for high-skilled workers is more competitive than the market for low-skilled labor.
    b. The demand for high-skilled workers exceeds the demand for low-skilled workers.
    c. The number of high-skilled workers exceeds the number of low-skilled workers.
    d. Low-skilled workers often are in the process of acquiring more human capital.

14. Technological change has _____ the demand for low-skilled workers and _____ the demand for high-skilled workers.
    a. increased; increased
    b. increased; decreased
    c. decreased; increased
    d. decreased; decreased

15. Globalization has _____ the demand for low-skilled workers and _____ the demand for high-skilled workers.
    a. increased; increased
    b. increased; decreased
    c. decreased; increased
    d. decreased; decreased

16. Comparing the wage rates between never-married men and women with equal human capital, researchers have found that the wage rates are
    a. farther apart than the wage rates of other men and women in the labor force generally.
    b. the same as wage rates of other men and women in the labor force generally.
    c. equal.
    d. not comparable because men and women work at different jobs.

17. Contests among superstars
    a. are a reason why technological change has decreased income inequality.
    b. have been diminished by the on-going globalization.
    c. need the prizes of the winners to be similar to the prizes of the losers in order for them to have incentive effects.
    d. explain why top business executives are paid such high incomes.

18. Assortative mating _____ the distribution of income.
    a. makes the distribution of income more equal.
    b. makes the distribution of income less equal.
    c. has no effect on the distribution of income.
    d. might make the distribution of income more equal or less equal.

Income Redistribution

19. Government tax and redistribution programs
    a. generally redistribute income away from the poor and give it to the rich.
    b. have no net redistributive effects.
    c. generally redistribute income away from the rich and give it to the poor.
    d. are dwarfed by the scale of government programs designed to give away goods and services below cost.

20. The idea that increasing the equality of the income distribution reduces economic efficiency is called the
    a. negative tax trap.
    b. progressive tax problem.
    c. big trade-off.
    d. problem of poverty.

■ Short Answer Problems

TABLE 19.1

Market Income

Households grouped by income	Group income (dollars)	Percentage of total national income	Cumulative percentage
Lowest 20%	$200,000	5%	5%
Second lowest 20%	300,000	____	____
Middle 20%	500,000	____	____
Second highest 20%	1,000,000	____	____
Highest 20%	2,000,000	____	____

1. Table 19.1 gives information regarding the distribution of market income in Microland, a small nation with 100 residents.

   a. Complete the table.

   b. Based on Table 19.1, plot the Lorenz curve for this nation in Figure 19.4.

2. The government of Microland imposes a progressive income tax. Only those in the highest 20 percent income bracket pay the tax, and they must pay 30 percent of their income. From the tax receipts, the government gives 1/3 to the lowest 20 percent group, 1/3 to the next lowest, and 1/3 to the next lowest (the middle 20 percent group).

   a. If none of the groups in the economy alter their behavior — so that their market incomes remain the same as those in Table 19.1 — finish Table 19.2 for the post-tax, post-transfer income distribution.

   b. In Figure 19.4 draw the new Lorenz curve showing the distribution of income *after* the government redistribution program.

   c. When is income distributed more equally: before or after the government program?

3. What is the difference between wealth and income? If you know one of these for an individual, can you calculate the other?

4. Jake has human capital worth $100,000 and stocks and bonds worth $100,000. James has only human capital worth $200,000. The return on both types of capital is 15 percent.

   a. What is Jake's income? James's income? Who has more income?

FIGURE 19.4

Short Answer Problems 1 and 2

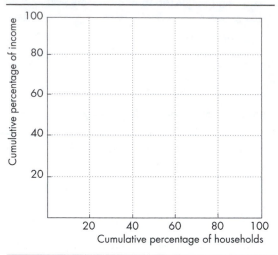

TABLE 19.2

Group Income After Redistribution

Households grouped by income	Group income (dollars)	Percentage of total national income	Cumulative percentage
Lowest 20%	____	____	____
Second lowest 20%	____	____	____
Middle 20%	____	____	____
Second highest 20%	____	____	____
Highest 20%	____	____	____

   b. Suppose that human capital is not measured. What is Jake's capital? James's capital? According to this measure, who has more capital?

   c. If income can be measured correctly, will Jake's and James's income or capital appear to be less equally distributed?

5. How does the distribution of income in the world compare to the distribution within the United States? How has the difference between these two distributions changed over the last three decades?

6. Suppose that new technology is developed that increases the demand for high-skilled workers. In Figure 19.5 (on the next page) illustrate the effect the increase in demand has on the wage rate paid to high-skilled workers. If the new technology does not affect the demand for low-skilled workers, how

FIGURE **19.5**

Short Answer Problem 6

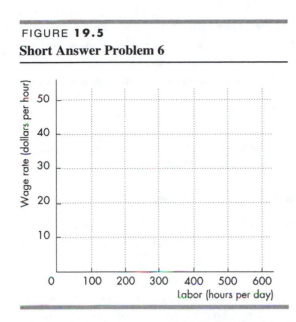

is the relative wage rates paid high-skilled and low-skilled workers affected?

7. Igor currently works as a mid-level manager for Midnight Express, a global over-night package delivery company. Igor is one of 50 mid-level managers. Each of them is willing to work extremely hard if they have a 2 percent chance of being named a top executive making a salary of $1,000,000. Suppose Midnight Express expands, perhaps by making day deliveries. The number of mid-level managers increases to 100. What must happen to the salary paid a top executive to give Igor and the other mid-level managers the incentive to work extremely hard?

8. Return to Problem 2. With the redistribution policy discussed in Problem 2, what are the likely reactions of the recipients of the tax money? Of the taxpayers? How do these reactions affect your answer to part (c) of Problem 2?

■ You're the Teacher

1. "No citizen of the United States should be forced to live in poverty!" Comment on this assertion. Do you think attaining this goal is likely? Why or why not?

Answers

■ True/False Answers

Economic Inequality in the United States

1. **F** Income in the United States is skewed, with relatively few people earning above-average incomes and many people earning below-average incomes.

2. **F** Income is less equally distributed than the question states: The poorest 20 percent receive less than 4 percent of total income and the richest 20 percent receive more than 50 percent of total income.

3. **F** The *closer* the Lorenz curve to the line of equality, the more equal the income distribution.

4. **F** The *smaller* the Gini ratio, the more equal the income distribution.

5. **T** Over the past four decades, the distribution in the United States has become less equal.

Inequality in the World Economy

6. **F** Compared to other nations, the distribution of income in the United States is neither extremely equal nor extremely unequal.

7. **T** Since 1970, average incomes in very poor nations such as India and China have increased, thereby increasing the equality of the world distribution of income.

The Sources of Economic Inequality

8. **T** The labor demand curve is the *MRP* curve. Because the *MRP* of low-skilled workers is less than high-skilled workers, the demand for low-skilled workers is less than that for high-skilled workers.

9. **T** In general, people with more human capital have higher wages, so more schooling and more work experience generally lead to higher wages.

10. **F** There might be discrimination, but there are other possibilities, such as specialization, that can account for wage differentials.

11. **T** Globalization has increased the size of the pool of job candidates, which has, in turn, increased the size of the "award" won by the winner.

12. **F** Inheritances make the income distribution less equal.

Income Redistribution

13. **F** A progressive income tax is one whose average tax rate *increases* with income.

14. **T** Government redistribution programs increase the income of poorer households and decrease the income of richer households.

15. **T** The trade-off results because more redistribution, and hence more equal incomes, lessens incentives to work, thereby creating inefficiency.

■ Multiple Choice Answers

Economic Inequality in the United States

1. **b** Mean household income in the United States is a little less than $70,000.

2. **d** This answer defines the line of equality.

3. **b** The line of equality shows the income distribution if everyone received the same income.

4. **b** Follow the dotted line up from 60 percent of the households to the Lorenz curve and then left to determine that these households have about 37 percent of the nation's total income.

5. **c** The farther away the Lorenz curve is from the line of equality, the less equally income is distributed.

6. **d** If human capital were included in the measured wealth distribution, the distribution would be more equal.

7. **c** Over people's lifetimes, the degree of inequality is less than in any given year.

8. **c** White households have the highest average income.

9. **b** According to the government's measure of poverty, 46 million Americans lived in poverty.

Inequality in the World Economy

10. **a** Incomes in the world range from the extremely poor, who live on less than $2.50 per day, to the very rich, who live in industrialized countries.

11. **c** Although income within most nations has become distributed less equally, the overall world distribution of income has become more equal because incomes within very poor countries have grown relatively rapidly.

The Sources of Economic Inequality

12. **d** The vertical distance between the supply curve of high-skilled labor and of low-skilled labor equals the cost of acquiring the skill.

13. **b** Because the demand for high-skilled workers exceeds the demand for low-skilled workers, high-skilled workers have a higher wage rate.

14. **c** Technological change has increased the demand for high-skilled workers and thereby raised the wage rates and incomes rate of high-skilled workers.

15. **c** Globalization also has increased the demand for high-skilled workers and so is a second reason why their wages and incomes have increased.

16. **c** Never-married men and never-married women have the same degree of specialization in market work and their wage rates are the same.

17. **d** The executives who "win" the contest and become top executives are paid enormous incomes as their "prize."

18. **b** Assortative mating refers to "like marrying like," thereby making the distribution of income less equal.

Income Redistribution

19. **c** These government programs result in income after redistribution being distributed more equally than market income.

20. **c** The big tradeoff points out a cost of increasing income equality: decreasing economic efficiency.

■ Answers to Short Answer Problems

1. a. The answers are in Table 19.3. To calculate the answers, first add all the groups' income to get the total income in the nation, $4,000,000. The percentage earned by the second lowest 20 percent is $300,000/$4,000,000, which equals 7.5 percent. The cumulative percentage for the second group equals the percentage earned by it and all lower groups, which in this case is only the bottom 20 percent group. The cumulative percentage therefore is 5 percent + 7.5 percent = 12.5 percent. The rest of the answers in the table are calculated similarly.

    b. Figure 19.6 shows the Lorenz curve for Microland.

TABLE 19.3
Short Answer Question 1

Households grouped by income	Group income (dollars)	Percentage of total national income	Cumulative percentage
Lowest 20%	$ 200,000	5.0%	5.0%
Second lowest 20%	300,000	7.5	12.5
Middle 20%	500,000	12.5	25.0
Second highest 20%	1,000,000	25.0	50.0
Highest 20%	2,000,000	50.0	100.0

FIGURE 19.6
Short Answer Problem 1

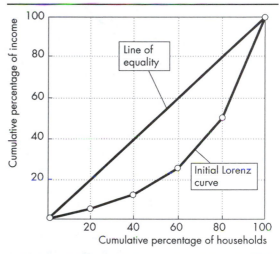

TABLE 19.4
Short Answer Problem 2

Households grouped by income	Group income (dollars)	Percentage of total national income	Cumulative percentage
Lowest 20%	$ 400,000	10.0%	10.0%
Second lowest 20%	500,000	12.5	22.5
Middle 20%	700,000	17.5	40.0
Second highest 20%	1,000,000	25.0	65.0
Highest 20%	1,400,000	35.0	100.0

2. a. Table 19.4 shows the income distribution after the government redistribution. The richest 20 percent of households are taxed 30 percent of their income, which equals $600,000. Their af-

ter-tax income therefore equals $1,400,000. Then, $200,000 ($1/3$ of the total $600,000) is given to the lowest 20 percent, so their income rises to $400,000; another $1/3$ is given to the next lowest group, so their income rises to $500,000; and the final $1/3$ is given to the middle group, so their income rises to $700,000. The percentages are calculated in the same way as in problem 1.

FIGURE **19.7**

Short Answer Problem 2

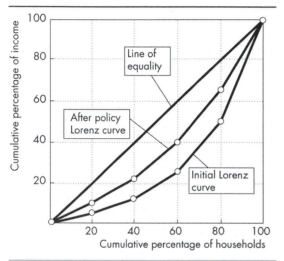

b. Figure 19.7 shows both Lorenz curves.
c. Income is distributed more equally after the government programs. The Lorenz curve for income after the government redistribution is closer to the line of equality than the Lorenz curve showing market income before the redistribution.

3. Wealth is the stock of assets owned by an individual, whereas income is the flow of earnings received by an individual. These concepts are connected because an individual's income is the earnings that flow from the person's stock of wealth. If we know the person's stock of wealth and rate of return, we can calculate his or her income flow. If we know the person's income flow and the rate of return, we can calculate his or her stock of wealth.

4. a. Jake's income equals the return on capital, 15 percent, times the amount of capital. Hence Jake's income equals $30,000. James's income equals $30,000, so the incomes are the same.

b. Jake's capital is measured as $100,000. James's capital is measured as $0 because human capital is not included when capital is measured. Jake seems to have more capital.
c. Capital *appears* to be less equally distributed. The two measured incomes are equal but the two measured capitals are different. This line of reasoning helps explain the difference between the measured income distribution and the measured wealth distribution in the United States.

5. The distribution of income in the world is less equal than the distribution of income within the United States. The world distribution of income has become more equal over the last three decades, while the U.S. distribution of income has become less equal. These changes mean that the difference between these two distributions has decreased.

FIGURE **19.8**

Short Answer Problem 6

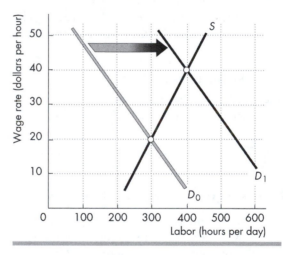

6. The increase in the demand for high-skilled workers shifts the demand curve rightward as shown in Figure 19.8, where the shift is from D_0 to D_1. With this change, the wage rate rises from $20 per hour to $40 per hour. The wage rates of low-skilled workers are not directly affected, so the relative wage rate of high-skilled to low-skilled workers rises.

7. The increase in the number of mid-level managers decreases the probability of any particular mid-level manager being named to the top job. The decrease in the probability of winning the contest decreases Igor's incentive to work hard. To restore Igor's and the other mid-level managers' incentive to work ex-

tremely hard, the "prize" in this contest—the salary paid the top executive must rise.

8. The recipients of the tax money likely will work less. If they were to work more, they might earn enough to move into a higher income bracket and lose the money the government is giving to them. The taxpayers also will tend to work less. The government is taxing them so that they must pay 30 percent of their income as taxes. As a result, they will tend to cut back on their work because the income they get to keep for themselves from working, their after-tax income, has fallen. On both counts, people work less and so the nation's total income decreases.

Both of these effects illustrate the force of the big trade-off. By making incomes more equal, the government program has blunted people's incentives to work and thereby lessened economic efficiency and decreased the overall size of the nation's income. These big trade-off effects indicate the cost to redistributing income. They should play at least a minor role in your decision whether you think the income distribution before or after the redistribution is best.

■ You're the Teacher

1. "Oh come on, you can't really be serious about this statement, can you? Think of the amount of redistribution it would take to insure that no one has less than the poverty-level income and then think about the idea of the big tradeoff that we studied. The opportunity cost of this policy would be immense because it would really blunt people's incentives to work — both the high-income people who would have to pay heavy taxes and the low-income people who would lose a lot of transfer payments if they earned more income. I think the big tradeoff points out that this suggestion, appealing in concept, simply isn't practical in reality."

Chapter Quiz

1. The median household income in the United States is closest to
   a. $17,000.
   b. $29,000.
   c. $50,000.
   d. $102,000.

2. In the United States, the 20 percent of families with the highest incomes receive about ____ of total income.
   a. 20 percent
   b. 35 percent
   c. 50 percent
   d. 66 percent

3. The closer the Lorenz curve for income is to the line of equality, the
   a. larger is the nation's total income.
   b. smaller is the nation's total income.
   c. more equally are incomes distributed.
   d. larger the fraction of the nation's income received by the richest families.

4. Which of the following makes the distribution of income more equal?
   a. Inheritances
   b. Progressive income taxes
   c. Assortative mating
   d. The fact that people paid higher wage rates work more hours

5. Government tax and transfer payments generally
   a. shift the Lorenz curve toward the line of equality.
   b. shift the Lorenz curve away from the line of equality.
   c. have no effect on the Lorenz curve.
   d. shift the Lorenz curve away from the line of equality at low incomes and toward it at high incomes.

6. The big tradeoff
   a. would not exist if income taxes were proportional.
   b. points out that the redistribution of income increases people's incentives to work.
   c. says that economic efficiency is decreased as more redistribution is undertaken.
   d. says that richer families trade off more hours at work for more income.

7. The supply curve of high-skilled workers lies ____ the supply curve of low-skilled workers.
   a. above
   b. on top of
   c. below
   d. below at low wage rates and above at high wage rates

8. Over the last decade, globalization has ____ the demand for high-skilled workers and ____ the demand for low skilled workers.
   a. increased; increased
   b. increased; decreased
   c. decreased; increased
   d. decreased; decreased

9. The distribution of income in Brazil is ____ the distribution of income in Finland.
   a. more equally distributed than
   b. distributed the same as
   c. less equally distributed than
   d. not comparable to

10. Because the measured distribution of wealth does not consider the role of human capital, the measured wealth distribution
   a. is more equal than measured income distributions.
   b. is less equal than measured income distributions.
   c. is more equal than actual wealth distributions.
   d. cannot be compared to the actual wealth distribution.

The answers for this Chapter Quiz are on page 346

Key Concepts

■ Decisions in the Face of Uncertainty

Decisions made in the face of uncertainty depend on expected wealth, risk aversion, the utility of wealth, and expected utility.

◆ **Expected wealth** is the money value of what a person expects to own at a point in time. For instance, if a person has a 60 percent chance of having $100 and a 40 percent chance of having $200, expected wealth, *EW*, is $(0.6 \times \$100) + (0.4 \times \$200) = \$140$.

◆ **Risk aversion** is the dislike of risk. Most people are risk averse. The utility of wealth curve helps make measurement of risk aversion more concrete.

◆ *Utility of wealth* — the amount of utility a person has from different amounts of wealth. Figure 20.1 illustrates a utility of wealth curve. The curve shows diminishing marginal utility of wealth—the utility gain from gaining a dollar of wealth is less than the utility loss from losing a dollar of wealth. The "pain from a loss exceeds the pleasure from a gain of equal size" so the person is risk averse.

◆ **Expected utility**, *EU*, is the utility value of what a person expects to own at a point in time. Expected utility might differ from the person's actual utility, which is the amount of utility the person actually gets.

In an uncertain situation, people maximize expected utility. A person calculates the expected utility for the possible choices and then selects the action with the highest expected utility.

An individual's cost of risk (the amount by which expected wealth must be increased to give the same expected utility as a no-risk situation) can be measured using the utility of wealth curve. In Figure 20.1 Katie faces the risky situation of receiving wealth of $10,000, with utility of 30, or $20,000, with utility of 50. Both outcomes have a 50 percent chance of occurring. The expected wealth is $15,000 and the expected utility is

FIGURE **20.1**
Utility of Wealth and Cost of Risk

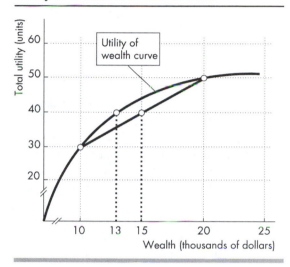

40. Figure 20.1 shows that the risky situation has the same utility, 40, as receiving certain wealth of $13,000. The difference in wealth between the risky and the sure case, $15,000 - $13,000 = $2,000, is the cost of the risk.

■ Buying and Selling Risk

Previous chapters have demonstrated how *both* buyers and sellers can gain a surplus from buying and selling in markets. Risk can also be bought and sold in markets and both buyers and sellers can gain.

Insurance is a method of buying and selling risk.

◆ People buy insurance to reduce risk (they sell risk). They trade off the certainty of paying a (relatively) small insurance premium to avoid the potential uncertain outcome of a large loss.

◆ Insurance works by pooling a large number of risks so that the total number of adverse outcomes is relatively certain. Insurance companies can calculate how much they will pay out in claims.

◆ Firms find selling insurance profitable because

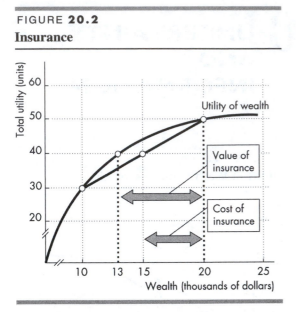

FIGURE **20.2**

Insurance

people are risk averse and will pay to reduce their risk. That is, people will pay a smaller sum to be sure that they will not incur a larger loss.

In Figure 20.2, Katie owns a car worth $20,000 and has a 50 percent chance of being in an accident, which decreases the car's value to $10,000. Katie has expected utility of 40. Katie has the same utility, 40, if she pays $7,000 for insurance and has (certain) wealth of $13,000, so Katie is willing to pay up to $7,000 for insurance. The $7,000 is her value of insurance. The expected value of the car is $15,000 so the cost of the insurance to the insurance company is $5,000. If the price of the insurance is between $7,000 and $5,000 both Katie and the insurance company gain from trade. Insurance is not possible if the risk of one individual's loss is not independent of everyone else's risk or if the risky event is not observable to both the buyer and seller.

■ **Private Information**

Private information is information about the value of an item being traded that is possessed by only buyers or sellers. A market in which buyers or sellers have private information has **asymmetric information**. Asymmetric information creates two problems:

♦ **Adverse selection** — the tendency for people to *enter into agreements* in which they can use their private information to their own advantage and to the disadvantage of the less informed party.

♦ **Moral hazard** — when one of the parties with pri-

vate information *after an agreement is made* has the tendency to use the information for their own benefit and at the cost of the less informed party.

Adverse selection and moral hazard create the used car market's **lemons problem**, the problem that in a market in which it is not possible to distinguish reliable products from lemons, too many lemons and too few reliable products are traded.

Information problems can be partially overcome through **signals**, when the informed person takes actions that send information to uninformed parties. A warranty on a used car is an example of a signal. The equilibrium when only one message is available and an uninformed person cannot determine quality is a **pooling equilibrium**. The equilibrium when signaling provides full information to a previously uninformed person is a **separating equilibrium**.

♦ In the loan market, banks face **credit risk** or **default risk** that the borrower (the creditor) will not repay the loan. Signals (e.g., length of time on the job) can help overcome moral hazard and adverse selection problems in this market. Banks also use **screening**, inducing an informed party to reveal relevant private information, by requiring that all borrowers reveal the signaling information.

♦ In the market for insurance both adverse selection and moral hazard exist. Insurance companies use signals and screening. For instance, for automobile insurance a driver's past driving record (a signal) and the amount of the deductible payment (a screen because high-risk drivers choose a small deductible payment while low-risk drivers choose a large deductible payment) limit adverse selection and moral hazard.

■ **Uncertainty, Information, and the Invisible Hand**

Do uncertainty and incomplete information mean that the invisible hand idea that self-interested choices promote social interest is incorrect? There is no definitive answer to this question.

The efficient amount of information to gather is the amount that sets the marginal benefit of information equal to the marginal cost.

If there are monopoly elements in markets dealing with information, such as insurance, there is underproduction arising from the inefficiency created by monopoly.

Helpful Hints

1. **WHY DID WE PREVIOUSLY IGNORE UNCERTAINTY AND RISK? :** Until this chapter we have ignored uncertainty when examining firms' and consumers' behavior. That is not to say that uncertainty does not exist; on the contrary, it is pervasive in the real world. Often, however, it does not change what is important about the situation. For instance, the key factor in how a business chooses its level of output is that it maximizes its profit and produces at $MC = MR$. The firm may be uncertain about its MC and MR, but it still tries to equate MC to MR to maximize its profit. If we had incorporated the role played by uncertainty into our analysis of firms, we might have missed the result that setting MC equal to MR gives the maximum profit. The models that we have studied before ignore uncertainty and risk because including these factors would obscure the important conclusions these models illuminated.

2. **A COLLEGE EDUCATION AS A SIGNAL :** Because people dislike uncertainty and the ensuing risk, they take actions to limit the extent of uncertainty. Signals play a significant role in this process. One relevant example of a signal is your college degree. Its possession signals to prospective employers that you have enough persistence, enough initiative, and enough intelligence to complete four (or more) years of a rigorous endeavor to attain a long-term goal. Persistence, initiative, and intelligence are productivity boosting traits. Hence a college degree raises your skills and also signals information about aspects of your character and personality.

Questions

■ True/False and Explain

Decisions in the Face of Uncertainty

1. Risk aversion is the dislike of risk.

2. The marginal utility of wealth diminishes as wealth increases.

3. For a risk averse person, expected wealth and expected utility are the same.

4. In a risky situation, risk averse people maximize their expected wealth.

5. Jane's cost of risk in an uncertain situation equals the difference between Jane's expected wealth and the certain wealth that gives her the same utility as the expected utility in the uncertain situation.

Buying and Selling Risk

6. In the insurance market, only the sellers benefit.

7. Insurance pools risks.

8. Insurance can increase a risk averse person's utility.

9. All risk can be insured.

Private Information

10. Adverse selection occurs when one party enters into a contract with private information that shows the agreement will give that party more benefit and the other party to the contract less benefit.

11. In a used car market with a lemons problem, too many good cars are offered for sale.

12. Traffic tickets are an example of a signal.

13. A separating equilibrium occurs when signaling provides full information to previously uninformed people.

14. Signals and screening are used to try to create a pooling equilibrium.

Uncertainty, Information, and the Invisible Hand

15. Information is unique because more can be produced at decreasing marginal cost.

16. The efficient quantity of information is always as much as possible.

■ Multiple Choice

Decisions in the Face of Uncertainty

1. Burt thinks that after a year he has a 30 percent chance of owning wealth of $20,000, a 20 percent chance of wealth of $40,000, and a 50 percent chance of wealth of $60,000. Burt's expected wealth is _____.
   a. $60,000
   b. $44,000
   c. $40,000
   d. $36,000

2. Erika's utility with $2,000 of wealth is 5,000 and her utility with $2,001 of wealth is 5,005. Her marginal utility from gaining the additional $1 of wealth is ____.
   a. 5,005
   b. 2.5
   c. 5,000
   d. 5

3. If Al is risk averse, as his wealth increases, his total utility of wealth ____ and his marginal utility of wealth ____.
   a. increases; increases
   b. increases; decreases
   c. decreases; increases
   d. decreases; decreases

4. Soran is risk averse. If her wealth falls by $100, her total utility decreases by 300. If her wealth increases, her total utility will increase
   a. by more than 300.
   b. by 300.
   c. by less than 300.
   d. but the amount of the increase cannot be determined without more information.

5. In a risky situation, people maximize their
   a. expected wealth.
   b. wealth.
   c. expected utility.
   d. benefit from risk.

6. In a risky situation, Jasmine has expected wealth of $8,000 and expected utility of 600. If Jasmine had certain wealth of $6,000 her utility would be 600. Jasmine's cost of risk is
   a. $14,000.
   b. $8,000.
   c. $6,000.
   d. $2,000.

Buying and Selling Risk

7. Insurance companies
   a. pool risk and thereby lower people's utility.
   b. never can earn a profit.
   c. can increase risk averse people's utility.
   d. pool utility of wealth curves.

8. When Sardar buys insurance, on net he
   a. gains if the value of the insurance is greater than the price he pays the insurance company.
   b. loses because the price must pay the insurance company lowers his expected utility.
   c. gains because his actual wealth with the insurance is greater than his expected wealth without the insurance.
   d. loses if the price of the insurance equals his expected loss from a bad outcome.

9. Vanessa has an automobile that is worth $30,000. If she is in an accident, the automobile will be worthless. The probability of an accident is 0.10. To the insurance company, what is the cost of insuring Vanessa's automobile?
   a. $2,700
   b. $3,000
   c. $27,000
   d. $30,000

Private Information

10. The tendency for a person to make an agreement and then behave after the agreement in a way to increase his or her benefits and harm the other party to the agreement is called
    a. signaling.
    b. adverse selection.
    c. moral hazard.
    d. the cost of contracting.

11. Ben becomes more likely to play with matches after he has fire insurance. This situation illustrates the idea of
    a. moral hazard.
    b. adverse selection.
    c. the lemon problem.
    d. the "don't play with fire" principle.

12. Which of the following is an example of a signal?
    a. Membership in a professional society
    b. A history of promptly paying bills when they come due
    c. Informal clothing worn by a job applicant to a formal job interview
    d. All of the above are signals.

13. JCPenney guarantees to refund a customer's money if the customer returns poorly made clothing. This guarantee on clothing is an example of
    a. the adverse selection problem.
    b. the moral hazard problem.
    c. the cost of risk.
    d. a signal.

14. If buyers cannot assess the quality of used cars and if there are no warranties,
    a. too many lemons are sold.
    b. too many good used cars are sold.
    c. good used cars are sold at a higher price than lemons.
    d. there is no adverse selection problem.

15. The used car market
    a. is more efficient with a separating equilibrium than with a pooling equilibrium.
    b. is more efficient with a pooling equilibrium than with a separating equilibrium.
    c. is equally efficient with a separating equilibrium as with a pooling equilibrium.
    d. cannot have a separating equilibrium.

16. Banks require people applying for a loan to complete a form detailing their credit history
    a. because the banks are not trying to maximize their profit.
    b. to insure a pooling equilibrium.
    c. to signal to the borrowers that they have funds to loan.
    d. to help screen low-risk and high-risk borrowers.

17. If the loan market equilibrium is a separating equilibrium, then high-risk borrowers pay a _____ interest rate and low-risk borrowers pay a _____ interest rate.
    a. high; low
    b. low; high
    c. low; low
    d. high; high

18. If you have private information that you are a riskier driver than your record indicates, you are likely to buy an insurance policy with
    a. a higher than average deductible.
    b. a lower than average deductible.
    c. an average deductible.
    d. none of the above.

Uncertainty, Information, and the Invisible Hand

19. Information can be thought of as a
    a. non-economic piece of data.
    b. violation of the invisible hand idea that the pursuit of self-interest promotes social interest.
    c. good whose marginal benefit is infinite.
    d. good whose marginal benefit decreases as more information is acquired.

20. Which of the following statements is correct?
    a. Because information is different from typical goods and services, it cannot be provided in a market.
    b. The marginal benefit from more information does not decrease.
    c. Too much information is provided if the market for information is a monopoly.
    d. Too much information can be inefficient.

■ Short Answer Problems

FIGURE **20.3**
Lisa's Utility of Wealth

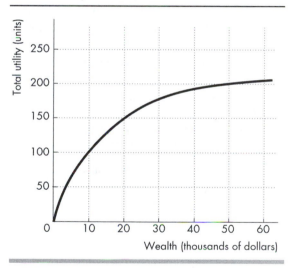

1. Figure 20.3 shows Lisa's utility of wealth curve. She is considering an investment that will pay her either $10,000 with a probability of 50 percent or $50,000 with a probability of 50 percent.
    a. What is Lisa's utility if she receives $10,000? Her utility if she receives $50,000? Her expected wealth, *EW,* and her expected utility?
    b. What is the cost of this risk to Lisa? Carefully explain what is meant by "the cost of risk."

TABLE 20.1
Leonard's Utility of Wealth

Wealth (dollars)	Utility
$0	0
4,000	52
5,000	60
8,000	79
10,000	87
15,000	98
20,000	104

2. Table 20.1 presents Leonard's utility of wealth schedule. Leonard is considering an investment that will pay either $0 or $20,000 with equal probability, that is, there is a 50 percent chance of obtaining $0 and a 50 percent chance of gaining $20,000.

   a. What is Leonard's expected wealth from the investment?

   b. What is Leonard's expected utility?

   c. What is Leonard's cost of risk for this investment opportunity?

   d. Is Leonard willing to make the investment if it costs him $5,000?

TABLE 20.2
Igor's Utility of Wealth Schedule

Wealth (dollars)	Utility
$100	400
80	350
60	280
40	200
20	110
0	0

3. Igor owns a valuable bat worth $100. Unfortunately, this species of bat has a 20 percent annual probability of dying and becoming worthless — even to Igor.

   a. Igor's utility of wealth schedule is given in Table 20.2. What is Igor's utility if his bat lives? If it dies? What is Igor's expected utility?

   b. It is potentially fortunate for Igor that he is able to purchase bat insurance. Bat Farm Insurance Company is willing to sell him a policy that costs $40 a year and promises to replace his bat if it dies. Might Igor buy insurance from Bat Farm?

   c. Is Igor willing to pay $20 for bat insurance? Why or why not?

   d. Igor eventually buys insurance from the All Bat Insurance Company. Suppose that Igor knew his bat was already sickly, but that All Bat did not know this, and so charged Igor the premium that applies to healthy bats. Who expects to gain more than usual from this policy? What does this situation illustrate?

4. When is the used car market more efficient: With a pooling equilibrium or a separating equilibrium? Why?

5. Why do banks often lend more readily to people who have credit cards and have previously borrowed from the bank than to people who have always paid in cash and have never borrowed?

6. Larry and Harry have private information about their safety as drivers. Larry is a safe driver; he never speeds and comes to a full stop at every stop sign. Harry believes that speed limit signs give the minimum speed and that yellow lights mean "full speed ahead."

   a. If you owned an automobile insurance company and had to charge everyone the same rate, who would you most want to insure?

   b. You want to sell insurance to safe drivers, like Larry, for $500 a year and to risky drivers, like Harry, for $1,500 a year. In other words, Larry is expected to have accidents costing an average of $500 a year and Harry $1,500 a year. Of course, in any particular year, Larry may have accidents that cost more (or less) than $500 and Harry may have accidents costing more (or less) than $1,500. Because you cannot determine who is safe and who is risky, you offer both Larry and Harry insurance for $1,000 a year with no deductible. Is Harry likely to buy the insurance? Is Larry? Does Larry's decision depend on whether he can convince another insurance company that he is a safe driver? If he does so, what problem do you face?

c. Suppose that you decide to sell two types of insurance policies: one costs $1,300 a year and has a $100 deductible (so that the car owner pays the first $100 of any claim) and the other costs $300 a year and has a $1,500 deductible. Which type of insurance is Harry most likely to buy? Larry? Why?

d. What do your answers to part (c) tell you about the role played by deductibles?

■ You're the Teacher

1. "I understand all this signaling stuff, but it's just not fair. The best person should get the job or the loan or whatever, even if he or she doesn't have the best signal!" This student raises an interesting point. Comment on the fairness of the role played by signals and on the efficiency of using signals.

Answers

■ True/False Answers

Decisions in the Face of Uncertainty

1. **T** The question gives the definition of risk aversion.

2. **T** The diminishing marginal utility of wealth means that the increase in utility from a dollar gain of wealth is less than the decrease in utility from a dollar loss of wealth.

3. **F** Expected wealth is the amount of wealth the person expects to own while expected utility is the amount of utility a person expects to receive.

4. **F** People maximize their expected utility.

5. **T** Jane's cost of risk essentially indicates the maximum she is willing to pay to avoid the risk.

Buying and Selling Risk

6. **F** As is the case in most markets, *both* buyers and sellers benefit from their trade.

7. **T** By pooling risks, an insurance company can collect enough revenue to compensate its customers that have bad outcomes and have revenue "left over" as the company's profit.

8. **T** Because insurance can increase their utility, risk-averse people are willing to buy insurance.

9. **F** Risk must be independent across buyers and must be observable by both buyers and sellers to be insurable.

Private Information

10. **T** The question shows why the person with the private information is likely to enter into the contract.

11. **F** The lemons problem leads to too *few* good cars being offered for sale.

12. **T** Traffic tickets signal that the person is a riskier driver than someone without the tickets.

13. **T** A separating equilibrium occurs when everyone participating in the transaction is informed.

14. **F** Signals and screening are used to try to create a separating equilibrium.

Uncertainty, Information, and the Invisible Hand

15. **F** Information is similar to other goods and services: More can be produced but at increasing marginal cost.

16. **F** The efficient amount of information is the amount that sets the marginal benefit of information equal to the marginal cost of information.

■ Multiple Choice Answers

Decisions in the Face of Uncertainty

1. **b** Burt's expected wealth equals $(0.3 \times \$20,000) + (0.2 \times \$40,000) + (0.5 \times \$60,000) = \$44,000$.

2. **d** Erika's marginal utility equals the change in her total utility, $5,005 - 5,000 = 5$.

3. **b** An increase in wealth raises total utility and decreases the marginal utility of additional wealth.

4. **c** Diminishing marginal utility means that the decrease in utility from a loss in wealth is larger than the increase in utility from a similar gain in wealth.

5. **c** By maximizing their expected utility, people are making themselves as well off as possible if the situation is repeated many times.

6. **d** Jasmine's cost of wealth equals the difference between her expected wealth and the certain wealth that gives her the same utility.

Buying and Selling Risk

7. **c** Insurance reduces people's risk, which increases their utility.

8. **a** Sardar benefits from the insurance if he values the decrease in risk he enjoys more than the price of the insurance he pays.

9. **b** The cost of the risk to the insurance company is 10 percent of $30,000, or $3,000, because 10 percent of automobiles will have an accident.

Private Information

10. **c** The fact of moral hazard makes uninformed people less likely to enter agreements.

11. **a** Moral hazard exists when, after entering into a contract, one party acts to gain more benefits and thereby lessen the benefits to the other party.

12. **d** All are signals because all convey some information about the individual.

13. **d** JCPenney is signaling that it sells high quality clothing.

14. **a** In this case, adverse selection and moral hazard combine to cause the lemons problem in which only bad used cars are sold.

15. **a** The separating equilibrium means that high-quality cars sell for a higher price than do lemons.

16. **d** If banks could perfectly discriminate between high-risk and low-risk borrowers, they would charge high-risk borrowers a higher interest rate than low-risk borrowers.

17. **a** With a separating equilibrium, banks *can* discriminate between high-risk and low-risk borrowers and charge high-risk borrowers a higher interest rate than low-risk borrowers.

18. **b** A lower deductible reduces the cost of having an accident; because you are more likely to have an accident, you want a lower deductible.

Uncertainty, Information, and the Invisible Hand

19. **d** Similar to other goods, the marginal benefit of information decreases as the quantity of information increases.

20. **d** The efficient quantity of information to gather is the is amount that sets the marginal benefit of information equal to the marginal cost of information.

■ Answers to Short Answer Problems

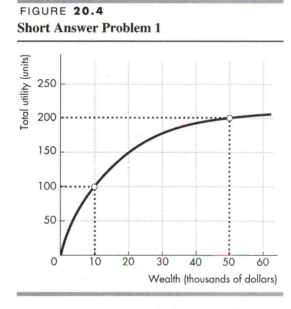

FIGURE **20.4**
Short Answer Problem 1

1. a. Figure 20.4 shows that Lisa's utility if she receives $10,000 is 100. The figure also shows that if she receives $50,000, her utility is 200. Lisa's expected wealth, *EW*, equals $10,000

multiplied by the probability of receiving $10,000 plus $50,000 multiplied by the probability of receiving $50,000. In this case, each probability is 0.5, so Lisa's expected wealth equals $30,000. Similarly, Lisa's expected utility equals the utility if she receives $10,000 (100) multiplied by the probability of receiving $10,000 (0.50) plus the utility if she receives $50,000 (200) multiplied by the probability of receiving $50,000 (0.50). Hence Lisa's expected utility is 150.

b. The difference between Lisa's expected wealth and the certain wealth that gives her the same utility, that is, *EW* − *W*, is her cost of risk. In the risky situation, Lisa's expected utility is 150. From the utility of wealth curve in Figure 20.4, if Lisa received certain wealth, *W*, of $20,000, she would have the utility of 150. The cost of risk to Lisa is $30,000 − $20,000 or $10,000.

The cost of risk reflects the fact that Lisa dislikes uncertainty. The outcome of Lisa's investment is uncertain; it may pay off in a big way (wealth of $50,000), or it may pay off only a little (wealth of $10,000.) The expected (average) wealth from this investment is $30,000 and the expected utility is 150. Because Lisa dislikes risk, she can achieve the same utility if she receives a certain wealth of $20,000, which is $10,000 less than the $30,000 of expected, but uncertain and therefore risky, wealth. The difference between the risky wealth and the certain wealth with the same utility is Lisa's cost of risk for this opportunity.

2. a. Leonard's expected wealth is
($20,000 × 0.5) + ($0 × 0.5) = $10,000.

b. Leonard's expected utility is
(104 × 0.5) + (0 × 0.5) = 52.

c. The situation with uncertain wealth of zero or $20,000 yields expected wealth of $10,000 and expected utility of 52. Table 20.2 shows that certain (no-risk) wealth of $4,000 also yields utility of 52. The cost of risk is $6,000 ($10,000 − $4,000), the amount by which (expected) wealth in the risky case exceeds the no-risk wealth with the same utility.

d. For Leonard, the foregone utility, 60, of the $5,000 cost of the investment is greater than the expected utility of the risky project, 52. Leonard is not willing to make the investment.

3. a. If Igor's bat lives, he has utility of 400; if it dies, he has utility of zero. Igor's expected utility equals his utility if the bat lives multiplied by the probability it lives plus his utility if the bat dies multiplied by the probability it dies. The expected utility is $(0.8 \times 400) + (0.2 \times 0) = 320$.

   b. If Igor buys insurance from Bat Farm, he is guaranteed wealth of $60 (wealth of $100 minus the insurance payment of $40). Certain wealth of $60 gives Igor utility of 280. That amount of utility is less than the expected utility Igor gets from being uninsured (320), so Igor will not buy insurance from Bat Farm.

   c. Igor is willing to pay $20 for bat insurance. If he pays $20 for insurance, his wealth is $80, which gives utility of 350. This level of utility exceeds the expected utility of 320 when he is uninsured.

   d. Igor expects to gain more from the policy because the probability of his bat dying exceeds the normal probability of 20 percent. Thus the probability that All Bat will need to pay off on the policy exceeds 20 percent. This situation illustrates the adverse selection problem from private information: The people who most want to buy bat insurance are those who have sickly bats.

4. The market is more efficient with a separating equilibrium. With a pooling equilibrium, both high-quality cars and lemons sell for the same price. Less than the efficient quantity of high-quality cars are sold and more than the efficient quantity of lemons are sold, so there is a deadweight loss for both types of cars. With a separating equilibrium, high-quality cars sell for a high price and lemons sell for a low price. The efficient number of high-quality cars is sold and the efficient number of lemons is sold. Neither type of car has a deadweight loss.

5. Banks have more information about the ability and willingness to repay loans from people who have previously borrowed from them or from other financial institutions. A good loan repayment record is evidence (a signal) that the customer is a low-risk borrower. If a customer has never borrowed before, the bank must find other ways to assess whether the customer is a high-risk or a low-risk borrower.

6. a. You most want to sell insurance to Larry because you expect that his policy will be more profitable than Harry's policy.

   b. Harry is likely to buy the policy. If Harry does not buy the policy, he expects to pay $1,500 a year for his accidents. If he buys the policy, he pays only $1,000, a saving to Harry of $500. Larry may or may not buy a policy. If he is very risk averse and cannot obtain a lower price from another company, he will buy your insurance. But, if he is only a little risk averse, he may decide to do without insurance. If another company can recognize him as a safe driver, it will offer him a less expensive policy. Larry then will buy from your competitor. Indeed, if all safe drivers can find other companies that realize they are safe drivers, you might wind up insuring only risky drivers for $1,000 a year and incurring an economic loss because their claims will cost you an average of $1,500 a year.

   c. Harry probably will buy the first policy; Larry likely will buy the second. From Harry's standpoint, the second policy is more expensive than the first. Harry, the risky driver, is likely to have an accident and thereby incur the $1,500 deductible. However, Larry realizes that he is unlikely to have an accident and is not likely to have to pay the deductible. Larry therefore is more likely to opt for the second policy because, if he has no accident, he pays only $300 rather than $1,300 for his insurance.

   d. In general, insurance companies can use deductibles to separate risky and safe drivers. Safe drivers generally prefer a low premium/high deductible policy because they realize that they are not likely to have an accident and be forced to pay the deductible. However, risky drivers prefer a high premium/low deductible policy because they know that an accident is probable and they do not want to be hit with a high deductible payment. High-risk drivers know that they are accident prone and they are willing to pay higher premiums for nearly full coverage, but low-risk drivers know that they seldom have accidents so they will choose lower premiums with lower coverage. With deductibles, the adverse selection problem of high-risk people driving low-risk people out of the market is less likely to occur. The insurance company can charge differential premiums that reflect the different risks that it is insuring

■ **You're the Teacher**

1. "Well, it's hard to know what's fair. Let's take a concrete example. (This, incidentally, is a true story drawn from the experience of the author of your study guide.) While Mark was an undergraduate, he used to work for a county government. In those pre-Internet days, the government posted job openings on a wall. The left side had jobs that required graduation from high school; the right side required graduation from college. Mark graduated from college on Saturday. Thus on Friday before he graduated, he was ineligible for the jobs on the right side of the wall but on Monday when he returned to work, he was eligible. Had Mark changed over the weekend? Was he suddenly more productive or more intelligent as a result of the graduation ceremony? No; indeed, Mark did not even go to the graduation ceremony. The only difference now was that Mark possessed a signal: he had graduated from college. So, even though he was the same person, one day he was ineligible for certain jobs and the next day was eligible. Was this fair? At the time, Mark didn't think so."

"But, suppose that a department advertising a position that was listed as requiring a college degree was forced to accept all applications. Would it have been fair to force the people in the department to look through hundreds or thousands of applications for the possibility that they might find someone without a college degree who could handle the job? Because fairness is a normative issue, the question cannot be answered with certainty."

"However, with respect to efficiency, signals and reliance on them may enhance efficiency. In particular, the department advertising the opening that required a college degree was guaranteed by this screening requirement that a high proportion of the applicants would be qualified to hold the position. The department would not waste time and resources sorting through the many applications from people who would not work out in the job. Thus by requiring a college degree (relying on a signal) the department increased its efficiency and did not squander society's scarce resources."

Chapter Quiz

1. If you have a high-quality used car for sale, you would prefer a _____ equilibrium in the used car market but if you have a lemon, you would prefer a _____ equilibrium in the used car market.

   a. separating; pooling
   b. pooling; separating
   c. pooling; pooling
   d. separating; separating

2. People who have a genetic predisposition toward cancer are more likely to demand insurance against cancer. Insurance companies are aware of this _____ problem and _____ potential customers by asking for their relatives' health history.

   a. moral hazard; signal
   b. moral hazard; screen
   c. adverse selection; signal
   d. adverse selection; screen

3. Daniel will earn $21,000 with a probability of 1/3 or $30,000 with a probability of 2/3. Daniel's expected income equals

   a. $21,000.
   b. $27,000.
   c. $30,000.
   d. None of the above.

4. Cynthia will buy insurance as long as

   a. she is risk averse.
   b. the value of insurance exceeds the cost of insurance.
   c. there is a separating equilibrium in the insurance market.
   d. the risky event can be observed by her but not by the insurer.

5. The cost of risk is the amount by which expected wealth must increase to give the same _____ as a no-risk situation.

   a. marginal wealth
   b. marginal utility
   c. expected utility
   d. expected wealth

6. A diagram with a utility of wealth curve has utility on the vertical axis and wealth on the horizontal axis. On this diagram, the dollar value of the cost of risk can be shown as

   a. a horizontal distance.
   b. a vertical distance.
   c. the area of a triangle.
   d. the area of a rectangle.

7. The efficient amount of information to acquire is

   a. as much as possible.
   b. as little as possible.
   c. the amount that sets the marginal benefit of information equal to its marginal cost.
   d. the amount that sets the moral hazard of information equal to its adverse selection.

8. Private information does **NOT** create the problem of

   a. risk.
   b. moral hazard.
   c. adverse selection.
   d. None of the above because private information creates all of the above problems.

9. James buys insurance for his boat. As a result of this purchase, his utility with insurance is _____ his expected utility without insurance and his wealth with insurance is _____ his expected wealth without insurance.

   a. greater than; less than or equal to
   b. greater than; greater than or equal to
   c. equal to; less than
   d. less than; less than

10. For a person who is risk averse, which has higher utility: Expected wealth of $15,000 or certain wealth of $15,000?

   a. Certain wealth of $15,000 has greater utility.
   b. Expected wealth of $15,000 has greater utility.
   c. The utility of expected wealth of $15,000 equals the utility of certain wealth of $15,000.
   d. It is impossible to tell because it is impossible to compare the utility from certain wealth to the utility from expected wealth.

The answers for this Chapter Quiz are on page 346

FACTOR MARKETS, INEQUALITY, AND UNCERTAINTY

Mid-Term Examination

■ **Chapter 18**

1. An increase in the demand for a factor _____ its equilibrium price and _____ its equilibrium quantity.
   a. lowers; decreases
   b. raises; increases
   c. lowers; increases
   d. raises; decreases

2. As a firm increases the quantity of labor it employs, the marginal product of labor _____ and the value of marginal product _____.
   a. increases; increases
   b. decreases; decreases
   c. increases; decreases
   d. decreases; increases

3. The future price of a nonrenewable natural resource, such as oil, is expected to
   a. fall in the future when the resource is depleted.
   b. equal the current equilibrium price.
   c. rise at a rate equal to the interest rate.
   d. fall at a rate equal to the rate of technological advance.

4. The labor supply curve bends backward if the
   a. substitution effect outweighs the income effect.
   b. income effect outweighs the substitution effect.
   c. demand for labor is elastic.
   d. demand for labor is inelastic.

5. Compared to a competitive labor market, a monopsony pays a _____ wage rate and employs _____ workers.
   a. lower; fewer
   b. lower; more
   c. higher; more
   d. higher; fewer

■ Chapter 19

6. Distributions of wealth that include human capital
   a. are more equal than distributions of wealth that exclude human capital.
   b. overstate the degree of income inequality.
   c. understate the degree of income inequality.
   d. None of the above.

7. The high-skilled labor demand curve lies _____ the low-skilled labor demand curve and the high-skilled labor supply curve lies _____ the low-skilled labor supply curve.
   a. above; above
   b. above; below
   c. below; above
   d. below; below

8. On average, compared to women, men are _____ specialized in earning an income in the market and receive _____ pay as a result.
   a. less; lower
   b. less; higher
   c. more; lower
   d. more; higher

9. If the average tax rate rises with income, the tax is
   a. a sales tax.
   b. an excise tax.
   c. a regressive tax.
   d. a progressive tax.

10. The distribution of income within the United States is _____ the world distribution of income.
    a. more equally distributed than
    b. as equally distributed as
    c. less equally distributed than
    d. not comparable to

■ Chapter 20

11. Jeanna is a risk averse. For her, an increase in wealth _____ her total utility and _____ her marginal utility.
    a. raises; raises
    b. raises; lowers
    c. lowers; raises
    d. lowers; lowers

12. A warranty on a used car is an example of a signal. Only people who are risk averse are willing to send signals.
    a. Both sentences are correct.
    b. The first sentence is correct and the second sentence is incorrect.
    c. The first sentence is incorrect and the second sentence is correct.
    d. Both sentences are incorrect.

13. Kris is risk averse. She has the opportunity to invest $5,000 in an investment that will return $10,000 with probability of 50 percent and $0 with probability of 0 percent. Kris will
    a. definitely make the investment.
    b. definitely not make the investment.
    c. make the investment half the time and not make it half the time.
    d. More information is needed to answer the question.

14. The market for loans has low-risk and high-risk borrowers. If there is a separating equilibrium in this market, then
    a. low-risk borrowers pay a lower interest rate than do high-risk borrowers.
    b. high-risk borrowers pay a lower interest rate than do low-risk borrowers.
    c. both low-risk and high-risk borrowers pay a low interest rate.
    d. both low-risk and high-risk borrowers pay a high interest rate.

15. If an auto insurance company offers a policy that it thinks will appeal to safe drivers but instead the policy appeals to risky drivers, the company faces _____ problem.
    a. a moral hazard
    b. a risk-averse
    c. an adverse selection
    d. a signaling

Answers

■ Mid-Term Exam Answers

1. b;   2. b;   3. c;   4. b;   5. a;   6. a;   7. a;   8. d;   9. d;   10. a;
11. b;   12. b;   13. b;   14. a;   15. c.

Exam 1

1. A decrease in supply shifts the supply curve _____; a decrease in demand shifts the demand curve _____.
   a. rightward; rightward
   b. rightward; leftward
   c. leftward; rightward
   d. leftward; leftward

2. Which of the following can lead a perfectly competitive market to produce *less* than the efficient level of output?
   a. The market is perfectly competitive, producing a product with no externalities.
   b. The good or service being produced has an external benefit (for example, education).
   c. The good or service being produced has an external cost (for example, producing the product creates pollution).
   d. None of the answers offered above causes a perfectly competitive market to produce less than the efficient level of output.

3. New cars are a normal good and people's incomes increase. As a result of the increase in income, the equilibrium price of new cars _____ and the equilibrium quantity _____.
   a. rises; increases
   b. rises; decreases
   c. falls; decreases
   d. falls; increases

4. A natural monopoly has no deadweight loss when
   a. it is left unregulated.
   b. it is regulated so that it sets its price equal to its average cost (that is, $P = LRAC$).
   c. it is regulated so that it sets its price equal to its marginal cost (that is, $P = MC$).
   d. Both b and c are correct answers.

5. If the U.S. government imposes a tariff on memory chips used in computers, U.S. producer surplus _____, U.S. consumer surplus _____, and a deadweight _____ created.
   a. increases; increases; is
   b. increases; decreases; is
   c. increases; decreases; is not
   d. decreases; increases; is

6. Which type of industry is characterized by having a few, mutually interdependent firms?
   a. Perfectly competitive
   b. Monopolistically competitive
   c. Oligopoly
   d. Monopoly

7. A 10 percent increase in the price of clothing results in a 2 percent decrease in the quantity demanded. Hence the price elasticity of demand equals
   a. 20.0.
   b. 5.0.
   c. 2.0.
   d. 0.2.

8. A feature of the labor supply curve is that it, unlike most supply curves,
   a. is always upward (positively) sloped.
   b. is always downward (negatively) sloped.
   c. might "bend backwards" so that at low wages it has a positive slope and at high wages it has a negative slope.
   d. None of the above.

9. Production points outside the production possibilities frontier are
   a. efficient and attainable.
   b. inefficient and attainable.
   c. inefficient but not attainable.
   d. not attainable.

10. With no international trade, the U.S. price of corn is less than the world price. If international trade is allowed, the United States _____ corn and U.S. producer surplus _____.
    a. imports; decreases
    b. imports; increases
    c. exports; decreases
    d. exports; increases

11. Suppose the government taxes a product. The decrease in the quantity consumed is *smaller* when the elasticity of demand is _____.
    a. higher
    b. lower
    c. the premise of the question is wrong because the elasticity of demand has nothing to do with the reduction in the quantity demanded.
    d. the premise of the question is correct, but more information is needed to answer it.

12. Compared to an otherwise identical perfectly competitive market, a monopoly firm will hire _____ workers.
    a. more
    b. the same number of
    c. fewer
    d. sometimes more and sometimes fewer workers, depending on whether the monopoly finds that MR exceeds or is less than P.

13. Which of the following does <u>NOT</u> shift the production possibilities frontier (*PPF*) rightward?
    a. An increase in the nation's capital stock.
    b. An increase in technology.
    c. A decrease in inefficiency (so that the nation moves from an inefficient production point to an efficient point).
    d. All of the above shift the production possibilities curve rightward.

14. Suppose that the cost of acquiring a skill rises. As a result of the increase in cost, the wage rate paid people with that skill will
    a. rise.
    b. not change.
    c. fall.
    d. probably change but in an ambiguous direction.

15. In the long run, firms in what type of market structure can earn an economic profit?
    a. Perfectly competitive
    b. Monopolistically competitive
    c. Monopoly
    d. Both monopolistically competitive and monopoly

16. In a natural monopoly,
    a. the firm's MC curve remains above its $LRAC$ curve until the curves cross the demand curve.
    b. it is hard for a *small* second firm to compete with a *large* established firm because the small firm's average cost is higher than the large firm's average cost.
    c. society faces the problem of trying to insure that several firms compete and do not form a cartel.
    d. the MC curve is not defined because the firm is required to produce the quantity set by the regulators.

17. The closer a Lorenz curve for income is to the line of equality,
    a. the more competitive is the industry.
    b. the less competitive is the industry.
    c. the more equally is income distributed.
    d. the less equally is income distributed.

18. The following conditions characterize what type of firm? $P > MR$, $P > ATC$.
    a. Perfectly competitive in the short run.
    b. Perfectly competitive in the long run.
    c. Monopolistically competitive in the long run.
    d. Monopoly in the short run.

19. When MR exceeds MC by the greatest possible amount, the firm is
    a. maximizing its profit.
    b. not maximizing its profit.
    c. earning an economic profit if $P < ATC$.
    d. both answers a and c are correct.

20. When an increase in income shifts the demand curve for a good leftward, the good is _____.
    a. an inferior good
    b. a normal good
    c. a complementary good
    d. a substitute good

21. Which of the following influences does <u>NOT</u> directly shift the supply curve?
    a. An increase in income
    b. Development of new technology
    c. An increase in the cost of producing the product
    d. A decrease in the number of sellers

22. Which of the following is <u>NOT</u> an argument used in favor of protectionist policies?
    a. The infant industry argument.
    b. The claim that protectionist policies save American jobs.
    c. The rich nations exploit developing countries argument.
    d. The comparative advantage frequently switches argument.

23. The cost of wheat used to produce bread rises. As a result of the increase in cost, the equilibrium price of a loaf of bread _____ and the equilibrium quantity produced _____.
    a. rises; increases
    b. rises; decreases
    c. falls; increases
    d. falls; decreases

24. A nation can *produce* at a point outside its *PPF*
    a. when it trades with other nations.
    b. when it is producing products efficiently.
    c. when there is no unemployment.
    d. never.

25. More states pass "green" laws that require ethanol to be mixed with gasoline before it is sold to consumers. These laws _____ the equilibrium price of ethanol and _____ the equilibrium quantity of ethanol.
    a. raise; increase
    b. raise; decrease
    c. lower; increase
    d. lower; decrease

26. The government breaks up a monopoly so that the industry becomes perfectly competitive. As a result of the government action, the price of the product _____, the level of the industry's total output _____, and the deadweight loss _____.
    a. rises; increases; decreases
    b. falls; decreases; increases
    c. rises; decreases; decreases
    d. falls; increases; decreases

27. Suppose Microsoft will sell its Windows operating software to computer manufacturers only if the manufacturers buy Microsoft's Word software. If Microsoft's policy substantially lessens competition, it is
    a. illegal under the exclusive dealing clause of the Clayton Act.
    b. illegal under the tying contracts clause of the Clayton Act.
    c. legal.
    d. None of the above.

28. Due to many workers taking early retirement, the supply of labor decreases. As a result, the equilibrium wage rate _____ and quantity of employment _____.
    a. rises; increases
    b. rises; decreases
    c. falls; increases
    d. falls; decreases

29. Suppose consumers become convinced that eating chicken is healthy while at the same time the price of chicken feed increases. Then, in the short run the equilibrium price of chicken will _____ and the equilibrium quantity will _____.
    a. rise; probably change, but in an ambiguous direction
    b. probably change, but in an ambiguous direction; decrease
    c. rise; increase
    d. not change; probably change, but in an ambiguous direction

30. The demanders of a good pay all of a sales tax when the demand for the good is
    a. perfectly elastic.
    b. more elastic than the supply.
    c. more inelastic than the supply.
    d. perfectly inelastic.

31. Jon will buy insurance if
    a. he is risk averse.
    b. the insurance decreases the uncertainty about his income.
    c. the insurance decreases his expected wealth.
    d. his expected utility with the insurance is greater than his expected utility without it.

Exam 2

1. The price of meat used to produce tacos rises. As a result, the equilibrium price of a taco ____ and the equilibrium quantity ____.
   a. rises; increases
   b. rises; decreases
   c. falls; decreases
   d. falls; increases

2. The total cost of producing 6 pizzas is $24. The total cost of producing 7 pizzas is $35. The marginal cost of the 7th pizza is
   a. $4.00.
   b. $5.00.
   c. $11.00.
   d. None of the above.

3. Which form or forms of business organization have limited liability?
   a. Only sole proprietorship
   b. Only partnership
   c. Only corporation
   d. Both sole proprietorships and partnerships

4. A firm in what type of industry is necessarily characterized by the following conditions? $P = ATC$, and $P = MR$.
   a. Monopoly in the short run.
   b. Monopolistic competition in the long run.
   c. Perfect competition in the short run.
   d. Perfect competition in the long run.

5. For lunch you decide to eat either a slice of pizza or a taco; these are your only two alternatives. Last year, a slice of pizza cost $3 and a taco cost $3; this year, a slice of pizza cost $4 and a taco cost $4. The opportunity cost of a slice of pizza is
   a. highest last year.
   b. highest this year.
   c. the same in both years.
   d. None of the above.

6. A perfectly competitive firm
   a. produces a product identical to those of its competitors.
   b. has $P > MR$.
   c. can earn an economic profit in the long run.
   d. may incur an economic loss in the long run.

7. A good with perfectly elastic demand has a demand curve that is
   a. upward sloping, but not horizontal nor vertical.
   b. downward sloping, but not horizontal nor vertical.
   c. vertical.
   d. horizontal.

8. Because of technological advances, the price of a DVD player falls. Simultaneously, technological advances take place in the production of DVDs. As a result, the equilibrium price of a DVD ____ and the equilibrium quantity ____.
   a. rises; increases
   b. falls; increases
   c. rises; probably changes, but in an ambiguous direction
   d. probably changes, but in an ambiguous direction; increases

9. The equilibrium amount of output equals the efficient amount in a ____ market producing a good or service with ____.
   a. perfectly competitive; no externalities
   b. perfectly competitive; an external cost
   c. perfectly competitive; a external benefit
   d. monopoly; no externalities

10. Of the following, which good would have the most elastic demand?
    a. Pepsi
    b. food
    c. insulin
    d. oil

11. Which of the following statements about the *PPF* is correct?
    a. Technological growth moves the economy from producing at a point in the interior of the *PPF* to a point nearer the *PPF* itself, but does not change the *PPF* itself.
    b. The *PPF* shows that it is not possible for a nation to produce unlimited amounts of all products.
    c. The *PPF* shows that it is not possible for a nation to change the mixture of what it produces.
    d. The *PPF* shifts inward when the labor force grows because the unemployment rate rises.

12. If income is distributed so that everyone has exactly the same income, the Lorenz curve
    a. is horizontal.
    b. is vertical.
    c. lies on the line of equality.
    d. none of the above.

13. E-mail and regular mail are substitutes. Suppose that technological advances lower the price of E-mail. As a result, the equilibrium price of regular mail _____ and the equilibrium quantity _____.
    a. rises; increases
    b. rises; decreases
    c. falls; increases
    d. falls; decreases

14. Leonardo's Pizza, a local restaurant selling pizza, discovers that a 10 percent increase in the price of their pizza decreases the quantity demanded 5 percent. As a result, the 10 percent increase in the price of pizza
    a. increases Leonardo's total revenue.
    b. does not change Leonardo's total revenue.
    c. decreases Leonardo's total revenue.
    d. increases Leonardo's average total costs

15. If Sue is risk averse, then an increase in her wealth _____ her total utility of wealth and _____ her marginal utility of wealth.
    a. increases; increases
    b. decreases; decreases
    c. increases; decreases
    d. decreases; increases

16. With the advent of AIDS, the demand for latex used to make gloves has increased. As a result, the equilibrium price of latex _____ and the quantity _____.
    a. rises; increases
    b. rises; decreases
    c. falls; increases
    d. falls; decreases

17. Which of the following directly shifts the supply curve?
    a. A rise in the wage rate paid workers.
    b. An increase in consumers' incomes.
    c. People deciding they want to buy more of the product.
    d. A decrease in the number of demanders.

FIGURE 1

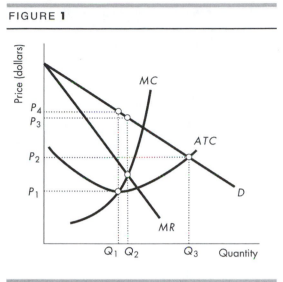

18. In the figure, a profit maximizing monopoly that does not price discriminate will set its price equal to
    a. P_1.
    b. P_2.
    c. P_3.
    d. P_4.

19. In the figure, a profit maximizing monopoly that does not price discriminate will produce how much output?
    a. Q_1
    b. Q_2
    c. Q_3
    d. Q_4

20. Suppose that the Board of Directors of Ford and General Motors are the same. This situation is
    a. legal.
    b. illegal under the Sherman Act.
    c. illegal under the Clayton Act.
    d. illegal under the Rule of Reason.

21. An increase in the minimum wage rate above the equilibrium wage rate will
    a. increase employment.
    b. not change employment.
    c. decrease employment.
    d. increase employment only if the price of the product does not change.

22. Which of the following definitely indicates that a company is earning an economic profit?
    a. $MR = MC$
    b. $MR > MC$
    c. $P = ATC$
    d. $P > ATC$

23. Compared to a similar perfectly competitive industry, a single-price monopoly produces _____ output and charges a _____ price.
    a. more; higher
    b. more; lower
    c. less; lower
    d. less; higher

24. A monopolistically competitive restaurant sells 3 meals for $5 a meal for total revenue of $15. If it sells 4 meals, its marginal revenue from the 4th meal equals
    a. $20.
    b. $15.
    c. $5.
    d. some amount that cannot be calculated because not enough information is given

25. The difference between the maximum price consumers are willing to pay for a good and the price they actually pay the good is called the _____ on that unit of the good.
    a. deadweight surplus
    b. consumer surplus
    c. producer surplus
    d. total surplus

26. Technological advances make labor more productive, that is, the marginal product of labor increases. As a result, the equilibrium wage rate _____ and equilibrium amount of employment _____.
    a. rises; increases
    b. rises; decreases
    c. falls; decreases
    d. falls; increases

27. Which of the following illustrates the concept of external cost?
    a. Bad weather decreases the size of the wheat crop.
    b. A reduction in the size of the wheat crop decreases wheat farmers' incomes.
    c. Smoking harms the health of the smoker.
    d. Smoking harms the health of nearby non-smokers.

28. Suppose biologists perfect a tomato plant that is resistant to diseases and bears more tomatoes than before. As a result, the equilibrium price of a tomato would _____ and the quantity produced would _____.
    a. rise; increase
    b. rise; decrease
    c. fall; increase
    d. fall; decrease

29. The production possibilities frontier reveals that if less developed countries want to grow by producing more capital equipment, they must forego some consumption goods. But in the affluent countries of Europe and North America, the production possibilities frontier shows that this opportunity cost is not necessary.
    a. Both sentences are true.
    b. The first sentence is true and the second sentence is false.
    c. The first sentence is false and the second sentence is true.
    d. Both sentences are false.

30. Exports _____ the nation's total surplus and imports _____ the nation's total surplus.
    a. increase; decrease
    b. decrease; increase
    c. increase; increase
    d. decrease; decrease

31. A crowded public parking lot is a _____ because it is _____.
    a. private good; rival and nonexcludable
    b. public good; nonrival and nonexcludable
    c. common resource; rival and nonexcludable
    d. public good; nonrival and excludable

Answers

■ Final Exam 1 Answers

1. d;   2. b;   3. a;   4. c;   5. b;   6. c;   7. d;   8. c;   9. d;   10. d;
11. b;   12. c;   13. c;   14. a;   15. c;   16. b;   17. c;   18. d;   19. b;   20. a;
21. a;   22. d;   23. b;   24. d;   25. a;   26. d;   27. b;   28. b;   29. a;   30. d;
31. d.

■ Final Exam 2 Answers

1. b;   2. c;   3. c;   4. d;   5. c;   6. a;   7. d;   8. d;   9. a;   10. a;
11. b;   12. c;   13. d;   14. a;   15. c;   16. a;   17. a;   18. c;   19. b;   20. c;
21. c;   22. d;   23. d;   24. d;   25. b;   26. a;   27. d;   28. c;   29. b;   30. c;
31. c.

A n s w e r s   t o   Q u i z z e s

Answers

■ Chapter 1
1. c; 2. c; 3. c; 4. a; 5. d; 6. a; 7. c; 8. c; 9. d; 10. d.

■ Appendix 1
1. c; 2. c; 3. a; 4. c; 5. c; 6. c; 7. c; 8. d; 9. b; 10. b.

■ Chapter 2
1. b; 2. d; 3. b; 4. d; 5. a; 6. a; 7. d; 8. b; 9. c; 10. d.

■ Chapter 3
1. d; 2. d; 3. b; 4. b; 5. c; 6. b; 7. c; 8. a; 9. b; 10. b.

■ Chapter 4
1. d; 2. d; 3. c; 4. a; 5. a; 6. d; 7. c; 8. a; 9. d; 10. a.

■ Chapter 5
1. d; 2. a; 3. c; 4. b; 5. b; 6. b; 7. d; 8. b; 9. c; 10. b.

■ Chapter 6
1. c; 2. a; 3. a; 4. d; 5. c; 6. a; 7. d; 8. c; 9. d; 10. a.

■ Chapter 7
1. a; 2. d; 3. c; 4. b; 5. a; 6. c; 7. a; 8. d; 9. d; 10. a.

■ Chapter 8
1. b; 2. d; 3. b; 4. c; 5. d; 6. b; 7. c; 8. b; 9. d; 10. c.

■ Chapter 9
1. c; 2. c; 3. c; 4. a; 5. d; 6. a; 7. c; 8. d; 9. a; 10. a.

■ Chapter 10
1. d; 2. a; 3. d; 4. c; 5. c; 6. b; 7. c; 8. d; 9. c; 10. c.

■ Chapter 11
1. a;   2. d;   3. c;   4. b;   5. b;   6. a;   7. b;   8. a;   9. b;   10. b.

■ Chapter 12
1. a;   2. c;   3. d;   4. c;   5. a;   6. d;   7. b;   8. a;   9. a;   10. b.

Chapter 13
1. c;   2. d;   3. c;   4. a;   5. c;   6. b;   7. b;   8. b;   9. c;   10. b.

Chapter 14
1. d;   2. a;   3. d;   4. d;   5. a;   6. b;   7. b;   8. c;   9. c;   10. a.

Chapter 15
1. d;   2. a;   3. d;   4. d;   5. c;   6. b;   7. b;   8. c;   9. c;   10. a.

Chapter 16
1. b;   2. c;   3. c;   4. a;   5. a;   6. b;   7. a;   8. c;   9. a;   10. b.

Chapter 17
1. b;   2. c;   3. c;   4. d;   5. b;   6. d;   7. c;   8. d;   9. b;   10. b.

Chapter 18
1. d;   2. c;   3. c;   4. c;   5. a;   6. c;   7. a;   8. d;   9. c;   10. c.

Chapter 19
1. c;   2. c;   3. c;   4. b;   5. a;   6. c;   7. a;   8. b;   9. c;   10. b.

Chapter 20
1. a;   2. d;   3. b;   4. b;   5. c;   6. a;   7. c;   8. a;   9. a;   10. a.

SHOULD YOU MAJOR IN ECONOMICS?*

Should You Take More Economic Courses?

Now that you have learned about supply and demand, utility and profit maximization, employment and unemployment, and good old Igor (at least in the Study Guide you learned about Igor!), it is time to look to the future.

♦ Should studying economics be part of your future?

♦ Should you take more classes or maybe even major in economics?

♦ What about graduate school in economics?

Economists generally assume that people make rational choices to maximize their own well-being. There is no reason to drop this assumption now. The purpose of this chapter is to help you make that rational maximizing choice by providing low-cost information. Let us assess the benefits and see whether they outweigh the costs of studying economics.

Benefits from Studying Economics

■ Knowledge, Enlightenment, and Liberation

As John Maynard Keynes, a famous British economist, said, "The ideas of economists ... both when they are right and when they are wrong, are more powerful than is commonly understood. Indeed the world is ruled by little else. Practical men, who believe themselves to be quite exempt from any intellectual influences, are usually the slaves of some defunct economist." Studying economics is a liberating and enlightening experience.

---

* This section was written by Robert Whaples of Wake Forest University and updated by Mark Rush.

It's better to bring your ideas out in the open, to confront and understand them, rather than to leave them buried.

■ Knowledge, Understanding, and Satisfaction

Many of the most important problems in the world are economic. Studying economics gives you a practical set of tools to understand and solve them. Every day, on television and in the newspapers, we hear and read about big issues such as economic growth, inflation, unemployment, international trade relations, the latest moves by the Fed, the most recent tax or spending bill, the environment, and the future of Social Security. Your introduction to economics shows that learning economics will let you watch the news or pick up a newspaper and better understand these issues. As an added bonus, economics helps you understand smaller, more immediate concerns, such as: How much Spam should I buy? Is skipping class today a good idea? Should I put my retirement funds in government bonds or in the stock market? After all, as the famous author George Bernard Shaw put it, "Economy is the art of making the most of life." Mick Jagger, the lead singer of the "Rolling Stones" and who dropped out of the London School of Economics, complains that he "can't get no satisfaction." Maybe he should have studied more economics? The economic way of thinking will help you maximize your satisfaction.

■ Career Opportunities

All careers are not equal. While the wages in many occupations have not risen much lately, the wages of "symbolic analysts" who "solve, identify, and broker problems by manipulating symbols" are soaring.[1] These people "simplify reality into abstract images that can be rearranged, juggled, experimented with, communicated to other specialists, and then, eventually, transformed back into reality." Their wages have been rising as the globalization of the economy increases the demand for their insights and as technological developments (especially computers) have enhanced their productivity. Economists are the quintessential symbolic analysts as we manipulate ideas about abstractions such as supply and demand, cost and benefits, and equilibrium.

You can think of your training in economics as an exercise regimen, a workout for your brain. You will use many of the concepts you will learn in introductory economics during your career, but it is the practice in abstract thinking that will really pay off.

In fact, most economics majors do not go on to become economists. They enter fields that use their analytical abilities, including business, management, insurance, finance, real estate, marketing, law, education, policy analysis, consulting, government, planning, and even medicine, journalism, and the arts. A recent survey of 100 former economics majors at my university included all of these careers. If you want to verify that economics majors graduate to successful and rewarding careers, just ask your professors or watch what happens to economics majors from your school as they graduate.

Census statistics show that across the nation, economics majors earn more than most other majors. That's the long-run picture. The short-run view looks much the same. In 2009-2010 the average annual starting salary of economics majors was $50,507. While this is lower than the salaries for those with degrees in computer science, engineering, and some other sciences, it is a couple of thousand dollars higher than salaries for those with more general degrees in business administration/management. Moreover, the entry-level salary of economics majors beats the entry-level salary of social science and humanities majors by a wide margin, as Table 1 shows. In addition, the employment rate of economics majors is higher than that of many other majors, such as those in the humanities and other social sciences.

The widening earnings gap between economics and similar majors helps explain why enrollments in economics are climbing. Since 1996 the number of economics degrees awarded in the United States has jumped about 14 percent, with similar trends in Canada and Australia.[2]

Even if you aren't planning on getting a job right out of college, economics can be a valuable major. Economics degrees are looked upon very favorably by MBA programs and law schools. Over one-third of economics

TABLE 1

Average Annual Starting Salary Offers by College Major, 2009-2010

Chemical Engineering	$65,920
Computer Engineering	61,069
Physics	61.075
Economics	**50,918**
Finance	50,150
Information Systems	50,041
Mathematics	47,230
Geology	45,014
Management	43,936
Marketing	43,169
Architecture	40,119
Secondary Education	38,243
History	37,481
Criminal Justice	36,511
Political Science	35,939
Sociology	34,737
English	33,766
Psychology	33,622
Elementary Education	32,995
Biology	31,849

Source: National Association of Colleges and Employers.

graduates enter professional programs within two years of their undergraduate degree, divided equally between business and law. In fact, an analysis of Law School Admission Test (LSAT) scores from 2002-2003 showed that among the twelve college majors with more than 2,000 students taking the exam, economics majors did the *best*. The average score of 156.6 topped second-place Engineering (155.4), as well as English (154.3), Psychology (152.1), Political Science (152.1), Communications (150.5), Sociology (150.2), and Business Administration (149.6).[3]

A *Wall Street Journal* article announced that "Economics, Once a Perplexing Subject, Is Enjoying a Bull Run at Universities." Economics is not a vocational training program, preparing you for a single line of work. Instead, the career benefits of an economics major are so great because economics teaches you to *think* and thinking is what's ultimately rewarded in our dynamic economy.

The Costs of Studying Economics

Because the "direct" costs of studying economics (tuition, books, supplies) aren't generally any higher or lower than the direct costs of other courses, indirect costs will be the most important of the costs to studying economics.

■ Forgone Knowledge

If you study economics, you can't study something else. This forgone knowledge could be very valuable.

■ Disutility

If you dislike studying economics because you find it boring, tedious, or unenlightening in comparison to other subjects, then the opportunity cost is even higher because your overall level of satisfaction falls. (I know that this is rare, but it does occasionally happen).

■ Time and Energy

Economics is a fairly demanding major. Although economics courses do not generally take as much time as courses in English and history (in which you have to read a lot of long books) or anatomy and physiology (in which you have to spend hours in the lab and hours memorizing things), they do take a decent amount of time. In addition, some people find the material "tougher" than most subjects because memorizing is not the key. In economics (like physics), analyzing and solving are the keys. The rigor of the major is an obstacle for many.

■ Grades

As Table 2 shows, grades in introductory economics courses are usually a notch lower than grades in some other majors, including other social sciences and the humanities.[4] On the other hand, grades in economics are generally higher than grades in the sciences and math. Grades in introductory economics courses are generally a hair lower than grades in introductory courses to other majors, including other social sciences and the humanities.

TABLE 2

Average Grades and Grade Distribution by College Major

Department	Mean Grade	% Above B+	% Below B−
Music	3.16	44	21
English	3.12	27	12
Psychology	3.02	28	23
Philosophy	2.99	29	21
Art	2.95	29	24
Political science	2.95	24	23
Economics	2.81	20	31
Chemistry	2.66	17	44
Math	2.53	22	46

Caveat Emptor (Buyer Beware): Interpreting Your Grades Is Not Straight Forward

High grades provide direct satisfaction to most students, but they also act as a signal about the student's ability to learn the subject material. Unfortunately, because the grade distribution is not uniform across departments, you might be confused and misled by your grades. You might think that you are exceptionally good at a subject because of a high grade, when in fact nearly everyone gets a high grade in that subject. The important point here is that you should be informed about your own school's grade distribution. Just because you got a B in economics and an A in history does not necessarily mean that your comparative advantage is in learning history rather than economics. Everyone — or virtually everyone — might receive an A in history. Earning a B or a C in economics could mean that it is the best major for you because high grades are much harder to earn in economics. It is fun to have a high GPA in college, but maximizing GPA should not be your goal. Maximizing your overall well-being is probably your goal, and this might be obtained by trading off a tenth or so of your GPA for a more rewarding major — perhaps economics.

In assessing the tradeoffs, you'll notice that mean departmental grades are higher where average earnings are lower. Employers know which departments grade harder. A recent article on grade patterns concluded that "those students who attend college primarily as a route to a better paying job should understand that 'easy' courses may be no bargain in the long run."[5]

Potential Side Effects from Studying Economics

Studying economics has some potential side effects. I'm not sure whether they are costs or benefits and will let you decide.

■ Changing Ideas about What Is Fair

A recently completed study compared students at the beginning and end of the semester in an introductory economics course.[6] It found that by the end of the semester, significantly more of the students thought that the functioning of the market is "fair." This was especially true for female students. The results were consistent across a range of professors who fell across the ideological spectrum.

For example, the proportion of students who regarded it as unfair to increase the price of flowers on a holiday fell almost in half. The proportion that favored government control over flower prices, rather than market determination, fell by over 60 percent. The study argues that these responses do not reflect changes in deep values, but instead represent the discovery of previous inconsistencies and their modification in the light of new information learned during the semester.

■ Changing Behavior

Many people believe that the study of economics changes students' values and behavior. Some observers think that it changes them for the worse. Others disagree. In particular, it is argued that economics students become more self-interested and less likely to cooperate, perhaps because they spend so much time studying economic models, which often assume that people are self-interested. For example, one study reports experimental evidence that economics students are more likely than nonmajors to behave self-interestedly in prisoners' dilemma games and ultimatum bargaining games.[7]

This need not mean that studying economics will change you, however. Another study compares beginning freshmen and senior economics students and concludes that economics students "are already different when they begin their study of economics."[8] In other words, students signing up for economics courses are already different; studying economics doesn't change them. However, there are reasons to question both of these conclusions, because it is not clear whether these laboratory experiments using economic games reflect reality. One experiment asked students whether they would return money that had been lost. It found that economics students were more likely than others to say that they would keep the cash.

However, what people say and what they do are sometimes at odds. In a follow-up experiment, this theory was tested by dropping stamped, addressed envelopes containing $10 in cash in different campus classrooms. To return the cash, the students had only to seal the envelopes and mail them. The results were that 56 percent of the envelopes dropped in economics classes were returned, while only 31 percent of the envelopes dropped in history, psychology and business classes were sent in.[9] Perhaps economics students are less selfish than others!

Obviously, no firm conclusions have been reached about whether or how studying economics changes students' behavior.

Costs versus Benefits

Suppose that you've weighed the costs and benefits of studying economics and you've decided that the benefits are greater than or equal to the costs. Obviously, then, you should continue to take economics courses. If you can't decide whether the benefits outweigh the costs, then you should probably collect more information — especially if it is good but inexpensive. In either case, read the rest of this section.

The Economics Major

The study of economics is like a tree. The introductory microeconomics and macroeconomics courses you begin with are the tree's roots. Most colleges and universities require that you master this material before you go on to any other courses. The way of thinking, the language, and the tools that you acquire in the introductory course are usually reinforced in intermediate microeconomics and macroeconomics courses before they are applied in more specialized courses that you take. The intermediate courses are the tree's trunk. Among the specialized courses that make up the branches of economics are econometrics (statistical economics), financial economics, labor economics, resource economics, international trade, industrial organization, public finance, public choice, economic history, the history of economic thought, mathematical economics, current economic issues, and urban economics. The branches of the tree vary from department to department, but these are common. It will pay to check your college bulletin and discuss these courses with professors and other students.

Graduate School in Economics

■ Preparing for Graduate School in Economics

You can prepare for graduate school in economics by taking several math classes. This would probably include at least two years of calculus plus a couple of courses in probability and statistics and linear/matrix algebra. Ask your advisor about the particular courses to take at your college. In addition, the mathematical economics and econometrics courses in the economics department are essential. (*Helpful hint*: Even if you aren't going to graduate school, these mathematical courses can be valuable to you, just as more economics courses can be valuable for nonmajors.)

If your school offers graduate level economics courses, you might want to sit in on a few to get accustomed to the flavor of graduate school.

Most graduate programs require strong grades in economics, a good score on the Graduate Record Examination (GRE), and solid letters of recommendation. It is a good idea to get to know a few professors very well and to go above and beyond what is expected so that they can write glowing letters about you.

■ Financing Graduate School

Unlike some other graduate and professional degree programs, you probably won't need to pile up a massive amount of debt while pursuing a Ph.D. in economics. Most Ph.D. programs hire their economics graduate students as teaching or research assistants. Teaching assistants begin by grading papers and running review sessions and can advance to teaching classes on their own. Research assistants generally do data col-lection, statistical work, and library research for professors and often jointly write papers with them. Most assistantships will pay for tuition and provide you with enough money to live on.

■ Where Should You Apply?

The best graduate school for you depends on a lot of things, especially your ability level, geographical location, areas of research interests, and, of course, financing. You should talk with your professors about ability level and areas of research. In addition, a number of web sites contain information you should probably read. Ask a professor or reference librarian to help you track them down.

■ What You Will Do in Graduate School

Most graduate programs in economics begin with a year of theory courses in macroeconomics and microeconomics. After a year you will probably take a series of tests to show that you have mastered this core theory. If you pass these tests, in the second and third year of courses you will take more specialized subjects and perhaps take lengthy examinations in a couple of subfields. After this you will be required to write a dissertation —original research that will contribute new knowledge to one of the fields of economics. These stages are intertwined with work as a teaching and/or research assistant, and the dissertation stage can be quite drawn out. In the social sciences the median time that it takes for a student to complete the Ph.D. degree is about 7.5 years.[10] Be aware that a high percentage (roughly 50 percent) of students do not complete their doctoral degree.

■ What Is Graduate School Like?

Graduate school in economics comes as a surprise to many students. The material and approach are distinctly different from what you will learn as an undergraduate. The textbooks and journal articles you will read in graduate school are often very theoretical and abstract. A good source of information is sitting in on courses or reading the reflections of recent students. See especially *The Making of an Economist* by Arjo Klamer and David Colander (Boulder, Colo.: Westview Press, 1990).

The Committee on Graduate Education in Economics (COGEE) undertook an important review of graduate education in economics and reported its findings in the September 1991 issue of the *Journal of Economic Literature*. COGEE asked faculty members, graduate students, and recent Ph.D.s to rank the most important skills needed to be successful in the study of graduate economics. At the top of the list were analytical skills and mathematics, followed by critical judgment, the ability to apply theory, and computational skills. At the bottom of the list were creativity and the ability to communicate. If you are interested in economic issues but do not have the characteristics required by graduate economics departments, consider other economics-related fields, such as graduate school in public policy. Many economics majors go to business schools to obtain an MBA and are often better prepared than students who have undergraduate degrees in business.

Economics Reading

If decide to make studying economics part of your future, or if you're hungry for more economics, you should immediately begin reading the economic news and books by economists. Life is short. Why waste it watching TV?

The easiest way to get your daily recommended dose of economics is to keep up with current economic events. Here are a few sources to pick up at the newsstand, bookstore, or library over your summer or winter break.

■ The *Wall Street Journal*

Many undergraduates subscribe to the *Wall Street Journal* (WSJ) at low student rates. Join them! Your professor will probably have student subscription forms. Not only is the WSJ a well-written business newspaper, but it also has articles on domestic and international news, politics, the arts, travel, and sports, as well as a lively editorial page. Reading the WSJ is one of the best ways to tie the economics you are studying to the real world and to prepare for your career.

■ Magazines and Journals

The Economist, a weekly magazine published in England, is available at a student discount rate. Pick up a copy at your school library and you will be hooked by its informative, sharp writing. *Business Week* is also well worth the read.

Also recommended are *The American Enterprise, The Cato Journal, Challenge,* and *The Public Interest*, four quarterlies that discuss economic policy. Finally, there is the *Journal of Economics Perspectives*, which is published by the American Economic Association. The *Journal of Economic Perspectives* is a professional journal, but many of the articles are written to be accessible to undergraduate economics students.

■ Books by Economists

I recently asked a group of economics professors from across the country the following question: "A bright, enthusiastic student who has just completed introductory economics comes up to you, the professor, and asks you to recommend an economics book for reading over the summer. What do you suggest?"

Here is what they suggested that you, the bright, enthusiastic student, should read:

■ Top Choices

Milton Friedman, *Capitalism and Freedom.*

Steven Levitt and Stephen Dubner, *Freakonomics.*

Steve Landsburg, *The Armchair Economist: Economics and Everyday Life.*

■ Other Good Choices

Alan Blinder, *Hard Heads, Soft Hearts: Tough-Minded Economics for a Just Society.*

Hernando de Soto, *The Mystery of Capital: Why Capitalism Triumphed in the West and Failed Everywhere Else.*

Robert Frank, *Luxury Fever: Why Money Fails to Satisfy in an Era of Excess.*

David Friedman, *Hidden Order: The Economics of Everyday Life.*

Susan Lee, *Hands Off: Why the Government Is a Menace to Economic Health.*

Pietra Rivoli, *The Travels of a T-Shirt in the Global Economy: An Economist Examines the Markets, Power, and Politics of World Trade*

In addition, Adam Smith's *The Wealth of Nations* is a must read for every student of economics. Written in

1776, it is the most influential work of economics ever. Its insights are still valuable today.

■ Economic Fiction

For those with a taste for fiction, choices include:

Marshall Jevons, *Murder at the Margin, The Fatal Equilibrium*, and *A Deadly Indifference*. A trio of economics-based murder mysteries. Use your economic theory to solve the crime.

Russell Roberts, *The Invisible Heart*. An economics-based romance novel! "Can Laura love a man with an Adam Smith poster on his wall?"

Russell Roberts, *The Choice: A Parable of Free Trade and Protectionism*.

Jonathan Wight, *Saving Adam Smith: A Tale of Wealth, Transformation, and Virtue*.

Endnotes

1. This term is used by Robert Reich in *The Work of Nations*. The quote is from p. 178.

2. John J. Siegfried and David K. Round, "International Trends in Economics Degrees during the 1990s," *Journal of Economic Education*, Vol. 32, no. 3, Summer 2001, pp. 203-18.

3. Michael Nieswiadomy, "LSAT Scores of Economics Majors: The 2003-2004 Class Update," *Journal of Economic Education*, Vol. 35, Spring 2006, pp. 244-47.

4. Richard Sabot and John Wakeman-Linn, "Grade Inflation and Course Choice," *Journal of Economic Perspectives*, Vol. 5, no. 1, Winter 1991, pp. 159–170.

5. Donald G. Freeman, "Grade Divergence as a Market Outcome," *Journal of Economic Education*, Vol. 30, no. 4, Fall 1999, pp. 344-51.

6. Robert Whaples, "Changes in Attitudes about the Fairness of Free Markets among College Economics Students," *Journal of Economic Education*, Vol. 26, no. 4, Fall 1995.

7. Robert H. Frank, Thomas Gilovich, and Dennis T. Regan, "Does Studying Economics Inhibit Cooperation?" *Journal of Economic Perspectives*, Vol. 7, no. 2, Spring 1993, pp. 159–171.

8. John R. Carter and Michael D. Irons, "Are Economists Different, and If So, Why?" *Journal of Economic Perspectives*, Vol. 5, no. 2, Spring 1991, pp. 171–177.

9. "Economics Students Aren't Selfish, They're Just Not Entirely Honest," *Wall Street Journal*, January 18, 1995, B1.

10. See Ronald Ehrenberg, "The Flow of New Doctorates," *Journal of Economic Literature*, Vol. 30, June 1992, pp. 830–875. If breaks in school attendance are included, this climbs to 10.5 years. Of course, some students attend only part time, and most have some kind of employment while completing their degrees.